GW01458492

Kingston upon Hull City Libraries
WITHDRAWN
FROM STOCK

FOR SALE

HULL LIBRARIES

5 4072 02222662 9

John Nash
Architect of the Picturesque

John Nash
Architect of the Picturesque

Edited by Geoffrey Tyack

ENGLISH HERITAGE

Published by English Heritage, The Engine House, Fire Fly Avenue, Swindon SN2 2EH
www.english-heritage.org.uk
English Heritage is the Government's lead body for the historic environment.

© The individual authors 2013

The views expressed in this book are those of the authors and not necessarily those of
English Heritage.
Images (except as otherwise shown) © English Heritage or © Crown copyright. EH.

First published 2013

ISBN 978-1-84802-102-0

Product code 51665

British Library Cataloguing in Publication data
A CIP catalogue record for this book is available from the British Library.

The right of the authors to be identified as authors of this work has been asserted by them in
accordance with the Copyright, Designs and Patents Act 1988

All rights reserved
No part of this publication may be reproduced or transmitted in any form or by any means,
electronic or mechanical, including photocopying, recording, or any information storage or
retrieval system, without permission in writing from the publisher.

Application for the reproduction of images should be made to English Heritage. Every effort
has been made to trace the copyright holders and we apologise in advance for any
unintentional omissions, which we would be pleased to correct in any subsequent edition of
this book.

For more information about English Heritage images, contact Archives Research Services,
The Engine House, Fire Fly Avenue, Swindon SN2 2EH; telephone (01793) 414600.

Brought to publication by David M Jones, Publishing, English Heritage.

Typeset in 9.5 on 11.75pt Charter

Edited by Louise Wilson
Indexed by Alan Rutter
Page layout by Francis & Partners
Printed in Great Britain by Butler Tanner and Dennis Ltd, Frome and London

Frontispiece: Portrait of John Nash by Sir Thomas Lawrence, exhibited at the Royal Academy
in 1827. He is shown in his Gallery at No. 14 Regent Street (The Principal and Fellows of Jesus
College, Oxford).

CONTENTS

The early 19th century witnessed the increasing prosperity, at least of the middle classes, that was so marked in the 18th century in Britain. Concerns over the threats of the Napoleonic War proved unfounded and there was every reason to want an architecture that was full of confidence and a desire to express our imperial ambition that was beginning to encircle the globe, in spite of setbacks in North America!

John Nash is the Regency architect *par excellence*, a friend of Prinny himself, and the designer of some of the most opulent and visually seductive buildings in England – the Brighton Pavilion, Buckingham Palace, the Regent's Park terraces. It was Nash who changed the face of the West End of London by the building of Regent Street; Nash who first applied picturesque ideas to the layout of the urban park; Nash who designed what is arguable the prototype villa suburb. And it was Nash who, more successfully than any other architect of his era, showed how picturesque aesthetics could transform domestic design, from cottages to aristocratic castles. It is now more than 30 years since Sir John Summerson brought out his *The Life and Work of John Nash, Architect* (1980). Since then, new scholarship has revised and expanded our knowledge of Nash's achievement. This book is intended to bring this knowledge to a wider public. Incorporating papers from a symposium organised by the Georgian Group in London in September 2009, it reinterprets the work of this most varied and fascinating of British architects for a 21st-century readership.

His Royal Highness The Duke of Gloucester

ACKNOWLEDGEMENTS

Many people have helped make this book possible. First, I would like to thank the Georgian Group for its generosity in giving a financial subvention towards the cost of photography, and Robert Bargery, the Secretary, for organising the symposium on Nash at the Paul Mellon Centre in London in September 2009, which provided the inspiration for the project, and for his constant support subsequently. At English Heritage John Hudson, Robin Taylor and David Jones have been consistently helpful, both in embracing the idea of publication and in producing the book to the highest standards. Thanks are also due to Louise Wilson for her copy-editing, to Geoff Francis for design, to Andrew Donald, Derek Kendall and Paul Backhouse for helping illustrate chapters 5 and 6, and to Alan Rutter for the index. English Heritage has also kindly allowed free reproduction of the unparalleled collection of images in the National Monuments Record at Swindon, and I am grateful to its staff, and especially Clare Broomfield, Graham Deacon and Emma Whinton-Brown, for their help in identifying and supplying images from the collection.

Among other suppliers of images I would like to thank Kate Holyoak of the Royal Collection, Sheila O'Connell of the British Museum, Dr Julius Bryant and Nazek Ghaddar of the Victoria and Albert Museum, Jeremy Smith of London Metropolitan Archives and Myke Clifford of the Cambridge University History of Art department. Among the many archivists and librarians who have given helpful advice I would particularly like to mention Richard Smout of the Isle of Wight Record Office, Katherine Jones of the Royal Institute of British Architects drawings collection, Owen McKnight of Jesus College, Oxford, Robin Darwall-Smith of Magdalen College, and the staff of the Royal Archives.

My main debt of gratitude is to the contributors to this volume, who have proved exceptionally accommodating in sharing the fruits of their knowledge and encouraging its publication. Other Nash scholars and enthusiasts who have contributed in different and invaluable ways include James Anderson, Sue Berry, Edna Dale-Jones, Melvin Hirst, Caroline Knight, the late Peter Laing, Leanne Langley, Tom Lloyd, Marion McGarry, John Newman, Malcolm Pinhorn, Ian Sherfield, Malcolm Tucker and Gareth Williams. I am also grateful to Sir Terry Farrell for his efforts in increasing public awareness of Nash's work in London; to Jeremy Musson and John Goodall for featuring Nash's buildings in the pages of *Country Life*; and to Andrew Saint for reading and commenting on some of the chapters.

This book could not have been written without the help of owners and occupiers of Nash buildings who have kindly arranged and facilitated access. They include David Beevers at the Brighton Pavilion, Loreley Burkill, Sir Charles Burrell, Gill Burton, the Rev Alan Cross, Norman Devlin, Andreas Gestrich of the German Historical Institute in London, Hero Grainger-Taylor, Sir David Hoare, Marion Kamlish, Sarah Kay and David Duckham at Attingham and Cronkhill, Lord Lloyd George, Jan Lucas-Scudamore, Howard Rees, Edward Somerville, John Vaughan and Julian Williams.

Geoffrey Tyack

CONTRIBUTING AUTHORS

Jonathan Clarke was a Senior Investigator with English Heritage's Investigation and Analysis Division. His interests include the history of 19th- and early 20-century buildings and structures, especially their constructional aspects, and he is currently finishing an illustrated book on early structural steel in London buildings.

Joe Mordaunt Crook is a former Slade Professor and Waynflete Lecturer at Oxford, and a former Public Orator and Professor of Architectural History at London University. His many writings include *The Greek Revival* (1972), *The Dilemma of Style* (1997), *The Rise of the Nouveaux Riches* (1999), *The Architect's Secret* (2003), *Brasenose* (2008) and a revised and expanded edition of *William Burges and the High Victorian Dream* (2013).

M H Port, Emeritus Professor of Modern History, Queen Mary, University of London, was co-author of *The History of the King's Works, VI, 1782–1851* (HMSO 1973), and subsequently has written extensively about royal and public buildings.

Richard Suggett, FSA, is Senior Investigator at the Royal Commission on the Ancient and Historical Monuments of Wales (RCAHMW). His account of the early career of John Nash was published as *John Nash. Architect in Wales* (National Library of Wales 1996). His other architectural studies include *Houses and History in the March of Wales* (RCAHMW 2005) and *Introducing Houses of the Welsh Countryside* (RCAHMW and Y Lolfa 2010).

Geoffrey Tyack, FSA, is a Fellow of Kellogg College, Oxford, Director of the Stanford University Centre in Oxford, and editor of the *Georgian Group Journal*. His books include *Sir James Pennethorne and the Making of Victorian London* (1992). He is also co-author of the revised Berkshire volume in the Pevsner *Buildings of England* series (2010).

David Watkin is Emeritus Professor of the History of Architecture at the University of Cambridge and Vice-President of the Georgian Group. His many books include *Sir John Soane: Enlightenment Thought and the Royal Academy Lectures* (1996), winner of the Sir Banister Fletcher Award.

David Whitehead, FSA, is a schoolmaster who has lived and taught in Herefordshire for 40 years and has published extensively on the architecture of the West Midlands. He is presently Honorary Secretary of his local antiquarian society – the Woolhope Naturalists Field Club.

Rosemary Yallop read Law at Cambridge before working in investment banking for 12 years and then training as a book conservator. After some years of independent research she is now undertaking a DPhil in Architectural History at the University of Oxford, focusing on the Italianate style in early 19th-century Britain.

List of commonly used abbreviations

BL – British Library
LMA – London Metropolitan Archives
NA – The National Archives, Kew
NLW – National Library of Wales
NMR – National Monuments Record
ODNB – Oxford Dictionary of National Biography
PD – Parliamentary Debates
PP – British Parliamentary Papers
PRONI – Public Record Office of Northern Ireland
RA – Royal Archives, Windsor
RCAHMW – Royal Commission on the Ancient and Historic Monuments of Wales
RIBA – Royal Institute of British Architects

INTRODUCTION: FROM LAMBETH MARSH TO BUCKINGHAM PALACE

GEOFFREY TYACK

John Nash was born in 1752, while George II was still on the throne, and died at the age of 83 in 1835, two years before the accession of Queen Victoria. During Nash's lifetime, Britain experienced the loss of a substantial part of one Empire, in America, and the acquisition of another, in India, followed by 22 years of almost uninterrupted warfare with revolutionary and Napoleonic France. Britain's economy was transformed by industrialisation, its towns and cities by massive population growth, its politics by administrative and Parliamentary reform, its religious life by Evangelicalism, and its culture by Romanticism. Nash's architectural achievement cannot be understood without taking into account these momentous developments.

Nash's origins have always been somewhat mysterious, not least because he took pains to obscure them. Recent research has clarified the picture, and the results are summarised in chapter 1. He grew up in Lambeth, on the industrial south bank of the Thames in London, where his father, who came from Wales, was a millwright, probably designing waterwheels for pumping water to reservoirs and breweries.[1] A 'wild, irregular youth', as he described himself in middle age,[2] he went at the age of 15 or so into the office of Sir Robert Taylor (1714–88), one of the first architects to run a practice on recognisably modern lines[3]; echoes of Taylor's work appear repeatedly in Nash's later buildings. On leaving Taylor's office, he set up business in Lambeth,[4] making a bid for fame in 1777–8 by designing a pair of larger houses in Bloomsbury Square, and a more modest row of terraced houses in Great Russell Street, close to the British Museum. But the houses failed to sell and in 1783 he went bankrupt. He made matters worse by trying to divorce his wife after she had allegedly run up debts and imposed two spurious children on him. But the divorce was not confirmed by the House of Lords and the suit failed.

In 1785, Nash, now aged 33, moved to Carmarthen – at the time, the largest town in Wales.[5] At first he made a living as a builder and supplier of materials, but in time he built up a successful architectural practice among the South Wales gentry, discussed in detail in chapter 1. Originally in partnership with Samuel Saxon (1757–1831), a pupil of Sir William Chambers, he began to take assistants and pupils himself, starting with Robert George, who acted as clerk of works for some of his early commissions;[6] George left in 1796 and was succeeded by James Morgan (c 1773–1856), who remained Nash's chief office assistant for the rest of his career. Nash also made use of the services of Auguste (Augustus) Charles Pugin (1768/9–1832), an émigré from revolutionary France who received an artistic training at the Royal Academy Schools in London in 1792, and who developed a talent for producing coloured perspective drawings. Pugin continued to work intermittently for Nash after moving to London in about 1796, where he opened a drawing school.[7]

Through his extensive and varied practice in South Wales and the Welsh Borders, Nash fortuitously came into contact with the three most important advocates and practitioners of the picturesque approach to architecture and landscape design: Uvedale Price (1747–1829), Richard Payne Knight (1751–1824) and Humphry Repton (1752–1818). These encounters transformed his career, and their initial implications are explored in chapter 2. Repton went into partnership with Nash in or about 1796, and wrote in his autobiography: 'Two such congenial minds were never brought together since David and Jonathan … We acted as one joint soul! Our homes … our carriages, our offices … were as the property of both'.[8] One of Repton's aims was to ensure that his sons had an architectural training: first John Adey Repton (1775–1860), and then, after the partnership with Nash broke up, John's younger brother George (1786–1858). George Repton eventually became Nash's chief design assistant and remained with him until 1817 when, to the older man's chagrin, he secretly married the daughter of the Lord Chancellor, Lord Eldon, and set up practice on his own.

By the mid 1790s, Nash had become an important figure in Carmarthen society. He lived in a large house on the site of the present Ivy Bush Hotel in Spilman Street, and owned property that included a small theatre in which he himself acted.[9] He developed close contacts with the Whig interest in what was politically a notoriously fractious town, but his litigious and mercenary temperament made him enemies, and in 1798 he was threatening to sue the Carmarthenshire magistrates for non-payment

Fig 0.1
Nash's house at
No. 29 Dover Street, London
photographed c 1934
(CC 39_00382)

x

of fees. In the same year, Uvedale Price told the collector and connoisseur Sir George Beaumont that Nash was 'uncommonly quick & full of resources … & very docile. He is reasonable in his charges but don't trust to my estimates but get some other person to execute his designs'.[10]

In 1797 Nash left Carmarthen for London, settling first in Duke Street, St James's, and then in the following year at No. 29 Dover Street, north of Piccadilly.[11] His new house, facing down Hay Hill to Lansdowne House and Berkeley Square, was a surprisingly ambitious residence for a middle-aged provincial architect with a somewhat questionable past, who had only recently arrived in the capital (Fig 0.1). From here, with Humphry Repton's help, he succeeded in attracting a succession of lucrative domestic commissions, mostly from *nouveaux riches* in search of villas in artfully improved sylvan surroundings close to the capital.[12] He also built a villa for himself: East Cowes Castle on the Isle of Wight. It was begun shortly before his second marriage, which took place on 17 December 1798 to Mary Anne Bradley, the attractive daughter of a coal merchant from Abingdon Street, close to the Palace of Westminster, one of Nash's early business associates. There is no evidence for the often-repeated story that the second Mrs Nash, who was some 20 years younger than her husband, was a cast-off mistress of the Prince of Wales, whom Nash is not known to have met for at least another 10 years.[13] But it seems unlikely that the marriage was without some financial benefit to Nash, and, having built his island retreat, he and his wife regularly moved there for three months or so each summer, sometimes accompanied by his pupils and assistants.

The Repton partnership broke up acrimoniously in 1800, after Nash had (according to Repton) failed to pay his share of the seven per cent fees charged to their joint clients.[14] Over the next decade, Nash went on to build up a large country-house practice of his own, mainly among the landed gentry and aristocracy, who were profiting from rising wartime food prices. From 1800 to 1811 he worked on 37 houses, an average of three or more a year, the most important of which are discussed in chapters 3 and 4. In or about 1805 he told the wife of one of his clients, Colonel Stewart of Killymoon, Co. Tyrone, that he had been 'constantly travelling' for two months, and the diarist and gossip Joseph Farington recorded him as saying in 1821 that he had travelled

11,000 miles a year throughout the kingdom during this period and spent an annual £1,500 in coach hire.[15] It is often assumed that he delegated much of the work to assistants, but this assumption is not supported by the evidence, at least from the early years of his practice. He paid no fewer than 39 visits to Corsham Court, Wiltshire, his first job in partnership with Repton, between 1778 and 1810,[16] and between 1800 and 1804 he went 28 times to The Warrens, a relatively minor commission in Hampshire.[17] His *fa presto* methods of design and his willingness to experiment with new methods of construction certainly led to a litany of complaints from clients. But they continued to beat the path to his door in Dover Street, and his career prospered accordingly.

Growing up among millwrights, pump-makers and engineers at a time of rapid industrial growth and change, Nash became a pioneer in the use of structural woodwork and iron – a subject discussed in chapter 8 – and he also made extensive use of new materials such as Coade stone.[18] But his houses were notable most of all for their inventiveness in planning and for their stylistic variety, unusual even by the standards of the time. He could work within the loosely Palladian idiom in which he had been trained, as his villas of the 1790s and some of his later country houses show.[19] In his classical interiors, he followed popular taste by developing a rich and lavish style exemplified in the staircase and Picture Gallery at Attingham Park, Shropshire (1806–9; *see* Fig 8.4) and subsequently reappearing at the Brighton Pavilion and Buckingham Palace. But his creative talents were stimulated above all by more 'pictorial' styles, whether derived from medieval England (*see* chapter 3) or from the Italian rural vernacular that he knew only at second or third hand (*see* chapter 4). The best of these houses display a wit, grace and practicality that have rarely been equalled, and which still delight those fortunate enough to live in them.

Nash's working methods were not very different from those of prolific contemporaries such as James Wyatt (1746–1813), or of Victorian architects with large practices, such as Sir Gilbert Scott. Once the style and location of a house was selected, Nash made preliminary drawings, often showing different possible treatments of a project.[20] The chosen design was then worked up as a perspective by one of the assistants – often George Repton, who also recorded several designs in his notebooks:

an invaluable record of Nash's domestic work.[21] Working drawings were then prepared in the office before being transmitted, often with Nash's annotations, to the clerk of works on site.[22] Some of Nash's clerks of works went on to build up successful careers in their own right, including James and Richard Pain (c 1779–1877 and c 1793–1838, respectively), from a family of London builders, who went on from Lough Cutra Castle, Co. Galway (1811–17) to become two of the leading architects in south-west Ireland.[23] Later, at the Brighton Pavilion, it is difficult to see how Nash's innovative structural ideas could have been adopted into practice without the help of William Nixon, a carpenter who acted as clerk of works there and subsequently at Buckingham Palace.

Some of Nash's houses were beset by structural problems, often related to his choice of recently devised materials, such as Dehl or Hamelin's mastic used in place of lead for flat roofs. At his first large country-house job, Corsham Court, the cellar joists collapsed in 1800 under the weight of his new gallery, and part of the ceiling of the music room fell in because of water seepage through the flat roof.[24] At Rockingham, Co. Roscommon, Nash was dismissed once the main structure was complete in 1810 following disagreements with his client, Viscount Lorton, and was replaced by his clerk of works.[25] But he treated criticisms with studied nonchalance – infuriating some clients and amusing others. In 1816, following complaints about leaking roofs and smoking chimneys, he reminded Lord Caledon, a former Governor of Cape Province, 'that Caledon [Co. Tyrone] with all its charms, has not the climate of Italy, but that Providence considering fruitful soil a greater blessing than a dry house, has given you a horrid atmosphere'.[26] Yet Lord Caledon later went on in 1827 to employ him for his new town house in Carlton House Terrace.

A minor but important part of Nash's domestic practice involved the design of gate lodges, cottages and other estate buildings (see chapter 2). Such buildings, with their connotations of seigneurial *noblesse oblige*, exhibited in concentrated form the qualities most admired by artists and writers influenced by picturesque aesthetics. The apogee of this attractive genre was reached at Blaise Hamlet, near Bristol, in 1810–11, where, along with George Repton, to whom had been given a 'moiety of the cottages' from the office, he designed a complete 'village' for the retired estate workers of a banker,

J S Harford (see Figs 9.16 and S.1).[27] Here he appealed to the fashionable rural nostalgia of a rapidly urbanising society, anticipating in the process not only the Victorian estate village but also the garden cities and garden suburbs of the 20th century.

By 1812, when he reached his 60th birthday, Nash had established himself as one of the most successful architects of his time. In 1802 he bought a farm at Hamstead, five miles west of East Cowes, and he later established brick and lime kilns there, together with a *cottage orné* for his and his wife's occasional use.[28] In 1808–10 he enlarged East Cowes Castle (Fig 0.2), laying out elaborate gardens and entertaining extensively; in 1814 the architect James Spiller (not, it seems, one of Nash's guests) commented: 'who would cast a thought upon the marshes of Lambeth amidst the Circean voluptuousness of the Isle of Wight ... I have heard of such gourmandizing and drinking that the recital has created a vertigo; whence came the original supplies I wonder, and by what means are architectural compositions prepared under a sick headache?'[29]

With a flourishing domestic practice, Nash might now have been expected to settle gradually into a comfortable semi-retirement. Instead, a new official career opened up. In 1806 he had been appointed as joint salaried architect, with James Morgan, to the Office of Woods and Forests, the government department responsible for managing the Crown Estate. Then, in 1811, the Commissioners of Woods and Forests – recently amalgamated with the Office of Land Revenues – commissioned him to redevelop Marylebone Park, on the north-western edge of London's built-up area. This became Regent's Park, the prototype of urban parks throughout the world; it is the subject of chapter 5. And in the same year, he prepared his first design for what became Regent Street, the most ambitious programme of urban improvement so far undertaken in London, and arguably the most successful ever. This is discussed in chapter 6.

In 1813, when the legislation for Regent Street was finally passed, the Prince of Wales (by now Prince Regent) employed Nash as his private architect at Royal Lodge, a vast thatched *cottage orné* in Windsor Great Park. And, following the sudden death of James Wyatt in the same year, he went on to extend the Prince's London residence, Carlton House. The precise circumstances of Nash's introduction to the Prince are not known, but by 1813 he was said to be 'in great favour' with him,[30] acting as an intermediary in his fruitless negotiations with his former political allies, the Foxite Whigs, and with his estranged wife, Caroline of Brunswick. In 1814, Nash was employed to design a bizarre group of temporary structures in the grounds of Carlton House and St James's Park as part of the celebrations for a visit by the allied sovereigns following what was to be only the temporary defeat of Napoleon at the Battle of Leipzig, and the subsequent Treaty of Paris. But his most spectacular commission for the Prince was the remodelling of the Brighton Pavilion, in 1815–23, in what he called an 'Eastern' style. This improbable pleasure dome is the *ne plus ultra* of picturesque architecture, capturing the hedonistic spirit of the age in its most exuberant form. It is described, together with Nash's other commissions from royalty, in chapter 7.

Peace with France enabled Nash to travel to Paris, first in 1814 and again, following Napoleon's escape from Elba and the Battle of Waterloo, in 1815. Here he met A C Pugin's brother-in-law, Louis Lafitte, designer of the

panels on Percier & Fontaine's recently erected Arc du Carrousel in front of the Tuileries, and he went to Paris again in 1817–18.[31] These visits – Nash's only known foreign excursions – occurred while he was involved in the design of the buildings along Regent Street, work on which started in 1815; he continued to be heavily involved in the development of Regent Street and the surroundings of Regent's Park throughout the 1820s. He was also was a leading promoter and the largest shareholder in the Regent's Canal, opened in 1820 to link the Grand Union Canal and the industrial Midlands with the London docks,[32] and was responsible for the development of the artisan area south of the basin formed to the east of Regent's Park. Then, in 1824, he leased a tract of land at the north-eastern corner of the Park, where he laid out the Park Village, a planned development of middle-class houses that anticipates the form and character of much subsequent villa suburbia on both sides of the Atlantic (*see* chapter 5).[33]

Nash continued to take private commissions during the 1810s and, to a lesser extent, the

Fig 0.2
The south front of East Cowes Castle
(George Brannon, Views of the Isle of Wight, *1824).*

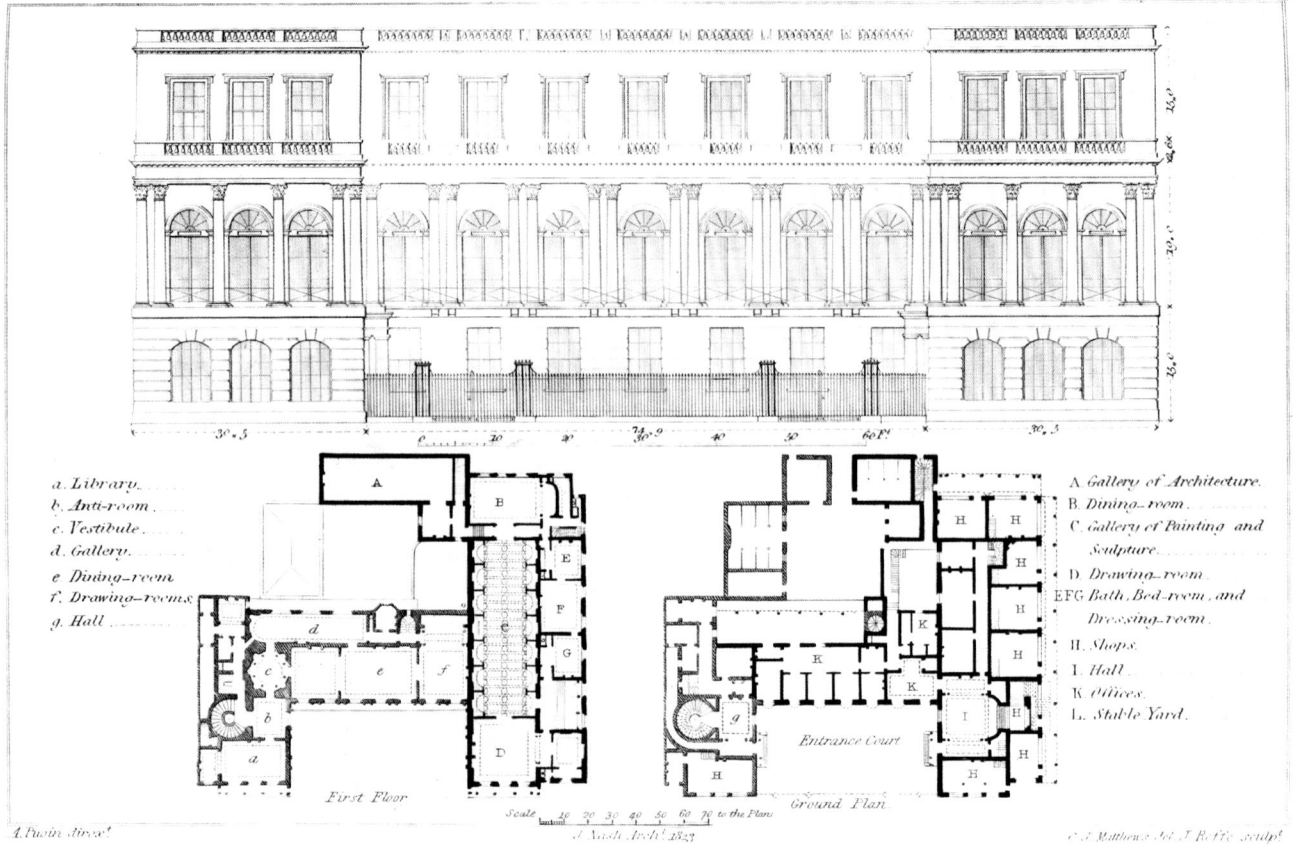

a. Library
b. Anti-room
c. Vestibule
d. Gallery
e. Dining-room
f. Drawing-rooms
g. Hall

A. Gallery of Architecture.
B. Dining-room.
C. Gallery of Painting and Sculpture.
D. Drawing-room.
EFG. Bath, Bed-room, and Dressing-room.
H. Shops.
I. Hall.
K. Offices.
L. Stable Yard.

First Floor

Scale 10 20 30 40 50 60 70 to the Plan

Ground Plan

Entrance Court

A. Pugin dirext
J. Nash Arch.t 1823
C.J. Matthews del. J. Roffe sculpt

The Houses of John Nash and John Edwards Esq.rs Regent Street

John Weale, Architectural Library, 59 High Holborn.

Fig 0.3
Nos 14–16 Regent Street, from Britton and Pugin, Illustrations of the Public Buildings of London *II, 1828 (BB 65_02595).*

1820s. His Guildhall at Newport, Isle of Wight (1814–16), is a competent but modest essay in the Renaissance manner, and in about 1812–14 he rebuilt Rheola, near Neath, a villa for his cousin John Edwards (*see* Fig S.4); its long, low, rendered profile uncannily anticipates some of the houses designed by C F A Voysey at the end of the century. Most of Nash's few churches date from this period too, three of them displaying a high degree of originality, if not eccentricity: St Mary, West Cowes, where in 1816 he added a startlingly austere Grecian tower (the closest he ever came to neoclassical minimalism) which doubled up as a mausoleum for the Ward family of the neighbouring Northwood House (*see* Fig S.8); St Paul, Cahir, Co Tipperary (1817–20), in an unconventional version of Gothic;[34] and All Souls, Langham Place, London (1822–4), where he reused elements from his model designs of 1818 for new churches to be erected with Government money by the newly established Church Commissioners.[35]

In 1820 the Prince Regent became King. He soon decided that 'he did not like Carlton House standing in a street',[36] and in 1825 it was demolished in favour of what was to become Buckingham Palace. Nash then redeveloped the site, going on to redesign St James's Park along picturesque lines, and to supervise a second phase of Government-sponsored Metropolitan Improvements, which started in 1826 (*see* chapter 6). Buckingham Palace turned out to be Nash's nemesis. Unlike Royal Lodge and the Brighton Pavilion, it was funded by the Treasury through the Office of Works, in which Nash, following a reorganisation in 1815, was one of three 'attached architects'.[37] As a public employee, he was now placed in the invidious position of having to take his orders from the King, while being ultimately responsible to Parliament and the taxpayer. Work began in 1825, and criticism mounted as the costs escalated. In 1828 he was questioned by a Commons Select Committee about the management of the public projects on which he was employed;[38] following further attacks in Parliament in 1829, attention turned to his speculative developments on Crown land. In both cases he was exonerated from blame, but the 1829 Committee concluded nevertheless that it was 'undesirable for official architects to acquire a financial interest in property for which they might be called upon to give a valuation':[39] an important milestone on the road towards the separation of the architectural profession from the occupations of builder and surveyor. The King attempted to reward Nash with a Baronetcy on the grounds that he had been 'most infamously used'[40], but he was thwarted by the Prime Minister, the Duke of Wellington – a clear example of the limits of the royal prerogative in an age of growing Parliamentary independence. Following the King's death in 1830 and the installation of a Whig Government, in 1831, at the age of 79, Nash was hauled before a more hostile Select Committee.[41] Although vindicated in his use of structural ironwork, he was accused of 'inexcusable irregularity and great negligence' in framing the accounts for Buckingham Palace, and was forced to relinquish his official appointments.

Nash's London home from 1822 to 1834 was at No. 14 Regent Street (Fig 0.3), one of the most ostentatious houses ever built by a British architect (see chapter 6). Here he had his drawing office, and here he housed his extensive library,[42] and his pupils. These pupils included Charles Mathews (1803–78), son of an actor who had performed in Nash's private theatre in Carmarthen,[43] and Charles Lee (1804–80), who became a well-known London surveyor, and who spoke warmly of Nash's 'constant gentlemanly and considerate demeanour'.[44] The scope of Nash's activities is revealed by an office ledger, containing accounts with 120 people, most of them suppliers and contractors.[45] He had no children by his second marriage, but he groomed Thomas Pennethorne, son of his wife's second cousin, a Worcester hop merchant, as a possible successor to the practice. Thomas died young, and in 1820 his place was taken by his younger brother, James (1801–71), whom Nash sent on an extended study tour to France and Italy in 1824–6. On James's return he became Nash's chief assistant, and in 1834 he took over the remnants of Nash's practice, going on to become the most important Government architect of the mid-19th century.[46]

Portraits of Nash painted by Sir Thomas Lawrence and Richard Evans in the mid-1820s show him as an alert-looking man, short in stature and almost bald.[47] Worldly, extrovert and seemingly lacking in vanity, he described himself in 1822, to his near-contemporary John Soane (1753–1837), as a 'thick, squat, dwarf figure, with round head, snub nose and little eyes.[48] Mrs Arbuthnot, wife of the First Commissioner of Woods and Forests, described him in 1824 as 'a very clever, odd, amusing man, with a face like a monkey's but civil and good-humoured to the greatest degree'.[49] One of his few obituarists said that he was 'singularly natural and simple', and praised his kindness to struggling artists.[50]

Nash and his wife were very gregarious; the artist Benjamin West told Joseph Farington in 1818 that there were rarely fewer than 20 people sitting down to dinner with them at East Cowes, and in 1822 C R Cockerell (1788–1863), whose father had been one of Nash's fellow-pupils in Sir Robert Taylor's office, remarked, following a dinner party, that Nash was 'always [the] same, merry amusing naïve, but making the same quotations, telling the same stories'.[51] The architect William Porden (1755–1822) recorded Nash's response to a fellow guest at another dinner party who chaffed him about his Welsh origins and lack of 'family': 'I am lineally descended from Naish, King of the Amorites, and you will find my Ancestors in Scripture'.[52] Nash later told Farington that 'he wd. live happily in a single room having his books about him'. And in 1821, when he was in his 70th year, he remarked that 'if it were not for the King he would quit his profession … He felt indifferent to what might be his estate. He could live or die. He could fall to low estate without repining'.[53] Such comments should probably be taken with a pinch of salt, and Soane told him in 1822 that there were 'few persons more anxious of fame, and who would make more sacrifices at the altar of public opinion' than Nash[54] – a comment that has a ring of truth about it.

Money was important to Nash, but the financial underpinning of his expansive, and expensive, lifestyle is difficult to reconstruct. He received the normal commission of five per cent on his architectural work, augmented by extra charges for giving advice to potential clients.[55] He also made money from surveying, and he became involved, not always profitably, in property speculation and brickmaking. He had a close working relationship in such enterprises with his relative John Edwards junior

(1772–1833), a lawyer who went into partnership with Nash's own solicitor, James Lyon;[56] both were closely involved in the Regent's Canal Company, and Edwards was Nash's next-door neighbour at No. 16 Regent Street. Early in 1821, following the building of the pair of Regent Street houses at a cost (shared with Edwards) of £34,000, Nash was said to be 'at a stand in money matters', owing between £800,000 and £1m.[57] But this did not prevent him from furnishing his new house, or from sending the young James Pennethorne to Italy. He had, according to one contemporary, 'extraordinary habits of persistence',[58] and, so long as his professional income lasted, he seems to have found little difficulty in borrowing money in order to pay his bills.

Dependent on royal and official favour, Nash's career collapsed when both were removed. By 1831, when he was dismissed from his official positions, he was nearing the age of 80, and he subsequently spent most of his time on the Isle of Wight. His tranquil but still sociable life there is recorded in the only two of his diaries that survived the destruction of his personal papers following his death.[59] In 1834 he suffered a major financial crisis following his failure to repay a loan; his capital, he said, was 'embarked in Houses, and in materials for Building, both of which, at the present epoch, were most difficult to turn into cash.'[60] He therefore sold his house in Regent Street, dismantling its magnificent gallery and re-erecting it within the long conservatory at East Cowes Castle. And in 1834, at the age of 82, he handed over the remnants of his architectural practice to James Pennethorne. He died on 13 May 1835 and was buried at St James, East Cowes, where an austere Grecian monument next to the tower marks the grave. He left his property, together with debts of £15,000, to his wife, who sold East Cowes Castle, together with most of its contents.[61] She then moved, along with her companion Ann Pennethorne, James's unmarried sister, to Hamstead, where she died in 1851. Nash's castle and its grounds vanished beneath a housing estate in the 1960s.

Nash's architecture appeals more to the eye than to the mind, and that is both its strength and its weakness. His buildings were vitiated in the eyes of contemporary pundits and of some modern critics by a somewhat superficial glamour and a fundamental lack of seriousness. And, by the demanding standards of Karl Friedrich Schinkel, John Soane and C R Cockerell – a comparison explored in chapter 9 – his buildings lack the 'Attribute of eternal' that Sir Christopher Wren had regarded as essential in architecture of the highest quality.[62] Though well read, Nash showed little interest in abstract thought or in academic theory. His talents were those of an improviser, and as such were well attuned to a culture that sought novelty, sensation and spectacle and was prepared to pay for it. He was a superb domestic planner and a town planner of genius, adept at relating buildings to their surroundings and grouping them for scenic effect, both on a small scale, as at Blaise Hamlet, and on a larger scale, as in Regent Street and in the Regent's Park terraces. Even today, his visual surprises – such as the unexpected vision of the Italianate Cronkhill in the Shropshire countryside, the Royal Pavilion in the heart of Brighton, or the triumphal arches at either end of Chester Terrace in Regent's Park – can draw a sharp and pleasurable intake of breath from the viewer. Few British architects have shown more sensitivity to the urban and rural environment than John Nash, and few have better understood the capacity of architecture to give pleasure.

Notes

1   Moher, J G 1988 'The London Millwrights and Engineers. 1775–1825'. Unpublished PhD thesis, U London, *passim*

2   MS diary of Wiliam Porden, Derbyshire Record Office, Gell of Hopton papers, 03311/4/5, 3 July 1812

3   Binney, M 1984 *Sir Robert Taylor*. London: George Allen and Unwin

4   He was associated with developments in Royal Row (now Royal Street), near the eastern end of Westminster Bridge, where he was living in 1776, and in Lambeth Road (Pinhorn (ed) 2000 II, 103–8).

5   Spurrell, W 1879 *Carmarthen and its Neighbourhood*. Carmarthen: William Spurrell; James, T 1980 *Carmarthen: An Archaeological and Topographical Survey*. Carmarthen: Dyfed Archaeological Trust

6   Suggett 1995, 15. For another of Nash's early assistants, Charles Heather, see chapter 2.

7   ODNB; Hill, Rosemary 2007 *God's Architect*. London: Penguin Books, 14–15. See also Ferrey 1861, 1–25. Nash also had a connection in Carmarthen with Robert Lugar (c 1773–1855), whose *Architectural Sketches* (1805) illustrate several of his own Nash-influenced houses: Colvin 2008, 661–2.

8   Gore and Carter (eds), 76; see also Daniels 1999.

9   Suggett 1995, 15–16; Price, C 1948 *The English Theatre in Wales*. Cardiff: University of Wales Press, 75, 82, 88

10 Watkins and Cowell (eds) 2006, 121, 8 March 1798

11 Cwmgili papers, NLW, letter of 17 Dec. 1796; Summerson 1980, 30–2

12 For example, Southgate Grove (1797), for a brandy merchant (*see* Figs S.5 and S.6; Sundridge Park, Bromley (*c* 1796–7), for a corn merchant who supplied grain to the British army (*see* S.7); Casina, Dulwich; and Bank Farm (sometimes called Point Pleasant) on the banks of the Thames at Kingston

13 Davis 1973, 56–9; Summerson 1980, 151. Nash exhibited a design for a conservatory for the Prince at the Royal Academy in 1798.

14 Farington *Diary*, Garlick *et al* (eds) 1978–1984 **III**, 1106. Nash claimed that the money went towards providing board and lodging for Repton's sons. Payments of £900 from Repton in 1806 may represent premiums for his son George, who continued to work for Nash (Pinhorn (ed) 2000 **II**, 148, quoting an account book in the Isle of Wight RO, Store 61.1)

15 PRONI, D/3187/A/42; Farington *Diary* (*see* note 14) **XVI**, 5746

16 Harcourt, L 1976 *Corsham Court: A Gothick Dream*. London: Gothick Dream, 30

17 Temple, N 1988 'Pages from an architect's notebook'. *Proc Hampshire Field Club* **44**, 97

18 Kelly, A 1985 'Coade stone in Georgian architecture'. *Architect Hist* **28**, 85–8. The top floor added to his house in Dover Street in 1814 was embellished with Coade stone figures of Geometry, Music, Painting and Poetry.

19 For example, Witley Court, Worcestershire (*c* 1806), Caledon, Co. Tyrone (1806 or 1808–11) and Rockingham, Co. Roscommon (1809–10)

20 For example, at Aqualate Hall, Staffordshire (English Heritage Archives Collection, JCB01)

21 RIBA, SD 110/1 and SKB 246/4; Temple 1993. Other pupils in Dover Street included Francis Greenway (1777–1837), later one of the pioneer architects in Australia, to which he was transported after being found guilty of forgery in 1812 (Colvin 2008, 449–50). There is no way of telling how many assistants Nash had in his office at any one time.

22 For example, Ravensworth Castle (RIBA, SB 54/5)

23 www. dia/ie/architects/view640

24 Ladd 1978, 111, 117, quoting Methuen MSS; Harcourt 1976, 40–46

25 Wheeler, G 'John Nash and the building of Rockingham', *in* Reeves, T and Oram, R (eds) 2003 *Avenues to the Past*. Belfast: Ulster Architectural Heritage Society, 172–80. His replacement was John Lynn, founder of a dynasty of architects in Ireland: www. dia/ie/architects/view3279.

26 PRONI, quoted www. caledon. org. uk/estate_ history, php

27 Temple 1979

28 Pinhorn (ed) 2000 **II**, 137–143; Sherfield, I 1994 *East Cowes Castle: A Pictorial History*. Camberley: Business by Design, 68–70

29 Bolton 1927, 196–7; Spiller to Soane, 13 March 1814A

30 Romilly, S 1840 *Memoirs of the Life of Sir Samuel Romilly*, London: J. Murray, **III**, 86

31 Farington *Diary* (*see* note 14) **XV**, 5134, 1 Jan 1818

32 Spencer, H 1961 *London's Canal*. London: Putnam. James Morgan was engineer to the canal company, designing Macclesfield Bridge over the canal in 1815–16 and the machinery for the Diorama in Park Square in 1823 (Colvin 2008, 703; Skempton, A (ed) 2002 *A Biographical Dictionary of Civil Engineers in Great Britain and Ireland*. London: Thomas Telford Publishing, **I**, 452).

33 The ideal of a planned development of middle-class villas had already been realised, in a less architecturally coherent form, on the Eyre estate in St John's Wood, to the west of the Park: see Galinou, Mireille 2011 *Cottages and Villas*. New Haven and London: Yale University Press

34 The site was given by the Earl of Glengall, builder of the nearby Swiss Cottage (1810–14), the finest surviving *cottage orné* in the British Isles, whose architect has eluded detection, despite repeated attempts by historians to link it to Nash. Nash designed Harriet Lodge at West Cowes on the Isle of Wight for Glengall's daughter the Countess of Belfast *c* 1832 (Pinhorn (ed) 2000 **I**, 89)

35 Liscombe, R 1970. *Architect Hist* **13**, 43–56. St Mary, Haggerston, in the East End of London (1826–7: demolished), drew on one of his Gothic designs for the Commissioners.

36 R[anger], W A 1836; I am grateful to Jon Clarke for this reference.

37 The other two were Sir John Soane and Robert Smirke

38 *PP* 1828 **IV**, 44–74

39 *PP* 1829 **III**, 4

40 *Despatches … of the Duke of Wellington* (ns 1867–80), ed 2nd Duke of Wellington. London: John Murray, **V**, 616

41 *PP* 1831 **IV**, 6

42 Catalogue 1835 (copy in Sir John Soane's Museum)

43 Colvin 2008, 683

44 *Builder* **13** (8 Dec 1855), 585

45 RIBA, MS Nas/1

46 Tyack 1992, 7–15

47 There is a less flattering drawing of *c* 1830 by Edwin Landseer in the National Portrait Gallery.

48 Bolton 1927, 351–5

49 Bamford, F (ed) 1950 *Journal of Mrs Arbuthnot 1820–32*. London: Macmillan, **I**, 334

50 *Gentleman's Magazine* 1835, 438

51 Farington *Diary* (*see* note 14) **XV**, 5161, 20 Feb 1821 and **XVI**, 5745, 6 Nov 1821; Watkin 1974, 68

52 MS diary, Derbyshire Record Office, Gell of Hopton papers, 03311/4/5, 3 July 1812

53 Farington *Diary* (*see* note 14) **XVI**, 5579–80, 12 Nov. 1820; 5746, 7 Nov. 1820

54 Bolton 1927

55 His scale of charges was set out in a memorandum to Lord Lorton of Rockingham (*see* Wheeler 2003, in note 25 above, 185–6).

56 Pinhorn (ed) 2000 **I**, 73; **II**, 117–8. Edwards was the son of Nash's cousin John Edwards, a millwright and pump-maker, latterly of Belvedere House, Lambeth (on the site of Waterloo Station); he was a friend of Alexander Milne, Secretary to the Commissioners of Woods and Forests and to the New Street Commissioners, and was MP for Glamorgan from 1818–20 and for Wells 1830–2.

57 Farington *Diary* (*see* note 14) **XVI**, 5624, 26 Feb. 1821; Summerson 1980, 186

58 *Builder* **14** (16 August 1856), 442

59 They are transcribed in Pinhorn (ed) 2000.

According to Pennethorne family tradition, most of his papers were burned on the order of the Duke of Wellington (personal communication).

60 Summerson 1980, 186

61 NA, PROB 11/1851, f. 507 (will). The will was disputed and led to proceedings in Chancery, from which it emerged that the main debts consisted of mortgages of properties owned by Nash. I am grateful to Malcolm Pinhorn for this information.

62 Wren, C and Wren S 1750 *Parentalia*. London: T Osborne and R Dodsley, 261

John Nash before fame and fortune*

RICHARD SUGGETT

John Nash was one of the greatest Regency architects, but he was a paradoxical figure. There were two sides to his reputation – respectable and disreputable. The portrait by Sir Thomas Lawrence (*see* Frontispiece), which he presented to Jesus College, Oxford, where it still hangs in the hall, shows how he wanted to be remembered.[1] It captures him at the height of his fame in the 1820s as architect to the King. Lawrence, the foremost portraitist of the day, was credited with the ability to capture the essential character of his sitters, and yet his Nash is curiously enigmatic. This is, of course, the point. Despite Nash's immense success, there was something not quite 'sound' about him.

Nash in his later years was rich and extraordinarily successful as architect to the Prince Regent (the future George IV), and the designer of the Brighton Pavilion, Regent Street and Regent's Park, and a string of admired country houses. Scandal, however, always threatened to puncture his respectability. In his early career, there had been bankruptcy, a strange divorce, unfortunate speculation and building disasters. It was widely believed that his later and (to some of his contemporaries) surprising success was a reward for marital complaisance: his second wife was supposed to have been the Prince Regent's mistress. No evidence for their liaison has ever been adduced, and the affair might have been an invention of the satirists of the day. A scurrilous but undeniably funny broadside depicts Prinny in the saloon of his royal yacht, braces dangling, informing a corpulent Mrs Nash: 'I like to visit all parts of my kingdom'.[2] A miniature survives, which shows the 'other' Nash in about 1798 (Fig 1.1). It was probably painted on the occasion of his second marriage, when he was on the verge of great professional success. It shows an interesting face, although Nash later described himself self-deprecatingly as having a 'dwarf figure, with round head, snub nose, and little

Fig 1.1
John Nash after his return to London, aged about 46 (photograph of a miniature, private collection).

eyes.'[3] Nash may have thought of himself as unprepossessing, but he certainly had a strong personality: you either took to him or you did not. A revealing diary entry by a Miss Butt, who encountered him at the dinner table in 1795, records how she found 'the little man ... pert, impudent and ugly'. But this sort of shallow aversion must be countered by the rueful comment of Humphry Repton, the famous landscaper and Nash's discarded business partner, who was captivated by Nash at their first meeting in 1792, and recalled that 'he had powers of *fascination* beyond anyone I have ever met with'. If a client fell under Nash's spell – as many did – it was never clear quite how it would all end, although the results were sometimes unexpected and usually expensive.[4]

Although Nash was a leading figure in the architectural profession until the 1830s, there was no 19th-century biography of him. This is somewhat surprising given his extraordinary success. There was of course a reaction against

* Nash's early biography is more fully considered, with extracts from his divorce papers, in the *Transactions of the Honourable Society of Cymmrodorion* for 2008. Nash's architectural work is discussed and referenced in my *John Nash – Architect in Wales: Pensaer yng Nghymru* (NLW & RCAHMW, 1995). I have taken the opportunity to note here some additional references. I must thank fellow Nash enthusiasts, especially Edna Dale-Jones (over many years), Tom Lloyd and Geoffrey Tyack, for sharing some of their discoveries with me.

Regency taste, which Victorians regarded as frivolous and indulgent. Nash's preference for stucco was regarded with some horror as the antithesis of architectural honesty, suspected of disguising inferior materials and workmanship. Nevertheless, as a professional man, Nash had the qualities of self-help and perseverance admired by the mid-Victorian Samuel Smiles' school of moral biography. Pugin held up Nash as a model of determination and industry, repeating for his pupils original anecdotes (a 'mixture of gravity and drollery')[5] to show how he was never deterred by the many difficulties in his early life. But for the Victorians there were probably too many disreputable elements in his career, which had ended with his ignominious dismissal from public service. In any case, the raw materials for a biography were just not available after his death, as several brief but error-strewn memoirs showed.[6]

Nash seems to have done his best to suppress knowledge of his early life and career, though Britton revealed obliquely that he was 'guilty of some irregularities and eccentricities'. In later life, he reinvented his early biography, presenting himself in rehearsed fashion as a gentleman with a small estate in Wales, whose architectural achievements had been attained rather effortlessly and almost as a diversion after John Vaughan of Golden Grove had challenged him as a *jeu d'esprit* to design a cold bath. In fact, Nash came from a family of artisans and was driven to succeed. He had flair in abundance, he worked quickly, and his apparently effortless success in later life rested on two decades of relentless application in London and Wales.

Early life

John Summerson's pre-War biography (1935) effectively rehabilitated Nash's architectural reputation, and the revised biography (1980) gave the outline of his surprising early career for the first time.[7] It is now possible to piece together more, but certainly not all, of his remarkable early life.

Characteristically, one of the key pieces of the biographical jigsaw is missing: it remains to be established exactly when and where Nash was born, and the name of his mother is unknown. Almost certainly, however, he was born in September 1752, probably in London but possibly in South Wales, to Welsh parents. His cousins, with the surname Edwards, were millwrights and engineers from the Neath area.

The Welsh poet and antiquarian Iolo Morganwg knew the family, describing how for several generations they had been 'greatly distinguished for their genius and skill' in constructing machines.[8] On the paternal side, Nash's forbears were artisans whose mobility had followed the changing geography of the 18th-century industrial dynamic. A genealogy, possibly compiled for a grant of arms, shows that they came from Broseley, near Ironbridge, an early industrial centre on the River Severn.[9] At about the turn of the century, Thomas Nash, the architect's grandfather, followed Sir Humphrey Mackworth from Shropshire to Glamorgan. He settled in Neath, apparently bringing with him several families of Broseley artisans attracted by Mackworth's development of industrial undertakings on his wife's estate. Thomas Nash eventually became a surveyor or agent of Mackworth's coalworks, and remained at Neath for the rest of his life. He had several sons and daughters, including John Nash (1714–72), a millwright and the architect's father. His daughter, Mary Nash, married Humphrey Edwards, a millwright and engineer, and the fortunes of both families became interlinked. The architect therefore had a large cousinage in Neath, many sharing his surname, but the Edwards family proved to be his most important relatives.[10]

Around the middle of the 18th century, John Nash senior, followed by his nephew John Edwards, migrated to London. Both were millwrights, and both settled in Lambeth, the bustling commercial area on the south bank of the Thames. Here there were numerous opportunities for the capable artisan. John Edwards seems to have specialised in the engineering required by the water companies supplying the needs of the expanding metropolis. He is described variously in the London directories as a pipe-borer and millwright, engine- and pump-maker, and latterly (1794–1800) as millwright and engineer of Vine Street, off Belvedere Road.[11] The family were successful and inventive: it was said that John Edwards invented the first water-cart used in the streets of late-Georgian London; and by 1794 he had acquired Belvedere House, a former pleasure garden and house, in whose grounds Lambeth Water Works was established in 1785 (on the site of the present Waterloo station).[12]

John Edwards senior, eventually styled esquire, lived on until 1818 at Belvedere House. His gravestone in the old Lambeth burial ground recorded that he died in his 80th year after '56 years an Inhabitant of this parish'.[13] John Nash senior's career, by contrast, was cut short by his relatively early death in 1772. Nevertheless, the family had the means to apprentice – or, more strictly, to indenture as a pupil – John Nash junior to Sir Robert Taylor, one of the principal architects of the day, and responsible, more than anyone else of his generation, for taking the design of the English villa out of its Palladian straitjacket.[14] Here, as Summerson observed, Nash had the opportunity to learn the best that architectural practice in England could offer.[15] Documentary confirmation of his apprenticeship has proved elusive, but it is confirmed by the recent rediscovery of John Nash senior's will. The will of John Nash of St Mary Lambeth, styled millwright (and evidently a widower), was witnessed in July 1772, and in it he bequeathed everything to his son, John Nash, described as 'now living with Robert Taylor Esquire of the parish of St Martin in the Fields, Architect'.[16]

Having finished his apprenticeship in 1774 or 1775, Nash set up on his own account as a surveyor and – a most important distinction – an architect. An architect was still a rarity in the 1770s. Later, during his painful litigation in the 1780s, Nash insisted that he was 'by profession an architect', although his professional earnings were small, and he denied that he was ever in trade as a carpenter or builder.[17]

We can imagine Nash as very much at home in later 18th-century Lambeth 'Marsh', the commercial area between Lambeth Palace and Southwark, defined by a loop of the Thames, which provided many services for London and beyond. Thomas Pennant was impressed by the range of industrial undertakings in north Lambeth, which included mills (with the Albion Flour Mills under construction in the 1780s), potteries, glassworks, wineries and distilleries with 'Brobdignagion' vats and vast barrel-yards. Mrs Coade's famous artificial-stone works had been established in Lambeth since 1767, and Nash was undoubtedly familiar with the range of architectural ornament produced there. On the riverside there were wharfs and great timber-yards, and Nash was involved in a significant partnership with a prosperous timber merchant, Richard Heaviside. He was also retained as the surveyor of a brew-house and vinegar yard at Vauxhall.[18] Besides, Lambeth had been a centre for entertainment and sociability since the 17th century, with taverns, public pleasure gardens (some disreputable), and

theatres. Contemporaries agreed that Nash was very sociable, and, as he prospered, he was able to indulge his taste for the theatre, eventually acquiring an interest in the playhouse in Carmarthen and taking the stage there as a gentleman-amateur, probably against a backdrop painted by the elder Pugin.[19]

Marriage and divorce

The 22-year-old John Nash, styled architect, was married by licence on 28 April 1775 in the parish church of St Mary Newington (since demolished), south of the present Elephant and Castle. His bride was Jane Elizabeth Kerr, the daughter of a Surrey surgeon, Hugh Kerr of Dorking, who had a practice in Walworth. The witnesses were Abraham Ewings of Newington, described as a gentleman and probably a business associate; William Blackburn, a fellow architect who later became a pioneer of modern prison design; and Ann Burrowes, presumably a friend of the bride's.[20] It was the match of an up-and-coming professional man to an established professional man's daughter. The Nashes lived in Ewings' house until Christmas 1775 when they set up home in Lambeth at Royal Row (Road), south of the present St Thomas's Hospital.

The couple were quite prosperous. Later litigation revealed that Nash had leasehold property worth a significant amount, as well as valuable household goods. He estimated his professional earnings at £200 a year on average, but Richard Woodings, who seems to have known the couple intimately and may have been Nash's clerk, said they amounted to between £500 and £1000, a substantial sum. Nash was described in the same legal proceedings as 'in a very extensive way of business as a surveyor, builder and carpenter', in partnership with the well-connected timber merchant, Richard Heaviside, and receiving an annual salary as surveyor of Thomas Fassett's vinegar-maker's factory in Lambeth.[21]

John and Jane Nash lived together in Lambeth for several years. The registers of the Church of St Mary, Lambeth record the baptisms of their two children: John on 9 June 1776, and Hugh on 28 April 1778.[22] The Nashes were, to all intents and purposes, a conventional married couple, naming the children after their paternal and maternal grandfathers. Then, in June 1778, they separated, Nash alleging that because of his wife's 'ill conduct' he had found it necessary to send her to Wales 'in order to work a reformation in her.'[23]

What had happened? Nash made two allegations against Jane, one commonplace but the other extraordinary.[24] The first complaint was that made by innumerable husbands against their wives: Jane Nash was accused of extravagance. Unknown to her husband, she had (Nash alleged) run up millinery bills of nearly £300, which her husband had been obliged to pay in 1777. Richard Woodings claimed both to have paid several bills on her behalf, and that her husband had been arrested for the non-payment of two milliners' bills, each for about £80. Nash said that he had repeatedly remonstrated with her, and that he decided to send her to stay with relatives in Wales where there would be fewer opportunities for extravagance, believing that her expenses in London were more than he could support.[25] The second allegation was astonishing. John and Jane Nash were acknowledged (as already noted) to be the parents of two children who were baptised in 1776 and 1778. But Nash then repudiated the children, making the extraordinary claim that Jane had 'imposed two spurious children on him as his and her own, notwithstanding she had then never had any child'.[26] In plainer terms, he claimed that Jane had simulated pregnancy and had bought or otherwise acquired the infants, passing them off as her own. His allegations, made in the Bishop of London's Consistory Court, were reported in the press. The original report has not been found, but it re-circulated several years later when Nash was petitioning for his divorce. According to *The World* in 1787, Mrs Nash 'was the dame [a somewhat derogatory term], of whom a very extraordinary tale was not long ago related in the newspapers. She used to impose upon her husband with a simulation of pregnancy, and actually bought children whom she brought up as her own, to carry on the imposture.'[27] It is now impossible to know what the exact circumstances were. However, as in cases of child abduction or baby-snatching reported in the 20th century, Jane might have bought or stolen babies in an attempt to retrieve an already failing marriage. Interestingly, even in the 20th century – as in the 18th century – husbands were readily deceived by these mock pregnancies and fake births.

Nash initiated divorce proceedings (separation from bed and board) against his wife in the Bishop of London's Consistory Court in 1782, and she seems to have been resigned to the separation. It emerged that during her exile in South Wales she had had an affair with the chaperone selected by Nash to show her 'the sights of the country'.[28] The couple were observed *in flagrante* on Aberavon beach and at Jane's lodgings. She became pregnant and gave birth to a girl at Neath in December 1779. The other children, John and Hugh Nash, seem already to have been completely rejected and are never referred to again; presumably they were removed from Nash's household when Jane was sent to Wales. Jane apparently remained penniless in Neath until 1785, when she was awarded maintenance of £10 quarterly from Doctors' Commons (ie the consistory court). Definitive sentence of divorce from bed and board was finally read on 26th January 1787. Jane made a further petition for her maintenance and that of her child, now aged seven, on 20th March 1787, after which nothing more was heard of them.[29]

Bankruptcy

Nash's personal life had been in turmoil since 1778, but his business affairs were also failing. Nash's personal answer to the consistory court shows how he felt that his personal and business lives were interconnected. According to Nash, Jane's extravagance and deceptions had induced his creditors to demand payment of outstanding bills amounting to some £5,000. Unable to pay their demands, Nash had been obliged to mortgage his properties in Lambeth and Bloomsbury. The details of his interests in Lambeth are obscure, but the nature of his building speculation in Bloomsbury can be established.[30]

Nash was anxious to make an impact, as well as a profit, on the metropolitan building scene, as both architect and speculative builder. In September 1777 he had agreed with Sir John Rushout (a Worcestershire squire) to redevelop Rushout's town-house in Bloomsbury Square with some adjoining land. This would allow a new residential block on the north-west corner of Bloomsbury Square with Great Russell Street. The development formed two larger houses (Nos. 16–17) in the square, and six smaller houses (Nos. 66–71) on the south side of Russell Street. The design of the elevations was to be approved by Thomas Leverton, an older and more experienced surveyor and architect. The agreement between Nash and Rushout was supported by a bond with a penalty of £2,000 for non-completion of the development by September 1778. Nash's sureties were two business associates: Abraham Ewings, who had been witness at his wedding, and Richard Heaviside, the timber merchant. The building lease was presumably of the standard type, with the developer responsible for a substantial ground rent after completion until the houses had been sold.[31]

The development must have been substantially finished by September 1778, when rates were levied on the houses. Nevertheless, they remained unoccupied and became a target for thieves. Large quantities of lead were stolen from the roofs, and eventually Nash's foreman apprehended a suspect who was found guilty at the Old Bailey of stealing 42lb (19kg) of lead.[32]

The completed development (Fig 1.2) with its relatively novel stuccoed front (encouraged by the 1774 Building Act), dignified by pilasters above the rusticated ground floor on the Bloomsbury Square side, was a 'humble imitation' (as Summerson put it) of the river frontage of old Somerset House, then attributed to Inigo Jones.[33] But it was also a significant pointer to the future. The ingeniously planned interiors included boldly cantilevered stairs, an octagonal room of the type that Nash was to favour in his Welsh villas, and the radial fluted motif that appears in much of his later work.[34] Nash's houses were undeniably stylish but, none the less, they failed to sell in a well-supplied market. Nash himself moved into one of the empty houses.[35]

Nash was in an increasingly difficult financial situation, and his creditors lost patience. It is clear that the Bloomsbury building speculation had stretched Nash to breaking point, and at the end of September 1783 he was declared bankrupt. In particular, he owed a considerable sum to the Adam brothers' firm for Liardet's patent cement or 'composition', William Adam & Co having applied the stucco to the house fronts in Bloomsbury Square (in 1778) and then

Fig 1.2
Nash's development
on the corner of
Bloomsbury Square and
Great Russell Street
(DP104374).

to the Great Russell Street houses (in 1779) at a total cost of £688 12s 6d. According to litigation over the stucco patent, this was one of several debts run up by persons in the building trade that would not have been incurred had Messrs Adam been better acquainted with the characters of those concerned. Nevertheless, the Adams went on to lend Nash £2,000 on the security of the Bloomsbury Square houses. Nash had evidently charmed the businesslike brothers into a temporary rescue of his finances, but, significantly, there was never any further association between Nash and the Adam brothers. Nash, according to his personal answer, assigned the whole of his property to his creditors in about May 1782, and was allowed three years to pay off his debts. But, oppressed by debts and legal charges, he was insolvent, and, on 30 September 1783, he was declared bankrupt. He managed to reach an accommodation with his creditors and was discharged on 31 December 1783, but by then his business reputation was in ruins.[36]

Carmarthen

Nash disappeared from the London building scene in 1784. He is next heard of in Carmarthen. It is possible that he already knew the west Wales town and had worked there as an apprentice on Sir Robert Taylor's Carmarthen guildhall (Fig 1.3). Be that as it may, we know exactly what brought Nash to west Wales in 1785: he responded to a small advertisement placed in the provincial press by the church-wardens of St Peter's, Carmarthen, seeking contractors for a new church roof.[37] The church-wardens accepted Nash's estimate of £670 for taking down the old roof and erecting a new double roof of oak, with lead gutters and ridge and Pembrokeshire slates, and for making a plain plaster ceiling. The contract was signed on 22 June 1785 by Nash and his business partner, Samuel Saxon.[38] The profit margin was probably quite small; visiting antiquarians complained that Nash's workmen had ground up irreplaceable alabaster monuments, presumably

Fig 1.3
The Guildhall, Carmarthen, by Robert Taylor 1767–77 (RCAHMW: Crown Copyright).

to save money on plaster. With the project successfully completed, Nash decided not to leave. Carmarthen was a regional capital, 'the resort of the aristocracy and gentry of the surrounding neighbourhood', and Nash saw that it would be possible to rebuild his career there.[39]

The early years in Carmarthen were probably difficult for Nash. He was primarily a contractor and supplier of building materials rather than an architect, as the evidence of Nash's litigation suggests. The very fortunate survival of the bill-book of his attorney, the acquisitive and sometimes patronising Herbert Lloyd, shows that Nash was involved in a web of litigation that extended from the Carmarthen Mayor's Court to the assizes and the central Westminster courts.[40] Nash was not perhaps especially litigious, but he understood that legal action enforced agreements and prompted the settlement of debts. Moreover, in 1787, in an extraordinary episode that shows Nash's determination to effect a complete break with the past, he sought – but failed – to obtain a Parliamentary divorce.[41]

Lloyd, the attorney, knew Nash's affairs better than most, and referred to him condescendingly as a 'jobber' (rather than a gentleman). His jobs included a new watermill for Lloyd in Carmarthen, the construction of which he supervised, ensuring that the millwrighting and smith's work were undertaken by his uncle, Humphrey Edwards of Neath.[42]

It took time for Nash to establish his credentials as an architect, and at first he was at a disadvantage vis-à-vis established metropolitan architects. In 1788, the Cardiganshire magistrates initially turned to William Blackburn when they sought a plan and estimate for the new county gaol. Blackburn, a witness at Nash's wedding, was already a successful architect specialising in advanced prison design following the Gaols Act of 1784, and had won the first prize in the National Penitentiary competition.[43] The Howardian-inspired Gaols Act prompted the rebuilding of many gaols and houses of correction. The turning point in Nash's Welsh career was reached in 1789, when his proposed designs for the new county gaol at Carmarthen were accepted.[44] The gaol was completed rapidly, and an idiosyncratic inscription on the portico announced that it had been begun in 1789 and finished in 1792. By then Mr Nash of Carmarthen, architect, was becoming a well-known figure in west Wales, building a new house in the town and

eventually indulging his theatrical tastes by adding a little theatre.[45]

By the later 18th century, a successful architect need not live in London but could be based in a provincial town. Nash took full advantage of the building opportunities provided by the improving Georgian towns and the magistrates' enthusiasm for new public buildings. During his residence in Carmarthen, Nash designed three prisons, a market-hall, a poorhouse, an asylum and several bridges. These were large projects, which Nash handled with flair. Supervision of their building provided Nash with a regular income, and brought him into prolonged and profitable contact with the magistrates who approved and scrutinised the projects.[46]

Nash's gaols provide some interesting contrasts. Cardigan had a severe, pedimented classical front and was large and impressive; so much so that Richard Colt Hoare wondered if paupers might exchange their cottages for lodgings in this palatial gaol.[47] Carmarthen was more theatrical. The main front was a compressed version of London's Newgate Prison (1770–95), complete with garlands of felons' chains. These are clearly shown in a drawing by C R Cockerell (1806), who conceded that the gaol, though 'affected', was 'gen[e]rally and commonly admired'.[48] The main front of Hereford Gaol (Fig 1.4) was similar to Carmarthen with its theatrical and intimidating portico, but it had the added refinement of a hanging platform on the flat-roofed lodge (partly shielded by a three-sided cupola) which was used almost immediately. Hereford was a new prison on a new site, and it allowed Nash to demonstrate his flair for planning. His gaol was a version of the panopticon, where a central octagonal observatory allowed views into the wings and airing courts where different classes of prisoners were segregated.[49]

Prisons were large buildings that took years to reach completion, so Nash sought a quicker route to celebrity through bridge building. Nash's bridges were, by and large, conventional – such as the multi-arched bridge at Aberystwyth – but when there was an opportunity to be innovative, he seized it. The opportunity arrived in 1791, with the competition for a new bridge across the Usk at Newport, Monmouthshire. The river is tidal at this point, with a large rise and fall in water levels. As a convenience for shipping, Nash boldly proposed building a huge single-arched stone bridge some three hundred

Fig 1.4 (right)
*The street frontage of
Hereford Gaol (1792–6)
(Hereford Guide, 1827).*

Fig 1.5 (below)
*St David's Cathedral before
Nash's restoration
(Pembrokeshire County
Library).*

Fig 1.6
St David's Cathedral
after Nash's restoration
of 1790–3
(Pembrokeshire County
Library).

feet in diameter with the crown 50ft (15m) above high water. Had the bridge been built, it would have been the largest single-span bridge in Britain, certainly with a span greater than the famous single-arched bridge at Pontypridd. Work began on the cofferdams for the abutments but the contractors and magistrates seem to have lost their nerve, and Nash was paid off.[50]

The proposed restoration of St David's Cathedral (Fig 1.5) provided another opportunity for Nash to play to the gallery. He was appointed to survey the Cathedral in 1789, but it was expected that James Wyatt would devise the scheme for stabilising the cathedral nave, where settlement was pushing out the west front in an alarming way. In the event, Nash completely outsmarted Wyatt, charming the Chapter into accepting his proposals for restoring the Cathedral after persuading them that they needed a new chapter house.[51] He shored up the nave, encased the shores in massive buttresses, and rebuilt the west front in a picturesque Gothic style (Fig 1.6). He probably saved the nave from collapse, but his eclectic design for the new front was despised by later Gothic purists, particularly Gilbert Scott, who erased all visible traces of Nash's work in the 1880s.

Nash also persuaded the Chapter to allow him to commission a series of perspective paintings showing the Cathedral before and after restoration. These were large and dramatic watercolours by J A Repton (then working in Nash's office) and Augustus Pugin (who seems to have included a tiny self-portrait; Fig 1.7).

Fig 1.7 (left)
An artist sketching the restored St David's Cathedral; possibly a self-portrait by Auguste Pugin (Pembrokeshire County Library).

1a

1b

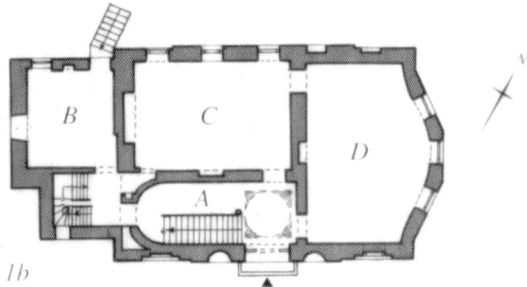

1c

2c

2a

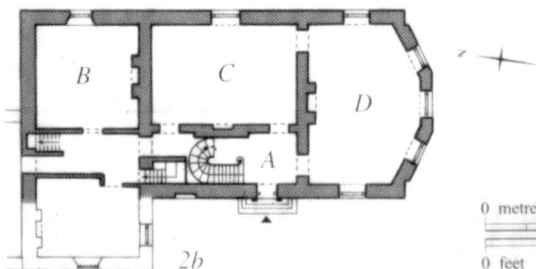

2b

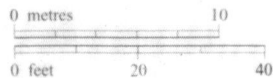

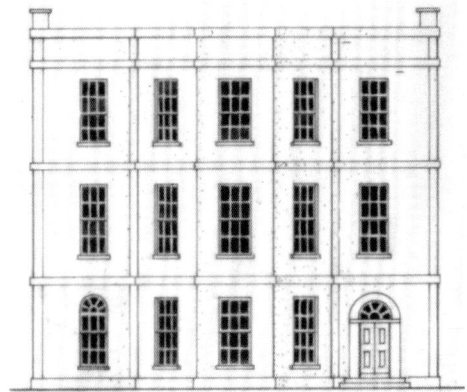

3a

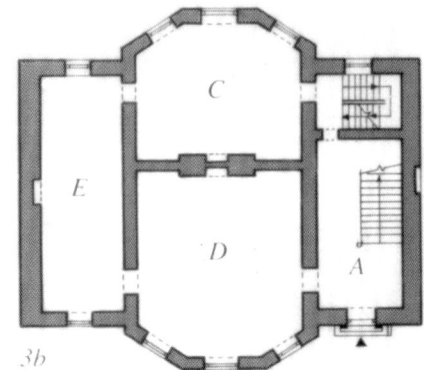

3b

4a

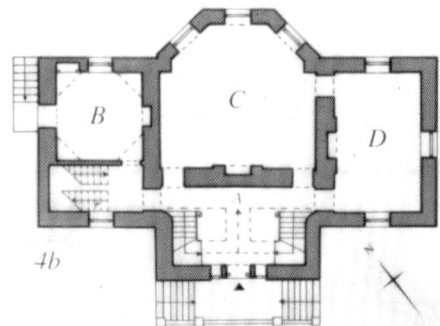

4b

Pugin, like Nash, was busy reinventing his biography and career, having fled from revolutionary France in 1792, and he was to have a lifelong association with the architect.[52] The drawings were intended as a fund-raising exercise, but they were excellent publicity for Nash, and were shown by him in London at the Society of Antiquaries. He eventually appropriated the drawings that belonged to the Chapter, and they seem to have been important to him. They certainly demonstrate that he was increasingly thinking about buildings pictorially: a transition that is also apparent in the design of Nash's houses.

Villas

Nash's public buildings were important because they brought him into prolonged contact with the magistrates who had commissioned them. Quite soon, Nash was rebuilding their houses in west Wales and beyond. It is difficult to establish a precise chronology for Nash's houses, but it is rewarding to distinguish stylistically between his earlier and later villas.

The earlier villas (Fig 1.8) include Glanwysc, near Crickhowell, Priory House in Cardigan, Foley House, Haverfordwest, and Zion House, Tenby.[53] With the exception of Glanwysc, they were built on the edge of towns, and, although having generous sites, the architectural emphasis is placed on the front elevation (Fig 1.9); the side and rear elevations are generally rather undistinguished. Sometimes, as at Whitson Court, Monmouthshire – an existing house 'finished' by Nash – screen walls and pavilions actually prevented the visitor from walking around the exterior of the house.[54] Most of these houses had canted bays in the style favoured by Sir Robert Taylor, sometimes placed rather incongruously as single-storeyed bays at the side of the house. In plan, they are quite conventional, with the principal doorway opening directly into a stair hall. Services were placed in a basement in the old-fashioned way.

Nash's later villas (Fig 1.10) are quite different: so different, indeed, that it is as if another architect has been at work. Ffynnone, Llysnewydd (Fig 1.11) and Llanerchaeron (Fig 1.12) are essentially cubes without a principal front and without the Taylorian projections of the earlier villas.[55] The fronts of the houses were essentially three-sided; the fourth side was taken up by the service courtyard, often a range of considerable charm (as at Llanerchaeron,

Fig 1.13), which displaced the service basement of the earlier villas. Subtle differences between the elevations were disclosed as the visitor walked around the outside. Whereas Nash's earlier villas had a single main front elevation, his later villas are best appreciated from a three-quarter view.

Nash's villas were like boxes full of surprises, since it was impossible to predict from the outside the arrangement of the rooms within. Llanerchaeron, the best of the surviving later villas, demonstrates this very well. One cannot deduce the arrangement of the rooms from a perambulation of the outside, especially as there are several false windows. On entering, a hidden light source draws the visitor from hall to inner-hall before the top-lit stair is encountered. The dramatic branching stair appears as if poured into the available space. The surprise stair, daringly cantilevered, was the key feature of Nash's later villas. Nash deliberately made it into a surprise feature by clever planning that ensured that a visitor could not reach any room without first traversing hall and inner-hall and encountering the stair.

Picturesque buildings

Ffynnone, Llysnewydd and Llanerchaeron lacked a considered relationship to the landscape beyond a parkland setting. But while Nash was designing these villas he was also designing buildings that were explicitly and theoretically picturesque. Nash designed three such buildings between 1791–4: Castle House, a marine villa at Aberystwyth for Uvedale Price, one of the theoreticians of the Picturesque; The Cottage, Newcastle Emlyn, a Gothic dower house built for

Fig 1.8 (opposite)
Nash's earlier villas,
from R Suggett, John Nash
– Architect in Wales:
1a–c Foley House;
2a–c Priory House;
3a–b Zion House;
4a–b Llanwysc;
A hall;
B morning room;
C dining room;
D drawing room;
E gallery
(RCAHMW: Crown Copyright).

Fig 1.9
Zion House, Tenby, showing the canted central bay,
(c 1790) engraving c 1850.

11

1a

2a

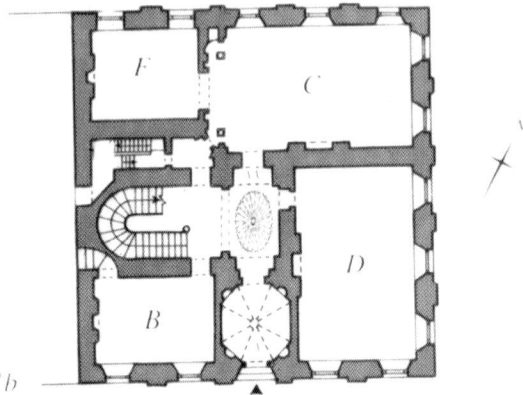

1b

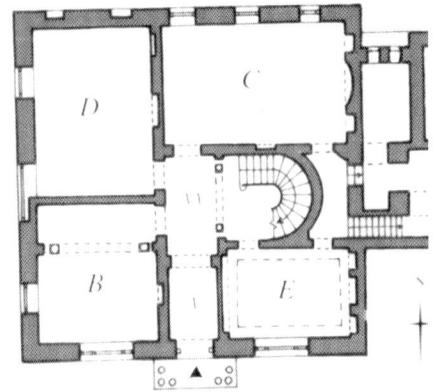

2b

3a

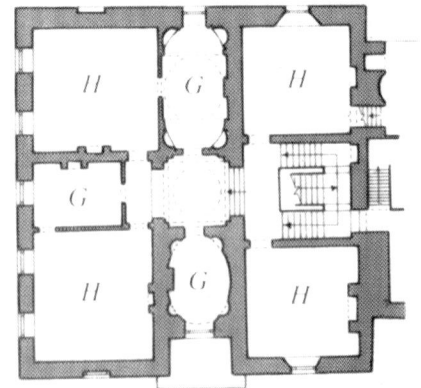

3c

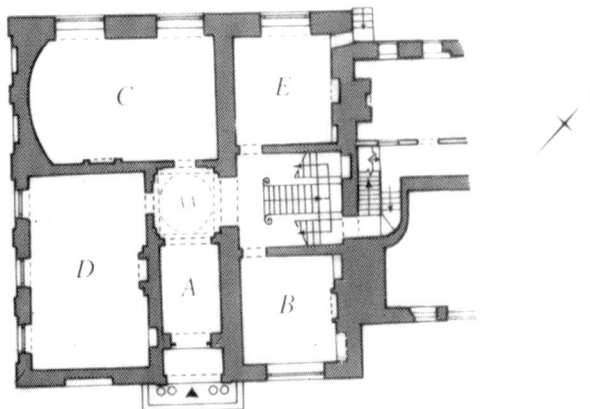

3b

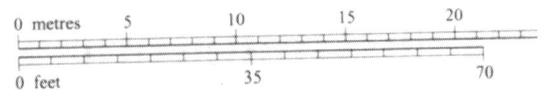

Fig 1.10 (opposite)
Nash's later villas, from
R Suggett, John Nash –
Architect in Wales:
1a–b Ffynone;
2a–b Llysnewydd;
3a–c Llanerchaeron,
ground and first floors;
A hall; AA inner hall;
B morning room;
C dining room;
D drawing room;
E library;
F ante-room;
G dressing room;
H bedroom (RCAHMW:
Crown Copyright).

Fig 1.11 (left above)
Llysnewydd (c 1795):
one of Nash's later villas
in a parkland setting
(RCAHMW: Crown
Copyright).

Fig 1.12
Llanerchaeron (c 1794)
after restoration
(Geoffrey Tyack).

Fig 1.13
An aerial view of
Llanerchaeron, showing the
relationship between the
house and service courtyard
(RCAHMW: Crown
Copyright).

13

the widow of a Carmarthenshire landowner and their unmarried daughters; and various additions to Hafod, the famously remote Cardiganshire country house, for Thomas Johnes, Richard Payne Knight's cousin and friend of Uvedale Price.[56]

A fourth villa must also be mentioned – Temple Druid at Maenclochog, Pembrokeshire – now known to have been commissioned by Barrington Price, Uvedale Price's brother.[57] Newly discovered documentation shows that the building contract for Temple Druid was agreed

Fig 1.14 (right)
A china model of Castle House, Aberystwyth (RCAHMW: Crown Copyright).

Fig 1.15 (below)
A reconstruction drawing of Castle House, Aberystwyth, the picturesque marine villa designed for Uvedale Price in 1791–4, from R Suggett, John Nash – Architect in Wales (RCAHMW: Crown Copyright).

in June 1791 according to designs prepared by Nash.[58] It is tantalising that no drawing of the house has been found that shows the villa before it was largely dismantled in the 1820s, but the design must surely have drawn on the 'druidic' associations of the place.

It was presumably Barrington Price who 'mentioned' Nash to his brother Uvedale, who had considered employing a 'common' Welsh carpenter to build a marine villa at Aberystwyth. Nash was introduced, and proposed building 'a square piece of architecture': no doubt a villa in his later style.[59] Price then explained that he wanted a house with the principal rooms orientated to the different viewpoints of castle ruins, the sea, and the view towards the Llŷn Peninsula. Price left Nash to work it out as best he could, and his solution was a three-sided villa: a geometrical tour de force that generally defeated the attempts of visiting artists to depict it.

Castle House is best appreciated three-dimensionally from an early 19th-century china model (Fig 1.14). It is essentially triangular in plan, but with octagonal towers rising from square bases at the points of the triangle,

Fig 1.16
*The Cottage, Newcastle
Emlyn (1792--4), the
entrance front* c *1800
(Thomas Lloyd collection).*

and turned to different viewpoints. There was a canopied balcony facing the sea, but it was not intended to be used merely for taking the air, so much as to experience the Sublime – of being safely frightened by the storms in Cardigan Bay. This explains why Castle House was deliberately sited right at the edge of the sea (Fig 1.15).

Stylistically, Castle House was an exercise in restrained towered Gothic, deferring to the ruins of the adjacent castle. At The Cottage (Fig 1.16), an elaborate Gothic single-storeyed entrance front signalled an ancient place of retirement. There were contrasting elevations. On the garden side, the house rose through two storeys, presenting a pedimented temple front with tall pointed arches. In section, it was somewhat like a nave between aisles, and no doubt was influenced by Nash's involvement with St David's Cathedral. In plan, it was an early exercise in ground-floor 'bungalow' planning, without a grand stair and having all the principal rooms, including the bedrooms, on the ground floor, and with the portico functioning as a verandah. A large drawing room with full-height sash windows allowed direct access to the temple portico and garden beyond, giving views across the river to the ruins of Newcastle Emlyn castle. This was an explicitly picturesque composition, with the castle and 'temple' facing each other in the manner of a landscape by Claude or Poussin.

At Hafod, the upland paradise created by Thomas Johnes, Nash was involved with remodelling the house and contributing to the extensive gardens and walks. It is clear that he dramatised an already interesting house – by Thomas Baldwin of Bath, 1786–8 – by moving the services behind a screen wall and placing a library and intercommunicating long conservatory in front (Fig 1.17).[60] Nash provided architectural incident in the extensive picturesque walks, but some of his schemes – including an elaborate bridge – were never realised. Nash showed his cleverness by successfully recycling earlier designs and motifs in ways that were far from obvious. The Adam and Eve gateways into Mrs Johnes's garden were urban doorways transposed from Bloomsbury, complete with keystones provided by Mrs Coade. The octagonal library and conservatory wing were extraordinarily successful, and visitors testified to the dramatic impact of the top-lit library and the conservatory with mirrored doors that presented a never-ending vista of delights. Nash allowed his rather pompous client to claim credit for the design. In reality, the design was a clever reworking of Nash's octagonal lantern over the central crossing at Hereford gaol.

15

Fig 1.17
Hafod, an idealised view
of c 1820, possibly based
on Nash's design drawings
of c 1793–4
(private collection).

Return to London

As Nash was finishing work at Hafod he was preparing to leave Carmarthen and return to London. He wound up his affairs in 1796–7, sold his house and theatre, and moved to Dover Street. The Carmarthen years have been regarded as Nash's 'lost' decade, but this was actually the period when Nash 'found' himself professionally. It was a decade of intense activity that had profound consequences for Nash personally and, more generally, for the future development of Regency architecture. Residence in Carmarthen allowed Nash to distance himself from the personal and professional disasters of his earlier career that might well have crushed a lesser personality. In Wales he was able to learn and to experiment. He had built very little in London, and Wales provided him with experience of a whole range of public and private building projects. His public buildings, especially the prisons, demonstrated his competence in handling large building projects. His villas showed his flair for planning. His earlier villas, with their bows and canted bays, inevitably reveal the influence of his old master, Sir Robert Taylor, but his later, box-like 'surprise' villas, shorn of projections, are entirely his own. He went on to build villas that were more explicitly picturesque, and a series of encounters with the theoreticians and enthusiasts of the Picturesque movement gave him the intellectual platform from which to become a brilliant and innovative metropolitan and countr house architect.

By the end of 1796, Nash was ready to return to London. He had formed a business partnership with Humphry Repton, the landscaper, that would allow him to work on a national stage. He returned briefly to Carmarthen in 1797, and in 1798 married Ann Bradley, after establishing his London home and office. Sir John Summerson refers rather grandly to Nash moving to a dignity and sophistication beyond the local Welsh gentry. There was a sense in which this was true, of course, but it has to be said that many of his clients were glad to see the back of this litigious and expensive architect. More fundamentally, one must emphasise that Nash's later sophistication was inseparable from his professional experience in Wales. His residence in Wales allowed him to rebuild a wrecked career. Without it, he might well have sunk without trace in the London building world. His great discoveries in Wales were his flair for planning, the importance of relating buildings to landscape, the capacity to design buildings that were explicitly picturesque, and the related freedom to be stylistically eclectic. These were the innovations that he brought to the metropolitan scene, reversing the usual direction of innovation. There was certainly something of the genius about Nash, but he was a genius in a hurry, and with lost time to make up. When, in 1796, he teamed up with Repton, they were – as Repton later recalled – ready to carry all before them.[61] The rest of Nash's story is well-established architectural history.

Notes

1   Garlick, Kenneth 1989 *Sir Thomas Lawrence: A Complete Catalogue of the Oil Paintings.* Oxford: Phaidon, pl 76, no. 592. For details of Nash's portraits, see Walker, Richard 1985 *Regency Portraits.* London: National Portrait Gallery **I**, 356–7.

2   George, M Dorothy 1952 *Catalogue of Political and Personal Satires* **X**. London: British Museum, no. 13, 854

3   Summerson 1980, 159 (Nash to Soane, 1822)

4   Quotations from Summerson 1980, 13, 17–18; Humphry Repton's Memoir, British Library (BL), Add MS 62112, f 87; and Gore and Carter (eds) 2005, 76. Repton actually adds that Nash's charm was all the more to be wondered at given that his personal appearance was 'far from prepossessing'.

5   Ferrey 1861, 10–12

6   'Nash, John', *in* Knight, C 1858, 430–2; Britton, J 1850 *The Auto-biography.* London: privately published, Part I, 345–6, corrected by Ferrey 1861, 14–15; *The Builder* **XIII** (1855), 585–7 and **XIV** (1856), 441–2

7   Summerson 1935; Summerson 1980

8   Williams, Edward 1818 *Vox Populi, Vox Dei! or, Edwards for Ever!* Swansea: J Harris, 10

9   'Genealogy of the Families of the Nashs as Extracted from the Register books of the Parish Church of Brosley in Shropshire', undated but watermarked 1818. The late Mr Peter Laing showed me this document, which was kept in Nash's trunk (marked 'John Nash, Hamstead, I of W 1835'). Related papers retained by the Edwards family (discovered by Malcolm Pinhorn) are in the Cameron (Vaughan-Lee) Papers, Somerset Record Office.

10   The details of Nash's paternal ancestry and the connection with the Edwards family have been established by Pinhorn 2000 **II**, 117–19 (Edwards family) and 120–3 (Nash family); see also Suggett 2009, 62, with genealogies at 81–2.

11   Summerson 1980, 1–2; Pinhorn 2000 **II**, 117

12   Phillips, D Rhys 1925 *The History of the Vale of Neath.* Swansea: privately published, 422. For Belvedere House, see *Survey of London* **XXIII** (London, 1951), 51 and pl 37a.

13   Somerset Record Office, Cameron (Vaughan-Lee) Papers, DD/CA/160. John Edwards had evidently arrived in Lambeth in 1762.

14   Binney, Marcus 1984 *Sir Robert Taylor: From Rococo to Neo-Classicism.* London: George Allen & Unwin, ch 3

15   Summerson 1980, 3–4

16   NA, Prob 11/981, cited by Tyack, *Oxford Dictionary of National Biography,* sn. Taylor's house was at 63 Spring Gardens, Charing Cross.

17   Suggett 2008, 77–8

18   *Survey of London* **XXIII**, 1–2; Pennant, Thomas 1813 *Some Account of London* (5th edn). London: J Faulder *et al*, 41–7; Gibberd, Graham 1992 *On Lambeth Marsh: The South Bank and Waterloo.* London: Jane Gibberd

19   Edna Dale-Jones's discovery that Nash was rated for the playhouse in Carmarthen is reported in *The Carmarthenshire Antiquary* **XXVIII** (1992), 117–19. On Nash's involvement with the theatre, see Price, Cecil 1948 *The English Theatre in Wales in the Eighteenth and Early Nineteenth Centuries.* Cardiff: University of Wales Press, 88–9. Pugin, whom Nash employed as a draughtsman, is specifically noted as a scene-painter at the Swansea Theatre in 1795 in Lewis, John 1851 *The Swansea Guide.* Swansea: William Matthias Brewster, 37.

20   Certified copy of the marriage entry in LMA, DL/C/559, f.105r

21   *Survey of London* **XXVI** (London, 1956), 41, notes that Fassett took over Sir Joseph Mawbey's distillery at Vauxhall in 1779–80 and probably built a house there. On Heaviside, timber-merchant of Parliament Street, Westminster, see Pinhorn 2000 **II**, 110.

22   Microfilm copies of register in the Greater London Records Office, ref X38/3–4

23   LMA, DL/C/179, f.335v

24   Libel dated 1 March 1781 in *Nash* vs *Nash* in the London Consistory Court, LMA, DL/C/179, ff.334r–339r

25   *Journals of the House of Lords* **37** (1783–7), 639, evidence of Mr Richard Woodings

26   LMA, DL/C/179, f.335r

27   *The World* 30 March 1787, cited by Summerson 1980, 11

28   *Journal of the House of Lords* **XXVII** (1783–7), 640

29   House of Lords Record Office, Large Parchment 279/48

30   But see Pinhorn 2000 **II**, 108 (note 6), for Nash's Lambeth interests.

31   Summerson 1980, 6 (citing documents in the Bedford Office); Olsen, Donald J 1982 *Town Planning in London: the Eighteenth and Nineteenth Centuries* (2nd edn). New Haven and London: Yale University Press, 27–38

32   Old Bailey Sessions Papers for 1779, 346–7, available on-line at www.oldbaileyonline

33   Mansbridge 1991, 35; reconstructed elevation in Davis 1966, fig 1. Somerset House (now generally attributed to John Webb) was demolished 1776 and replaced by the present building by Chambers, which echoes the original design in many ways. See generally Newman, John 1991 *Somerset House:*

Splendour and Order. London: Scala Books, especially 16–19, for Chambers's Strand front and Canaletto's view showing Old Somerset House from the Thames.

34 The interiors (as Geoffrey Tyack points out to me) show Taylor's influence, as would be expected, notably the downstairs passageways with plaster vaults and domes, and several upstairs ceilings are 'Taylorian'. There is also an octagonal room by Taylor at No. 4 Grafton St.

35 The Edwards family may have tried to rescue Nash's finances by acquiring an interest in the development. Summerson 1980, 26–7, points out that by 1810 John Edwards resided in Bloomsbury Square and his firm (Edwards and Lyons, attorneys) practised from 72 Great Russell Street.

36 The details of Nash's debts emerge in litigation over Liardet's stucco patent (NA, C12/921/11). See further, Kelsall, Frank 'Liardet versus Adam' in Newman, John (ed) 1984 *Design and Practice in British Architecture: Studies in Architectural History Presented to Howard Colvin, Architect Hist* [special volume] **27**, 118–26. Summerson 1980, 7–9, has further details of Nash's bankruptcy.

37 *Hereford Journal*, 17 March 1785

38 Carmarthenshire Archives Service, CDX/514

39 Spurrell, William 1879 *Carmarthen and its Neighbourhood.* Carmarthen: William Spurrell, 23

40 Nash's legal actions are listed in Suggett 2008, Appendix 2.

41 Summerson 1980, 8–11; report in *The Times* 30 March 1787

42 Thorne, R G 'Herbert Lloyd of Carmarthen'. *Trans Hon Soc Cymmrodorion* [vol for 1977], 111; National Library of Wales (NLW), G E Owen MS 139, 139–40

43 On Blackburn, see Brodie, Allan, Croom Jane, and Davies, James O 2002 *English Prisons: An Architectural History.* Swindon: English Heritage, 41–9.

44 NLW, Cardiganshire QS/OB/4, 28, 36; NLW, SD/Ch/B/8, 169

45 Suggett 1995, 15–16. A drawing showing Nash's house and theatre in Spilman Street has yet to be found.

46 For Nash's public buildings, see generally, Suggett 1995, ch 2.

47 NLW, MS 16989C, 504–6

48 RIBA, MS Coc/9

49 Further details of Nash's gaol are in Shoesmith, R and Crosskey, R 1994 'Go to Gaol … in Hereford'. *Trans Woolhope Naturalists' Field Club* **48**, 115–36, and pl XI–XIX.

50 Suggett 1995, 32–3

51 Nash's work at St David's is more fully considered in a forthcoming article in the *Georgian Group J* **XXI** [2013]

52 See generally, Hill, Rosemary 2007 *God's Architect: Pugin and the Building of Romantic Britain.* London: Penguin Books, 9–22.

53 For Nash's earlier villas, Suggett 1995, ch 3

54 Suggett 1995, 120

55 For Nash's later villas, Suggett 1995, ch 3

56 For Nash's picturesque buildings, Suggett 1995, ch 4. For a detailed account of Castle House see Watkins, Charles and Cowell, Ben 2012 *Uvedale Price (1747–1829): Decoding the Picturesque.* Woodbridge: The Boydell Press, 91–105

57 Research by Thomas Lloyd and Edna Dale-Jones

58 NLW, G E Owen MS 139, 137–8

59 The letter is quoted in chapter 3 below.

60 Suggett 1995, 76–80

61 Humphry Repton's Memoir, BL, Add MS 62112, ff 85–8; and Gore and Carter (eds) 2005, 76

2

Rebuilding a career: John Nash in Herefordshire 1790–1800

DAVID WHITEHEAD

John Nash's activities in South Wales were well known to the gentry of Herefordshire via *Pugh's Hereford Journal,* otherwise known, for its Welsh readers, as the *British Chronicle,* which was founded in 1770 and available at booksellers and stationers throughout the region. In the late 18th century, under the successive editorship of Charles Pugh, John Duncumb and David Walker, the principal architectural events in South Wales and the southern Marches were recorded either in advertisements or editorial commentary. Thus, on 19 October 1786, Nash made his debut when builders were invited to inspect the new plans for the Carmarthen House of Correction deposited by Messrs Nash and Saxon at Mr Ross's, the printers, Carmarthen. Other commissions for gaols at Carmarthen and Cardigan, the west front of St David's Cathedral, a poorhouse at St Clears, and a new single-arched bridge at Newport were all noticed in 1791, a year before Nash was engaged to build his third gaol at Hereford.

Meanwhile, Humphry Repton, with rather less publicity, also secured his first commissions in the southern Marches, producing a Red Book for Samuel Phipps of Ferney Hall, near Ludlow, in October 1789, which led to an abrasive encounter with Richard Payne Knight, the owner of the adjacent estate at Downton Castle. At about the same time, Repton was also employed by Dr John Matthews of Belmont, near Hereford, who had laid the foundation stone for his new house, designed by James Wyatt, in November 1788. The site, which had previously been occupied by a working farm called Old Hill, urgently required a new landscape and, perhaps, some architectural embellishments.

It was not surprising that Nash should meet Repton in Herefordshire. Both were approaching turning points in their careers when the meeting took place at Stoke Edith, early in the 1790s.

The moment is recorded, without any indication of date, in Repton's 'Memoirs', which state that:

> [the Hon Edward Foley] said in his peculiar manner – that he wanted to bring me acquainted with a very talented Architect, adding – 'If you two, whom I consider the two cleverest men in England, could agree to *act together* you might carry the whole world before you!' Now this was a bait exactly suited to my aspiring vanity! So I consented to the introduction to Mr Nash! – and *We met* – We were charmed with each other at the very first interview.[1]

Towards Hereford Gaol and an association with James Wyatt

Kedrun Laurie places Nash's meeting with Repton in 1790, but this seems a little early. Certainly, Repton received his first payment from Foley in July 1790, but the Red Book that materialised in January 1791 was for Prestwood, near Stourbridge, Foley's second home, where he had taken refuge with his second wife, Miss Hodgetts, after a celebrated divorce from the daughter of Lord Coventry.[2] Nash, meanwhile, was still busy in South Wales, where he would have been aware from the *Hereford Journal* that the Herefordshire magistrates were considering the rebuilding of the county gaol. Their choice of architect was William Blackburn, an old acquaintance of Nash, for whom he had recently provided a model for the new Carmarthan Gaol. Moreover, among the magistrates with delegated authority to supervise the construction of Hereford Gaol were Uvedale Price of Foxley and Richard Payne Knight of Downton Castle.[3] These two 'gentlemen professors' and 'arbiters of contemporary taste' – in matters of landscape and architecture – were already known to Nash. Knight was related to Thomas Johnes of Hafod, whose mother, Elizabeth Knight, was Payne Knight's aunt. As early as March 1792, the wife of Thomas Johnes, Jane, had written to her brother, Col John Johnes of Dolaucothi, recommending Nash as an architect for the rebuilding of his house.[4] Meanwhile, perhaps a year earlier, in 1791, Price had commissioned Nash to draw up plans for Castle House in Aberystwyth, which may have been completed by August 1792, when the *Hereford Journal* reported that Price was among the West Midland gentry who had 'built bathing houses at their own expense' in the resort.[5]

It seems very likely that Price and Knight recommended their Welsh protégé to their fellow magistrates, following the hiatus created by Blackburn's death in December 1790. But Nash also gained support from an unexpected quarter. His new plans for the gaol, which modified Blackburn's original proposal, required adjudication, and the magistrates asked James Wyatt, busy rebuilding the west end of Hereford Cathedral, to do this in the autumn of 1792. Wyatt supported the amended designs, and Nash was officially appointed the project architect. This affidavit from Wyatt, the most fashionable architect of the day, made Nash a fixture in Herefordshire for the next four years.[6]

Accompanying him were a number of influential craftsmen and assistants who promoted his talents and sustained a series of local contracts as he climbed back into prominence. Among these was Samuel Saxon, Nash's partner in South Wales, who maintained an office in London and was already known to Repton, having provided designs for Sir William Wake's house at Courteenhall, Northamptonshire, where Repton produced a Red Book in 1791.[7] In addition, Nash could call upon the services of his cousin, John Edwards of Lambeth, who was very skilled in acquiring materials; William Slack of London, an iron manufacturer; and James Yates, a prominent Hereford mason, who worked for him at St David's Cathedral in 1791. Finally, he had two assistants who, in his absence, could act as clerks of the work: William Walker and Robert George.[8]

The lessons in picturesque architecture conveyed to Nash by Uvedale Price in his instructions for Castle House at Aberystwyth were initially superfluous. Although the façade of the county gaol in Hereford, with its heavily rusticated stonework and iron bars, set in Piranesian apertures, distilled some of the 'sublime' qualities of a place of execution and incarceration (*see* Fig 1.4), it had, in Uvedale Price's pithy phrase, 'a union of character and effect'.[9] Nash had missed three of the best architectural opportunities for working the picturesque magic in Herefordshire to James Wyatt. At Belmont in 1788, on a prominent hill overlooking the Wye and within sight of Hereford, Wyatt had erected a stunning neoclassical villa for Dr John Matthews, and, on the evidence of an illustration in the *Polite Repository* (1794), Repton had subsequently laid out the grounds. As Matthews was mayor of Hereford in 1794, and proprietor of its principal bank, he probably had some contact with Nash, and, with Repton's recommendation, he eventually picked up several commissions for cottages when Matthews extended the Belmont estate after 1810 into the defunct royal forest of Haywood.[10] In 1979, the late Nigel Temple

Fig 2.1 (below)
Knockerhill Farm, Callow, built on the Belmont estate in the 1820s, design in George Repton's Pavilion Notebook (Brighton Royal Pavilion and Museums PNB 102).

Fig 2.2 (below bottom)
Knockerhill Farm before demolition in 1967 (the late Nigel Temple).

identified at least six cottages by Nash, scattered widely over the estate, tentatively adding Knockerhill Farm on the basis of an old photograph that matched several plans and an elevation in the Pavilion Notebook. This attribution can now be confirmed from an entry in the account book of a Ross-on-Wye builder, John Tristam, who specialised in erecting farms and cottages. In 1827, he claimed that John Matthews owed him £22 1s 6d for work carried out earlier on Knockerhill Farm (Figs 2.1 and 2.2). This process of artisans interpreting the sophisticated designs of drawing-board cottages can also be followed in the Stoke Edith accounts.[11]

Two other commissions secured by Wyatt were Sufton Court (1789) and Garnons (1791). At the former, Anthony Keck seems to have acted as executant architect in Wyatt's absence, while, at Garnons, Repton's Red Book illustrates a Gothic design by Wyatt – but as John Geers Cotterell went off to war, and Wyatt was very dilatory in drawing up detailed plans, the scheme was dropped. In 1796, Repton tried to introduce Nash as architect but eventually, in the 1820s, William Atkinson designed the house and Nash, at the climax of his career, provided patterns for the stained glass windows.[12]

Stoke Edith

By the early 1790s, Repton was in need of an architect with the sort of flair Wyatt had initially displayed, and one who would be more attentive to the relationship between house and landscape. This sort of picturesque ensemble was essentially the notion being promoted by Price and Knight, and, as Repton had difficulty in convincing his critics that he was not simply recycling the Brownian landscape, it was doubly important to get the architecture right.

At Garnons, as Wyatt's involvement faded, he tried to promote the talents of William Wilkins senior, a competent artisan architect and owner and scenery-maker of the Theatre Royal, Norwich, for whom Repton, in an earlier life, had written plays. John Cotterell found Wilkins too pushy, and accused him of producing unsolicited plans. Subsequently, Repton had Wilkins with him when he visited Prestwood in October 1790 and Edward Foley employed him to design a new stable block. He was still in tow when Repton was finally called to Stoke Edith in June 1792,[13] and quickly produced a portfolio of cottage designs, to be grouped around a village green, on which was to be erected, as a centrepiece,

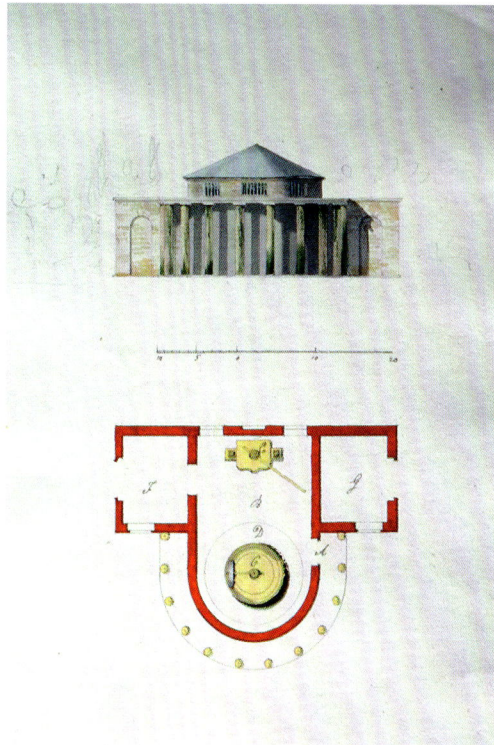

Fig 2.3
The proposed 'rude primitive temple' intended as the centrepiece for the new village at Stoke Edith, by William Wilkins, 1792 (Hereford Record Office).

a cider mill embellished 'by a colonnade of twelve trees with the bark on, giving the building an appearance of a kind of Rude Primitive Temple' (Fig 2.3).[14] This tribute to the fecundity of Foley's apple orchards was to be surrounded with some sturdy cottages of stone and slate, which appeared to take their cue from the local vernacular. However, Repton needed more than the painterly skills of Wilkins at Stoke Edith, as the late 17th-century house needed refurbishing after a fire in April 1789, which 'happened in the lower part of the house, and has very nearly destroyed the old steward's room and the parlour over it and did much damage to some other apartments'.[15] So, notwithstanding Repton's unqualified support in the Garnons Red Book for the 'acknowledged powers … of James Wyatt',[16] it was time to bring on John Nash.

An account book for the improvements at Stoke Edith was kept by John Edwards – presumably Nash's cousin – who was clearly skilled in budgetary matters. Nash made his first appearance on 13 October 1793, and received his final payment in November 1796. In total, £1,579 was spent in making the house habitable. No major rooms were touched except for the parlour, where a London plasterer called Poultney was employed for the decorative work, and John Yates, the mason, came from Hereford and set up the marble chimney piece,

Fig 2.4
Stoke Edith House, from
Humphry Repton's Red
Book, 1792. The range to
the right reflects Repton's
aspirations for his future
partner John Nash; Nash's
assistant Charles Heather
completed it in a less
metropolitan style in 1830
(Stoke Edith Estate).

carved by the Worcester statuary, William Stephens (Fig 2.4).[17] Unfortunately, none of the available literature illustrates this room, which tragically succumbed to fire in 1927.

In 1796, the new partners were at Corsham Court in Wiltshire, and the warmth of their friendship was such that Repton's sons – George Stanley and John Adey – found themselves in Nash's expanding office. Among the picturesque creations in George's RIBA Notebook is a thatched 'cottage for Mr Foley'. This irregular building survives today as the Game Keeper's

Cottage, situated in a wooded dell, half a mile above the mansion at Stoke Edith (Figs 2.5 and 2.6).[18] Repton returned to Stoke Edith in about 1799 and provided a plan for a carriage drive to show off the varied scenery of the Woolhope Hills. On this route, other cottages were built with overhanging thatched roofs, contrasting with the more down-to-earth vernacular of Wilkins' cottages. Repton, it seems, had convinced his employer that the new village around the Bacchanalian temple on the turnpike road was likely to be unpopular with Foley's

Fig 2.5 (right)
Cottage for Mr Foley,
from George Repton's
RIBA notebook
(RIBA drawings collection).

Fig 2.6 (far right)
Keeper's Cottage, sketched
by Madeleine Hopton
in 1835
(Hereford Record Office).

Fig 2.7
Kentchurch Court,
sketched by James Wathen
in August 1794
(Hereford City Library).

tenants in an age of revolution. If a Georgic poem, published by the Revd Luke Booker in 1797, is to be believed, Foley's tenants were pleased with their smart accommodation and, invigorated by 'sparkling store of rich Pomona's beverage', toasted their benefactor and reaffirmed their loyalty to Britannia. This must have been of considerable comfort to Foley – and Repton and Nash – in the year that the 'tyrannical' French landed in Pembrokeshire.[19]

Restoring Kentchurch Court

In 1795, Nash was to be found at Kentchurch Court in south-west Herefordshire, where John Scudamore, rather late in the day, decided to complete the work of restoration commenced by Anthony Keck (c 1726–97) in 1772. Keck had modernised the interior of the medieval house but had left the rambling exterior untouched (Fig 2.7).[20] Scudamore was a prominent member of the local gentry, a member of the Gaol Committee and father-in-law of James Hereford of Sufton. He gave Nash a chance to improve a characterful house without destroying its picturesque qualities. No doubt, his erstwhile tutor, Uvedale Price – at this time preparing his *Essay on Architecture* – would have been watching from Foxley with more than a passing interest.

Nash appears to have started on an almost free-standing range, attached as a solar wing to the south-west of the medieval house. From James Wathen's sketch, taken from the north, it had a steeply pitched roof, high first-floor windows and a large external chimneystack. Nash removed the windows, subdued the roof with a battlemented parapet, but left the stack.[21] On the east front he added a pretty oriel window to the façade to illuminate a first-floor room, and round the corner, on the south, he provided three new mullioned windows, with 'coat-hanger' transoms, for the ground-floor drawing room. In a narrow range immediately to the west, a new lobby was created, which internally required the removal of another chimney breast. Beyond the lobby, the top of Keck's internal communications corridor was reached, where Nash was forced to engage in some creative planning.[22]

A flight of broad steps was necessary to bring the corridor up to the level of the new drawing room. At the top, the steps arrived at a Gothic screen (Fig 2.8) that, from below, framed a large Perpendicular-style window, more suitable in this era for the chancel of a church than for a country house. It seems to be a clone of the west window of St David's Cathedral, which had recently been designed by Nash; an association made more obvious externally where it has a slender turret with a crocketted finial to

Fig 2.8
Nash's Gothic screen
at Kentchurch Court
(Paul Larsen).

accompany it. In practical terms, it threw essential light down Keck's dark corridor, but, as a piece of theatre, it thwarted any chance of carrying the flight of stairs up to the first floor. Instead, two narrow staircases were squeezed into the sides of the Gothic screen. They came out on a landing, from which there was an even better view of the 'chapel' window – as it became known – from a cast-iron balustrade, pierced with lancets enclosing quatrefoils. Internally, this was an ingenious and most inventive use of an area in the house that had hitherto been a dark cul-de-sac.

Nash now moved on to the four-storey solar tower – a distant relative of the pele towers of the Scottish border, but relatively unique on the Welsh border (Fig 2.9). Like everything else at Kentchurch, this was a structure replete with a great deal of antique patina, much of which survives today and includes a garderobe chute, an extruded chimney and miscellaneous openings. Only on the west front did Nash give the tower uniform fenestration and, even here, on the top floor, an earlier multi-light opening with wooden mullions is still evident. However,

Fig 2.9
The tower and south-west
range at Kentchurch Court,
as left by Nash in 1796
(BB 98/16097).

as with the drawing room wing, Nash again submerged the roof behind his ubiquitous battlements, replacing a steeply pitched helm crowned with a fleche. Today we would regard this as a mistake, but spires were very much out of fashion with picturesque writers, and Uvedale Price, for one, would have applauded Nash's decision to apply battlements to the roofline.[23] The final addition to the tower was a convenient, attached, round staircase turret, rising out of the main range of buildings to the south.

Nash now embarked upon the rationalisation of the complex west front, where there was a great deal of brick from Keck's work, and two earlier timber bays. He managed to add only a metre or two of battlements before John Scudamore died in July 1796, when the work came to an abrupt halt. Thus, his sensitive treatment of the tower may simply represent a work uncompleted. If the drawing-room range provides any guidance, there was more tidying up to be done and the traces of times past, which remain on the walls of the tower today, might well have disappeared altogether. We can assume, however, that Price applauded Nash's work, for in the 1820s the wife of John Scudamore's grandson, Sarah Lucy-Scudamore (née Jones), hung a portrait of Price in the gallery corridor. But, in the immediate aftermath of John Scudamore's death there was a more pressing problem for Price: to get his son (also John) elected as the Whig member of Parliament for the city of Hereford. Price writes to Lord Abercorn that he deferred a visit to him in order to shake the hands of 'greasy butchers + fusty tailors + cobblers + fat alewives'[24] for the sake of the political career his friend's son – and for the Whig cause, which Price espoused. However, there were other dissenting voices, for when James Wathen, the local artist, sent a group of his sketches to the Fitzwilliam Museum in Cambridge, which included a view of Kentchurch, he wrote on it 'now altered and spoiled. This view taken 26th August 1795'.[25]

The Hereford Lunatic Asylum and a collection of bridges

Nash's work at Hereford Gaol ended in 1796, but he was closely involved in three further buildings in the city of Hereford: the Lunatic Asylum, the Wyebridge and Panson Cottage. William Parker, an indigenous artisan-architect, had designed the Hereford Infirmary in 1781, but without its planned Lunatic Asylum. The public subscription for this addition seems to have failed and Parker, also the proprietor of the Hereford Theatre, went bankrupt. But in 1793 the public subscription was revived and Parker's plan was quietly dropped. In July the foundation stone of the new asylum was laid by 'Mr (James) Knight, having contracted for the execution of Mr Nash's plan'. It is perhaps significant that Richard Payne Knight was the Steward of the Friends of Hereford Infirmary, and, when the Infirmary was first mooted, his surveyor at Downton Castle, Thomas Symonds, had been lined up to produce a design. In Knight's mind Nash was, perhaps, the natural successor to Symonds, who had died a few years earlier. The asylum was not an especially distinguished building and looked very much like a contemporary town house. In the language of the time, however, it was 'neat and convenient' and lasted, with some improvements, until *c* 1870.[26]

In April 1795 Repton was engaged at Sufton Court, a house designed by James Wyatt and, possibly executed by Anthony Keck, in 1789. No lodges or cottages were required, so there was nothing available for Nash. However, James Hereford, Repton's patron, had other matters on his mind. He was mayor of Hereford in February 1795, when an exceptional flood occurred on the Wye, which seriously damaged the city's river bridge. Two months later, while Repton was drawing up his Red Book for Sufton, the *Hereford Journal* carried an advertisement for qualified persons prepared to undertake repairs to the bridge 'according to a plan prepared by Mr Nash, Archt' (Fig 2.10).[27]

The flood also encouraged Nash to confer with Thomas Telford on an iron bridge at Bewdley, Worcestershire.[28] This project came to

Fig 2.10
Wyebridge, Hereford, sketched by George Wathen in August 1795 following Nash's repairs (Hereford City Library).

nothing because of the collapse later that year of another bridge designed by Nash a few miles away at Stanford-on-Teme. It appears that Nash had been introduced to Sir Edward Winnington of Stanford Court by his brother-in-law, Edward Foley, and he contracted to rebuild Stanford Bridge, with iron castings, probably made by the London iron-founder William Slack. The bridge collapsed just after it had been made passable for pedestrians on 26 September 1795, due, according to Nash in a letter to the Bewdley Bridge Trustees, to some wedges, which had moved 'improperly'. The ironwork was quickly replaced with castings made at Coalbrookdale, and Nash patented this system in 1797. This second bridge was a great success, and the *Hereford Journal* claimed that 'a more perfect piece of workmanship has never been exhibited since the discovery of cast iron for such noble purposes'.[29] The collapse of Stanford Bridge lost Nash the contract for Bewdley Bridge and, no doubt, unnerved the magistrates of Hereford, but Nash successfully patched up their medieval bridge, enabling it to be widened, and reconstructed more substantially, by the local bridge-builder John Gethin in 1815, and again in 1826.

There was, perhaps, one more bridge that Nash completed successfully. This was at Downton Castle, where the high single-arched Forge Bridge appears to be modelled on the famous bridge at Pontypridd (Glamorgan) and, more pertinently, on Nash's own aborted plan for Newport Bridge (*see* chapter 1). Alistair Rowan suggested in 1970 that Nash might have had a hand in Richard Payne Knight's castle, but this always seemed unlikely, and we know that Knight acted as his own architect, using the professional help of Thomas Farnolls Pritchard (1723–77) to survey the site, and Thomas Symonds of Hereford to act as his clerk of works.[30] Nevertheless, Knight was familiar with Nash's work, and, along with Price, continued to take an interest in his career in the late 1790s. Price informed Sir George Beaumont in 1798 that he had sent a draft of his *Essay on Architecture* and another on bridges to Nash who commented on them favourably and showed them to Repton. Two months later, Price recommended 'my little friend Nash' to Beaumont, who was considering rebuilding his house at Coleorton in Leicestershire. He further proposed that Beaumont should view Nash's 'new gothic front' at Corsham Court in Wiltshire,

Fig 2.11
Forge Bridge, Downton (Martin Griffiths).

and proposed that he would bring Knight along to make it a threesome. The initiative seems to have come from Nash who was 'anxious they should see his work'.[31]

The correspondence fails to confirm whether the visit took place, but in September 1799 Nash wrote to Paul Cobb Methuen at Corsham that he intended to come to Corsham, but would be visiting Attingham and Downton first.[32] With Repton busy at Attingham laying out a new park with new lodges and cottages required, Nash's attendance there is explained. But what was going on at Downton? Was it just a social visit? It seems unlikely. The only major structures on the estate without dates or architects are the Castle Bridge and Forge Bridge, both of which cross the River Teme. The former was drawn by Thomas Hearne in *c* 1780 and is exactly as it appears today. Thomas Farnolls Pritchard has been suggested as architect, but it seems likely that it was built by Thomas Symonds at the same time as the castle. He was apparently building a bridge at 'Stoke' while acting as clerk of works for Knight. The Forge Bridge was originally constructed in timber, when it was also sketched by Thomas Hearne in 1786, and subsequently issued as a print by B T Pouncy in 1798. Moreover, the local artist, James Wathen, also made a sketch dated 1796. During this time, Knight took a great interest in his iron forge, which worked continuously, and presumably in profit, throughout the French Wars. It seems most likely that the stone bridge was constructed in about 1800, or just before, as it was essential for the efficient working of the forge, which consumed fuel and other materials drawn from both sides of the river. Hearne's print of 1798, and Wathen's sketch of 1796, seem to mark the *terminus ad quem* for the old bridge. Wathen famously seems to have been very much aware of imminent changes to familiar buildings, and produced an undated sketch of the new bridge, perhaps soon after its completion.[33] Nash certainly deserves consideration as architect of the bridge, which fulfilled his dreams of a grand single-arched structure, first proposed at Newport in 1791 (Fig 2.11).[34]

Panson Cottage, Putson, near Hereford

It seems probable that contact with James Hereford and Edward Foley brought about a further commission for a picturesque 'cottage' on the western outskirts of Hereford at Putson. This hitherto unnoticed product of Nash's office is to be found as a stray sketch in the library of the Dumbarton Oaks Foundation, Washington, DC, where it is attributed to Humphry Repton. On the reverse of the sketch is written: 'Panson Cottage to have been erected near Hereford'.[35] The sketch – in fact, a well-executed watercolour – shows a substantial house in the cottage style, standing close to the River Wye (Fig 2.12). It would have looked towards the north, with

Fig 2.12
Panson Cottage, a sketch attributed to Humphrey Repton c 1800 (Dumbarton Oaks Research Library and Collection, Rare Books Collection, Washington, DC).

Fig 2.13
Panson Cottage, Putson,
near Hereford, by James
Wathen c *1800*
(Hereford City Library).

uninterrupted views of Hereford Cathedral. Its eastern range is very similar to Rheola House, Glamorgan (*see* Fig S.4), designed by Nash *c* 1812–14 for his cousin and collaborator, John Edwards. A significant addition, however, is a veranda wrapped around the cottage on two sides. Separating this range from the service wing to the west is a two-storey round tower in the manner of Cronkhill (*see* chapter 4), but with wide tripartite fenestration, and without the ovals set under the Tuscan eaves. The 'cottage' is enhanced with a setting of mature trees and burgeoning shrubberies, suggesting the hand of a professional landscaper as well as an architect. The connection with Nash is perhaps confirmed by a sketch of the 'The Rev Mr Bird's Cottage, near Hereford', which appeared in the *Polite Repository* for September 1802 and was probably drawn by Repton. This image reflects quite accurately the three-part division of the house depicted in the Dumbarton Oaks view, although the perspective is more compressed, and the round tower is less distinct, and appears to have a steeply pitched roof. Three further views by the local artist, James Wathen, also dating from the early 19th century, confirm the presence of both the round tower and the veranda (Fig 2.13).[36]

The cottage was built for the Revd Charles John Bird, a member of a family of genteel solicitors who had prospered in Hereford during the 18th century, his father and elder brother, Thomas, having served as mayors of the city. Along with his brother, he was a serious antiquary, and was elected a fellow of the Society of Antiquaries in 1800. He also had a private museum of 'curiosities', which included 21

volumes of manuscript material of local interest, eventually inherited by the Hereford City Library. A further connection with Repton and Nash came when he was appointed rector of Mordiford in 1804, where his church and rectory stood, just beyond the pleasure grounds of Sufton Court, and which were appropriated by Repton in his Red Book to enhance the view from the principal rooms at the Court. Furthermore, Bird was the godson of Edward Foley of Stoke Edith, the lay patron of Mordiford rectory. Prior to his move to Mordiford, Bird had been the rector of Dinedor where he had been presented by Charles Howard, 11th Duke of Norfolk, the owner of Holme Lacy House. Uvedale Price was a regular visitor here in the 1790s, where a walk through the veteran oaks of the deer park was named after him. Thus, Bird can be placed among an influential group of gentry, engaged in picturesque improvement, and linked with its key practitioners. It is not surprising that he consulted Nash, or perhaps one of Repton's sons, to design his new cottage at Panson.

It seems that as there was no suitable rectory at Dinedor, Bird acquired eight acres of ground adjoining the river at Putson in *c* 1800, probably part of a larger holding which belonged to his elder brother Thomas, who was clerk to the Horse Tow Path Company, set up to facilitate transport up and down the Wye from Chepstow to Hereford. The site enjoyed proximity to the city but adjoined the parish boundary of Dinedor. The cottage was built before 1802, the date it appeared in the *Polite Repository*. Panson was not a local name, and appears to have been a whimsical invention of the Revd Bird, playing upon the township name of Putson. Indeed, on both the *Repository* sketches, and on one of those produced by Wathen, there appears to have been a Gothic temple to the east of the cottage, set at the end of a tree-lined walk. This was probably dedicated to 'Pan' and was later referred to as the 'grotto' in an advertisement of 1825. When the cottage was first put up for sale in 1804, a full description was provided:

> Panson cottage most desirably and beautifully situated on an eminence, on the bank of the River Wye, within a mile of the City of Hereford, of which and the adjoining countryside it commands a most delightful prospect; containing a Vestibule, two Sitting Rooms and a Kitchen on the ground floor, with other conveniences; and three Chambers and a Dressing Room on the first floor; together with an orchard planted with choice Fruit Trees, well stocked with beautiful Shrubs in high perfection, and a meadow adjoining extending along the bank of the Wye, with an avenue of Elms and Spanish Planes growing thereon planted parallel with the river; the whole containing about Eight computed Acres in the occupation of the Rev Mr Bird, the Proprietor.[37]

Soon after Bird became rector of Mordiford, he moved into the excellent early-Georgian rectory there and in August 1804 Panson Cottage was advertised for sale, being finally sold in 1806. It survived considerably extended, and known as Panson Villa, until it was demolished in the 1950s. Its early date suggests that it was something of a prototype, marking the first appearance of some of the key elements of the Claudian villa that was to be fully articulated at Cronkhill and Sandridge Park in Devon.

St Peter, Bromyard

It seems remarkable that Nash was apparently not involved in any ecclesiastical work in Herefordshire, especially after his endeavours at St David's between 1790–93. He missed an opportunity at Hereford after the fall of the west end of the Cathedral in 1786, where Keck was first on the scene, followed by Wyatt, with whom the Dean and Chapter signed a contract in 1788.[38] However, during the 1770s the dilapidated state of St Peter's church, Bromyard, was giving the churchwardens and the vestry considerable headache, which came to a climax in 1792 when the archdeacon insisted that competent architects should be consulted (Fig 2.14). Rather fortuitously, one of these was James Yates, Nash's mason at St David's, the Hereford Gaol and Stoke Edith, who happened to live in Bromyard. Naturally, he confirmed that the church was about to collapse, but the vestry were still uncertain of the solution when, in September 1794, John Barnaby of

Fig 2.14
St Peter, Bromyard in the late 18th century (Hereford City Library).

Brockhampton Court, near Bromyard, a member of the vestry, arrived with John Nash. With such influential support, Nash was engaged to carry out a further survey, which naturally confirmed his mason's findings.[39] He also found a further ally in another Bromyard resident, the mason/architect, Andrew Maund, who designed the new gaol at Brecon in 1780–1, and thus must have been well known to Nash.[40]

Maund was a member of the newly formed building committee and it seemed that, even the most reluctant members of the vestry, were carried along by his enthusiasm for a new church. In October 1794 Nash was asked to draw up a specification employing the 'plainest gothic forms' plastered inside with 'plain gothic mouldings' and a new tower with pinnacles. Late in December, a month beyond the agreed deadline, the plans were received, but without estimates, which the vestry committee insisted should arrive within 10 days. By late January the committee was looking for estimates from local workmen but was still determined to rebuild the church. The vestry began proceedings to sell some of the parish common land, and £3,000 was soon raised. After two years, Nash began to demand payment for his plans and eventually received £33, but in March 1797 the vestry appeared to get cold feet, and the decision was taken to just repair the old church. Ironically, it was Andrew Maund who supervised the work, which eventually cost £681.[41]

There is, however, a further line of potentially rewarding inquiry. What was John Nash doing in the company of John Barnaby? Upper Brockhampton House had been newly built by Thomas Farnolls Pritchard in 1765 but Barnaby still wanted a new chapel of ease to replace the old chapel beside the moated manor house at Lower Brockhampton. George Byfield (c 1756–1813) exhibited a design for a Gothic chapel at Brockhampton for J Barnaby at the Royal Academy of Arts in 1799, and it is generally accepted that the chapel that stands here today was Byfield's.[42] As an architect, he was fairly active in Hereford and Worcester during the 1790s, turning up at Kinnersley Castle in 1793 and Garnons in 1799. He was well known to Nash. Both men had served their indentures in the office of Sir Robert Taylor, and when Byfield got into difficulty over his fee for the House of Industry in Worcester in 1804, Nash acted as his referee.[43] But Byfield built no other church, and this is his only Gothic building. Could this be a church by John Nash? The east window has 'coat hanger' fenestration, which Nash used in much of his early Gothic work, for example, at Kentchurch, Corsham and Luscombe (Fig 2.15). There is very little early ecclesiastical work by Nash to compare it with, but the spire is similar to the one designed by Nash at Great Barr, Staffordshire (1800), which has links with Repton's employment at Prestwood for the Hon Edward Foley. The tall spirets occur on St John's

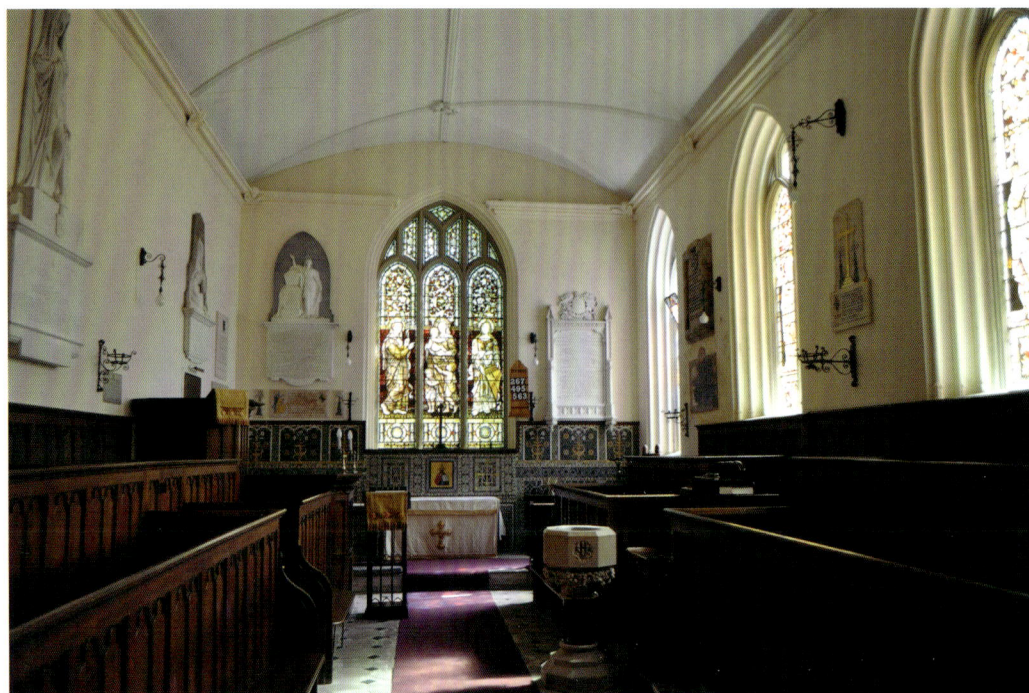

Fig 2.15
The interior of the chapel at Brockhampton-by-Bromyard (David Whitehead).

church at Caledon (Co. Tyrone), and there are other elements present in the later churches that Nash designed for the Church Commissioners in 1818.[44] Supporting documentary material is lacking, as the archive of the Barnaby family was destroyed when the estate was broken up in the 1950s.

Garnstone Castle and Charles Heather

There is one postscript to Nash's influence in Herefordshire. He left behind one of his assistants, Charles Heather (c 1774–1845), who, for the next three decades, continued to purvey his brand of neoclassicism and picturesque Gothic. Heather assisted Nash at Garnstone Castle in 1806, the one later commission he obtained in the county, apart from the cottages that periodically emerged from his office until c 1815.[45] His client at Garnstone was Samuel Birch Peploe, son-in-law of Sir George Cornewall of Moccas, for whom Nash had provided two lodges and a barn in 1804. The Tudor-Gothic 'castle' was very much a standard product of Nash's office at this time, but its massive staircase tower casts an eye towards the great tower at Downton (Fig 2.16). For serious castle builders of the next generation, the excessive fenestration was in conflict with its chivalric demeanour, but photographs taken just before its demolition in 1959 indicate how successful Nash was in illuminating the public spaces of the house

from above.[46] The building was generally despised during the 19th century, but Nash found an apologist in his old patron, Uvedale Price, whose lands abutted the Garnstone estate. Evidently, Price was seriously considering employing Nash in 1801 to rebuild Foxley – 'my castle in the air' – and was busy altering the grounds, 'preparing everything for its reception'. Nothing seems to have come of these aspirations, but in 1828, a year before he died, he wrote to the classical scholar Edmund Barker, rejoicing that his neighbour's house (Garnstone) was not 'an unvaried lump of brick' and, while regretting that it was not in the Grecian style, he regarded its Gothic character as an 'indigenous [and] beautiful exotic'.[47]

Charles Heather, Nash's clerk of works at Garnstone, was busy until 1810, probably supervising the laying out of the grounds. Thereafter, he followed his master to Ingestre Hall in Staffordshire and in 1812 he advertised his return to Herefordshire in the *Hereford Journal*.[48] He acted as clerk of works to Smirke at the Shire Hall (1815–17), and probably played a similar role at Pool Cottage (The Fosse) in Hereford, and similarly at the Homend, Stretton Grandison (1814–21). Here there is a lodge, dated 1825, modelled on the Oak Cottage at Blaise Hamlet, which clearly derived from his time in Nash's office (Fig 2.17). Unspecified work estimated at £350 was proposed at Garnons in association with William Atkinson (c 1820), and in 1830 he returned to Nash's old haunt, Stoke Edith, to a build a theatre,

Fig 2.16
Garnstone Castle
(1806–10), from the sale
catalogue of 1887
(Hereford Record Office).

which Repton appears to illustrate in the Red Book, and was thus, presumably instigated by Nash.[49] In 1825, he became Herefordshire's first County Surveyor and made himself useful building a classical pavilion as a focus for the Castle Green walks, a well-designed stuccoed terrace in St Ethelbert Street, and two schools, and restoring several churches in the wider county. He died in 1845.[50]

By this date Nash's work was very unfashionable, and in Herefordshire he was virtually forgotten. However, the Hereford Gaol remained a useful and memorable building – especially when public executions took place on a high platform designed by Nash – and when it was demolished in 1928 it was still referred to as 'Nash's Gaol'. Today it is still possible to enjoy the work of the architect of the Prince Regent in Hereford by visiting the loo or purchasing a bus ticket, both of which take place in the Governor's House, once in the middle of the gaol: the only piece of Nash's work to survive (Fig 2.18).

Fig 2.17
Homend Lodge, by Charles Heather, working for Robert Smirke (David Whitehead).

Fig 2.18
The former Governor's House at Hereford Gaol (David Whitehead).

Notes

1   BL, Add MS 62112, ff 5–7 reprinted in Carter, G, Goode, P and Laurie, K 1982 *Humphry Repton, Landscape Gardener 1752–1818*. Norwich: Sainsbury Centre for the Visual Arts, 135; Stroud, D 1962 *Humphry Repton*. London: *Country Life*, 94; Gore and Carter (eds) 2005, 75. The relationship between Humphry Repton and John Nash is pursued in greater detail in Whitehead 1992, 210–36.

2   Hereford Record Office (HRO), both the Red Book for Stoke Edith and Prestwood, Staffs are in the Foley Collection, E12.

3   Hereford City Library (HCL), *Hereford Journal* 13 May 1798; HRO Quarter Sessions 1782–91, ff 274, 295, 315, 328; 1792–7, ff 9, 17–24, 29; Summerson 1980, 6, 14

4   Jones 1939, 94

5   Watkins, Charles, Daniels, Stephen and Seymour, Susanne 1996 'Uvedale Price's Marine Picturesque at Aberystwyth, 1790–1829', *J Picturesque Soc* **14**, 4–7. *See also* chapters 1 and 3.

6   HRO, Quarter Sessions, 1792–97, ff 17–24

7   Summerson 1980, 10–11, 15; Colvin 2008, 906–7

8   For Edwards see Summerson 1980, 1; and Temple, N 1993, 9, 38–9, 139, 151–3. Nash tried to get employment for him at Abergavenny in 1794, where he is described as a 'pipe borer' (Gwent Record Office, D 874.1). William Walker was clerk of the works for Nash at Corsham Court (Ladd 1978, 101–18); and at Stoke Edith (HRO, E12 F 111). Robert George assisted at Carmarthen Gaol (Summerson 1980, 5); at Ffynone, Pembrokeshire *c* 1793 (Davis 1973, 26); and at Dolaucothi in 1794–6: Jones 1939, 94–5. Slack was at Hereford Gaol: HRO, Q/FV/6, ff 14, 38; at Corsham Court (Ladd 1978, 101–3 and note 65, where he supplied the gallery panels); Summerson 1980, 86, where he is called 'Slark'. John Yates was a prolific statuary (Roscoe, Ingrid 2009 *A Biographical Dictionary of Sculptors in Britain 1660–1851*. London: Yale University Press, 1433). For his involvement at St David's see Evans, W 1986 'St David's Cathedral: the forgotten centuries', *J Welsh Ecclesiastical Hist* 3, 88.

9   Price, Uvedale 1810 *Essays on the Picturesque*. London: J Mawman, **II**, 178

10 Whitehead, David 1995–6 'Belmont Herefordshire: the development of a Picturesque landscape', *J Picturesque Soc* **11–13**, *passim*

11 Temple 1993, 139 (PNB 100–3); HRO, M26/21

12 The Garnons Red Book is kept at the house; HRO, Garnons Coll D52/6/1, 5, 6; 9/4–5

13 HRO, Garnons Coll D52/5/1–13; Norfolk Record Office, Repton Accounts, f 28

14 HRO, B30/1 ('Designs for Lodges … Cot[t]ages' by William Wilkins)

15 *Hereford Journal* 15 April 1879

16 Garnons Red Book, transcribed in Fleming, L and Gore, A 1979 *The English Garden*. London: Michael Joseph, 150–5

17 HRO, E12 F111

18 RIBA Notebook, 'Cottage for Mr Foley', *in* Lever (ed) 1973

19 Booker, Luke 'The Hop Garden'. *Hereford Journal* 31 July 1799

20 HRO, M/26/614 – Keck's contract

21 Whitehead, David and Shoesmith, Ron 1994 *James Wathen's Herefordshire, 1770–1820*. Logaston: Logaston Press, unpaginated

22 The interior of Kentchurch is thoroughly described by Cornforth, John 'Kentchurch Court, Herefordshire'. *Country Life* 15 Dec, 22 Dec and 29 Dec 1966, 1632–5, 1688–91 1734–7.

23 Price 1810 (*see note 9*) **II**, 223, 360–1

24 The portrait of Price has since been sold but is noticed in *Country Life* 29 December 1966, 1734; Watkins and Cowell (eds) 2006, 88–9

25 Letter in the possession of the author sent originally to Nigel Temple by Jane Munrow, Senior Assistant of Paintings, Drawings and Prints at the Fitzwilliam Museum, dated 26 January 1995

26 *Hereford Journal* 8 August 1776; 18 July 1787; 30 May 1792; 25 September 1793; 25 December 1793; 7 May 1794. James Knight was executing Nash's proposals at Abergavenny for a suite of new markets and a drainage system for the town; Gwent RO, D.874, Abergavenny Improvement Commissioners Minute Book 1794–1822, *passim*

27 *Hereford Journal* 13 May 1795, 22 July 1795

28 Worcester Record Office, BA 4600/765, 705:550; Ruddock, Tom 1979 *Arch Bridges and their Builders*. Cambridge: Cambridge University Press, 149

29 *Hereford Journal* 30 September 1795; 11 November 1795; 3 October 1798; Ruddock 1979, 137–8. *See also* chapter 8.

30 Rowan, Alister 1970 'Downton Castle', *in* Summerson, John, Colvin, Howard and Harris, John (eds) *The Country Seat*. London: Harmondsworth Press, 172–3; Ionides, Julia 1999 *Thomas Farnolls Pritchard of Shrewsbury*. Ludlow: Dog Rose, 206–7; Whitehead, David 2009 'Artisan attitudes to Gothic in Georgian Herefordshire'. *Georgian Group J* **17**, 68–74

31 Watkins and Cowell 2006, 37, 121, 125

32 Ladd 1978, 111

33 Wall, Tom 1994 'The verdant landscape: the practice and theory of Richard Payne Knight at Downton Vale', *in* Daniels, Stephen and Watkins, Charles (eds) *The Picturesque Landscape*. Nottingham: Department of Geography, University of Nottingham, 63, fig 5; Ionides 1999 (*see note 30*), 267–7; Whitehead, David 2010 'Goths and Vandals: restoring historic buildings in Georgian Herefordshire'. *Georgian Group J* **18**, 127 (note 2)

34 Pouncy, B T 1798, *Six Picturesque Landscapes* – 'An Ironwork at Downton, Herefordshire' [a collection of engravings]; Penny, N 1982 'Richard Payne Knight: a brief life', *in* Clarke, Michael and Penny, Nicholas (eds) *The Arrogant Connoisseur: Richard Payne Knight, 1751–1824*. Manchester: Manchester University Press, 16; Van Laun, John 1987 'Industrial archaeology'. *Trans Woolhope Naturalists Field Club* **45**, 787; on Newport Bridge see Ruddock 1979, 124 and *Hereford Journal* 2 November 1791. Nash was still tendering for bridge-work in South Wales in 1805 when he produced a design for the Usk Bridge at Caerleon, but the justices chose the plan by John Hodgkinson: Cross-Rudkin, P S M and Shaw, P T 1999 'John Gethin, Surveyor of County Bridges'. *Trans Woolhope Naturalists Field Club* **49**, 416.

35 This sketch was drawn to the attention of the author by Prof Stephen Daniels, who refers to it in Daniels 1999, 260.

36 Whitehead, David and Shoesmith, Ron 1994 (*see note 21*).

37 Watkins and Cowell 2006, 107, 127, 128, 169; Eisel, John C 2007 'Duncumb, Bird and Bird'. *Trans Woolhope Naturalists Field Club* **55**, 26–7, 31–5; also *Hereford Journal* 29 August 1804 and 9 November 1825. Dr Eisel provided the author with these references.

38 Whitehead, David 2000 'The architectural history of Hereford Cathedral since the Reformation', *in* Aylmer, Gerald and Tiller, John (eds) *Hereford Cathedral*. London: Hambledon Press, 259–61

39 HRO, E38/4, Bromyard Vestry Minute Book 1723–1805; E38/2, Churchwardens' Accounts

40 Colvin 2008, 684

41 All signs of the Georgian restoration were removed during two phases of late Victorian improvements (Pearson, Edna 1993 *Two Churches, Two Communities*. Bromyard: Bromyard and District Local History Society, 55–8).

42 Ionides 1999 (*see note 30*), 98–101; Colvin 2008, 207; *Country Life* 4 January 1989, 50–1

43 Colvin 2008, 206; HRO, Garnons D52; Worcester Record Office, Quarter Sessions Order Book 8, ff 76, 80

44 Mansbridge 1991, *passim*

45 *Hereford Journal* 10 June 1812

46 Mansbridge 1991, 125–6; National Library of Wales, Moccas letters MS 21816D

47 Watkins and Cowell 2006, 144, 60

48 *Hereford Journal* 10 June 1812; 1 July 1812; and 14 October 1812

49 Rees, W J 1827 *The Hereford Guide*. Hereford: T E Watkins, 58; The Fosse – *Hereford Journal* 28 July 1824; The Homend – HRO, C95/B/4 and Temple 1993, 117–9; Garnons – HRO, D52/13; Stoke Edith – HRO, Foley Portfolio 12

50 Colvin, 2008, 510; HRO, pamphlet 202; *Hereford Journal* 10 February 1841; Ledger stone in the Venn's Graveyard, Commercial Road, Hereford; HCL, Minute Book of the Society of Tempers, 18 March 1819; Hereford Cathedral Library, Chapter Act Book 20, f 226

3

Domestic Gothic

GEOFFREY TYACK

The Gothic Revival started long before Nash began to practice as an architect.[1] When he left London for Wales in 1785 Horace Walpole's Strawberry Hill was all but complete and Sir Roger Newdigate's spectacular transformation of Arbury Hall in Warwickshire, the most impressive of all surviving 18th-century Gothic houses, nearing completion. The 1770s and 1780s saw a new upsurge of interest in domestic Gothic, encouraged in part by antiquarian enthusiasm, in part by the relatively new phenomenon of picturesque travel. William Gilpin's *Tour of the Wye* was first published in 1782, and in 1786, the year after Nash moved to Carmarthen, Sir Joshua Reynolds exhorted architects to introduce something of the irregularity, variety and 'intricacy' of medieval castles into their buildings, citing the work of Sir John Vanbrugh as especially worthy of admiration.[2] By then Robert Adam's Culzean Castle in Ayrshire, begun in 1777, and, Richard Payne Knight's Downton Castle in Herefordshire (*c* 1772–8) (Fig 3.1) had already demonstrated the picturesque potential of the castle style. James Wyatt meanwhile, at Lee Priory, Kent (*c* 1785–90: demolished), and elsewhere, showed how the architecture of medieval abbeys could be exploited to similar expressive effect.[3]

Nash's years in Wales, that land of castles, nurtured his interest in the picturesque possibilities of medieval domestic architecture. His *cottage orné* for Mrs Brigstocke (1792–4) was built to overlook the ruined castle at Newcastle Emlyn on the wooded banks of the River Teifi, and there may have been medievalist references in the tantalisingly unrecorded Temple Druid in Pembrokeshire.[4] Then, in 1791, Uvedale Price asked him to design Castle House (*see* Figs 1.14, 1.15), a villa on the seafront at Aberystwyth.[5] Castles, Price later wrote, were 'the most picturesque *habitable* buildings' of the Middle Ages,[6] and his new house, which stood

Fig 3.1
Downton Castle from the
south-west c 1780, drawing
by James Sheriff
(AA 48_05225).

close to a genuine, albeit ruined, late 13th-century castle, was intended evoke something of their visual appeal. Even more important, as he later told Sir George Beaumont, it would enable him and his wife to enjoy the spectacular views north over Cardigan Bay:

Lady Caroline and I found ourselves always at the spot, always looking at the waves breaking against the near rocks, & at the long chain of distant mountains with their monarch Snowden [sic] at their head, & we thought how charming it would be to look comfortably from one's own window in all weathers, instead of being driven away 'when the stormy winds do blow' just when the waves are the most magnificent … At first I thought merely of running up two or three nutshells of rooms, & got a plan from a common welch [sic] carpenter: then Nash was mentioned to me, & he had a mind to build me a larger house indeed, but a square bit of architecture. I told him however, that I must have not only some of the windows, but some of the rooms turned to particular points … I explained to him why I built it so close to the rock, shewed him the effect of the broken fore-ground & its varied line, & how by that means the foreground was connected with the rocks in the second ground; all of which was lost by placing the house further back. He was exceptionally struck with these reasons, which he said he had never thought of before … & he has I think contrived the house most admirably for the situa-tion, & the form of it is certainly extremely varied from my having obliged him to turn the rooms to different aspects.[7]

As a description of one of the main principles of picturesque house-planning – the alignment of the house to the view – this can hardly be bettered. An architect, wrote Price, should 'be obliged to do what so seldom has been done – to accommodate his building to the scenery, not make that give way to the building'.[8] Nash quickly took this advice to heart.

The triangular plan of Castle House echoed – whether consciously or otherwise – the diamond or lozenge shape of the nearby Aberystwyth Castle, as well as later triangular eccentricities such as Longford Castle, Wiltshire (1591); Gibbs's Gothic Temple at Stowe, Buckinghamshire (1741–4); and Midford Castle, just outside Bath (c 1775).[9] Its medievalism was implicit rather than overt – the three turrets were not crenellated, and the doorways and windows were round-arched, like those of Vanbrugh's own castellated house on the edge of Greenwich Park, begun in 1718. There were more obvious medieval references in the

octagonal library and conservatory added by Nash in 1793–4 to Hafod (see Fig 1.17), Thomas Johnes's spectacular but ill-fated pleasure dome high in the mountains to the east of Aberystwyth;[10] there were even more at Kentchurch Court, Herefordshire, which Nash remodelled in 1795 (see Figs 2.6 and 2.7). Thomas Johnes was Payne Knight's cousin, and John Scudamore of Kentchurch was a fellow-member with Knight of the committee for Nash's new gaol at Hereford.[11] Nash's first recorded visit to Knight's Downton Castle was in 1799,[12] but it would be surprising if he had not seen it before then, and its influence can be seen in all his castle-style houses.

Robert Southey called the picturesque 'a new science for which a new language has been invented'.[13] Knight's poem The Landscape – one of the key documents of this science, or pseudo-science – was published in 1794, the same year as Price's Essay on the Picturesque, and a year before Humphry Repton's Sketches and Hints on Landscape Gardening. Repton's publications, based on his famous Red Books, showed how the ideas of Price and Knight – the value of irregularity as opposed to classical symmetry, of oblique over axial vistas, of rough surfaces over smooth, of indigenous over imported models, of broken and varied over simple outlines – could be applied in specific circumstances. When, in 1796, Nash and Repton went into partnership, Nash's role was to give these ideas practical architectural expression. Their first joint work was at Corsham Court, Wiltshire (1797–1802), an Elizabethan H-plan house containing a notable collection of Old Master paintings amassed by the Methuen family. In 1761–4, 'Capability' Brown had landscaped the grounds and designed a new gallery for the pictures, where they can still be seen. Soon after inheriting, in 1795, Paul Cobb Methuen sought designs for further enlargements from James Wyatt, by then the leading champion of 'Modern Gothic' in England. But it was Nash, six years younger than Wyatt, who gained the commission, aided in preparing the designs by Repton's older son, John, who had already shown a penchant for medieval detailing. The gabled Elizabethan façade was retained, as was Brown's picture gallery, but Nash created an elongated staircase hall in the existing central range, 'fitted up as an old baronial hall',[14] albeit with iron galleries and staircases. There was also a new suite of reception rooms on the garden front in the rich late-Perpendicular

style employed by Wyatt at William Beckford's Fonthill Abbey (begun 1796), the *ne plus ultra* of the Gothic Sublime (Fig 3.2). At the centre was an octagonal Saloon, like a miniature version of Henry VII's chapel at Westminster Abbey, with flying buttresses clustered around a clerestory made up of Perpendicular-traceried windows which would, according to Britton, catch the rays of the sun and 'illumine the gloom of a northern aspect'. The alterations cost £25,662 – a tenth of what was spent by Beckford on Fonthill Abbey.[15] But the house was plagued by structural problems, and most of Nash's work perished in a ponderous rebuilding of 1846–9.[16]

Most of Nash's houses of the 1790s were in the classical idiom, but in 1798, the year of his second marriage, he returned to what Repton called 'Castle Gothic' in the villa he designed for his own use on the Isle of Wight.[17] The island had long been a popular destination for seekers after the picturesque, quite close to London but gratifyingly wild in parts.[18] When war with France broke out in 1793, the Isle of Wight gained an added patriotic significance as one of

the outer defences of the realm; the fleet in the Solent could be seen from the towers of Nash's house, which rose up among trees to the east of the busy Medina River.[19] As first built in 1798, East Cowes Castle (Fig 3.3) was a playful *jeu d'esprit* rather than a quasi-fortress, its rooms grouped around a circular staircase that might have been on the site of an old windmill. But over the next few years Nash became a substantial local landowner,[20] and in about 1808–10 he added extra rooms and two more

Fig 3.2 (above top)
The north front of Corsham Court as rebuilt by Nash in 1797–1802 (John Britton, Historical Account of Corsham Court, *1806).*

Fig 3.3 (above)
The west front of East Cowes Castle as first built in 1798, from William Cooke, New Picture of the Isle of Wight, *1808 (Isle of Wight Record Office).*

Fig 3.4
East Cowes Castle, the entrance front looking towards the Medina River, by John Buckler 1815 (© Trustees of the British Museum, 1886,0903.1).

towers, one square, the other octagonal (Fig 3.4; and *see* Fig 0.2). The castle now acquired 'more importance as a distant object', echoing Downton and rivalling the neighbouring Norris Castle, built to Wyatt's designs for Lord Henry Seymour in 1799.[21] Price singled out an 'appearance of splendid confusion and irregularity' as one of the most attractive qualities of medieval buildings,[22] and when the work was

finished Nash could tell one of his clients: 'We have not a Pallace [*sic*] … but we have elbow room & (really) a Castle'.[23]

Visitors to the enlarged East Cowes Castle approached it by a winding drive from North Lodge, an essay in the cottage vernacular that has survived the destruction of the house itself.[24] On arrival they were confronted by an array of towers and battlements, but the medievalism

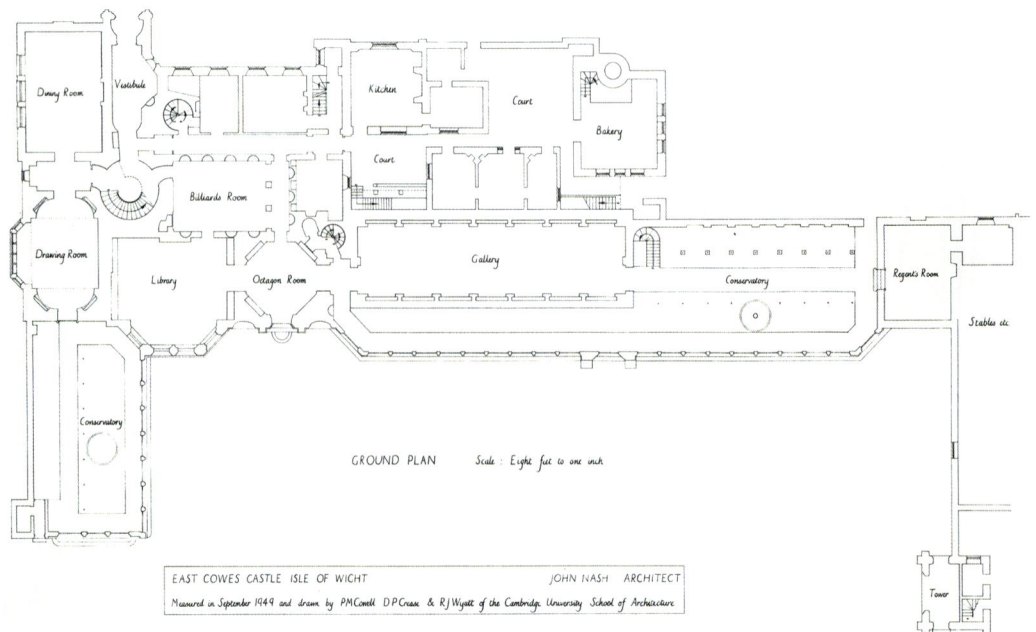

Fig 3.5
Plan of East Cowes Castle drawn in 1949 (BB 76_03338).

Fig 3.6
The drawing room at East
Cowes Castle c 1900
(AA 50_03869).

stopped at the front door. Knight pronounced, no doubt with the classical interiors of Downton in mind, that:

> A house may be adorned with towers and battle-ments, or pinnacles and flying buttresses; but it should still maintain the character of a house of the age and country in which it is erected; and not pretend to be a fortress or monastery of a remote period: for such false pretensions never escape detection; and, when detected, necessarily excite those sentiments, which exposed imposture never fails to excite.[25]

Nash's interior likewise presented a loosely arranged sequence of rooms, none of them very large, in a variety of classical styles (Fig 3.5, plan). When the artist and diarist Joseph Farington paid an unannounced call on 6 Sept 1817 he was first shown the dining room, 'genteely set for dinner for 7 persons'[26] and hung with pictures of houses designed by Nash. Then came the drawing room (Fig 3.6), where he found the architect sitting with his guests.[27] The conservatory and library followed, and then the Octagon Room, added c.1808-10 and hazily evoked in an unfinished painting by J M W Turner, who stayed at the castle for six weeks in 1827, and visited it again in 1832 (Fig 3.7).[28] Finally there was the billiard room, top-lit with little glass domes identical to those that Nash

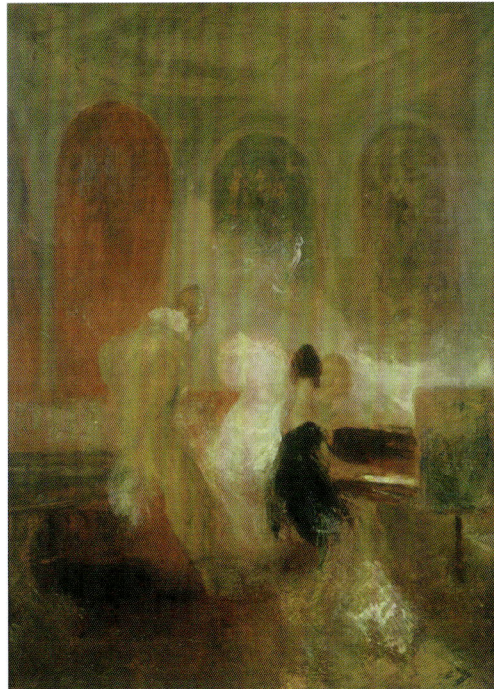

Fig 3.7
'Music Party, East Cowes
Castle', by J M W Turner
c 1835
(© Tate, London 2012).

was later to employ in the picture gallery at Buckingham Palace. The staircase, in the middle of the house, was also top-lit, with fluted walls: a motif later used in the staircase at Attingham, Shropshire (1805–7). The main rooms all commanded views, the dining room and drawing room looking west over the river,

Fig 3.8
*Perspective view, probably
by A C Pugin, of one of
Nash's designs for a second
courtyard at Magdalen
College, Oxford, 1801
(The President and Fellows
of Magdalen College,
Oxford).*

with the little town of West Cowes in the distance; the conservatory looked eastwards over a lawn, and the library and Octagon Room faced south, along with a second, 140ft-long (43m) conservatory added *c* 1821–4, in which Nash enjoyed walking long distances in his old age.[29] The lawn formed part of a pleasure garden laid out with clumps of trees and shrubs after the fashion of the garden at the Brighton Pavilion, created by Nash and the royal gardener William Aiton for the Prince Regent, who paid a visit to the Castle in 1817.[30] And it was from here that the castle was revealed in its most imposing aspect (*see* Fig 0.3).[31]

East Cowes Castle was not just a comfortable weekend retreat; it was, like Nash's house in Dover Street, an advertisement for his architectural skills. Between 1798 and 1811, when he drastically scaled back his private practice in order to work on Regent's Park, he designed eleven more castellated houses – seven in England and four in Ireland – as well as two houses in the late-Perpendicular or Tudor-Gothic idiom, and several remodellings of 16th- or 17th-century houses in a more-or-less faithful version of the original style.[32] His clients did not come from the highest reaches of the aristocracy, who generally preferred the Wyatt clan, but neither were they, like Nash himself or most of his clients of the late 1790s, *nouveaux riches*. Most were country squires enjoying increasing agricultural revenues at a time of rising wartime prices, sometimes reinforced by the proceeds of

commerce and industry. Gothic houses and castles proclaimed the primacy of landed property in an age of rapid and transformative economic change; William Porden, writing to Lord Grosvenor about his proposed transformation of Eaton Hall, Cheshire, claimed that Gothic was preferable to Classical styles 'on the score of preserving that Distinction of Rank and Fortune, which it is the habit of the age to diminish'.[33] For the Protestant ascendancy in Ireland, following the convulsions of the 1790s and the Union of 1801, castles acquired further resonance as symbols of authority and security among a potentially hostile population, which had looked to England's enemies for succour.[34] Above all, houses in the medieval style could express a shared sense of indigenous cultural values threatened, but not suppressed, by the might of Napoleonic France.

Nash's success as a domestic architect derived in large measure from his ability to give his clients what they wanted, not what he thought they ought to want. In the summer of 1801, he was asked by Robert Burton of Longner Hall, Shropshire, to prepare designs for a new house to replace the dilapidated Elizabethan building in which his family had lived for many generations. Burton was asked to 'put down in words and figures the names of the rooms you should like to have and nearly their sizes and if you have any preference as to the shapes of the rooms'. Then came the choice of style. There were, Nash wrote, seven 'characters suitable to a house', five of them drawing upon the architecture of the Middle Ages or the 16th century: 'the gothic of the time of Elizabeth called house gothic'; 'the gothic of Henry the 6th & 7th, of which character are many of the collegiate houses'; 'the monastic gothic of which are most of the religious houses'; 'the cathedral gothic which is a mixture of towers and turrets'; and finally the 'Norman or Saxon castle'.[35]

The most picturesque houses, Nash told, Burton, were those 'whose tops are enrich'd with towers, turrets, battlements and pinnacles'. Antiquarians had long shown an interest in castles, and Nash owned copies of Hearne's *Antiquities of Great Britain* (1786) and Carter's *Ancient Architecture of England*, the first volume of which came out in 1795.[36] The castles he designed himself were inspired, at least in their outward appearance, by late medieval examples such as Raglan (Monmouthshire), Bodiam and Herstmonceaux (Sussex), Nunney (Somerset) and Warwick, all featuring high stone curtain walls interrupted by towers of varied shapes, often capped with corbelling or machicolation.[37] For his internal Gothic detailing, when it was requested, he drew mainly upon late medieval ecclesiastical and collegiate architecture, especially that of Oxford, where he produced a lavish but unexecuted scheme in 1801 for remodelling and extending the 18th-century New Building at Magdalen College, clothing it in a Tudor-Gothic garb loosely based on the style of the college's surviving 15th-century core (Fig 3.8).[38] Here he followed recent practitioners of the genre such as James Wyatt, aided by drawings from his assistants, several of which were published by Augustus Pugin in 1821 as *Specimens of Gothic Architecture*, and dedicated to Nash.

Nash's main challenge in designing Gothic houses for a modern clientele was to reconcile the need for a suitably romantic and picturesque exterior with a growing demand for domestic comfort. Changes in manners had already led to a relaxation of the formality that had characterised early 18th-century country-house life, as noted in a doggerel verse by Humphry Repton:

> No more the cedar parlour's formal gloom
> Where dullness chills, 'tis now the living room,
> Where guests to whim, to task or fancy true
> Scatter'd in groups, their different plans pursue.[39]

Elements of formality still survived in Nash's houses, often in the form of a ceremonial route leading from a *porte-cochère* to the staircase hall. But the most important consideration was now to supply a sequence of differently shaped ground-floor reception rooms – usually a dining room, drawing room and library, together with extra rooms in grander houses – commanding views over the garden, which was often accessed, as at East Cowes, through French windows or a conservatory: a relatively novel innovation made desirable by the recent influx of exotic plants and possible by improvements in heating technology. The first floor of Nash's houses was always given over to bedrooms, and the servants' quarters were usually placed asymmetrically to one side of the house, often around embattled courtyards. Such irregular arrangements had already been recommended by Price, who believed that they 'would suggest to an artist of genius, no less varied and picturesque effects within; and that the arrangement of rooms, would oftentimes be at least as convenient as in a more uniform plan'[40] – an insight later shared by Frank Lloyd Wright. And in arranging rooms in a convenient and visually satisfying way, Nash showed a flair matched by few of his contemporaries.

Luscombe, Devon (1799–1804) (Fig 3.9) is the most engaging of Nash's medieval-inspired houses. It was built for Charles Hoare, younger son of Richard Colt Hoare of Stourhead, who had recently extended his Palladian villa in Wiltshire, and who was a partner in the family bank that still flourishes in Fleet Street.

Fig 3.9
Luscombe (1799–1804),
the garden front
(BB 73_06897).

Fig 3.10
The entrance front
at Luscombe
(BB 73_06895).

Like Price's house at Aberystwyth, and Nash's on the Isle of Wight, it is a monument to the late Georgian cult of the seaside. Since 1795, Hoare and his valetudinarian wife had been in the habit of visiting Dawlish to enjoy the mild air of the South Devon coast, and the house went up on a small estate they had purchased in a dry valley running steeply up from the village.[41] A villa rather than a full-scale family seat, costing some £12,500 – half the cost of the alterations at Corsham Court – it occupies a sheltered site,

invisible from the public road and framed by what Repton – writing just before the termination of his partnership with Nash – called 'an adequate foreground of highly Dressed Lawn and Pleasure Garden', with views across its valley to 'a bank of Lawn, beautifully broken by large trees, & skirted by a bold sweeping line of plantation.'[42] Repton harboured no doubts about the suitability of the castle style, contrasting it in his Red Book to the blandness of a typical stuccoed villa:

> [The] Character of a Castle, … by blending a chaste correctness of proportion, with bold irregularity of outline; its deep recesses & projections producing broad masses of light & shadow, while its roof is enriched by turrets, battlements, corbles [*sic*] & lofty chimneys, has infinitely more picturesque effect than any other stile of building … Its very irregularity will give it consequence, which the offices, & meer [*sic*] walls which in a modern building it would be essential to conceal, by partaking the Character of the Castle, will extend its Scite [*sic*], & make it an apparently considerable pile of building.

The house is built of rough local stone and is defiantly asymmetrical, with a square tower over the *porte-cochère* close to the steep northern slope of the valley (Fig 3.10), and an octagonal one over the drawing room on the garden side. There is a Gothic-arched loggia (later glazed as

Fig 3.11
Luscombe, ground plan
(redrawn by EH from Mark
Girouard 1978 Life in the
English Country House.
New Haven and London:
Yale UP, 226. The original
source is a drawing in the
Hoare family archives in
Hoare's Bank, Fleet Street).

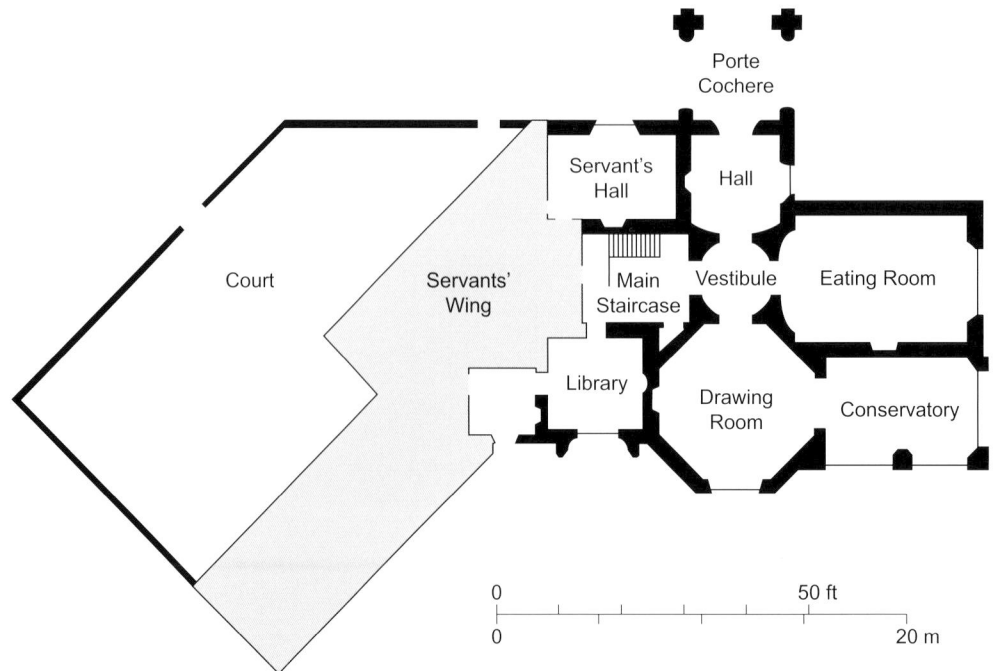

Fig 3.12
*Killymoon Castle (1803–9)
from the west
(Malachy Coney).*

a conservatory) to one side of the octagonal tower, allowing views down the valley to the sea; on the other side, at an angle of 45 degrees, is the service wing, terminated by a square tower, increasing the 'apparent extent' of the building. The interior is compactly planned (Fig 3.11, plan), but more coherently than East Cowes Castle, with a formal route leading from the entrance through a hall to a circular central vestibule. It gives access to the drawing room straight ahead, its canted windows commanding views across the valley, with the library (formerly the dining room) and main staircase on either side: a looser version of the ingenious planning of Nash's Welsh houses of the early 1790s.[43] Summerson regretted the lack of 'studied ornament' in the vestigially classical decoration of the rooms. But Luscombe was a holiday home built for occasional recreational use, and elaborate interior decoration was neither desired nor necessary, sufficient visual incident coming from the pictures and the furniture, supplied by the Chippendale firm, much of which survives *in situ*.

Nash's first Irish house, Killymoon Castle (Fig 3.12), just outside Cookstown in Co. Tyrone, is about the same size as Luscombe and was designed only a year or two later. But it is very different in character. This is partly because it is faced with the grey ashlar used in so many Irish buildings, and partly because of the external detailing: round-headed windows enclosing grouped wooden lancets, and, in the *porte-cochère*, neo-Norman round arches, conceivably alluding to the Anglo-Norman settlement of Ireland. Nash's client was James Stewart, descendent of a family that had come from Scotland in the 17th century and a leading light in the Irish Volunteer movement of the 1780s.[44] His house burned down in or about 1801, the year of the Union, and in 1802 the Earl of Selkirk expressed the hope that Nash's replacement would serve as 'an introduction to a good taste of Architecture in your quarter of the Kingdom'.[45]

Killymoon stands in a carefully planted landscape by the banks of the Ballinderry River, close to the hilltop fort of Tullaghoge on which the O'Neill kings of Ulster had once been

Fig 3.13 (right)
West Grinstead Park
(c 1806–8), the dining room
in 1954, shortly
before demolition
(AA 54_02061).

Fig 3.14 (below)
The garden front of
Knepp Castle (1808)
(OP 10360).

crowned; a neighbour, John Burges, wrote in 1824 that 'its equal is not to be found in any country for the most perfect combination of wood, water, mountain and undulation of ground … The grandeur of the timber, particularly the oaks and sycamore, quite give you the idea of a scene of Claude Lorraine's.[46] Work got under way in 1803, when Stewart's wife lamented that 'Mr Nash is more magnificent in his finishings than we need be'; the house was still being furnished in 1809.[47] The interior is more formally arranged than that of Luscombe, with a ceremonial route rising from the entrance to a spacious staircase hall lit from above by a lantern filled with painted armorial glass. The detailing here is in the late-Perpendicular style of Corsham; the Library – in a surviving wing of the older house – is in the same vein. But the octagonal dining room and the oval drawing rooms are decorated in the restrained neoclassical manner that came equally easily to Nash, their shapes reflected in the round and octagonal towers which, with the *porte-cochère*, form the most dramatic features of the exterior.

Nash's career as a domestic architect came to a climax between 1806 and 1810: a time when landed profits were being augmented by the effects of the Napoleonic blockade. Most of his clients opted for castles, with towers of varying sizes and shapes grouped for picturesque effect; examples included the rather foursquare Garnstone, deep in the Herefordshire countryside (*c* 1806–10; *see* Fig 2.16: demolished); Childwall Hall, in what are now the outskirts of Liverpool (1806–13: demolished), a derivative of East Cowes; and Kilwaughter Castle (1807), near the north-east coast of Co. Antrim, now a ruin approached through a farmyard, and incorporating parts of an early 17th-century tower house with Scottish-style bartizans at the corners.[48] There were also two castles on adjoining estates in Sussex. West Grinstead (*c* 1806–8) was a castellated version of Nash's slightly earlier Italianate villa at Cronkhill, Shropshire (*see* page 68), with a round and a square tower on either side of the main façade, linked by a round-arched loggia. It was entered from the side through a *porte-cochère* which led to a corridor or gallery running behind the main reception rooms, some of them decorated in a vestigially Gothic fashion (Fig 3.13), others in a neo-Jacobean style; the staircase, of the double-return variety used at Corsham and Killymoon, led off from the corridor.[49] Nash's client here was Charles Burrell, whose father, the Sussex

county historian, had inherited a fortune and a baronetcy from his own father-in-law.[50] The same fortune, augmented by the proceeds of the sale of the former family home, The Deepdene in Surrey, allowed Charles's brother Sir Walter Burrell to spend some £13,500 on building Knepp Castle (1808), only a mile away, the choice of style inspired perhaps by an isolated tower from a long-abandoned Norman castle on the estate.[51] Knepp is built of brick and stucco and looks out onto a lake, originally a hammer-pond for the local iron industry. The rooms here are disposed on either side of a central route leading from the *porte-cochère* to a circular staircase inside a round tower, and it is from this side of the house that Nash's compositional skills are best displayed (Fig 3.14).[52]

Nash was sometimes asked to restore an 'Old English' character to medieval and Tudor houses that had been altered in the 18th century. At Helmingham Hall, Suffolk, the moated courtyard house of the Tollemache family, he was employed in 1800 to reverse a series of changes wrought by the 4th Earl of Dysart between about 1745 and 1760. The 16th-century porch was rebuilt, its 18th-century Venetian window over the entrance replaced by a convincing-looking oriel, and a handsome iron bridge thrown across the moat. The rest of the house was meanwhile coated in stucco (subsequently removed) and enlivened with bay windows, pinnacled gables and battlements (Fig 3.15), and the interiors remodelled with plain Elizabethan-style plaster ceilings.[53] A similar makeover occurred at the 16th-century Parnham, near Beaminster in Dorset – a smaller house to which Nash gave a convincingly authentic-looking external treatment in 1807–11, accompanied by a thorough internal remodelling at a total cost of about £25,000, equivalent perhaps to about £1,500,000 today.[54] And at Ingestre Hall, Staffordshire, he refashioned the entrance front in about 1808–13 in a manner almost indistinguishable from that of the genuinely Jacobean south front it was designed to imitate. In these commissions Nash anticipated countless 19th- and 20th-century restorations designed to impose stylistic consistency, however spurious, on older houses that had undergone later alterations.

Nash also designed two completely new houses in versions of what, in his letter of 1801 to Robert Burton of Longner Hall, Shropshire, he called 'the gothic of Henry the 6th & 7th': the style of his alterations to Corsham Court and of

Fig 3.15
Helmingham Hall,
remodelled c 1800–3,
north-east view showing
Nash's gabled kitchen wing
and one of his two cast-iron
bridges over the moat.
Nash's stucco has been
removed from the house
(© Country Life 1956).

Fig 3.15
Helmingham Hall,
remodelled c 1800–3,
north-east view showing
Nash's gabled kitchen wing
and one of his two cast-iron
bridges over the moat.
Nash's stucco has been
removed from the house
(© Country Life 1956).

Fig 3.16
A drawing of Longner Hall,
probably by George Repton
(AA 60_00583).

Fig 3.17 (opposite)
The staircase at
Longner Hall (1805–8)
(AA 60_00576).

his unexecuted scheme for Magdalen College, Oxford. The irregular, pinnacled elevations of the new Longner Hall (Fig 3.16), begun in 1805, anticipate those of many Victorian parsonages and villas, though the interiors, with their plaster fan and lierne vaults – reminiscent of those at Arbury Hall (1763, etc) and the earlier chapel at Brasenose College, Oxford (1657–63) – would no doubt have appalled later Gothic zealots. Here, as in so many of Nash's houses, the layout was determined by the view. The main rooms command views of the distant hills of the Welsh borderland, framed by a pointed-arched loggia (later glazed), and the entrance was placed at the back of the house, from which a vestibule leads to a vaulted corridor with a double-return staircase rising up to a Perpendicular Gothic window, its stained-glass figures recalling the heroic exploits of the family (Fig 3.17).[55] Aqualate Hall, Staffordshire (1806–9), not far from Longner, was also built to 'command a prospect' – in this case a lake

Fig 3.18 (above)
The entrance front of
Aqualate Hall (1806–9),
late 19th-century
photograph
(BB 82_01838).

Fig 3.19 (right)
Aqualate Hall (1806–9),
the library in 1857,
watercolour
(FF 82_00063).

(hence the name). The owner, John Boughey Fletcher, originally contemplated building a classical house of brick with stone dressings, but, after extensive correspondence with Nash, he settled for a stuccoed Gothic design with rows of small triangular gables on the roofline – a favourite Nash motif, used previously in the outbuildings at Corsham and at Helmingham Hall. The most striking features were two large ogee-topped octagons, one at each end of the house, inspired perhaps by the western chantry chapels of St George's Chapel, Windsor, or Sir Christopher Wren's Tom Tower at Christ Church, Oxford (Fig 3.18). One octagon surmounted the Library, the other the drawing room (Fig 3.19); both rooms had views over the lake, and both were upholstered and decorated in the rich classical manner Nash also used in the interiors of Attingham, not far away.[56] The other impressive interior was the long gallery running across the spine of the house, separating the 'public' from the more private rooms. It was fan-vaulted in plaster, like Horace Walpole's gallery at Strawberry Hill, but was lit from above by skylights, and at one end was a double-return

staircase: an arrangement anticipated at Corsham and repeated a few years later, in more exotic guise, at the Brighton Pavilion.

Nash returned to the elongated galleried layout of Aqualate in two castles designed in 1808. Sir Thomas Liddell, the builder of Ravensworth Castle, just outside Newcastle, came from a family which had owned the estate since 1607; he was MP for County Durham until 1807, when he retired and 'devoted himself to the erection of his noble seat and the development of the coal mines on his estate', and was raised to the peerage as Lord Ravensworth in 1821.[57] The existing house, remodelled by James Paine in a delicate Gothic style in the mid-18th century, stood on the site of a late medieval castle, of which four corner towers and a curtain wall survived.[58] Nash's replacement was much larger, with a north-facing entrance range separated by a long gallery from the main reception rooms, which overlooked a wooded valley (Fig 3.20). The outside was punctuated by towers; there was also a large service courtyard incorporating two of the towers of the medieval castle and, beyond it, a stable courtyard

Fig 3.20
Ravensworth Castle,
begun 1808, aerial view
(EPW019815).

Fig 3.21
The Gallery at Ravensworth
Castle in the 1920s
(NRO 722/A/11/3,
Reproduced by kind
permission of the Berwick-
upon-Tweed Record Office,
part of the Woodhorn
Trust).

entered through an imposing gatehouse. Nash's working drawings show an extensive use of structural iron girders – hardly surprising in one of the nurseries of the Industrial Revolution – and an ingenious system of reversed arches in some of the foundations, employed later at All Souls Church, Langham Place in London;[59] the flat roofs were covered, like those of most of the castles, with a composition material, probably Dehl's mastic. Building was unduly drawn-out, and several changes were made to the original design. First, a plaster Gothic vault was substituted for the glazed classical saucer-domes originally proposed for the gallery (Fig 3.21).[60] Then in about 1818 the west end of the house was reconfigured, possibly at the suggestion of Liddell's son Thomas who, in Britton's words, 'devoted some years to the pleasing and arduous task of superintending [the] works';[61] Thomas Liddell was almost certainly responsible for redesigning the north range, part of which was given over to a magnificent staircase hall with a hammer-beam roof, much more 'correctly' detailed than any of Nash's interiors elsewhere in the house.[62] But the coal mining whose profits funded the house proved its undoing, for in 1953

subsidence led to its almost total demolition, save for the stable and parts of the service courtyards,[63] and the castellated entrance lodge that still stands within sight and earshot of the A1 road.

Caerhayes Castle, another house with a central top-lit gallery, still survives in its highly picturesque setting on the south coast of Cornwall. The builder, John Bettesworth Trevanion, briefly Whig MP for the rotten borough of Penryn, near Falmouth, was 'a complete man of fashion in the best sense of the word … the very *arbiter elegentiarium*'.[64] His grandfather, John Bettesworth, who came from Sussex, had married the heiress of the Trevanions, an old Cornish gentry family; his younger brother, a naval captain who had carried Nelson's dispatches from Antigua, was killed in action in 1808, the year the house was begun; and the poet Lord Byron was his cousin.[65] The new house replaced an older one, which was allegedly damp and presumably insufficiently picturesque. This was not a criticism that could be levelled at Nash's castle (Fig 3.22), which made the most of the potential of the site; for one contemporary commentator it presented

Fig 3.22
Caerhayes Castle, begun
1808, from the south
(AA 53_00709).

'with considerable correctness, the features of the semi-castellated dwellings of our ancestors; and very scientifically harmonizes with the picturesque wildness of the surrounding scenery'.[66] As in many of his castles, Nash used local materials: granite for the walls, and parapets and quoins of china-clay.[67] Towers proliferate: a low, square one over the *porte-cochère*; a round one anchoring one corner of the south front, overlooking the sea; a larger square one on the far side at the junction with the service courtyard; and a miniature circular one with a little turret at the corner of a lower terrace, allegedly laid out to reinforce the foundations on the sloping site.[68] There is also an outer line of mock-fortifications with cruciform arrow slits next to the bay, recalling the diminutive outer fortifications to the 15th-century Great Tower at Raglan. The interiors, according to Neale, preserved 'the same style, as far as can be consistently adapted to the required arrangement of modern society', with painted glass windows casting a suitably dim medieval light into the entrance hall, dining room and staircase, which rose up from the far end of the central gallery (Fig 3.23).[69] The house was still unfinished in 1824, and little of Nash's interior decoration survived Trevanion's bankruptcy and flight to Belgium in 1840, followed by gradual dereliction, from which it was fortunately

rescued in 1853 by a new owner whose descendants live there today.[70]

Nash's last two medieval-inspired houses were built in Ireland, a land thought by one later commentator to be peculiarly suitable for modern castle-building:

> This bold and harsh, but splendid species of design is well adapted to the recluse parts of Ireland, where nature reigns in wild and mysterious majesty. The towers, the ramparts and long irregular lines of military grandeur, which characterise the castellated house, assimilate with the lofty mountains and widespread lakes of this romantic island.[71]

These scenic qualities were well exemplified at Shanbally, Co. Tipperary, begun *c* 1809–10 for Cornelius O'Callaghan, second Baron and first Viscount Lismore. He was the representative of an old Irish family that had made an accommodation with the new political establishment after the Glorious Revolution, and had gone on to improve the estate, which lay in pastoral country between the Galty and Knockmealdown Mountains, and to develop the nearby town of Clogheen.[72] Nash's plan (Fig 3.24) was a variant of that employed at Ravensworth and Caerhayes: a south-facing range of reception rooms separated from the entrance range by a gallery with the main

Fig 3.23
The hall and staircase
at Caerhayes Castle
(AA 53_00720).

staircase at one end.[73] The internal decoration, as in most of Nash's later castles, was consistently Gothic, and, so far as one can judge from photographs, represented his finest achievement in that genre. From the *porte-cochère*, a passage led through an entrance hall to the gallery, lit by roof lights supported on plaster rib vaults. At one end was a double-return staircase surmounted by a plaster fan vault, at the other a doorway leading into a vestibule between the octagonal dining room and the circular drawing room, both facing west. On the south front, overlooking a lake, were the common parlour and library, the former with a lierne vault and pendants like those of the 15th-century Divinity School in Oxford, the latter with repetitive late Gothic panelling on the ceiling similar to that on the drawing room ceiling at Arbury.[74] Beyond this was a conservatory. The internal layout was reflected in the exterior, seen at its best from the south, with round and octagonal towers anchoring it at each end, and the

Galty Mountains as a backdrop. Now nothing remains, the Irish Land Commission having gratuitously blown up the remains of the house in 1960.

Lough Cutra, Co. Galway, the last of Nash's castles, was begun in 1811, just after Nash had enlarged his own castle at East Cowes.[75] The builder, Charles Vereker (later second Lord Gort), had been, like the O'Callaghans of Shanbally, a supporter of Grattan in the doomed Dublin parliament, and, as a colonel in the Limerick Militia, played an important part in halting the French invasion of western Ireland in 1798; he was elected to Westminster in 1802 as MP for Limerick, a city where his family had long exercised influence.[76] The castle (Fig 3.25) was built on a virgin site, surrounded by newly planted woodland and facing south-east over a lake towards the mountains that separate Connaught from Munster, and presented a telling contrast to the abandoned tower houses of the Catholic landlords who had dominated

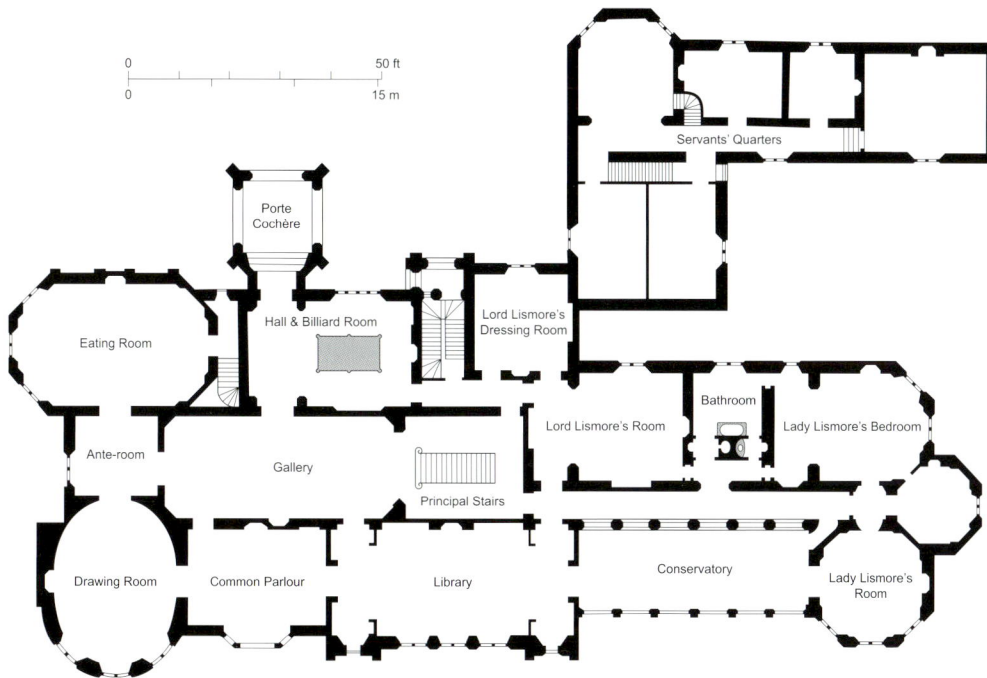

Fig 3.24
Shanbally Castle (c 1810–19),
plan (redrawn by EH from
Mansbridge 1991, 218.
The original source is George
Repton's RIBA notebook:
SD 110/1).

the area until the Battle of the Boyne.[77] Smaller than Shanbally, it has a rectangular plan, with the central block taken up by the entrance hall and saloon placed back-to-back and the other reception rooms in towers overlooking the lake; the staircase, next to the entrance hall, winds sinuously within the walls of another, circular, tower, as at East Cowes – which Vereker had visited – and Shanbally. The interiors, notably the lierne-vaulted entrance hall and the saloon, with a Coade stone chimneypiece based on one at Windsor Castle,[78] are now among the best surviving examples of Nash's domestic Perpendicular Gothic. But by 1811 he was already becoming preoccupied by the Metropolitan Improvements which were, along with his work for the Prince Regent, to dominate the last phase of his career, and the completion of the building was placed in the hands of the Pain brothers, who later employed the castle style with great panache at Dromoland (Co. Clare), Mitchelstown (Co. Cork) and elsewhere.[79]

Fig 3.25
Lough Cutra Castle
(1811–17), the entrance
front and lake
(© National Inventory of
Architectural Heritage,
Ireland).

Nash's great achievement as a domestic architect, whether in the medieval idiom or in the Italianate villa manner discussed in chapter 4, was to reconcile the growing taste for the picturesque with the demand for a more comfortable lifestyle. Neither a pioneer nor a prophet of the Gothic Revival, he has been too easily dismissed as a dilettante.[80] His use of medieval detailing was certainly unoriginal and often unscholarly, lacking the 'archaeological' accuracy prized increasingly by pedantic critics. And for A W N Pugin, son of his chief illustrator, the very idea of modern Gothic as understood by Nash's generation was an absurdity:

> How many portcullises which will not lower down, and drawbridges which will not draw up! – how many loopholes in turrets so small that the most diminutive sweep could not ascend them! – On one side of the house machicolated parapets, embrasures, bastions, and all the show of strong defence, and round the corner of the building a conservatory leading to the principal rooms, through which a whole company of horsemen might penetrate at one smash into the very heart of the mansion! – for who would hammer against nailed portals when he could kick his way through the greenhouse?[81]

These criticisms miss the point of Nash's architecture. His approach to medieval buildings, as to classical buildings, was intuitive rather than academic, pragmatic rather than emotional, associative rather than rationalist. He was an *architetto-pittore*, in Uvedale Price's words, unusually sensitive to the *genius loci*, and alert to the demands of a society in which universal standards of taste had broken down. His best houses show a gaiety and lightness of touch absent in the work of later, more prosaic, architects. Fortunate to come into contact with the main ideologues of the picturesque at a crucial stage in his career, he gave their principles practical application, and so helped shape the way in which we view the domestic environment today.

Notes

1   Among many treatments of the subject, see Eastlake, C L (Crook, J Mordaunt ed) 1970 *The Gothic Revival.* Leicester: Leicester University Press, especially the Introduction; Brooks, Chris 1999 *The Gothic Revival.* London: Phaidon; McCarthy, M 1987. *The Origins of the Gothic Revival.* New Haven and London: Yale University Press; Rowan, A 1965 'The castle style in British domestic architecture'. unpublished PhD thesis, University of Cambridge.

2   Wark, R (ed) 1975 *Discourses on Art.* New Haven and London: Yale University Press, 242–3

3   For Culzean, and other Adam castles, see Rowan, A 1974 'The Adam Castle Style'. *Roy Soc Arts J* **CXXII**, 679–94; Astley, S 2000, *Robert Adam's Castles.* London: The Soane Gallery. The best discussion of Downton Castle is in Ballantyne, A 1997 *Architecture, Landscape and Liberty: Richard Payne Knight and the Picturesque.* Cambridge: Cambridge University Press; also Whitehead, David 2009 'Artisan attitudes to Gothic in Georgian Herefordshire'. *Georgian Group J* **17**, 70–2. Knight, who designed the house himself, always denied that he was trying to imitate a medieval castle. For Lee Priory, Robinson, J M 2012 *James Wyatt, Architect to George III.* New Haven and London: Yale University Press, 220–3.

4   *See page 23*

5   Lloyd, T Orbach, J and Scourfield, R 2006 *The Buildings of Wales: Carmarthenshire and Ceredigion.* New Haven and London: Yale University Press, 406–8, 412–4; also Webster, J R 1995 *Old College, Aberystwyth.* Cardiff: University of Wales Press; Watkins, C and Cowell, B 2012 *Uvedale Price (1747–1829): Decoding the Picturesque.* Woodbridge: The Boydell Press, 91–105. The house was demolished in 1896.

6   Price, Uvedale 1810 *Essays on the Picturesque.* London: J Mawman, **I**, 52–3, 181–2. The 1810 edition incorporates Price's 'Essay on Architecture and Buildings', published in 1798 as a supplement to his *Essay on the Picturesque.*

7   Watkins and Cowell (eds) 2006, 121–2, 18 March 1798. The reference to nutshells may allude to *Oikidia, or Nutshells* (1785), by James Peacock (under the pseudonym Jose Mac Packe), which includes a design for a triangular house. Nash had a copy in his library.

8   Price 1810 (*see note 6*) **II**, 268–9

9   Midford Castle was designed by John Carter, a passionate propangandist for the preservation of English medieval architecture (Crook, J Mordaunt 1995 *John Carter and the Mind of the Gothic Revival.* London: Soc Antiq, 50–1).

10 The library was mentioned by C R Cockerell in 1806, and was recorded in a perspective view, probably by Frederick Nash (Suggett 1995, 78–80 and fig 43). A watercolour by J M W Turner in the Lady Lever Art Gallery, Port Sunlight, may represent a Nash scheme for remodelling the whole house.

11 *See page 23; Country Life* 15 and 22 Dec 1966, 1632–5, 1688–91; Whitehead, David 2010 'Goths and Vandals: restoring historic buildings in Herefordshire'. *Georgian Group J* **18**, 123–7. Work ceased when the owner died in 1796 but was resumed in 1825 by a 'Mr Tudor', who may have followed Nash's original design.

12 Letter quoted in Ladd 1978, 111

13 Southey, Robert 1808 *Letters from England.* London: Longman, Hurst, Rees and Orme. I am grateful to Rosemary Yallop for this reference.

14 Britton, J 1806 *Historical Account of Corsham House.* London: privately published, 106

15 Ladd 1978, 162; Wilson, R and Mackley, J 2000 *Creating Paradise.* London and New York: Hambledon and London, 241. *See also* chapter 8.

16 Britton 1806 *(see note 14),* 107; also Ladd 1978, 75–119, and Harcourt, L 1976 *Corsham Court: a Gothick Dream.* London: Gothick Dream. The Saloon may have been inspired by Nash's library at Hafod. His library at Corsham still survives, as do an octagonal dairy and some other outbuildings.

17 Repton 1803 *Observations on the Theory and Practice of Landscape Gardening.* London: J Taylor. A plaque in the house recorded that it was 'designed and built by John Nash 1798' (Sherfield, Ian 1984 *East Cowes Castle.* Camberley: Business by Design, 22, 24).

18 Boynton, L 1996 'The Marine Villa', *in* Arnold, Dana (ed) *The Georgian Villa.* Stroud: Sutton Publishing, 118–28

19 The first datable view is in Cooke, W 1808 *New Picture of the Isle of Wight.* London: Vernor, Hood and Sharpe

20 Sherfield, Ian 1984 *(see note 17),* 22

21 Cooke 1808 *(see note 19).* The octagonal tower resembled the 15th-century Guy's Tower at Warwick Castle and Sanderson Miller's Edge Hill tower, Warwickshire, built in the 1740s. For Norris Castle, Robinson, J M 2012 *(see note 3),* 232. Thomas Pennethorne drew both East Cowes and Norris Castle in 1815: Sherfield 1984 *(see note 17),* pls 1 and 3.

22 Price 1810 *(see note 6)* **I**, 52–3

23 Aqualate Hall papers, William Salt Library, Stafford, letter to J F Boughey, Nov 1810

24 For Nash's lodges and cottages see Temple 1979.

25 Knight 1805 *Analytical Inquiry into the Principles of Taste.* London: Thomas Payne, 223–4

26 Farington, J *Diary* (ed Garlick et al 1978–1984) **XIV**, 5078–9 (6 September 1817). Farington returned in November 1821 and spent two nights in the Castle. For pictures taken when the house was in an advanced state of dereliction before its final demolition in the 1950s, see *Builder* 1 September 1950, 270–4, and NMR photographs.

27 Some early 20th-century photographs are reproduced in Sherfield 1984 *(see note 17),* figs 7–9.

28 Pinhorn (ed) 2000 **I**, 82, and Pinhorn (ed) 2002, 5–7; Youngblood, P 1983 'Three misidentified works by J M W Turner'. *Burlington Magazine* **125**, 615–9. Another of Turner's unfinished paintings, long described as an 'Interior at Petworth' and hailed as a progenitor of Impressionist art, is now thought to show the drawing room (Horzee, R (ed) 2007 *British Vision: Observation and Imagination in British Art 1750–1950.* Ghent: Mercatorfonds and Museum vor Schon Kunsten, 325–8). Turner also did two oil paintings of the Medina estuary (in the Victoria and Albert Museum, and in the Indianapolis Museum of Art, USA) showing the castle's towers rising above the trees.

29 Pinhorn 2000, eg 1 Dec 1832: 'walked in the Conservatory four miles'

30 Jones, M 2005 *Set for a King.* Brighton: Royal Pavilion, Museums and Libraries, 70–1, 96–105. Part of the East Cowes conservatory was adapted in 1834 to incorporate the gallery from his house in Regent Street. A step leading into it survives today, hidden by a clump of shrubs within the housing estate that now sprawls over the site of the house and grounds.

31 Brannon, George 1824 *Views of the Isle of Wight.* London: Colnaghi, Walker and Clay

32 Hawarden, Flintshire (1807) was built by Thomas Cundy, largely to Nash's designs

33 Acloque, G and Cornforth, J 1971 'The eternal Gothic of Eaton'. *Country Life* 11 Feb 1971, 304

34 eg Charleville Forest (1801) and Killeen Castle (1803–13), by the Dublin architect Francis Johnson, and Tullynally, begun in 1801, by Johnson and Morrison (Rowan 1965 *(see note 1),* 185–6, 238–247; Brooks 1999 *(see note 1),* 176–7)

35 Private collection, letter dated 31 July 1801; Tyack, G 2004 'Longner Hall, Shropshire' *Georgian Group J* **14**, 199–213

36 Catalogue in Sir John Soane's Museum

37 Thompson, M W 1991 *The Rise of the Castle.* Cambridge: Cambridge University Press, 157–78; Thompson, M W 1987 *Decline of the Castle.* Cambridge: Cambridge University Press, 71–85; also Goodall, John 2011 *The English Castle.* New Haven and London: Yale University Press

38 White, R 2001 *The Architectural Drawings of Magdalen College, Oxford.* Oxford: Oxford University Press, 31–8. Repton, whose partnership with Nash had broken up by 1801, produced another set of designs for the college, also unexecuted.

39 Loudon, J C 1840 *The Landscape Gardening … of the late Humphry Repton.* London: Longman & Co, 460–1

40 Price 1810 *(see note 6)* **II**, 269

41 Hussey, Christopher 1958 *English Country Houses: Late Georgian.* London: *Country Life*, 55–65

42 Red Book (Private Collection); account book in Hoare's Bank, Fleet Street. The cost of forming the gardens is not included.

43 As noted by Summerson 1980, 38–9

44 Thorne 1986, 273–4; www.proni.gov.uk/records/private/stewart/htm

45 Letter to Stewart, quoted in Davis 1973, 45

46 PRONTI, T/1282/1

47 By Thomas Tatham of London (Davis, 1973, 45; PRONI, D/3167/2/167, /174–6, /213–14). Nash supplanted an Irish architect, Robert Woodgate.

48 Twycross, E 1847 *The Mansions of England and Wales: the County Palatine of Lancashire.* London: Ackermann & Co, **III**, 22–3; Jope 1956, 124–7. For Garnstone Castle, *see* chapter 2.

49 Temple 1993, 28–9, 161–5; NMR photographs

50 Cartwright, E 1830 *Parochial Topography of the Rape of Bramber.* London: J Nichols and son, **II** (2), 295–8, 308; Rowan, 1965 *(see note 1),* 259

51 Affidavit from Nash in West Sussex Record Office; the cost excludes Nash's fees and the carriage of materials. I am grateful to Mary Miers for this reference.

52 Cartwright 1830 *(see note 50),* 298, states that the house was built 'partly from the design of Mr Nash', suggesting that another architect was involved at an earlier stage; also *Country Life* 17 July 2003, 66–71. The house burned down in 1904, but was rebuilt in a style remarkably faithful to the original.

53 *Country Life* 23 August 1956, 378–81. Two 'before and after' elevations in the house record the changes.

54 *Country Life* 14 July 2005, 72–7; Wilson and Mackley 2000 (*see note 15*), 383, note 64. Nash's interiors were swept away by a later owner, but there are photographs in the NMR.

55 Tyack 2004 (*see note 35*), 199–213. Before settling on Nash's design Burton consulted Repton, who tried in vain to persuade him to remodel the existing building.

56 Temple 1993, 56–9; MSS and photocopied drawings at the NMR. Remnants of an earlier Jacobean building were incorporated into the service quarters.

57 Cockayne, G E *et al*, 1945 *Complete Peerage.* London: St Catherine Press, **X**, 745–6 and note

58 Mackenzie, E and Ross, M 1834 *View of the County Palatine of Durham.* Newcastle: Mackenzie and Dent, **I**, 149–50

59 RIBA, SB 54/5, SB 55/1. Similar arches were used by Sir Christopher Wren in the library at Trinity College, Cambridge.

60 RIBA, SB 54/5/2

61 Quoted in Colvin 2008, 651. Nash originally intended to place a semicircular staircase projection, like that at Knepp, at the west end. Liddell later designed Beckett Park, Berkshire, for his brother-in-law Lord Barrington and was a member of the committee selecting the design for the new Houses of Parliament in 1835.

62 RIBA, SB 56/1/49–51

63 www.bpears.org.uk/Albums/Ravensworth

64 Thorne 1986 **III**, 203

65 Rowse, A L 1978 *The Byrons and Trevanions.* London: Weidenfeld & Nicholson, 147, 187, 196

66 Neale, J P 1818 *Views of Seats.* London: Sherwood, Neely and Jones, **I**, unpaginated

67 Gilbert, C S 1820 *Historical Survey of Cornwall.* London: Longman, Hurst, Rees, Orme and Brown, **II**, 845–6

68 There is a similar tower at Slanes Castle, Co Antrim, on the northern shore of Lough Neagh, where Nash carried out a never-completed remodelling of an earlier house that had been classicised in the C18 – Davis 1973, pl 29.

69 Neale 1818 (*see note 66*) **I**, unpaginated

70 Stockdale, F W 1824 (reprinted 1972) *Excursions in the County of Cornwall.* Truro: Barton, 51; Cornwall County Record Office, DDJ 242/4 (sales particulars, 1852)

71 Brewer, J N 1825–6 *Beauties of Ireland.* London: Sherwood, Gilbert & Piper, **I**, cxxxi

72 O'Riordan, E *Historical Guide to Clogheen*, quoted in www.galteemore.com; Smyth, W J 1976 'Estate records and the making of the Irish landscape'. *Irish Geog* **9**, 29–49. The estate totalled 42,206 acres in 1883 (Cockayne, G E 1932 *Complete Peerage.* London: St Catherine Press, **VIII**, 81).

73 There are plans and elevations in one of George Repton's notebooks (RIBA, SD 110/1, 1–4).

74 MacDonnell, Randall 2002 *The Lost Houses of Ireland.* London: Weidenfeld & Nicholson, 192–6

75 An elevation by Nash, dated October 1811, is preserved in the castle.

76 Thorne 1986 **V**, 447–8. He was described in 1803 as 'a very troublesome man, who is full of vanity, but warm in his attachments'.

77 Rait, R S 1908 *The Story of an Irish Property.* Oxford: privately published, 75–86; Guinness, D and Ryan, W 1971 *Irish Houses and Castles.* London: Thames and Hudson, 177–80; McNamara, M and Madden, M (eds) 1995 *Beagh: A History and Heritage.* Beagh, Co. Galway: Beagh Integrated Rural Development association, 80–1

78 Kelly, A 1985 Coade Stone in Georgian Architecture, *Architect Hist* **28** (1985), 86-7. There was another Coade stone chimneypiece at Ravensworth.

79 Work was continuing in 1817, when James Pain fell off the scaffolding (Lee, David 2005 *James Pain, Architect.* Limerick: Limerick Civic Trust, 57 and *passim*).

80 Nash's alleged remark, 'I hate this Gothic style … [One] window costs more trouble in designing than two houses ought to do' was wrongly attributed to Nash in Clark, Kenneth Clark 1962 *The Gothic Revival.* London: John Murray, 123, and the misattribution has been repeated by several later writers (McKendry, J 1988 'The attitude of John Nash toward the Gothic Revival style'. *J Soc Architect Hist* **47**, 295–6).

81 Pugin, A W N 1841 *True Principles of Pointed or Christian Architecture.* London: John Weale, 58–9

4

Nash and the *villa rustica*

ROSEMARY YALLOP

John Nash's architectural legacy is diverse in style, eclectic in its sources and often pragmatic in its response to the demands of a particular site, or client. His work ranges from castles to cottages, country villas to metropolitan terraces, by way of Gothic, neoclassical, rustic and oriental; attempts to divide it into distinct stylistic areas or to trace a chronological evolution towards a definitive signature are fraught with difficulty. He was not an intellectual architect, his designs springing more from bravura instinct than from a philosophical quest for a personal aesthetic. In his introduction to his catalogue of Nash's works, Terence Davis describes how he found the architect's work so varied and of such diverse quality that he fleetingly considered dividing his catalogue into such headings as Bizarre, Scholarly, Gloomy and Inventive.[1]

One small group of buildings that might have a legitimate claim to coherence is that which has been identified as constituting his 'Italianate' houses. Nash is credited with the introduction of the Italianate villa into Britain at Cronkhill, Shropshire, in the very early years of the 19th century. It was followed by two other examples of the style: Sandridge Park in Devon, and Lissan Rectory, Co. Tyrone. Of the many facets of Nash's interpretation of the picturesque aspiration, this group is often referred to as his 'Claudean' series by reference to the depictions by painter Claude Lorrain (1604–82) of the countryside around Rome, in which asymmetrical stuccoed villas, the vernacular of the Roman *campagna*, are artfully placed.[2]

Italianate architecture made its appearance in England in many forms, but a distinction must be made from the start between, on the one hand, inspiration derived from Palladio and reinterpreted in the grand country house, and on the other, the neo-Renaissance palazzo of the mid-19th century presented by Barry and followers, and used as much for public buildings

as for private residences. The Italian rustic vernacular style of Nash's villas, which predated the latter, is a world apart from both in scale and aspiration. In Nash's hands, this was an idiom employed for substantial, but not grand, houses for the well-to-do in picturesque rural settings. The Picturesque married freedom of form with an idealised, arcadian view of landscape, and the asymmetry of these vernacular buildings lent itself perfectly to this romantic aesthetic. In itself, a series of three country villas, however eye-catching, might not be considered evidence of an important innovation; their architectural significance lies in their characteristic details, which evolved over time into a successful template for more modest suburban dwellings for the aspiring Victorian middle class. The aim of this chapter is to take one example of the three Claudean villas – the little-known Sandridge Park (Fig 4.1) – and to examine the circumstances of its building, the principal elements of its design, and its characteristics as a *villa rustica*. It will be compared and contrasted with its siblings: the more celebrated Cronkhill, and Lissan Rectory, which has been somewhat neglected.

In 1800, Nash's country house practice was well established beyond the confines of Wales, where he had repaired his reputation after his early bankruptcy. In the mid-1790s, he became acquainted with the theory of the picturesque through the group of Herefordshire landowners who were then its main proponents. Houses were to be in empathy with the natural landscape in which they were placed, and if that landscape was seen as 'painterly' then it followed that the house needed to be so too: irregular in form and romantic in its allusions. The works of the great landscape painters such as Claude, with his depictions of the Roman *campagna*, rustic buildings and mythological subjects were a well-documented source of inspiration, although whether Nash would himself have used the word

Fig 4.1
Sandridge Park (c 1804–7)
following recent restoration
(Rosemary Yallop).

'Italianate' is debatable; his impressions of Italy would (unlike those of the well-travelled Joseph Gandy, for example) have been largely coloured by sight of paintings of the masters in British collections and engravings derived from them. His interpretation of the picturesque up to this point had manifested itself in the romantic form of the castle (*see* chapter 3); Luscombe, a charming example of the 'domesticated castle' some 20 miles from Sandridge Park, was begun in 1799, only two or three years before Cronkhill. The ground plans of the castles share some similarities to those of the Italianate villas, usually with a round tower anchoring one corner, but the nature of the catalyst for the change of mood from castle to sylvan villa is not clear.

Sandridge Park

As with so many of Nash's smaller houses, little survives to document the genesis of Sandridge Park, and until recently the house had not been the subject of detailed study.[3] Summerson photographed the house in the 1930s,[4] but in a 1956 letter to the historian E M Jope, which

Jope reproduced in his own article on Lissan Rectory,[5] he asserted that Sandridge Park had been demolished: an error which he repeated in the 1980 edition of his monograph on Nash,[6] and which further encouraged the house's lapse into obscurity. The facts of history and genealogy which left Sandridge Park bereft of a single family in unbroken continuous occupation over the decades, and the corresponding absence of archives, has undoubtedly exacerbated the problem. More recently however, research in connection with a programme of restoration has brought to light new information on the dates and circumstances of its construction, as well as confirming Nash's authorship. No original plans or working drawings have yet been located, but scattered documents relating to the estate have been found in a variety of public and private collections, and further avenues are still to be pursued.

The Sandridge estate stands on a rounded headland high above the eastern bank of the River Dart, in the Devonshire parish of Stoke Gabriel. It is equidistant between Totnes, some three miles upstream, and Dartmouth, a port of some antiquity where the river meets the English

Channel, downstream. The Sandridge estate has been inhabited since at least the time of Domesday, when the manor was held by the de Sandridge family as tenants of the Bishop of Exeter. By the 16th century it had passed into the hands of the Pomeroy family, and then by marriage to the Gilbert family of nearby Compton Castle. In Elizabethan times the Gilberts were noted seafarers; Adrian Gilbert of Sandridge, Sir Walter Raleigh's half-brother, obtained letters patent from the Queen to search for the North-West Passage. A branch of the Gilberts owned Sandridge until the last quarter of the 18th century, but with the death of Pomeroy Gilbert in 1770, his executors sold the estate shortly afterwards, to John Dunning of nearby Ashburton.

We know nothing of the houses of the earlier periods, and only a little about the house that immediately preceded Sandridge Park. The site had already attracted comment: 'A very healthy and pleasant seat it is, lifted up on a small hill or ascent, on the east side of the River Dart, which encompasses near three parts thereof.'[7] The location certainly caught John Dunning's eye. Dunning was born in 1731, the son of a country attorney at Ashburton, at the edge of Dartmoor, and his precocious intelligence and legendary capacity for hard work propelled him not only to a successful career as a barrister but also to a glittering life in public service, as Member of Parliament, Solicitor-General, and Chancellor of the Duchy of Lancaster, crowned by his ennoblement in 1782, for which he chose the title of Lord Ashburton. Along the way he acquired substantial wealth and accumulated land and estates in his native county. In 1772 he added the Sandridge estate to his portfolio, consisting, as far as can be determined, of a mansion house, ancillary farms and some 210 acres, for the sum of £6,100. His seat at the time was at Spitchwick, on Dartmoor, but it seems that the Sandridge purchase was more than a mere investment. Thanks to the journals of the Revd John Swete, a friend of Dunning's and a Devon cleric, whose parochial duties clearly took second place to jaunts around the county with journal and sketchbook in hand, we learn of Dunning's ambitions for the place, as Swete recorded on a visit made by river some four years after the purchase:

High placed among enclosures and ornamented with noble woods that spread themselves down the hills to the water's edge ... opened the elevated grounds and mansion of Sandridge ...

the situation is more exposed than any other on the river and to counteract the effect of storms ... the front hath been guarded by a case of slate ... the colour however of the stone being blue detracts from the consequence which it would have possessed when seen from the river, had it been white. Passing closer to Sandridge we skirted a cliff on which the young beech grew luxuriantly and the whole wooded hill, which rounded towards its summit, possessed as picturesque an appearance as can well be imagined ...We were all, I well remember, struck with the beauty and grandeur of the spot and his Lordship then expressed an intention of raising an house on it that should be more worthy than the present, of the situation.[8]

Another significant achievement of Dunning's was to marry rather well. In 1780 he secured the hand of Elizabeth Baring, daughter of a wealthy merchant in the city of Exeter. Two of her better-known brothers – John and Francis Baring – founded the eponymous bank and were political allies of Dunning. Two sons of the marriage were born at Spitchwick. But tragedy marred a life of intellectual and material success: their first son died at only 14 months, and just eight months later, in August 1783, John Dunning, first Lord Ashburton, already ailing but now fatally weakened by grief, died at Exmouth. After barely three years of marriage, Elizabeth was now a widow with only their surviving second son, Richard Barré Dunning, the new Lord Ashburton, a babe-in-arms, to console her in her double loss. So John Dunning never built his new house, the one 'more worthy of the situation', at Sandridge.

But 20 years later that is exactly what Elizabeth Ashburton, at the age of 60, decided to do, and her creation was a remarkable one. Recently discovered correspondence in the Baring Archives between the dowager Lady Ashburton and her son provides some illumination, though limited to a handful of letters. The irascible Richard was not enamoured of Devon, preferring to live in Scotland where he had attended university and was later to marry, and he makes clear his refusal to take any part in the design and execution of the project. He writes tetchily to his mother from Edinburgh:

I hope that for once by way of variety Devonshire may enjoy some fine weather to enable you to pursue your plans at Sandridge. I have made a resolution not to interfere at all ... I do not wish to bias your taste as I shall never reside there but at the utmost will only be an occasional visitor.

It is difficult sometimes to build a house so as to please one person – but to build a house so as to please two people, and of such entirely differing tastes as you and I, is a thing that may be pronounced impossible.[9]

Elizabeth's keen interest in the detailed planning of both house and grounds is apparent: it was a place that gave her much pleasure, and for which she had a deep affection. In July 1804, Richard, referring to her building and planting schemes as her 'favourite whim', advises his mother: 'I think the sooner you go to Devonshire the better, for although that county is to me a hell, it seems to be a paradise to you and when you are busy planting trees and laying out grounds your blue devils will fly away.'[10]

The reason for her choice of Nash is not clear. Perhaps it was nothing more than a well-connected dowager choosing the fashionable architect of the day. The Baring family were not otherwise patrons of Nash, whose only other work in Devon had been Luscombe Castle some four or five years previously, for Charles Hoare, a banker: the connection might possibly have been through the Hoare family. Humphry Repton had collaborated with Nash at Luscombe, and was rather more active in Devon (Endsleigh; Tavistock Abbey), but Sandridge Park dates from after the probable date of the dissolution of the partnership and so Repton is unlikely to have been the source of the introduction. Interestingly, at the same time as Elizabeth was building Sandridge Park, her brother, Francis Baring, was engaged on a more grandiose project. Having bought Stratton Park in Hampshire from the Russell family in 1800, he had asked Humphry Repton to design a new house and landscape. While he proceeded with the plans for the park, he rejected Repton's vision for the house, looking instead to George Dance the younger, who built for him a house firmly in the neoclassical tradition with a massive portico (which is all that remains today). Work on both house and grounds started in 1803, making Stratton Park exactly contemporary with Sandridge Park. The widowed Elizabeth was clearly more willing to be open-minded in matters of design than her more conventionally inclined brother.

The Ashburton letters are very helpful in dating the building. Sandridge Park is conventionally dated to 1805 because that was the year in which a drawing under that description ('a house for Lady Ashburton') was exhibited at the Royal Academy. Equally, the reference date for Cronkhill is given as 1802 for the same reason, for in this year George Stanley Repton's wash perspective of Cronkhill was exhibited there. But that drawing, which differs in significant details from the house as actually built, may precede its building, and certainly precedes its completion; work on Cronkhill seems to have begun in 1803 and was still continuing in the summer of 1807, although the house was inhabited by 1808.[11] Equally, from the letters from Richard to his mother we know that work on Sandridge Park was under way by the summer of 1804 and that the house was completed and inhabited by January 1809, as it was ready to be let furnished immediately after Elizabeth Ashburton's death, although final settlement to Nash was made by her executors.[12] So the strong implication is that the construction of both houses was closer in time than has been supposed, with Sandridge starting perhaps only a year later, and work running concurrently for part of that time. Also confirmed in this correspondence is the involvement in the construction of Sandridge Park of James Morgan – Nash's assistant, probably as draughtsman, but possibly in a wider capacity, as he is described as 'Mr Nash's Clerk'. Elizabeth's executor, her brother Sir Francis Baring, notes a disputed account of some £181 12s 4d with a carpenter, Horrell.[13] The Horrells were builders and cabinetmakers in Exeter, and Thomas Horrell had worked at Luscombe for Nash. The accounts of Nash's client there, Charles Hoare, show a first payment on account to Horrell in the autumn of 1799, and then annual payments thereafter until final settlement (making a total of some £8,675) in August 1804,[14] at which point construction at Sandridge Park was already under way. So it is also possible that the Horrells were employed by Nash at both houses simultaneously. In the absence of the original plans and the Royal Academy depiction, knowledge of the house as it was first built derives from one engraving, together with structural details revealed during renovation. There is also a 1935 sale catalogue for the estate that contains room descriptions and dimensions, but no plan. The engraving (Fig 4.2), after a drawing by Shepherd, appeared in 1829 in Moore's *History of Devonshire*, showing the south elevation from a point to the south east, with the River Dart over the artist's left shoulder. The house, which faces south-south-west, is asymmetrical, with the characteristic *villa rustica* feature of a round tower with conical roof (out of sight in the

SANDRIDGE, DEVONSHIRE.

engraving) to the west; a square tower over a garden door in the middle of the river elevation (the presumed front door); round-headed windows, some grouped in threes, to flood the house with light; a large conservatory in a prominent position to the south-east; and an abundance of external decorative features such as trelliswork and wreathed pilasters. The overall effect is playful rather than grand: the intention is to fill the onlooker with delight, rather than awe, as the house nestles amid trees on three sides, with sweeping views down to the river to the south, and an upstream view to the west through a cutting.

Sandridge was constructed directly onto the local limestone bed, with cellars to only about half of the ground floor, under the service wing to the east, where the soil structure includes more easily excavated clay. The ground-floor level is therefore identical with that of the grounds outside, increasing the feeling of connection with the exterior landscape. The walls, both external and the internal supporting walls, are of local stone rubble, rendered on the outside and lined with lath and plaster to the interiors, with window arches and flues and other structural, hidden features constructed in red brick. There are several ranges of chimneys – which originally totalled close to 30 – clustered

particularly over the service wing. In addition to the round and square towers there is a steeple-like smaller tower towards the rear of the service wing, used as a belfry in Victorian times, although its original function may have been different, or even purely ornamental, and not tall enough to earn the epithet of campanile.[15] The arrangement of towers means that the roof plan is quite complex, with great attention to detail such as diminishing courses of slates on the conical roof of the round tower and elsewhere. The broad eaves with double brackets came to be identified as a defining characteristic of the suburban villas that were built in such profusion some 40 years later.

The plan is L-shaped (Fig 4.3). As to the original layout, the room dimensions in the sale catalogue of 1935,[16] supplemented by the structural features revealed during restoration, show that in the western or 'polite' end of the house at least, the original interior floor plan is easily recognisable. There are three principal reception rooms in this wing. On the ground floor of the square tower there is a small octagonal room, created by angled walls enclosing triangular voids, which opens onto the drawing room to the left but also gives access to the conservatory to the right and, via a jib door on the north side, to the ground-floor corridor.

Fig 4.3
Plan of Sandridge Park
(redrawn by EH from Davis
1960, plan 12).

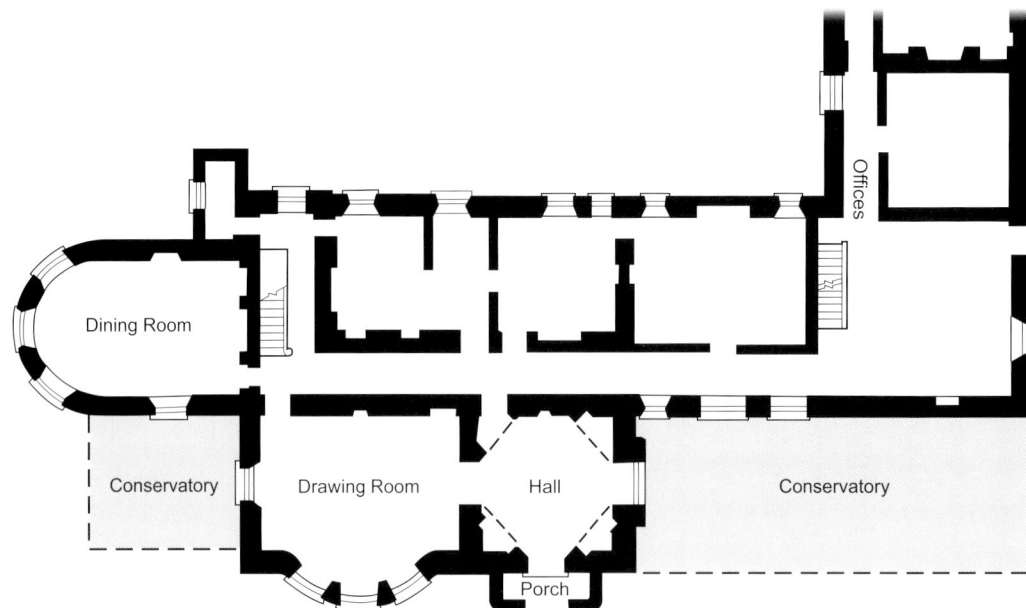

This octagonal room is assumed to have been the original entrance hall, although it has no direct connection with the stairs. The drawing room faces south, with sweeping views over the river (Fig 4.4), and has a triple-window bay set not into a straight wall but into a reversed curved wall, creating a small but graceful serpentine. When originally built, this room also gave onto a smaller glazed conservatory (lost in the 20th century) that filled the apex between the southern side of the round tower and the flat western wall of the drawing room. The third reception room is under the round tower, possibly intended as the dining room, although it is as large as the drawing room. Unlike Cronkhill, where the interior of the round tower has been squared off, this room is D-shaped – in plan, a square with a half-circle attached – and as well as sharing access to the smaller conservatory, it has a triple-windowed rounded bay looking out westwards through the cutting to an upstream view of the river (Fig 4.5). It seems that Nash blasted through the high, wooded rocky outcrop to create this view, leaving a picturesque grassy *allée* flanked by craggy rocks, topped by trees, to collect the evening sunlight and focus it into the room. The eastern wing of the house contained

Fig 4.4
Sandridge Park,
the drawing room
(AA 60/131).

Fig 4.5
*The round tower at
Sandridge from the west
(Rosemary Yallop).*

the kitchens, servants' hall and domestic offices on the ground floor, with staff bedrooms above. They were connected to the western 'polite' wing service by a corridor, masked by the conservatory.

The interior decorative style is restrained.[17] There is no detailing that could remotely be described as Italianate, vernacular, or anything other than classical Regency. The door reveals are deep, but architraves are simple; the ground-floor cornicing is of two main patterns, both of which are also found at Cronkhill, in gilded form at Attingham, and throughout other Nash houses: a line of wrapped acanthus, separated by a concave band of plaster from a small beaded string above. In both the ground-floor corridor and the bedroom corridor above, Nash dazzles us not with flamboyant plasterwork but with the complexity of the geometry used in laying out the vaulted ceiling: some shallow diagonal cross-vaults; some concave ovals; some ribs sitting on corbels, resembling an arcade (Fig 4.6). It has a spare, Soaneian feel. The ground-floor room, already referred to, in the square tower is a geometrical *tour de force*: the externally square room is octagonal inside, but rises to a round ceiling, giving the effect of being under a tented canopy (Fig 4.7).

The very wide splays to the round-headed windows act both to maximise the light and to frame the views. Other repeated details include the charming oval windows (seen in a variety of other Nash houses), particularly in the room on

the top floor of the round tower, which was clearly designed to be inhabited, for it contains a fireplace that follows the curve of the wall. Fireplaces in general (or at least those that survive) are very plain: the one in the former dining room, which is in dark grey marble with a stylised 'Egyptian' palm design, is identical to one at Southborough (Surrey), built some three years later, and although executed in different stone, appears as a much grander pair in the Picture Gallery at Attingham. Nash seemed to delight in the construction of wandering flues, which follow a seemingly random course around the walls and often snake right round a room. For example, the round tower fireplaces on both first and second floors are diametrically opposite the chimneys, presumably to spread the heat around the room (a similar arrangement is found on the wall of the conservatory at Luscombe) as well as enabling an optimal placement of the chimneys in the outline of the exterior on the inside flank of the round tower, where they are less conspicuous.

There are two puzzling features to the ground-floor plan, and they are connected. First, where and what was the front door? And second, how to account for the position of the staircase. Unlike many of Nash's other small houses, whether castles or villas, the principal rooms are not arranged around the staircase, which here is tucked away at the north-west end of the house, at the end of the central corridor. It is a plain staircase, not unlike that at

Fig 4.6 (above left)
The ground floor corridor
at Sandridge
(AA 60/129).

Fig 4.7 (above right)
The room under the square
tower, probably the original
Entrance Hall, at Sandridge
(AA 60/130).

Cronkhill in detail but less prominently placed, with remarkably shallow risers of some five and a half inches (140mm) – an old lady's staircase, perhaps – and a wide, floor-length, round-arched window on the half landing to illuminate this north-facing stairwell. But access to this corridor is either from the drawing room or the dining room or through a jib door in the octagonal room – the putative entrance hall or vestibule. Guests arriving at the front door would therefore either be conducted to their right, into the conservatory, or to their left, directly into the drawing room. Lady Ashburton herself would, on arrival, have had to go through either the jib door (most unlikely) or the drawing room in order to reach the stairs or even the other ground-floor rooms. All the evidence found in the course of restoration confirms that the staircase is indeed in its original position, but this arrangement does not quite ring true, and it remains a mystery.[18]

I have left almost until last one of Sandridge Park's most distinctive features, and one that differentiates it from both sibling houses: the conservatory. It disappeared at some time in the 1930s, but the 1829 engraving, together with the footings revealed during renovation, confirm that it was indeed a substantial structure, at 52ft long and 19ft wide (16m × 5.75m), with a roof height of 14ft (4.25m) to the ridge, matching that of the other reception rooms that it adjoins (Fig 4.8). One function is of course to mask the service wing behind, but its prominent

position suggests that it was designed to be an entertaining room in its own right. Its design was exactly repeated in the smaller conservatory (also lost) to the south-west corner of the house, in the angle between the drawing room and dining room. It is interesting to note that this is the one element of Sandridge Park for which we have contemporary drawings, neither of which is under the name of Nash, but each under those of his one-time assistants, the brothers George Stanley and John Adey Repton. This distinctive design – with pairs of tall glazed doors, wrapped 'bundles' of metalwork 'Egyptian' shafts, surmounted by square trellis and a spade-shaped cornice – appears both in George Stanley Repton's Pavilion Notebook,[19] where there are detailed working drawings, and in his RIBA notebooks.[20] Its intended location, however, remains mysterious: possibly Albury (Surrey) or Battlesden (Bedfordshire), where it appears in a painting of the estate,[21] although it does not seem to have been built at either location. Also in the Pavilion Notebook is a drawing of a square conservatory with identical glazing but a domed roof.[22] John Adey Repton's almost identical pen-and-wash depiction in the RIBA collection is interesting in that it is executed on paper watermarked 1810,[23] after the completion of Sandridge Park: was one of the brothers responsible for the original conservatory design?

In the realm of the smaller house, the latter years of the 18th century witnessed the evolution of the conservatory from its role as

Fig. 4.8
Sandridge Park from the
south-east: the conservatory
in 1933
(B42/1521).

a separate garden building in the grounds to that of a receiving room integral to the life of the house, often as a breakfast or morning room. Filled with exotic blooms rather than workaday produce, it was, some commentators have suggested, an attempt to bring the picturesque indoors. Nash had already employed a conservatory that was integral to the main house, rather than a linked but separate structure, at The Warrens, as well as at Luscombe and Longner Hall, though neither of the latter were originally glazed. The size of the conservatory at Sandridge Park, together with its prominence in the principal elevation, confirm its importance to the house as a whole; it is by no means a mere appendage.

Finally, even the stables were accorded particular prominence and attention to detail at Sandridge Park (Fig 4.9). The stables and coach-house complex, which also accommodated a large number of outdoor servants, is sited slightly further downhill from the house and slightly closer to the river: its extravagant design continues the Italianate vernacular, with an equally complex roof profile, with its characteristic shallow-pitched pyramids topping square towers, and broad eaves with double brackets. It had a substantial footprint almost as big as that of the main house, although today it is much reduced.

Sandridge Park is not a grand house: it is compact, elegant but restrained, and picturesquely placed. The generous windows not only admit the glorious southern and western light, but also lead the eye outside by framing the extraordinary views, and thus the house conducts a fluent conversation with the landscape. It approaches the epitome of the villa: not as an architectural style but as a state of mind, or at least an aspiration towards it.

Subsequent history of Sandridge

Sadly Elizabeth Ashburton did not live very long to enjoy her new creation, for she died in London in January 1809. Her son writes to Sir Francis Baring, her brother and executor in a character-istically robust and unsentimental manner:

> I have no wish to sell. I have been pestered with several proposals. Mr. Leach says it is difficult to know what rent to ask for Sandridge as so extraordinary a thing cannot be valued regularly

Fig 4.9
The stable block at
Sandridge, now Cross
Creek House
(Rosemary Yallop).

like a common farm, for which purpose he wishes to consult Nash. ... If you think it is desirable I would have Nash informed that Sandridge is to be let. Of course the greater rent it produces to me the greater glory it produces to the architect who built it and his fame and reputation will act as motives to puff it sufficiently.[24]

Indeed, by the summer, he had secured a tenant, Sir Robert Newman, who was to remain there for some 25 years before moving to a nearby estate, Mamhead, with a principal house that he commissioned Salvin to re-build, in a neo-Tudor style far removed from that of the Italian *campagna*. A quarter of a century at Sandridge had clearly not given him a taste for southern skies or rustic allusion.

Subsequently, the history of Sandridge Park was dogged by legal and financial problems. Intense squabbling among trustees and life tenants paralysed its proper management. This, together with the decline in agricultural incomes, saw a gradual deterioration in the condition of house, grounds and farms. By 1935, the death of the last, and by now very lateral, member of the family nominated under the second Lord Ashburton's convoluted will died

intestate and, for the first time in its life, Sandridge Park was a house that nobody wanted. Together with its contents, it was submitted to the ignominy of a public auction. The sale to a consortium for the development of hundreds of houses on the site left Sandridge Park teetering on the brink of extinction. However, economic conditions intervened, and the house was requisitioned for military use in the Second World War, being released in 1951, when it once again became a family home.

Neglect had taken its toll on the house: by the late 1930s the conservatory had already disappeared, and by the end of the war both house and grounds were in a sorry state. Its new owners rescued the estate from oblivion, but, in the post-war economy, rescue came at a cost, and compromises had to be made. There were two main phases of alterations: in the 1950s and then again, under different ownership, in the late 1980s. The most significant alteration was to divide the house physically into two separate parts by removing what was formerly the rear wall of the conservatory and the entire linking section between the two wings (a two-storey corridor that originally had been masked from view by the conservatory). In its place, a purely decorative archway was constructed, with a new front door inserted into the stub of the east wall of the main wing, which was now an external wall. The two parts of the house were now entirely separate, the archway allowing no access between (Fig 4.10). One secondary staircase was removed and another inserted elsewhere, windows were blocked and others created, and some fireplaces and detailing were lost. In the late 1980s, the most striking alteration was the loss of part of the first floor in the east wing to create a room of double height, into which was inserted an indoor swimming pool. All of the major alterations have now been reversed, and the lost conservatory replaced with a new structure modelled on the depiction in the Shepherd engraving of 1829, in the course of a programme of restoration completed in 2010. As a result, the footprint has now been restored to that of the original building.

The Claudean series

All three of the Claudean villas were built in the first decade of the 19th century: from *c* 1802 for Cronkhill, 1804 for Sandridge Park, and 1807 for Lissan Rectory. At some point work must have been progressing on all three houses simultaneously, which makes their points of difference just as interesting as their similarities.

It is worth considering the different purposes for which each of the three houses was built. Sandridge Park was a widow's belated fulfilment of her late husband's desire to build for his own occupation 'an house more worthy of the situation':[25] one of unparalleled natural beauty. By building it at a late stage in her life, and with an only son who had completely forsworn his native county, by definition it was never intended to be a family home. The question remaining to be answered is whether it was intended to be a permanent home, or instead to perform the true function of the *villa rustica* of antique Rome – a small estate with a farm and a house which together provided an occasional retreat from the press of the city and smart society into the solace of nature: a concept that had found much favour in contemporary England. Lord Ashburton, a shrewd investor in property, had purchased not just a site for a new house but a functioning and productive estate, if relatively modest in scale. If his widow, an elderly but impeccably connected dowager, regarded it as more

Fig 4.10
Sandridge in 1959
(AA 60/123).

of a villa than a principal seat for grand entertaining, that would go some way towards explaining its informality, the self-effacing staircase and the absence of a grand entrance.

At Cronkhill, the task of housing a gentleman land agent, not an obviously romantic project, is usually said to have been Nash's brief when Lord Berwick commissioned him to make alterations to the existing farmhouse on his Attingham estate in Shropshire at the start of the 19th century. It is not wholly convincing that Lord Berwick should have presided over the building of such an inventive and elaborate house solely for the occupation of his agent, even if a gentleman agent. Plans date from at least as early as 1802, and construction almost certainly from 1803, and Walford's employment in that capacity did not begin until 1804 (at which point he was barely 22 years of age). Could Francis Walford perhaps have been an illegitimate son of the family, or have enjoyed an intimate relationship with a Berwick son or daughter, which might have justified this indulgence? The correspondence of the second Mrs Walford laments her husband's miserliness and reluctance to engage in society; eventually even his professional competence came into question and he left the Berwicks' employ.[26] Much remains to be discovered about the mysterious Mr Walford.

Lissan Rectory (Co Tyrone) is the least-known and least characteristic member of the Claudean villa group, even allowing for the substantial alterations it has undergone, which obscure Nash's precise intentions and make it hard to draw meaningful comparisons with Sandridge and Cronkhill. It was built as (and remains) a rectory, albeit for a Rector of considerable social standing in the area. The Revd John Molesworth Staples (1776–1859), Rector of Lissan for some 60 years, was the son of the Rt Hon John Staples, Privy Councillor and Speaker of the Irish House of Commons, whose family descended from an English lawyer who had settled in Ireland in the early 17th century and had been granted an Irish baronetcy. They had built Lissan House as the family seat, and their Irish wealth derived initially from iron-founding, but was augmented by some fortunate marriages.[27]

John Molesworth Staples supplied part of the cost of the works from his own resources, but he also applied successfully, in 1804, for a loan from the Board of First Fruits, available for the building of a parsonage under the scheme instituted under Queen Anne to encourage the greater proliferation of Church of Ireland churches and glebe houses.[28] It seems that nearly half of the money came from this source, though it is not clear whether the church authorities had any say in the design, the records

of the Board of First Fruits having been destroyed in a fire in Dublin in 1922. A Rector's residence required room for a family, for the reception of visitors including even the bishop, and for a gentleman's library; it had to indicate status but not ostentation. The compact villa form was therefore entirely appropriate, although the unconventional style is perhaps more surprising. Disappointingly few archival traces remain to flesh out the circumstances of the house's conception, but the link to the architect is clear: Staples was a cousin of the Stewart family of Killymoon Castle, not far away, which Nash had begun in 1803 (*see* chapter 3).

All three of the 'Claudean' houses are of comfortable but not extravagant size. The plans show some similarities in the geometry of their three principal rooms, being, *mutatis mutandis,* square, rectangular and round – or at least incorporating a circle to a greater or lesser extent. In each case the dimensions are roughly similar, with, for example, a diameter for the round tower of some 18 to 20ft (5.5–6m), and

Fig 4.11
Cronkhill (c 1803–8)
from the south-east
(Rosemary Yallop).

the square room being a cube of approximately 18ft. But they are laid out differently and to different effect.

Cronkhill (Fig 4.1I) is usually referred to as the first and best-known example of Nash's Italianate country villas, whereas Sandridge Park by contrast is seen as a paler and unsatisfactory copy. Terence Davis thought that 'Sandridge must take second place to Cronkhill as a piece of design. The elements, although they make a pleasing group, are less thoughtfully disposed, the composition is less successful and the impact we feel at Cronkhill is missing.'[29] In fact both houses are extraordinary creations, and while they share a striking superficial (using the word in the literal sense) resemblance, there are points of difference that reflect perhaps both a difference in function and some evolution in Nash's approach to this style in the relatively brief period between the building of both houses.

Cronkhill is widely felt to be more original, more successful, purer in design. The parallels between the depiction of the design in the 1802 drawing and the buildings in Claude's 1645 'Landscape near Rome with a view of the Ponte Molle'[30] – always cited as the keystone of the inspiration for the Italian vernacular style – are indeed striking, if rather less convincing in the finished article. Davis preferred Cronkhill's more compact shape.[31] It must be said, however, that Cronkhill's compactness is rather illusory, as the villa element was grafted on to an existing building, a largely 17th-century half-timbered vernacular brick and timber farmhouse, which houses the service wing, and still plays a prominent part in the main 'show' elevation. To combine the two so visibly must have entailed some compromises, and, as the first in the series, a degree of experimentation in Nash's agile mind.

This is perhaps the most curious feature about Cronkhill: that for his first foray into the novel and eye-catching Italianate style Nash should have chosen to model it not *ab initio* but only as an extension of an existing house of a very different timbre. What Nash added was a wing in villa form, containing a suite of 'polite' rooms with bedrooms above, grouped around a spacious and elegant staircase hall and accompanying entrance vestibule. Externally, it has the feel of a theatrical set: the rendered facade of the new building's front elevation stops abruptly, to be replaced at the return by brick (now painted white), continuing as bare

brick on the untidy rear elevations (Fig 4.12), unlike the uniform exterior of Sandridge Park. Internally, the joins to the domestic offices in the older wing are effected by simple doors opening off at both ground- and first-floor level. In short, the new wing cannot escape an air of having been bolted on.

Was this somewhat awkward compromise the result of an instruction from a cautious client who could not quite commit himself to rebuilding completely from scratch, or who jibbed at the potential cost? Or was Nash himself only experimenting with the style at this point? This conjunction of villa and domestic offices (the latter screened by shrubbery) is clearly shown in George Repton's 1802 depiction, and this might be considered to be a more accurate representation of the ancient Roman villa. For whatever reason, by the time Nash was dealing with Sandridge Park he was much more bold and comprehensive in his vision, even if the result subsequently attracted criticism because the (illusory) sense of compactness had been lost.

Cronkhill is orientated to benefit from views towards the Wrekin, and also perhaps towards the Roman city of Wroxeter, whose remains lie directly across the fields.[32] This does, however, mean that the principal elevation faces more or less east, and the windows, flat-headed and under the loggia, do not entrap the light throughout the day to the same extent as at Sandridge Park. The later insertion of south-facing windows (there is an example in the dining room) gives a view only of the service wing. The staircase, prominently sited in the

Fig 4.12
The rear elevation of Cronkhill (Rosemary Yallop).

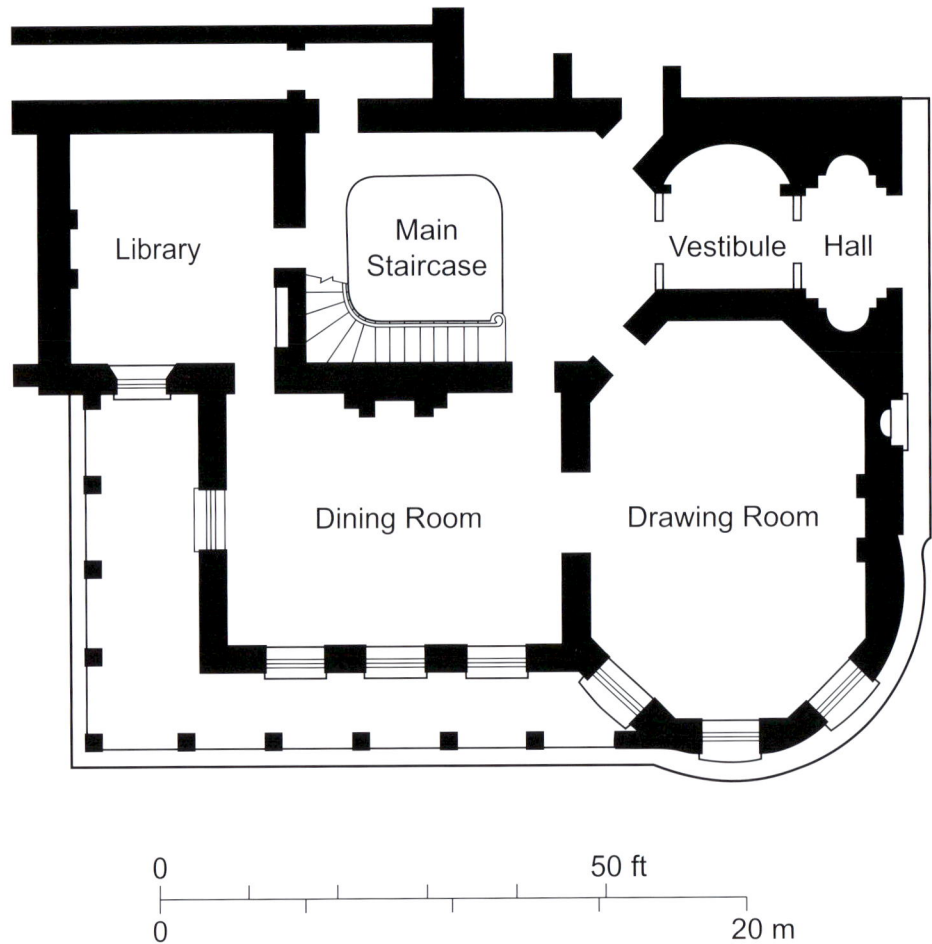

Fig 4.13
Plan of Cronkhill (redrawn by EH from Davis 1960, plan 4).

Fig 4.14
Cronkhill, the entrance and round tower. The drawing room is on the ground floor of the tower (Rosemary Yallop).

entrance hall, which Sandridge Park lacks, is a virtuoso cantilevered construction that makes an impact worthy of a much grander house. The compact form of the villa portion (Fig 4.13) means that there is no corridor to give scope for vaulting as at Sandridge Park, and the external shapes are not reflected in geometrical detailing inside: the round tower, for example, is transmuted inside into an elongated straight-sided lozenge (Figs 4.14 and 4.15). The absence of a conservatory changes the relationship with the landscape outside, which is conducted by means of the loggia, perhaps a more authentically Italian detail, reinforced by the use of chamfered Tuscan columns. Comparisons are of course odious, and it must be remembered that on its unveiling Cronkhill stood as an absolutely unique example of a new idiom: the impact of this extraordinarily innovative house must have been considerable.

Lissan must sadly be regarded as the Cinderella of the trio, not least because extensive alterations and neglect have diminished the

Fig 4.15
The drawing room at
Cronkhill
(AA 60_00563).

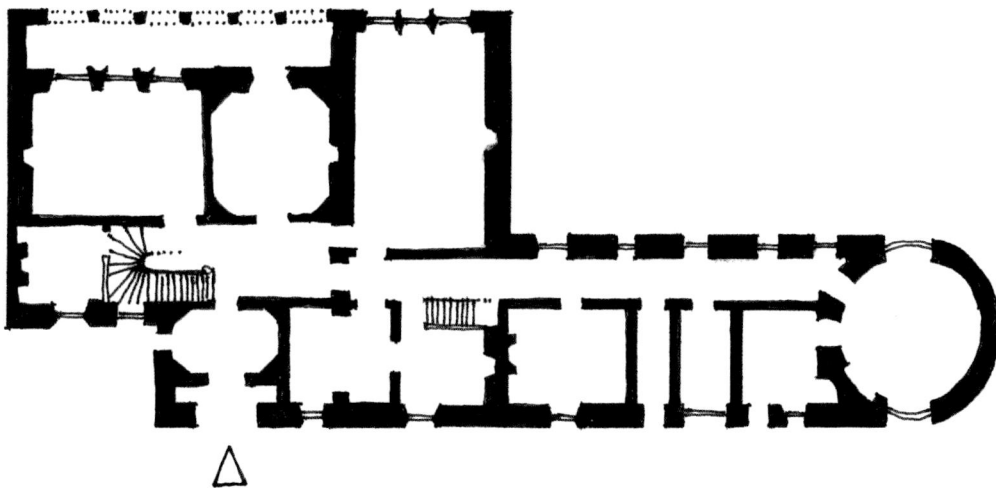

Fig 4.16
Plan of Lissan Rectory (1807)
(from Davis, Architecture
of John Nash, 1960).

original concept (Fig 4.16). Ironically, its original form is better documented than those of the other two houses, as plans and elevations survive in the notebook of George Repton in the RIBA collection,[33] showing a more sophisticated arrangement than is evidenced by the sad truncated relic standing today (and a more marked resemblance to the Cronkhill depicted in the view exhibited at the Royal Academy than Cronkhill as eventually built) (Fig 4.17). Curiously, the round tower (now lost) was much less prominent than in the other two houses, separated at some distance from the principal rooms by domestic offices, and marking a corner of the service wing and court (Fig 4.18). Like Cronkhill, but unlike Sandridge Park, the

Fig 4.17 (right)
Lissan Rectory today
(Rosemary Yallop).

Fig 4.18 (below)
The entrance front of Lissan
Rectory, c 1900, showing
the round tower
(Alan Cross).

entrance is well-defined, through an arch into a vestibule, before entering the staircase hall and the plain, classical interior, which includes an octagonal study. It shares with Cronkhill a loggia with chamfered stone columns, opening off the drawing room; in its long spinal corridor, ending in a plain, self-effacing staircase, it resembles Sandridge. The setting, while rural, lacks the impact of the landscape surrounding the other two houses, although the beauty of its original vistas may have been attenuated by the passage of time: it is built on a rise looking eastwards to Lough Neath, about eight miles distant,[34] and was apparently originally set within its own parkland.[35] Nevertheless, in the words of Professor Jope, 'although [the villa elements] are combined a little less skilfully [than at Cronkhill] it is a pleasing house to find in this mid-Ulster countryside.'[36] Or in Summerson's words: 'Among the surviving buildings in Northern Ireland which are of special significance in the history of British architecture as a whole, I would name Lissan Rectory [and Nash's Killymoon Castle] among the most interesting.'[37]

The end of the affair

This group of houses was not of course the end of the vernacular Italianate story, either in Nash's career or, more importantly, in the subsequent history of domestic, and particularly suburban, architecture. Imitators rapidly flattered Nash, among them Robert Lugar at Dunstall Priory in Kent only a few years later,[38] and perhaps at Wood Hall in Yorkshire,[39] both houses sporting a characteristic, copybook round tower, and few pattern-books in the rash of their publication in the mid-19th century were complete without their Italian villa. Indeed the style spread beyond British shores, to North America and to Australia, where a Nash pupil, Francis Greenway, was sent as a convict. Nash himself went on to repeat some of the detailing in other houses, such as Southborough Place, and made use of the asymmetrical, towered style to exuberant effect, although in reduced form and in the suburban setting of the Park Village at Regent's Park, some 15 years later (*see* chapter 5). But he produced no more villas in a landscape on the scale and with the impact of the original Claudian three.

We do not know with certainty what enticed Nash into this particular idiom at this particular time, nor why he then produced so few examples and only within a very limited period. All three houses raise intriguing questions about the nature of the process that takes place between client and architect in designing a house, and the balance – or tension, even – between expectation and outcome. Given their very different patrons, physical locations and intended functions, what are we to make of the fact that Nash devised three strikingly similar solutions?

In the construction of Sandridge Park, in particular, the tantalisingly limited glimpses we have of Elizabeth Ashburton's life and character tempt us to speculate about her influence as a client in matters of form, function and decoration. When she embarked upon her 'whim', one wonders to what extent she saw clearly what would emerge: was she intellectually engaged with the picturesque debate; was she less familiar with the detail of that debate and its influences but nevertheless consciously willing to embrace innovation; or was she simply content to place her trust in her architect and follow Nash's direction wherever it led? It is certain that she was passionate about her house and gardens: one can only hope that they afforded her as much pleasure and consolation as her son's letters suggest, and we should be grateful that she had the vision to engage John Nash to build a romantic house that so aptly fits its setting.

Notes

1 Davis 1960, 7
2 Italianate *detailing* is of course to be found in other Nash villa designs: Southborough Place, Surrey (1808), while largely neoclassical, deploys the characteristic bracketed eaves and bullseye windows of the Claudian trio, and the outbuildings with their short square towers topped with shallow pyramidal roofs resemble those at Sandridge Park. An even earlier house, The Warrens in Hampshire (1800–2), also made use of wide eaves on pairs of brackets, something of a signature detail of Nash, and an asymmetrical garden elevation incorporating a conservatory.
3 Yallop, Rosemary 2009 'An house more worthy of the situation'. *Trans Devonshire Assoc* **141**, 181–217
4 National Monuments Record, ref BF088468
5 Jope 1956, 121–30
6 Summerson 1980, 192
7 Prince, John 1810 *Worthies of Devon.* Plymouth: Rees & Curtis, 285
8 Swete, John (Gray, Todd and Rowe, M M eds) 1997 *Travels in Georgian Devon.* Exeter: Devon Books, **I**, 102

9   The Baring Archive, Northbrook Papers, NP.1.B.10.1

10   *ibid*

11   Tyack, Geoffrey 2004,'Cronkhill'. *Country Life* 19 February, 62–7

12   The Baring Archive Business Papers, NP1.B.10.3

13   *ibid*

14   Hoare family papers, quoted in Hussey, Christopher 1955 *English Country Houses: Late Georgian.* London: *Country Life*, 63

15   A similar spire can be made out over the service wing in the 1802 Repton watercolour of Cronkhill, although it was not built.

16   Devon Record Office, 867B/S22

17   Davis 1973, 43, calls it 'very severe indeed'.

18   By the 1930s the conservatory itself was described as the entrance hall; and at the turn of the 19th century the putative entrance hall is referred to only as the 'Octagon Room'.

19   Temple 1993, 183–5 (PNB 26–29)

20   The same design of shafts of bundled rods, together with square-section treillage appears in a drawing (undated) by Nash in the Royal Collection entitled 'Design for Mrs Jennings' house, Windsor Park'. The overall effect of the design (apparently unexecuted) is Oriental or Indian. It is reproduced in Morley, John 1993 *Regency Design.* London: Zwemmer, 199, fig 141), where Morley suggests that this detailing is derived from French sources.

21   Morley, John 1993 (*see note 20*), pl XIV; Temple 1993, 50

22   Temple 1993, 254–5 (PNB 98, 99)

23   RIBA, SE 20/12. Also reproduced in Temple 1993, 49, pl 40.

24   Baring Archive, Northbrook Papers, NP1.B.10.3

25   Swete 1997 (*see note 8*) **I**, 102

26   Shropshire Record Office, 49/840

27   John Staples's first wife was a Conolly of Castletown, Co Kildare, but the Revd J M Staples was the son of his father's second marriage to a daughter of Viscount Molesworth; his eldest son became the 10th Baronet. Lissan House became the home of the cadet branch from the mid-18th century, when the family inherited another estate at Dunmore, Co Leix. A succinct family history can be found in the general introduction to the Staples papers (ref D1567) held at the Public Record Office of Northern Ireland.

28   It was initially known as Muff Rectory, Muff being the older name for the village.

29   Davis 1973, 43

30   Birmingham Museum and Art Gallery. Acc 1955P111

31   Davis 1973, 43

32   Tyack 2004, 65

33   RIBA, SKB246/4. Watercolour plans of the ground and upper floors, and depictions of the house in its setting, are held in a private collection; three are reproduced in Mansbridge 1991, 136.

34   Jope 1956, 122

35   Listing particulars, Department of the Environment for Northern Ireland, ref HB09/03/001, rev 2008

36   Jope 1956, 123

37   Jope 1956, 121

38   Lugar, Robert 1805 *Architectural Sketches for Cottages, Rural Dwellings and Villas.* London: J. Taylor, pl 28

39   Pevsner, N and Neave, D 1995 *The Buildings of England Yorkshire: York and the East Riding.* London: Penguin Books, 400; Colvin 2008, 663 note. There is no evidence to support Mansbridge's attribution to Charles Mountain.

5

John Nash and the genesis of Regent's Park

J MORDAUNT CROOK

Writing history is an incremental process. We all stand on the shoulders of previous historians; sometimes I fear we stand on their toes as well. When, 50 years ago, I began work at the Public Record Office on *The History of the King's Works*, our knowledge of Regent's Park was more limited than we knew. True, we had Sir John Summerson's pioneering biography of John Nash. But in its first edition (1935), and in its second edition (1949), it took only the first steps towards an exploration of that phenomenal change in the evolution of urban planning which we now conveniently label picturesque. In the third edition (1980) – following general studies by Terence Davis (1960; 1966) and Ann Saunders (1969) – Summerson came much closer to a complete explanation of the genesis of Regent's Park. But even there he was still hampered by worrying lacunae in documentation. In 1992, after 30 years living and working in the Regent's Park area, I produced a survey of Nash's Metropolitan Improvements – building on my *Country Life* articles of 1968 – to accompany the exhibition, 'London: World City', staged that year at Essen in Germany. My 1992 essay treated Nash less as London's master-planner, more as an opportunist of genius, responding pragmatically to the pressures of political circumstance and the fluctuations of urban economics. I then followed this with a more considered text, my Soane Lecture delivered on 2 November 2000 and published by the Soane Museum the following year as *London's Arcadia*. This incorporated a good deal of new information, necessitating some re-thinking of Summerson's conclusions. Ten years after that came another opportunity for further correction and reconsideration. Here, therefore, unless still more evidence comes to light, are my final thoughts on what has turned out to be a tantalisingly complex topic: the conceptual development of Regent's Park.[1]

****

The metropolitan improvements of the early 19th century were the product of an alliance between the public and private sectors: public in the form of three government departments; private in the shape of individual builders and developers. The link between the two was indeed John Nash. But he arrived late on the scene. The genesis of these improvements lay with those three departments: thc Office of Works, the Land Revenue Office, and the Office of Woods and Forests.

The Office of Works had been purged and professionalised in 1782. It dealt with royal palaces and public buildings in so far as they were a charge on the taxpayer. Its impact on the face of Regency London was considerable: the British Museum, the General Post Office, the Mint, the Custom House, Somerset House, the National Gallery, Buckingham Palace – all these were, in different ways, Office of Works projects. But the involvement of the Office of Works with metropolitan improvement – that is, with the programme of development in the Regent's Park, Regent Street, Trafalgar Square and St James's Park areas – was, at most, tangential. The dynamic for change lay with the Departments of Woods and Forests and Land Revenues.

The idea of redeveloping Crown land in London grew – quite prosaically – out of the need to maximise revenue at a time of royal extravagance and unprecedented wartime expenditure.[2] In 1786 William Pitt set in motion a series of statutory inquiries. Seventeen reports were produced between 1786 and 1793;[3] four between 1797 and 1809;[4] and seven more between 1812 and 1830.[5] The heroes of this prolonged bout of investigation and reform were two busy Scottish civil servants: John Fordyce[6] and Sylvester Douglas, Baron Glenbervie.[7] Between them they transformed the administration of Crown lands into something like a modern government department.[8] But the plan did not go smoothly. Between Fordyce's first enunciation of the Crown Estate's grand strategy in 1793 and the suspension of operations 40 years later, in a flurry of royal scandal and extravagance, there were innumerable changes of plan, nearly always dictated by accident rather than design.

The first accident was the death of William Pitt in January 1806. That brought in the coalition Ministry of All the Talents. Their nominee as 'chief woodman' – at Woods and Forests – was an old gambling crony of Charles James Fox, Lord Robert Spencer, known as 'comical Bob'.[9] Spencer brought with him two figures of key significance in the history of the picturesque: John Nash and Uvedale Price. Nash was initially called in to investigate the incompetence of the current architect at Woods and Forests, John Harvey.[10] That might look like a case of the pot calling the kettle black. But Nash performed his task so thoroughly that he was immediately rewarded with Harvey's job.[11] The circumstances of Price's appointment are rather more obscure. Technically at least, he was the first and last Superintendent to the Deputy Surveyor of the Forest of Dean.[12] But, clearly, Spencer was simply looking after his Whig friends. And those friends happened to be devotees of the picturesque. It was Price who first explained to Nash the principles of that philosophy: during the planning of his triangular castle at Aberystwyth in 1795 (see chapter 3) he had expounded the optical benefits of linking architecture and landscape. Nash apparently 'never thought of [it] before in the slightest degree.'[13] Now, 10 years later, Nash and Price were in the same government department, no doubt still talking the language of the picturesque.

The second accident was a quite extraordinary coincidence. In April 1811 the leases on Marylebone Park fell in and reverted to the Crown. Two months before, in February 1811, George III had been finally declared insane, and the Regency formally began. Within weeks – in March 1811 – Nash's first scheme for Regent's Park was ready, and soon after that the Prince Regent was boasting that he would 'quite eclipse Napoleon'.[14]

The third accident was the sudden death of James Wyatt in a road crash in September 1813. Wyatt had been Surveyor General in the Office of Works, and a very negligent one too. At his death, the responsibilities of that office were therefore divided. In effect, Nash received the royal palaces, Soane was given Whitehall and Westminster, and Smirke the British Museum, Post Office, Royal Mint and London prisons. 'I [am] the King', Nash told Soane, 'you are the Lords, and your friend Smirke the Commons.'[15] More to the point, Nash now had the complete confidence of the Prince Regent, as well as a double position in Woods and Works.

To recapitulate, Nash arrived late on the scene of metropolitan improvement, thanks to a series of accidents. He inherited a financial strategy for exploiting the Crown estate. With that strategy came a major programme of urban renewal and road building. It was his job to give both strategy and programme architectural form. By the time he began work, in 1811, there was a body of thinking on the subject dating back 30 years.

****

That the Prince Regent and his architect should eventually think in Parisian terms was quite understandable. Here was a chance to set up permanent symbols of victory, as well as urban promenades that would rival the Rue de Rivoli. Unlike Soane, Nash was not a learned architect. Whether he actually read Ledoux's great folio of 1804, with its plan for a utopian *ville sociale*, must remain unproven.[16] What we do know is that in October 1814 Nash was in France, celebrating peace with a visit to the architectural delights of Paris.[17] He was there again in November 1815,[18] and again in January 1818 – making at least three visits in five years.[19] When, in 1825, he came to redesign Buckingham Palace, the Tuileries cannot have been far from his mind. Certainly Marble Arch owes something to the Arc du Carrousel. And when in the same year he was at last in a position to finalise one of Regent's Park's most conspicuous monuments – Chester Terrace – he noted with satisfaction that it would indeed be 'nearly as long as the Tuileries'.[20]

There was, however, another tradition: English, vernacular and picturesque. When it came to designing Regent Street, the High Street at Oxford would turn out to be a more useful precedent than the Palais Royal.[21] And when it came to planning Regent's Park, Nash had good reason to fall back on one very useful element in picturesque theory: surprise.

In the absence of any official metropolitan planning authority, the administrators of the Crown estate became *faute de mieux* coordinators of London's town planning; ancestors, in that respect, of the Metropolitan Board of Works, the London County Council and the Greater London Council. The grandest redevelopment scheme in London's history thus fell into the hands of an unelected group of civil servants, whose only official responsibility was to maximise the revenues of the Crown.[22] That they did so without neglecting public amenity tells us much about that political generation's sense of civic virtue, to say nothing of its aesthetic sensibility. In any case, it was Fordyce's reports to the Treasury – primarily those of 1793[23] and 1809[24] – which sketched out the parameters that one day Nash would follow: a redeveloped Marylebone Park (Fig. 5.1), with housing, sewerage, lighting, servicing and transportation; roads, canals, markets, hostelries, churches, shops and monuments, even perhaps a *valhalla*; at all events an urban precinct in North London linked to the centres of power and fashion – Mayfair, Charing Cross, Whitehall, Westminster – by a bold network of new thoroughfares.

Fordyce, of course, produced no designs; but he did sponsor a survey,[25] and an abortive competition.[26] And from that stemmed the first plan for 'Metropolitan Improvement': the elder John White's proposal of 1809.[27] In White's scheme were several features which – in modified form – recur in future plans: a 'grand crescent' near the head of Portland Place, with a major church at its centre; an 'Ornamental Water' sinuously laid out on picturesque principles to follow the contours of the land; and, around the park, a cordon of villas, accessible from a peripheral highway, forming the boundary of the entire estate. White was himself a local resident – his own house appears in the centre of the crescent – and he was surveyor to the Portland estate. His scheme shows real understanding of local topography. It is still a long way from the Regent's Park as built; but the germ is certainly there. In 1809 Fordyce's ideas were clearly still in the air; in October 1810, a few months after Fordyce's death, they formed the basis of a set of draft instructions prepared by the newly amalgamated departments. These guidelines were then sent out to the respective departmental architects: Leverton and Chawner for the Land Revenue Office, and Nash and Morgan for the Office of Woods and Forests. Both teams were directed to study Edinburgh and Bath as possible models, and accordingly, both produced schemes that contained only hints of picturesque planning.

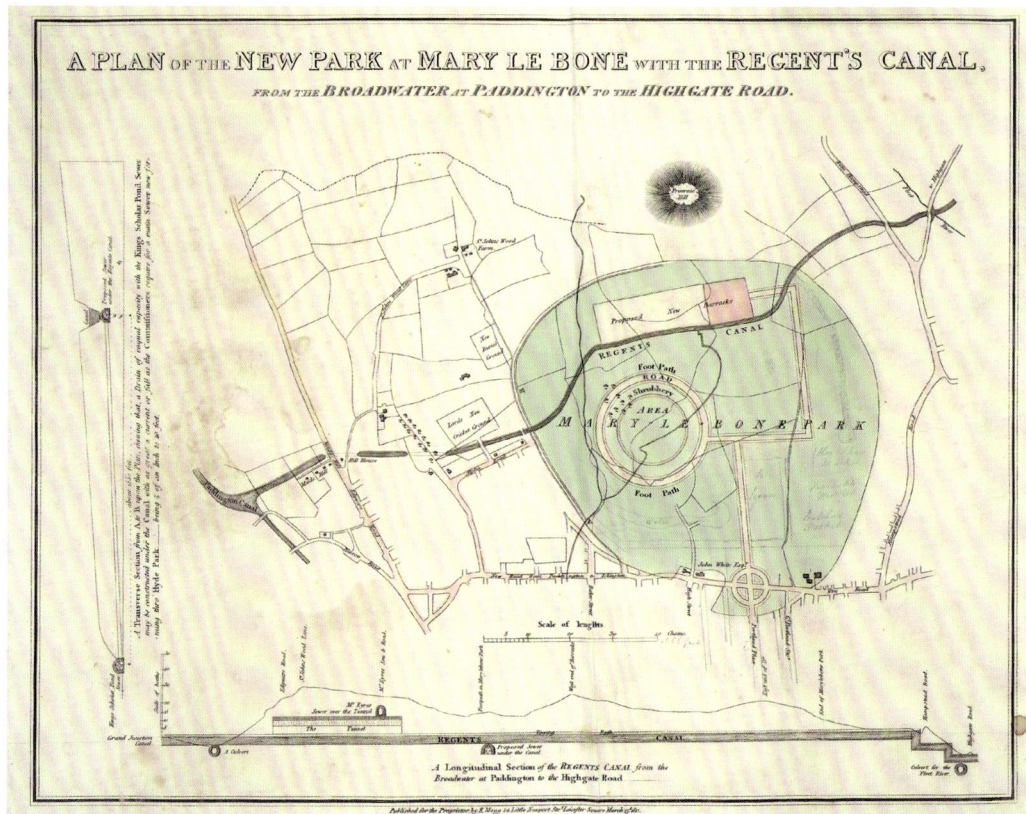

Fig 5.1
'A Plan of the New Park at Mary Le Bone' (watermark 1809). A preliminary proposal, prepared by the Regent's Canal Co for Parliamentary consideration, c 1810–11; published by Edward Mogg, 23 March 1812 (private collection).

Leverton and Chawner began with the kind of reticulated layout familiar from London's Georgian estates – Bedford, Portland, Southampton, Portman – and then combined it with the crescent (now reversed) and peripheral highway envisaged by White.[28] Following Fordyce's directional axes, they also proposed to link Marylebone to Westminster by means of a route – first proposed by them in 1808 – somewhat to the east of what was to become Regent Street.[29] It was a good scheme, in effect a new Bloomsbury. After all, Leverton had been involved in the design of Bedford Square. But it fell short as regards two features upon which Fordyce and his successors had clearly set their minds: civic dignity and public amenity. It was not yet a park.

Nash's plan – his first for what would, after 1813, become known as Regent's Park – was, like Leverton and Chawner's, dated March 1811.[30] In terms of density, this proved almost as urban as his rivals' scheme: a metropolitan annexe, laid out on geometrical lines, dominated by a circus and a double circus, with squares, avenues and crescents, plus a sinuous lake, fed by the Grand Junction Canal, and a scattering of villas within its interstices – just enough to create an illusion of rurality. It was a workable plan, with housing, canal, barracks and markets. But it looked back to John Wood and George Dance rather than forward with Humphry Repton towards the public parks of Joseph Paxton. Even so, it was cleverly packaged. It was speciously illustrated by two giant panoramas, first published in full by Summerson in 1977. They were probably prepared by A C Pugin and George Repton, and were designed to emphasise the picturesqueness of the scene.[31] At 16ft and 17ft long – but only three or four inches in height – they defy all but the cleverest photographer. But it was by such devices that Nash managed to satisfy the three Commissioners of Woods and Forests and Land Revenues: Lord Glenbervie, William Dacres Adams and Henry Dawkins.

The Treasury, however, was not deceived. Spencer Perceval, Chancellor of the Exchequer and Prime Minister, summoned Nash to Downing Street early in August 1811 and told him firmly to reduce the housing density: amenity was just as important as profit. What Perceval wanted was another plan with 'fewer Buildings and a greater extent of open ground ... [since the Treasury, as he put it] cannot approve of appropriating as much [land] to building.'[32] Now this was a matter on which the Tory government rightly felt vulnerable. Even after the balance of the plan had been shifted towards accessibility, Lord Brougham was able to protest vehemently against the Crown's virtual enclosure of Marylebone Park: a building programme like this, he complained, was 'trenching on the comfort of the poor for the accommodation of the rich.'[33] After all, this whole episode – the redrawing of the map of London's West End – could be interpreted as an exercise in social manipulation. It was the Treasury that controlled the leasing of Crown lands, and the Treasury, therefore, that became the target of political attack. Perceval set out to draw the teeth of such criticism by increasing the percentage of accessible parkland. First he corrected Nash's proposals, then he arranged for Glenbervie to square the Prince Regent with a visit to Carlton House in September 1811. Glenbervie in turn immediately took the Prince Regent's agreement back to Nash, at East Cowes Castle on the Isle of Wight.[34] The result was a revised scheme, prepared by Nash in the autumn of 1811, published in the Commissioners' Report of 1812 (see Fig 5.3).[35] Now, ever since Summerson's first edition of 1935, this plan has been hailed as a breakthrough into picturesque planning. It clearly led to the Regent's Park as built. But the conceptual and logistical origins of this layout have always been a little hazy. Between spring 1811 and autumn 1812, Nash clearly developed – or rather was forced to develop – a radically new approach. But what were the steps that took him there?

As far as Marylebone Park was concerned, the months between the spring of 1812 and the summer of 1813 were a period of vacillation and doubt. It is from this period that a group of documents recently discovered derives. Let us first recall the background. The Tories were in power at a time of economic crisis and civil unrest, fighting what was at the time the largest and most expensive war in English history, against the might of Napoleonic France. But domestic issues still exercised Parliament. By March 1812, MPs had been deliberating the future of Regent's Park for at least two years. In May 1812 the Prime Minister, Perceval, was assassinated. The Whigs, who had hoped to regain power after the replacement of George III by the Prince Regent in 1811, remained in the political wilderness. Among their causes of discontent, particularly in the summer of 1812, was one easy target: the government's plan to redevelop Marylebone Park. On the face of it, it did seem quite outrageous. An ancient open space, an area of useful husbandry, a place of recreation and fresh air, was to be turned into an exclusive suburb for the rich and royal, guarded by gates, hedges and fences. A commercial canal was to be driven through it, and among the Canal Company's shareholders was its architect, John Nash (with a personal stake of £10,000), and his political master, the Surveyor General of Crown Lands, Lord Glenbervie (with a personal stake of £3,500). Worst of all, a barracks was to be built – or rather two barracks, one for the Royal Artillery, one for the Royal Life Guards. This new Military Park, as the *Gentleman's Magazine* called it, was to cater for several thousand soldiers; 'a sort of Praetorian camp', in the words of one MP, costing an extraordinary £170,000 (that is £400 for every man and horse; £8,000 alone for a gravelled parade ground), all surrounded by a wall over one mile in length. And why? 'To keep down the national spirit,' cried Sir Francis Burdett in the House of Commons; 'to govern the people, not by law, but by the sword.'[36]

Prime Minister Perceval knew what had to be done. He whipped his parliamentary majority into place, and, in May 1812, just before he died, he managed to get the barrack bill through. To placate the Opposition, he had already made one key concession: 'he advised his Royal Highness [the Prince Regent] to surrender the 510 acres of ground which formed this new park, to the health and comfort of the inhabitants of this great metropolis, instead of [simply] making the greatest rent [out] of it by covering it with buildings.'[37]

What that meant in terms of architectural planning was this: Nash's first plan had already been ditched; so had his second plan (as we shall see); and his third plan, of autumn 1811, - still more his fourth and fifth plans of 1823 and 1826 - ended up bearing little or no relation to the project as he first conceived it. In effect, the Commissioners removed the canal, then the Commons put paid to the barracks. Meanwhile the economy ruled out the sort of densely packed housing programme originally conceived. Nash responded by rearranging his terraces and villas on picturesque lines, with a considerable degree of public access. Let's see how this happened.

Glenbervie's 1812 Report appeared late, in the autumn instead of the summer. In fact – using a device with which we have more recently become familiar – it was published during the Parliamentary recess. The intervening months, and the months immediately afterwards, were filled with acrimony, lobbying, and what today we call political 'spin'. And by the sort of miracle of which historians dream, three plans and a few manuscript fragments (notes prepared informally in 1811–12) somehow survived. Indeed they survived for nearly two centuries, rolled up in a library in deepest Shropshire (*see* Figs 5.1, 5.2 and 5.33).

When Glenbervie's 1812 Report eventually appeared it contained only one plan, instead of four. The chosen one was the one celebrated by Summerson in 1935 (*see* Fig 5.3) The other three plans were discreetly omitted. One of these referred merely to tree-planting, and we need not particularly lament its loss.[38] But the other two were more important. The first of these was Nash's March 1811 plan, the semi-formal, densely packed, housing programme rejected by the government. Summerson first came across this in the later 1960s – after its transfer to the Public Record Office (now The National Archives) from the Crown Estate Office in 1961 – and he published it for the first time in 1977. But the other plan he never found and never saw; in 1977, and again in 1980, he lamented its mysterious disappearance. But at last, in April 2000, it reappeared at auction in the version published by Edward Mogg at 51 Charing Cross Road on 24 May 1813 (Fig. 5.2).[39] What it shows is Nash responding pragmatically to political pressure. The barracks have been removed altogether; the canal has been pushed to the periphery, as have the majority of houses and terraces; to compensate, two more squares have been inserted, east and west of the central area; the serpentine lake has replaced the canal as the axis of the park; and the villas in the great double circle have been planned with alternating aspects, some looking in and some looking out of the dominating central focus.

The last of these arrangements clearly intrigued at least one of the MPs, who seems to have been studying it prior to publication. In a perfunctory way – on a scrap of paper accompanying the plan – he sketched out the system for the benefit of a less acute colleague: 'Circle in the middle of the Park', he writes; 'A. A. A. Villas with gardens looking into the Park. B. B. B. ditto, looking into the circle. I don't know the number or the proportions,' he adds; 'but this explains the principle.' Then, on the back of the same piece of paper, he records another sop to the sensibilities of the public:

Fig 5.2
'Plan of the Intended
Regent's Park, Marylebone'
(watermark 1813). Nash's
second alternative scheme,
prepared for Parliamentary
consideration in March
1812; published by Mogg,
24 May 1813; engraved by
William Faden, 4 June 1813
(private collection).

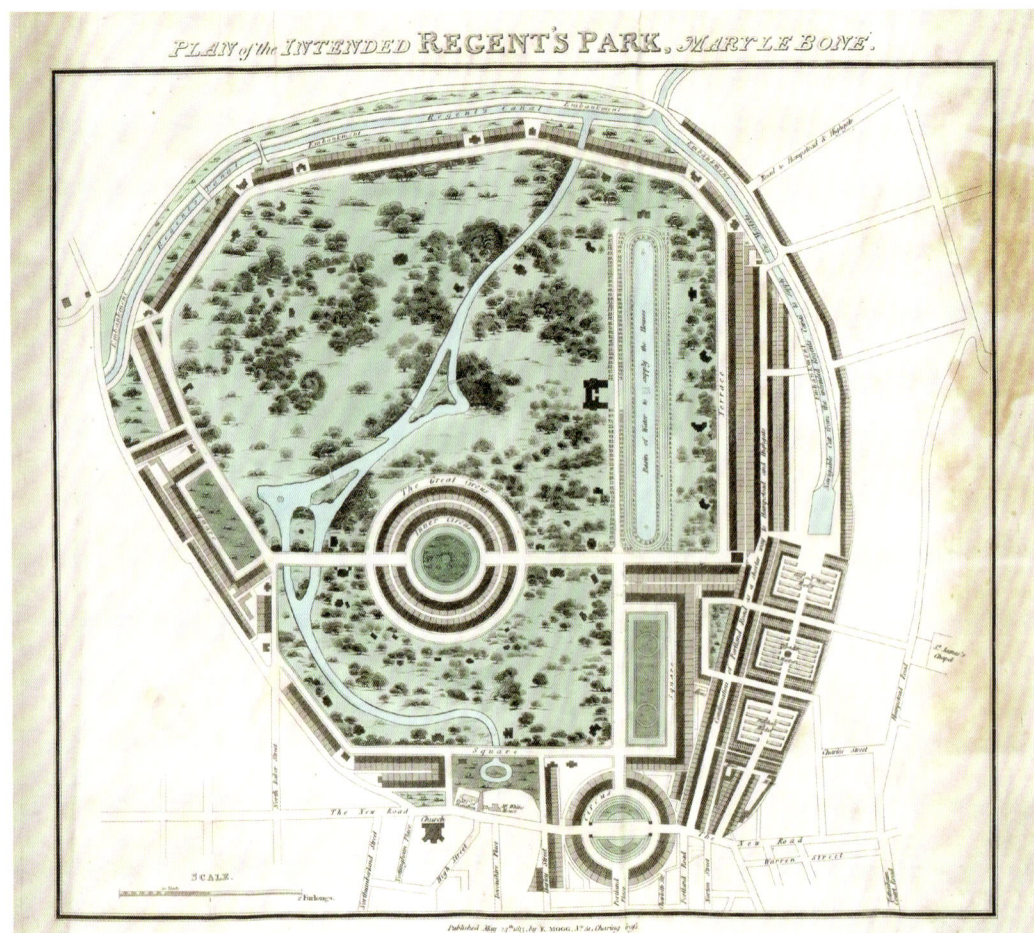

PLAN of the INTENDED REGENT'S PARK, MARYLEBONE.

a 'conservatory and flower house', along the New [Marylebone] Road, more or less on the site of the present Madame Tussauds, and planted – he notes optimistically – with 'beds of flowers as gay as possible.'[40] At the same time, he has faintly sketched in – on an outline plan of the new canal – a possible arrangement of squares and circles, villas and terraces, altogether a kind of shorthand *aide memoire*.

Who were these MPs, exchanging notes, during informal discussions at Westminster? One of them, I suggest – on the basis of rough directions for delivery – was Wilbraham Bootle, later Bootle Wilbraham, later still 1st Baron Skelmersdale (1771–1853) of Lathom House, near Ormskirk, Lancashire. Known apparently as 'Boo', he was the archetypal back-bench Tory. A couple of years before, Lord Boringdon had noted, Boo Bootle 'is not altogether without talent, his wit and judgement have however made but little progress … [since I knew him at Oxford; in fact] I scarcely can recollect an instance of any man's intellect remaining so stationary.'[41] From a House of Commons point

of view, he did have one redeeming quality: his sister tells us that he actually 'liked parliamentary attendance'[42] It was he, I suspect – attending diligently – who was the recipient of the explanation. The helpful explicator seems to have been a former backbencher with an even more improbable name: Sir Charles Boughton, later Boughton Rouse, later still Rouse Boughton, 1st and 9th Baronet (1747–1821) of Downton Hall, Hopton Cangeford (Hopton in the Hole), Shropshire. If only Summerson had visited Hopton in the Hole. Now, Boughton was also a Tory; but he was more than lobby-fodder. He did have a business background, in India; and for over 20 years he was a member of the Parliamentary Audit Commission. In other words, it was his business to check Glenbervie's figures. Finally, he was related, by marriage and by territory, to the apostle of the picturesque, Richard Payne Knight.[43]

From such inconsequential straws, a historian can construct the building blocks of historical explanation. In effect, I think we have found the missing link. Conceptually speaking –

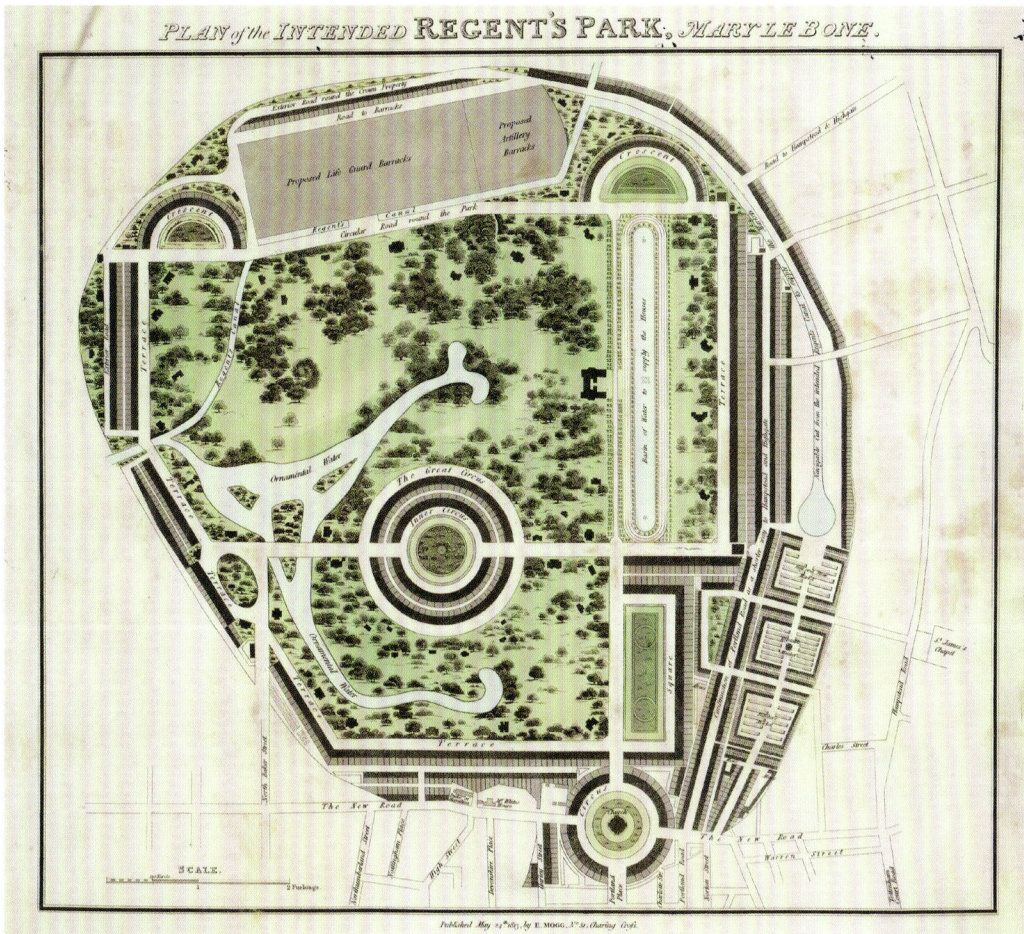

Fig 5.3
'Plan of the Intended
Regent's Park, Marylebone'.
Nash's third or definitive
scheme, engraved by James
Basire, printed by Luke
Hansard and Sons, by order
of the House of Lords and
House of Commons, 12–13
June 1812; published by
Mogg, 24 May 1813
(private collection).

if not chronologically – this new plan is the intermediate step between Nash's formal and informal plans for Regent's Park.

So now we can return to that familiar comparison between Nash's first plan and the so-called 'second plan of 1812' – which, in terms of formal evolution, we must now call his third or definitive plan – the plan in which he adumbrated for the first time the full implications of the urban picturesque. It was printed by House of Commons and House of Lords order on 12–13 June 1812, and then published by Edward Mogg on 24 May 1813 (Fig 5.3). It was here that Nash finally switched to the principles of 'picturesque beauty'.[44] Leverton and Chawner's plan, as James Elmes later explained, had been 'more urban and builder like'. Nash's first design had been a compromise between urbanity and rurality. His second, alternative plan (the missing link) tipped the balance towards rurality; his third or definitive plan 'embraced', in Elmes's words, 'those beauties of landscape gardening which his friend Humphry Repton so successfully

introduced'.[45] In this scheme there are fewer villas, perhaps no more than 50; fewer terraces too, and all tucked away around the circumference. The barracks are still there – remember this plan was prepared in 1811–12 – though their location was by then certainly in doubt. The circus and double circus are also still there, with monumental buildings – a church and a *valhalla* – at their centres; so is the royal pavilion, or *guinguette*, with its formal 'basin' or water garden; so are the crescents, though now they have been moved up to the northern boundary. But the tentacles of the Ornamental Water have been extended, and the serried plantations have given way to informal clumps and shrubberies. This is certainly picturesque, but it is an urban picturesque. 'The leading object,' Nash explained, is 'that of presenting from without one entire Park complex in unity of character and not an assemblage of Villas and Shrubberies like Hampstead, Highgate, Clapham Common and other purlieus of the Town … [But above all] the buildings and even the Villas should be considered as Town residences and not Country Houses.'[46] These terraces might be occupied by City magnates and professional people of middle rank, but they must look like metropolitan palaces.

Finally, the Regent's Canal has now been shifted definitively to the north-west corner of the park, only to emerge – functionally speaking – as a supply route to the markets and shopping areas on the Eastern rim. Not that Nash was totally averse to canals, which was why he made a feature of the one in his first plan. 'Many persons', he noted in 1812, 'would consider … Boats and Barges passing along the Canal as enlivening the Scenery, provided the Bargemen … were prevented from landing in the Parks … by fencing out the Towing Path on one side, and by stakes in the Water on the other.'[47] The Commissioners, however, clearly thought that the picturesque could not tolerate too much reality.

So here was a plan designed to maximise Crown revenue while increasing 'the beauty and salubrity of the metropolis.'[48] Nash had at last told his masters what they wanted to hear. 'Open space, free air, and the scenery of nature', Nash explains, will prove irresistible to 'the wealthy part of the Public.' An 'intermixture of Trees, Lawn and Water', will guarantee a 'unity of Park-like character.'[49] And Repton's principle of 'apparent extent' will in turn guarantee an illusion of space: 'no Villa should see any other,' Nash asserts, 'but each should appear to possess the whole of the Park'; and 'the Streets of Houses which overlook the Park should not see the Villas, nor the Streets of Houses overlook those of any other street.'[50] And then he played his trump card. By foregoing the majority of his 'Streets, Squares, Circuses and Villas', he had – inadvertently – secured not only 'a greater variety of beautiful scenery', but a higher level of leasehold value.[51] Nash's projected rental income from the new park was double that of Leverton's. And by tying this new park to an elegant New Street – linking the new park to the West End – the future worth of all these properties would be multiplied by facility of communication.[52]

Nash had now satisfied his ministerial masters, as well as the Prince Regent. He was now, in Creevey's phrase, the 'commander in chief'. But he had yet to satisfy the market. The immediate post-war property slump made new building unprofitable. 'The disposition to building', Nash explained in 1816, 'suddenly became paralyzed' by 'the sudden stoppage …

of credit.'[53] The roads, fences and plantations had been laid out, and the bed of the ornamental water excavated, but by 1819 only three sites of villas had been let, and two built: The Holme and St John's Lodge. By 1823, in Nash's fourth plan, the intended number had been reduced to 26.[54] By 1826, in Nash's fifth plan, the 26 had again been cut back, this time to a mere eight (Fig 5.4).[55] The *valhalla* had been quietly shelved. The number of terraces had been reduced as well. St Andrew's Terrace and Kent Terrace did not appear in their intended form. Garrick Terrace and Munster Terrace never even reached the drawing board. They – and the projected barracks – were replaced on the northern side by a novel entertainment: the Zoological Gardens (by Decimus Burton, 1826–41).[56] Note that, in a masterstroke of public relations, the barracks were replaced by the Zoo. Meanwhile, the Royal Life Guards had been relocated to the eastern perimeter, close enough to the royal *guingette* for military security, but discreetly out of the public eye, on the other side of what would become Albany Street. The Artillery were quietly moved to St John's Wood.

There were other changes too, financially rather than politically driven. The circus at the head of Portland Place became Park Crescent (1812–22) and Park Square (1823–5), after its initial contractor, Charles Mayor, went bankrupt in 1815–16.[57] The idea of a church as the focus of the crescent was then abandoned.[58] And the central double circus – centrepiece of Nash's first three plans in 1811–12 – was first slimmed down to a single circle (in 1826) and then (in 1828) came near to being turned into the site of King's College, London.[59] It ended up, more popularly, as the garden of the Royal Botanical Society (laid out by Decimus Burton in 1840–59).[60] A set of almshouses, St Katherine's Hospital, had already been added in 1826–8, to designs by Ambrose Poynter, much to Nash's displeasure.[61] Meanwhile the idea of a Long Walk, or avenue of trees, with its attendant 'Basin' had been first dropped (in 1826) and then tentatively reintroduced (in 1828) as a formal approach to the royal summer pavilion, at the time of the King's College scheme.[62] But in the end, the Regent's Park palace – once the *raison d'être* of the whole programme – turned out to be a mirage.

To recapitulate once more, Nash did not at first intend to design a public park. That eventuality was forced on him first by the good sense of his political masters, then by the pressure of market forces. As late as the summer of 1816, the future of the whole Regent's Park and Regent Street plan hung in the balance. 'The project', wrote Glenbervie, 'seems to be in a deplorable way, and Nash I hear is held in universal abhorrence, except by his royal master and dupe', the Prince Regent.[63] It was only royal favour – and Nash's incurable optimism – that kept the scheme afloat. From the start, the profitable urban precinct that Nash envisaged did involve a number of suburban features: self-sufficiency, good communications, and an illusion of rurality. Only gradually did it take on the characteristics of a popular recreational facility. But the pressure of public demand was certainly there. As early as September 1814, the painter Joseph Farington noted in his diary that

the new park was already popular with the public. 'The weather was remarkably fine today; the Thermometer at 73° – … multitudes of respectably dressed people, men with their wives and families … walking in … the Regency Park, or quietly sitting with Pipes and Ale in the open air at the small taverns … almost all the men dressed in Black or Dark Blue Cloaths … Boots [have clearly] become an article of Sunday finery even among the lower order of tradesmen and mechanics.'[64]

****

So the popularity of the picturesque was by no means an illusion. But illusion was certainly one of the chief ingredients in that cluster of ideas and attitudes that came to be labelled

Fig 5.4
'Plan of the Regent's Park Estate belonging to His Majesty' (watermark 1827). Nash's fifth amended scheme engraved by Basire, 12 May 1826 and printed by Hansard; re-published by Mogg in 1828 (private collection).

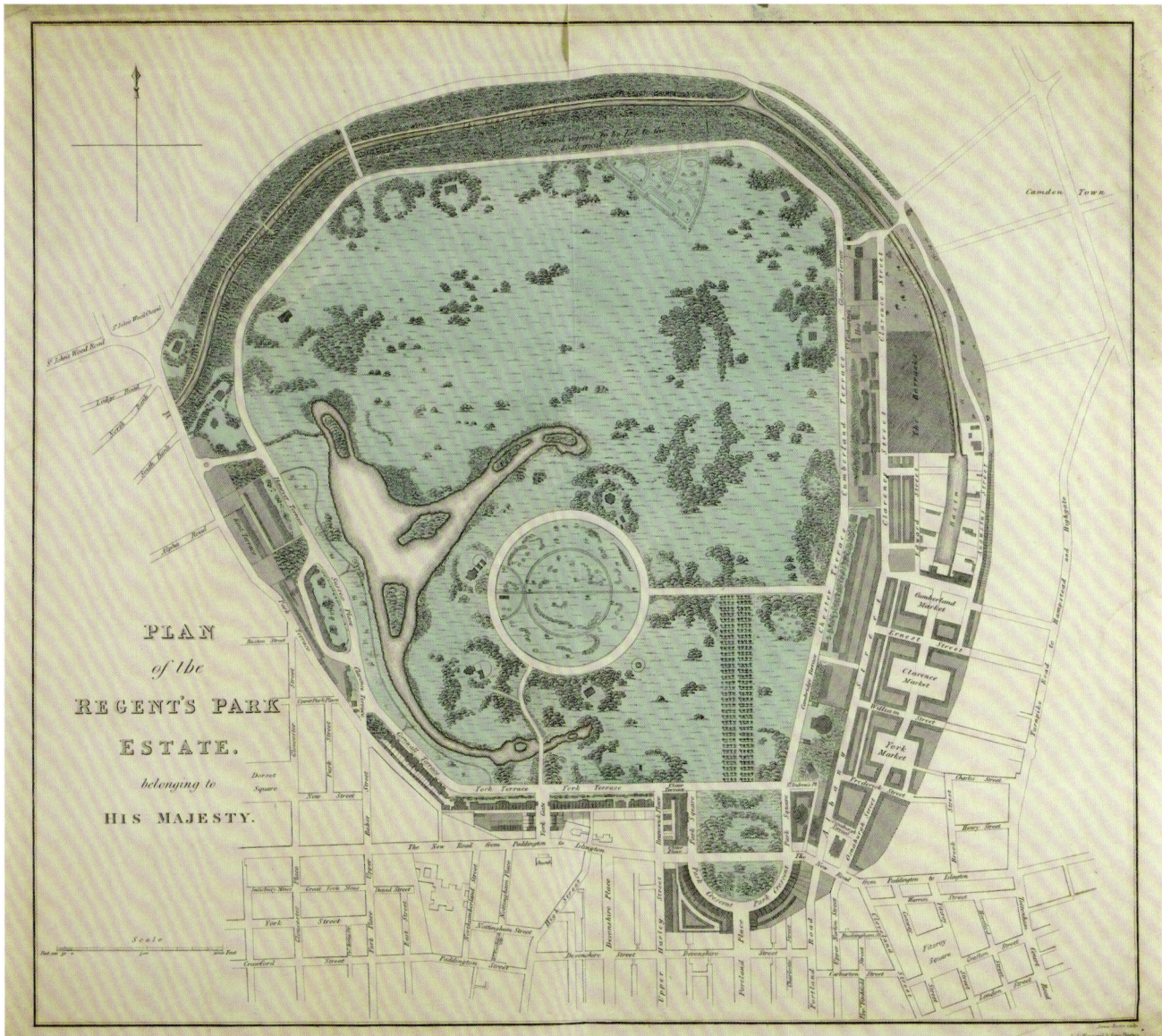

'picturesque theory'. Nash had been introduced to the picturesque by Uvedale Price, who later became a colleague in Woods and Forests, and Glenbervie, the First Commissioner, certainly knew both Price and Payne Knight. The picturesque, moreover, could be turned into a marketable commodity. Among the delights available in Regent's Park were two places of pictorial entertainment: the Colosseum and the Diorama. The Colosseum was a kind of *trompe l'oeil* travelogue: London in three dimensions. The Diorama was a distant ancestor of the modern cinema.[65] Outside, the Colosseum was a Roman Pantheon with a Greek portico. Inside – beneath a dome wider than St Paul's Cathedral – a sequence of giant perspective panoramas could be enjoyed. The Diorama featured a series of painted images, opaque or translucent,

Fig 5.5
Chester Terrace (1825) seen through the triumphal arch at the northern end (AA 098718).

which were shuffled like a kaleidoscope for the benefit of spectators seated in a dark, rotating auditorium. Here, James Elmes explains, is 'a display of architectural and landscape scenery, arranged … so as to exhibit changes of light and shade and a variety of natural phenomena in a really wonderful manner.' 'The delusion', he adds, 'is perfect and almost incredible.'[66] So, too, with Regent's Park. The magicians of the Colosseum and the Diorama – their 'pictorial enchanters' – were not architects but scene-painters: Messrs Horner and Parris, and Messrs. Bouton and Daguerre. But in Regent's Park itself, Nash was both architect and scene-maker. Like the Colosseum and the Diorama, his transformation of Marylebone fields was a compound of 'powerful pictorial illusions'.[67] In effect, it was a scenic conjuring trick.

That was certainly Nash's intention. As the drawings came in – from builders: James Burton, Jacob Smith, W M Nurse, Richard Mott, George Thompson, J M Aitkens; or from architects: Decimus Burton, James Thomson, J J Scoles, Ambrose Poynter – he inserted modifications in pursuit of picturesque effect. Decimus Burton's first design for Cornwall Terrace (1820–1), for example, was dismissed as altogether too monotonous: like 'a hospital, alms-house, work-house or some such building.' Nash failed to persuade the young architect to sub-divide the façade into several distinct units, 'each assuming the character of a nobleman's villa'; but he did secure a much more broken silhouette, with boldly projecting porticos.[68] And when it came to Chester Terrace (1825), he tolerated no half-measures, overruling his builder, James Burton.[69] We owe those transverse triumphal arches (Fig. 5.5) which multiply the terrace's theatrical effect, to Nash's personal insistence on picturesque values.[70] In 1935, Summerson thought those arches 'as badly detailed as a piece of realism in a provincial production of Julius Caesar'[71]. He later modified that view. But in any case theatricality – pictorial artifice – was all part of the picturesque system, and it was picturesque values that infused Nash's own designs – notably Sussex Place (1822–3; builder William Smith) and Cumberland Terrace (1826; executant architect James Thomson; builder W M Nurse) (Fig. 5.6). Both of these were virtuoso

Fig 5.6
Cumberland Terrace (1826)
from the south
(FF 003398).

Fig 5.7
Sussex Place (1822–3)
(DP104301).

orotund author of *Metropolitan Improvements* (1829). The architect's conception, Elmes explains, was essentially Reptonian.[73] The choicest views of The Holme (1816–18; Fig 5.8) – selected for himself by James Burton, and designed by his son Decimus – are framed in trees and reflected in 'the glassy surface of the lake', for all the world like sketches from 'the magic pencils of Ruysdael and Claude'.[74] South Villa (1818–19) and Albany Cottage (c 1822); Holford House (1832–3), St Dunstan's (1825–8) and St John's Lodge (1818–19); Hanover Lodge (1827) and Grove House (1822–4) – mostly by Burton under Nash's direction – all act as focal magnets of a 'picturesque group'; each, to the mobile spectator is part of a sequence of 'living pictures'.[75] Even St Marylebone Church (Thomas Hardwick, 1813–17) is transformed by Nash into a piece of theatre – a veritable 'stereotomous scene' – by being placed between York Gate's flanking terraces (1822; Fig 5.9); lit from East, West and North, explains Elmes, the result is 'an architectural pictorial symphony of three parts.'[76] Or, to vary the musical metaphor, by incorporating the church into the Park Nash makes it an overture to the visual cadenzas lurking deeper inside the landscape itself. Circular roads, winding paths; mazy walks, umbrageous pools: 'See!', exclaims Elmes, 'the sparkling undulating line of beauty.'[77] Cornice

performances in scenographic imagery. Sussex Place (Fig 5.7) alone consisted of 26 houses masked behind 56 columns, and shaped overall as a single palace. In modern jargon, it was a virtual palace. Nash saw all these terrace designs as discrete compositions; visually autonomous, like 'so many distinct pictures'.[72]

Nash's picturesque vision found its perfect expositor in the person of James Elmes, the

Fig 5.8
'The Villa of J Burton, Esq.'
(The Holme, 1816–18), seen from the western side of the lake, by G Cooke after J D Harding, 1827
(British Museum, Crace Collection **XXX**, 114).

Fig 5.9
St Marylebone Church from York Gate (1822) (DP104312).

and pilaster, bow and pediment; Cumberland Terrace's mighty colonnades, spotlit by sunbeams and shadowed by shifting light: 'see … how they play in … sunny coruscations'.[78]

Each terrace of houses appears to be a palace (Fig 5.10); each villa appears to be a country seat. The spectator's progress is a trail of continuous illusion. No urban scars can spoil this sylvan scene (Figs 5.11 and 5.12): the gardens of Park Crescent and Park Square are even linked by a tunnel beneath the traffic of Marylebone Road. These inner gardens, notes Elmes, are not picturesque according to the 'Gilpin school'. Even so, they are crammed with Reptonian devices: 'meandering walks', 'ambrosial shrubs', 'velvet turf', 'gay flowers', and – of course – 'serpentine walks':[79]

> As you are rowed [on the lake, sighed Charles Ollier in 1823], the variety of views … is admirable; sometimes you are in a narrow stream, closely overhung by branches of trees; presently you open upon a wide sheet of water like a lake, with swans sunning themselves on its bosom; bye and bye your boat floats near the edge of a smooth lawn fronting one of the villas; and then again you catch the perspective on the periphery of a range of superb edifices, the elevation of which is contrived to have the effect of a palace … [There is in fact, says Ollier] nothing like it in Europe … [Inside the park] the inhabitant of each [villa] seems, in his own prospect, to be the sole lord of the surrounding scenery. [For] in the centre of the park, there is a circular plantation of immense circumference, and in the interior of this you are in a perfect Arcadia.[80]

No wonder, when Disraeli imagined a Saracenic villa for *The Young Duke* (1829), he made its location Regent's Park.

By the 1840s, the social geography of Regent's Park was set firm. The grander terraces were occupied by commercial *nouveaux riches*; the villas by minor plutocrats; and the peripheral areas by respectable professionals. On public holidays the park attracted large numbers of clerks and shopkeepers, plus artisans and their families; at other times a smaller audience of genteel sensibility. Among the latter, certainly, we can count the poetess, Elizabeth Barrett. In May 1846, during a period of convalescence, she was driven from Wimpole Street to the Circle, and set foot in the park. She wrote to her fiancée Robert Browning:

> [Regent's Park] looked to me like a region of Arcady … the sun was shining with that green light through the trees, as if he carried down with him the very essence of the leaves, to the ground. We stopped the carriage, and I got out and walked [through a little iron gate], and I put both my feet on the grass … I gathered it in my hands – I laid it against my lips … It was like a bit of … Dreamland.[81]

****

So where does Nash's reputation stand today? He died in public disgrace, pilloried for 'inexcusable irregularity' and 'great negligence';[82] 'a jobber';[83] or at the very least 'a great speculator … a most suspicious character.'[84] To his accusers, Nash had a simple, and lordly,

Fig 5.10
Hanover Terrace (c 1822)
(DP104377).

reply: 'I am not a public accountant.'[85] His trump card was a brand of pragmatic vision that triumphed over the trivialities of finance. As one contemporary MP put it: 'if Mr Nash had not been speculator as well as surveyor, [Regent's Park and] Regent Street would never have been finished … at great risk and hazard [he] carried that noble project into complete execution.'[86]

As a neoclassical architect, Nash was neither an archaeologist nor a rationalist. In fact he was a self-confessed eclectic. One critic in 1820 called him 'not so much a designer as a collector of designs … he has taken them from all schools, more for their variety than for their beauty.'[87] 'An Ionic is an Ionic', he once told James Elmes, and he 'did not care which one his draughtsman used.' When an assistant queried the accuracy of drawings for some of the Regent's Park detailing – particularly around Gloucester Gate – he replied: 'Never mind, it won't be observed in the execution.'[88] Disraeli sensed an easy target. When, in 1829, the Duke of St James called for an architect, M Bijou de Millecolonnes seemed just the man:

Bijou de Millecolonnes laughed at the ancients … and had himself invented an order… 'The occasional retreat of a noble [he announced] should be something picturesque and poetical. The mind should be led to voluptuousness by exquisite associations, as well as by the creations of art…. Their luxury is rendered more intense by … reminiscences that add past experience to present enjoyment… what think you of Reviving the Alhambra?' Splendid conception! The Duke already fancied himself a Caliph. 'Lose no time, Chevalier! Dig, plant, build!'[89]

Such a cavalier approach in matters of detail was all part of the picturesque mentality. And it was this subordination of neoclassicism to the picturesque that particularly provoked a thoroughbred classicist like C R Cockerell. Nash's Regent's Park terraces certainly epitomise the precarious balance between neoclassical archaeology and picturesque theory. Their details are vestigially Grecian, as in Gloucester Terrace (1827); their composition posthumously Palladian, as in Hanover Terrace (c 1822); sometimes their forms might almost be described

Fig 5.11
View from Hanover Terrace looking north. In the distance is St Dunstan's villa (lithograph by unknown artist c 1850, coloured by hand; private collection).

Fig. 5.12
View from Hanover Terrace looking south. The dome of the Colosseum can be seen on the extreme left (lithograph by unknown artist c 1850, coloured by hand; private collection).

as Hollywood Baroque, as in the cinctured columns of Cambridge Terrace (*c* 1822). The impact of all this is largely dependent on scenic conjuring tricks. The Ionic order in Cumberland Terrace, for example, is neither archaeological nor rational, as Summerson pointed out more than 60 years ago. In more tolerant old age, however, he conceded that it was a 'composition of great energy and brilliance … a fantasia' on themes from Somerset House and Versailles.[90] Cockerell would have sided with the young Summerson. In 1825 he noted:

> The architecture of Regent's Park may be compared to the poetry of an *improvisatore* – one is surprised and then captivated at first sight with the profusion of splendid images, the variety of the scenery and the readiness of the fiction. But if as many were versed in the Grecian rules of this science as there are in those of Homer and Virgil this trumpery would be less popular.[91]

Even so, it is worth remembering that Cockerell in old age lived happily enough in Chester Terrace. 'Nash', he grudgingly concluded, 'always has original ideas.' And we in turn have to admit that if nothing else, the scale of the whole operation is prodigious: the lateral span of Chester Terrace alone is little short of 1,000 feet. If this is artifice, then – surely – let us have more of it.

****

What I have tried to do here is to explain, step by step, the process by which the plan of Regent's Park was formulated. What survives of Nash's scheme – unfinished, decayed, rebuilt; vandalised, bombed, redeveloped – is but a fragment of what he planned, and a shadow of what might have been. And much of what he actually did (and did not) build was forced upon him by political and economic pressure. Even so, there is no mistaking the imprint of his assimilative vision. The glorious panorama of Regent's Park survives as testimony to a master pragmatist, a virtuoso of scenographic art. Defying the swings and roundabouts of taste, Nash continues to rank with Wren as a maker of modern London. But his genius was essentially opportunism writ large.

Postscript: a note on Park Village East and West

Towards the end of his life, John Nash's greatest pleasure was to be driven in his carriage from his house at the bottom of Regent Street, along the full length of the grand processional route up Regent Street to Portland Place; then round Regent's Park, past the site of the Royal Palace that was never built, opposite Cumberland

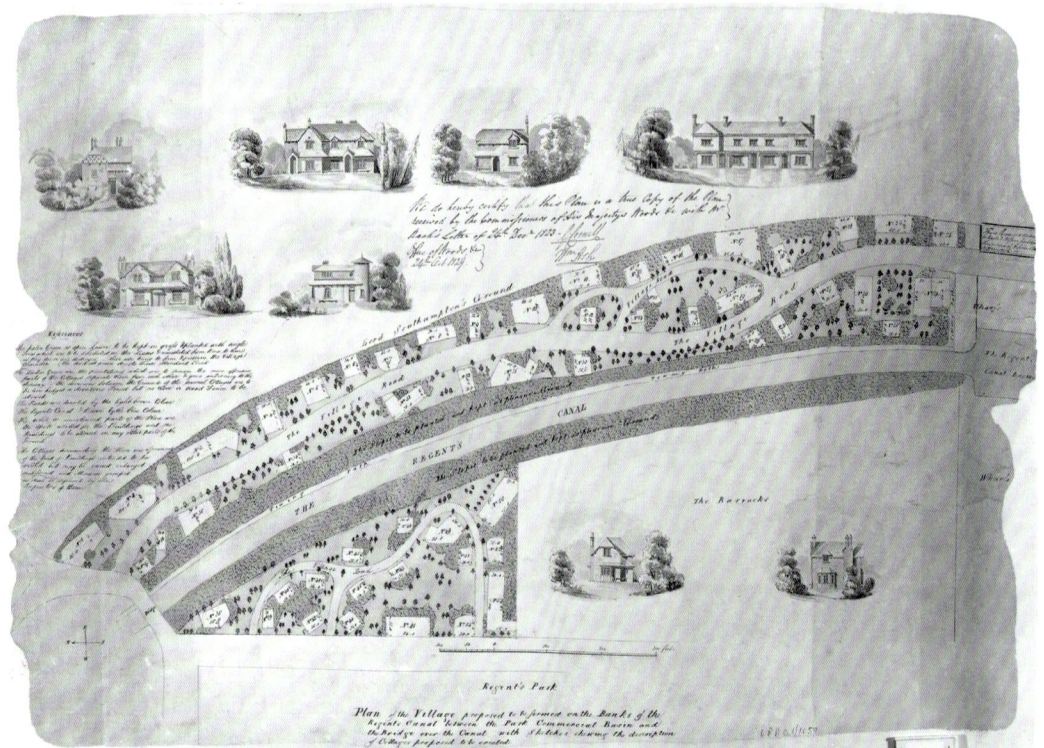

Fig 5.13
The first scheme for the Park Village, 1823 (The National Archives: ref MPE 911).

Terrace; and then back again to St James's Park and Buckingham Palace. Almost all the architectural features along the route were his own achievement. As he went he must have surveyed with satisfaction this greatest town-planning operation in the history of London. On 12 March 1832, aged 82 and by now very frail, he noted in his diary: 'Drove up to the Regent's Park and the Village with Mrs. Nash'. And again, on 24 March: 'Called … at the Village in the Carriage with Mrs. Nash'.[92] The Village in question was Park Village East and West, and its significance merits separate treatment here.

First of all, the chronology. Nash's first design for the site dates from 1823.[93] Park Village East was built first, in 1824–32. Park Village West followed in 1832–8.[94] By that time, Nash was in retirement – actually in disgrace – and the later work was directed by his young assistant James Pennethorne. Less than half now remains of Park Village East.[95] The houses on its eastern side were removed to accommodate the widening of the London and North Western Railway in 1883 and 1900–5; several of those on its western side were bombed in the Second World War.[96] In 1942–3 the access canal was filled in. In 1949–50 there was considerable restoration of both villages, on the advice of Sir Albert Richardson and Sir John Summerson.[97] And in the 1960s four additional villas were inserted on the Albany Street side of Park Village West.

What was Nash trying to do here? In that diary entry, he spelled 'Village' with a capital letter. He had been toying with 'village' design – that is, vernacular-style cottages in a picturesque context – since at least 1810. That was the year he began Blaise Hamlet, at Henbury, Gloucestershire, not far from Bristol. This had been built by J S Harford, a Quaker banker, for his retired servants. Its 10 cottages were decidedly picturesque: thatched roofs with irregular brick chimney stacks, and houses arranged around a village green (*see* Fig 9.16), all linked by an irregular pathway. They had names such as 'Rose Cottage', 'Oak Cottage' and 'Sweetbriar Cottage'. Something like this was clearly Nash's intention here too; but this time he was faced with an urban, or at least a suburban, site. The building land was no more than a residual slice on either side of that part of the Regent's Canal which provided access for goods to Cumberland Market. Blaise Hamlet had been a miniature model village in the country. By contrast, Park Village was designed for London, and was rustic, not bucolic. In this way it became the spiritual ancestor of the picturesque suburb.

The site was not promising: it lay alongside a commercial canal, close to a barracks, on the very edge of 'acceptable' London. Traditionally, Mayfair hostesses talk of 'the wrong side of the park', meaning Hyde Park. But Park Village was the wrong side of the wrong park. Nash took on this development partly as a personal speculation, partly for his own private amusement. His original proposal (Fig 5.13) showed a series of small rustic houses, 'scattered about in an irregular manner as Cottages with plantations between'. They were to be arranged along serpentine 'village roads', on either side of the branch waterway technically known as the Collateral Cut.[98] Originally these cottages were each assigned individual gardens, scattered among lawns and clumps of trees. That was soon altered, but in one respect the plan never changed. Each house was to be different in style, though similar in scale. Gothic, Tudor, Tuscan, Italianate: all these historical modes were represented. In art-historical language, their idiom was eclectically based. In visual terms, they were pictorially conceived on kinetic principles. Like Regent's Park itself, each village was designed for the mobile spectator. As the spectator perambulates, or drives, a sequence of images unfolds, kinetically adjusted and pictorially composed. That is Nash's concept of the urban picturesque.

For whom were these houses designed? What was the purpose of Park Village East and Park Village West? First, we must clear away several legends. They were not built for servants or tradesmen. Such people were accommodated in the area of Cumberland Market, to the east of Albany Street. They were not built for mistresses of officers at the barracks. St John's Wood would have been more discreet for that purpose. They were certainly not built for ladies of the night. (That comes later: by the 1880s – when the railway works were in full swing – several houses in Park Village East do actually appear to have operated as houses of ill fame.[99]) At No. 2 Park Village East, in the 1890s, lived and died one particularly notorious criminal: the man who in 1876 stole Gainsborough's famous portrait of Georgiana Duchess of Devonshire from Agnew's shop window in Bond Street. But the earliest inhabitants of both villages were decidedly bourgeois. At No. 12 Park Village West (Fig 5.14) – Tower House as it is often called, poised on a pivotal point in the plan – the first resident was

Fig 5.14
Tower House, No. 12 Park
Village West, c 1832
(DP104289).

Dr James Johnson, Physician to The Duke of Clarence, and Physician to John Nash himself. A later occupant of the same house was the artist W P Frith of 'Derby Day' and 'Paddington Station' fame. And later still, in 1861, the same house was the home of Thomas Duffus Hardy, Deputy Keeper of the Public Record Office. In the 1840s, one particularly learned Park Village West neighbour was the Rev Benjamin Webb, editor of the *Ecclesiologist*, at that time a curate at Christ Church, Albany Street. Just opposite him, at No. 17, the first Anglican convent – that is, the first convent established in England since the Reformation – was founded in 1845. In 1854 the Revd Henry Hart Milman, historian and future Dean of St Paul's, was living at No. 1. At the same time, James Wyld, geographer, MP and publicist, was living at No. 8. Soon afterwards a well-known etcher, R W Macbeth, was occupying No. 10 (Fig.5.15).

Except perhaps at the start, Park Village East (Fig 5.16) was always less desirable than Park Village West. Take again, as an example, one early occupant: Ebenezer Trotman the architectural journalist. He died there aged 56 in 1865.[100] By that date he was living in reduced circumstances, brought on by ill health. In all, there were originally some 50 houses in Park Village East, and they were never occupied by fashionable folk. At No. 14 in 1847–59 lived Frank Newman, brother of Cardinal Newman, but a man of rather different views. He was Professor of Latin at the 'godless' University College. Later on he was followed by a William Haywood, probably the architect of Holborn Viaduct. These villas in Park Village East were grouped around a winding carriageway called Serpentine Road; appropriately named, but no longer in existence. It disappeared when as many as 30 houses were demolished for the railway engineering works of 1883 and 1900–5. The only surviving images of those lost villas are some slight watercolour sketches now preserved in Swiss Cottage library. These removals left 20 villas remaining, which all survived into the Second World War. Fifteen of them are still there today, though very much restored (Fig 5.17).[101]

By the 1840s the social geography of Regent's Park was indeed established. The royal palace had never been built, so the courtiers never arrived, and nor did the inhabitants of Mayfair. Otherwise most classes were represented. The grander terraces around the park became the homes of upper-middle-class *rentiers*, the commercial *nouveaux riches*. There was little or

no old money: at No.1 Cumberland Terrace, for example, lived its builder-developer, W M Nurse. The separate villas inside the park – each with its own spacious garden – became miniature palaces for minor plutocrats, like James Holford and Sir Isaac Lyon Goldsmid. The market sector around Cumberland Basin – strictly speaking, outside the park – was for working people. And peripheral areas such as Park Village were profitably occupied by respectable professionals. On public holidays, from the start, the open sections of the park attracted crowds of clerks and shopkeepers, as well as artisans and their families. At other times there was sufficient peace and quiet to cater for a smaller audience of genteel sensibility: Elizabeth Barrett Browning, for instance, who – as we have seen – was occasionally driven up from Wimpole Street in an invalid carriage.

But to conjure up Park Village and its surroundings, we should imagine the area in its early days on a holiday weekend. Being not far from the Zoo, and accessible from Camden Town, the York and Albany public house (restored after long dereliction in 2009) must

*Fig 5.15
No. 18 Park Village West
(DP104288).*

Fig 5.16
Nos 6–16 Park Village East,
looking over the
Cumberland Market branch
of the Regent's Canal
(Shepherd & Elmes,
Metropolitan
Improvements, 1827).

have done good business. There was a tea garden behind it, at the entrance to Park Village East, where families could gather on a warm afternoon, perhaps to the sound of a band. On the edge of Park Village West, near the junction of Albany Street and Gloucester Gate Bridge – designed in 1877–8 by William Booth Scott, with sculpture by Fucigna – there was a pleasure garden, also for public use. Nash had guessed correctly that people had little objection to the appearance of canals. They enjoyed the proximity of water. In September 1814, 10 years before Park Village was begun, the painter Joseph Farington had already noted in his diary that the area round the new park was popular with the public on Sundays.

On weekdays, and in winter, there would have been rather less activity. At those quieter times, Park Village must have been a most agreeable retreat – at least, before the railway engineering of the 1880s. Those works brought with them a social decline into a world of lodging houses and transients. Then came revival.

By the time of The First World War, undesirables had been eased out; the professional classes had returned.

Finally, look at the address list for 1939. At that point there were still 16 houses in Park Village East, four of which (one quarter) were occupied by six doctors (physicians or surgeons). That is, one third of the residents there came from the medical professions. Of the other 12, one was an Oxbridge clergyman, another was a female CBE. So Park Village East had clearly recovered its respectability after that bad patch in the 1880s. Park Village West, on the other hand, had never really lost its bourgeois status. In that same year, 1939, there were 19 residents. Of these, one was the son of a peer, three were medical men, one was a doctor of music, and one was a retired colonel, CMG, DSO.[102]

✳✳✳✳

So how should the significance of Park Village be judged? It is difficult to overestimate the importance of Nash's idea. His concept of the

Fig 5.17
Nos 2–4 Park Village East
(DH104381).

urban picturesque was not a product of his own thinking. He was an intuitive designer, not a theorist; and he took his ideas from Richard Payne Knight, Uvedale Price and Humphry Repton, all of whom he knew. What he was – and it is worth repeating – was an opportunist of genius. Right at the end of his career he was able to put into practice – as it were in microcosm – those notions of the urban picturesque that he had already tried out in diluted form within the larger arena of Regent's Park itself. The two Park Villages, East and West, together came to form 'a miniature garden suburb in the very heart of London'.[103] In his biography of Pennethorne, Geoffrey Tyack rightly calls this 'perhaps the most original contribution of 19th-century London to urban civilisation'[104] Nash seems to have imagined, initially, that his 'cottages' would be occupied by artisans. In fact they quickly established themselves as desirable *pieds à terre*. And – apart from problems over prostitutes in the 1880s and 1890s – very desirable they have remained. In recent times, residents have included several public figures, notably Woodrow Wyatt and Peter Mandelson.

In terms of architectural theory, Park Village has become a classic of suburban imagery. In variety of style and irregularity of plan, both villages are striking exercises in picturesque theory. But it was theory with a purpose. In their function and setting, even in their inhabitants, they turned out to be prototypes of a universal suburbia. C R Cockerell, as we have seen, rather despised Nash as a charlatan. But he did himself choose to live in Chester Terrace. Perhaps we should leave him with the last word: 'Nash always has original ideas'.[105]

Appendix: Checklist of plans and proposals for Regent's Park

Abbreviations

  BL: British Library
  CCA: Canadian Centre for Architecture, Montreal
  NA: The National Archives, Kew
  PP: Parliamentary Papers
  sd: signed and dated
  WCA: Westminster City Archives
  wmk: watermark

Preliminary phase

1 'A Plan of Estates in the Parishes of St Mary le bone and Pancras'
   Surveyed by James Crew (1753)
   NA, MPE 315

2 'Plan of an Estate called the Maryebone Park Farm belonging to the Crown: taken by order of the Lords' Commissioners of HM's Treasury'. Drawn by George Richardson for John Fordyce, Surveyor General of Land Revenue; engraved by William Faden (August 1794)
   BL Maps, Crace Collection **XIV**, 28

3 'Plan showing the Improvements proposed in the Marylebone Park Estate'.
   Drawn by John White (1809); 'reduced and drawn from the original copy by Peter Potter, Kentish Town'; engraved by Neele, Strand, and re-published by John White Jr (1814; 2nd edn 1815 with plans showing layout of streets retrospectively updated); also engraved by I Bacon, 231 Holborn Hill for the *European Magazine*.
   NA, MPE 913 /1–3 [LRRO 1/1062/1–3]
   BL Maps, Crace Collection **XIV**, 15, 29
   WCA, T136 (35–6)
   Saunders 1969, 72 [plan from 1809 edn]

4 Outline plans for development; office of John Nash, 1810; superimposed on Richardson's survey of 1794; ns, nd, nwmk
   Canadian Centre for Architecture (CCA), DR 1984: 569.1

First phase

5 'Plan of … Marybone Park Farm', by Thomas Leverton and Thomas Chawner [March 1811]; engraved by James Basire; printed by Luke Hansard (13 June 1812)
   PP 1812 **XII** (1st Report), 429
   NA, MR 1108/1 [LRRO 1/1042/1]
   WCA, T136 (399)
   Saunders 1969, 89

6 Ditto, 'Reduced and drawn' by Peter Potter, Kentish Town; engraved by Neele, Strand, for John White Jr, *Proposed Improvements of the Western Part of London* [1814; 1815]
   BL Maps, Crace Collection **XIV**, 29

7 'A Plan of the New Park at Mary Le Bone with the Regent's Canal' [wmk1809; *c* 1810–11], 'Published for the Proprietor [Regent's Canal Co] by Edward Mogg, 14 Little Newport Street, Leicester Square, 23 March 1812, from a drawing made for a Committee of the Hon. House of Commons'. (Fig. 5.1)
   CCA, DR 1984, 569
   BL Maps, Crace Collection **XIV**, 31
   BL, King's Top Collection **XXVI**, 8a
   Crook, J M 2001 *London's Arcadia*. London: Sir John Soane's Museum, pl 1

8 'A Plan of the Proposed Regent's Canal through Marylebone Park' (13 June 1812)
   Engraved by James Basire; printed by Luke Hansard
   PP 1812 **XII** (1st Report), 470
   WCA, T136 (440)

9 'Plan of Marylebone Park, shewing the roads, fences, water and plantations' [as 'No. 1'] for
   PP 1812 **XII** (1st Report), 435; sd 'John Nash, Dover Street, March 1811'; not published
   NA, MPEE 58 [LRRO1/1060]
   Summerson, J 1977 'The beginnings of Regent's Park'. *Architect Hist* **20**, pl 17

10 'Marybone Park, Perspective View from the Double Circus in the Centre of the Park, by Mr Nash', and 'a view of the Park from the main circular Road': coloured Panoramas, drawn by (?) A C Pugin and G S Repton [1811], to illustrate 'No. 1' in *PP* 1812 **XII**, 435; not published
    NA, MR 1045 and 1047 [LRRO 1/1051 A and B]
    Summerson, J 1977 (*see* no. 9), pls 20–35

Second phase

11 Preliminary plan (?1811) for Marylebone Park; probably prepared March 1812 as an alternative 'No. 2' for *PP* 1812 **XII** (1st Report), 435; not published
CCA, DR 1984: 570.1

12 'Plan of the Intended Regent's Park, Marylebone' (wmk 1813); prepared in or about March 1812 as an alternative 'No. 2' for *PP* 1812 **XII** (1st Report), 435; published by Edward Mogg, 51 Charing Cross Road, 24 May 1813 (Fig. 5.2)
Crook, J M 2001, pl 2 [Nash's 2nd plan]

13 'Plan of the Improvements now executing in the Regent's Park, designed by J Nash Esq. Published with the Permission of the Commissioners of HM's Woods, Forests and Land Revenue, by W Faden, Geographer to HRH The Prince Regent, Charing Cross, 4 June 1813. D Wright, sculp Richard Street, Islington'
BL Maps 3620 (4)

14 'The Regent's Park, Late Mary le Bone Park with the Canal, Roads,
Plantations formed and forming'. 'Taken on the ground between the latter part of December last [1811] and 26 March [1812]'; 'the intended Canal is inserted from a Document laid before Parliament'.
BL Maps, Crace Collection **XIV**, 30
BL, King's Top, Crace Collection **XXVI**, 8b

Third phase

15 'Plan of an Estate belonging to the Crown called Marybone Park Farm, upon a Design for letting it out on Building Leases by John Nash' (29 August 1811); engraved by James Basire; printed by Luke Hansard (13 June 1812), *PP* 1812 **XII** (1st Report), 465
WCA 136 (398)
Summerson 1980, pl 32a

16 'Plan of the Intended Regent's Park Marylebone'. Published by Edward Mogg, 51 Charing Cross, 24 May 1813; Nash's 3rd, or definitive, plan engraved by Basire and printed by Hansard, by order of the Lords and Commons, 12–13 June 1812 (Fig. 5.3)
Crook, J M 2001, pl 3

17 Ditto. 'Reduced and drawn from the Original Copy by Peter Potter, Kentish Town' (nd); engraved by Neele, Strand
WCA. T136 (398), nd
BL Maps, Crace Collection **XIV**, 29 (3)

Fourth phase

18 Richard Horwood, Plan of London and Westminster (4th edn 1819)
BL Maps 33 e24

19 'Plan of the Crown's Mary-Bone Park Estate now called The Regent's Park; shewing the sites of the 26 Villas … intended to be built within the Area of the Park'. Engraved by James Basire; printed by Luke Hansard, *PP* 1823 **XI** (4th Report), Appendix 24, facing page 126 [Nash's 4th plan]
BL Maps 3620 (19) – (20)
Summerson 1980, pl 32b

20 Plans for Park Village, Regent's Park, 1823
NA, MPE 911 [LRRO 1/1059] and MR 1905 (1–4)
Summerson 1980, pl 37a

21 Ditto. By Philip Hardwick, 1829
NA, MPE 907 [LRRO1/1055]

Fifth phase

22 'Plan of the Regent's Park … as laid out by Mr Nash' (12 May 1826), showing eight Villas; engraved by James Basire; printed by Luke Hansard, *PP* 1826 **XIV** (5th Report), Appendix 22, facing page 136 [Nash's 5th plan] (Fig. 5.4)
BL, Crace Collection **XIV**, 32
Summerson 1980, pl 33a
Crook, J M 2001, pl 4

23 'Plan of the Regent's Park Estate belonging to His Majesty'. Published by Edward Mogg, 1828 (wmk1827)
Saunders 1969, 108

24 'Plan of the Regent's Park' (1828). With proposal in the Inner Circle for King's College, London
NA, MPE 912
Summerson 1980, 33b

Notes

1   For background, Anderson 1998; Crook, J M 1992, 77–96 and Crook, J M 1968 'The villas in Regent's Park', *Country Life* 4 and 11 July; Davis 1960 and 1973; Saunders 1969; Summerson 1949 and 1980

2   Pugh, R B 1960 *The Crown Estate* (London: Her Majesty's Stationery Office)

3   *Commons Journal* **XLII**, 310; **XLII**, 145, 559; **XLIV**, 126, 552; **XLV**, 120; **XLVI**, 97; **XLVII**, 141, 883, 1031; **XLVIII**, 267. See also Binney, J E D 1959 *British Public Finance and Administration, 1774–92* (Oxford: Clarendon Press).

4   1797, 1802, 1806, 1809: reprinted in *Parliamentary Papers* [hereafter *PP*] 1812 **XII**

5   Triennial Reports: *PP* 1812 **XII**; 1816 **XV**; 1819 **XIX**; 1823 **XI**; 1826 **XIV**; 1829 **XIV**; 1830 **XVI**

6   Fordyce – an Ayrshire farmer – was one of several Scottish administrators promoted under the aegis of that 'Caledonian Hercules', Viscount Melville: NA, WORK 16/40/3, 158 (27 June 1796); *Gentleman's Magazine* 1809 **II**, 658, 780.

7   For Glenbervie's departmental reform (NA, CRES 8/1 (1803); 8/2 (1805–6); 8/5 (1810); 8/7 (1812). For his life in Court circles, *Glenbervie Journals*, Sichel W (ed) 1910 (London: Constable) and Bickley, F (ed) 1928 *Diaries of Sylvester Douglas, Lord Glenbervie* (London and Boston: Constable & Co). John Thornborrow, senior clerk to Robinson and Glenbervie, is a good example of the new civil servant, apolitical and salaried – at £700pa (*Royal Kalendar*, 1814).

8   Despite ceremonial sinecurists; eg the Hereditary Lord Warden, or Ranger, of Whichwood Forest was the Duke of Marlborough, of Whittlewood Forest the Duke of Grafton, of Selsey Forest, Lord Ipswich (NA, CRES 8/2, 142, 146). In Windsor Forest the Duke of Gloucester was Head Keeper of Bagshot Walk, Princess Sophia of Gloucester of New Lodge Walk, and the Earl of Albemarle of Swinley Walk (NA, CRES 8/2, 421).

9   Thorne, 1986, 241–3

10   This was a post with a history of incompetence. Surveyors to the Land Revenue Office – John Marquand, Thomas Leverton, Thomas Chawner, Henry Rhodes – were departmental appointees, concerned only with mundane duties of house valuation, measurement and cartography; but architects to the Office of Woods – Charles Cole, John Soane, James Wyatt, John Nash, James Morgan – were Treasury appointees, subject to shifts of political patronage and responsible for potentially contentious works in royal parks. Soane resigned, Cole and Wyatt were dismissed, and Nash and Morgan were made redundant by the reorganisation of 1815.

11   Nash investigated the repair of a bridge at the head of the Serpentine near the middle of Rotten Row (NA, CRES 8/2, 505; 8/3, 11, 18, 35). Nash and Morgan were temporarily appointed on 23 October 1806 (NA, CRES 8/2, 515), and their position was confirmed on 23 March 1807 (NA, CRES 8/3, 147). See also *PP* 1813 V, 499, 501.

12   His duties were to strengthen the Deputy's hand in eliminating abuse of Forest land by yeomen and miners, while encouraging the growth of timber (NA, CRES 8/2, 386, 400, 405). Price's salary (1806–9) was £400pa. His post disappeared in the reorganisation of 1810 (NA, CRES 8/5, 19).

13   Price to Sir George Beaumont, 18 March 1798, quoted in Summerson 1980, 21. For Castle House, Mansbridge 1991, n 38; *see also* chs 1 and 3 in this volume.

14   Thomas Moore to James Corry, 24 October 1811, *in* Russell, J (ed) 1856 *Memoirs … of Thomas Moore* (London: Longman, Brown & Green) **VIII**, 97; Farington *Diary* (ed Garlick *et al* 1978–1984), XI, 3895 (18 March 1811)

15   Bolton 1927, 352

16   The idea is suggested in Summerson's introduction to Davis 1960, 14.

17   Ruch, J E 1968 'Regency Coade: a study of the Coade Record Books, 1813–21', *Architect Hist* **11**, 46 (n 20)

18   NA, CRES 8/10, 358 (23 May 1816)

19   Farington *Diary* (ed. Garlick *et al* 1978–1984) **XV**, 5134 (1–3 January 1818)

20   NA, CRES 2/1737 (1824–7)

21   *PP* 1812 **XII** (1st Report), Appendix 12B

22   As Nash put it, 'the main object of the Crown, I conceive to be, the Improvement of their own Estate, to augment and not diminish it, and not to sell any part of it; a magnificent Street for the Public would be the result, not the cause', *PP* 1816 **XV**, 122–4 (31 March 1813)

23   *PP* 1812 **XII** (1st Report), 517, 530–1, Surveyor General of Land Revenues, Appendix 3A (27 June 1793)

24   *PP* 1812 **XII** (4th Report), 718, 763–4, Surveyor General of Land Revenues, Appendix 3A (6 April 1809)

25   By George Richardson, engraved by William Faden (1794): NA, MR 324 [LRRO 1/479]; MR 1103 (2) [LRRO 1/1042 (2)]; BL Maps, Crace Collection **XIV**, no. 28. This work updated James Crew's survey of 1753 (NA, MPE 315).

26   £1,000 reward, open to 'every Architect of eminence in London' (*PP* 1812 **XII**, 517, 530–1 (27 June 1793)). Only John White submitted plans (*PP* 1812 **XII**, 355–6).

27   NA, MPE 918 (1)–(3) [LRRO 1/1062 (1)–(3)], *in* White 1814. See also BL Maps, Crace Collection **XIV**, nos. 15 and 29; Westminster City Archive, T.136 (35–6), engraved by I Bacon for the *European Magazine*. J White Jr later suggested that Marble Arch be moved to the entrance to the avenue in Regent's Park (*The Builder* **VIII** (1850), 490).

28   NA, CRES 2/1736

29   NA, MR 1108 (1) [LRRO 1/1042 (1)], in *PP* 1812 **XII** (1st Report), 429; drawn by Peter Potter, Kentish Town, March 1811

30   *PP* 1812 **XII** (1st Report), 419; Westminster City Archives T.136 (399)

31   NA, MPE 58 [LRRO 1/1000]; Summerson, J 1977 'The beginnings of Regent's Park', *Architect Hist* **20**, 56–62 and Summerson 1980, pl 22; 'Perspective Drawings … A View of the Parks from the main circular Road, and one of the inner Park from the

circular Road round the double Circus' (*PP* 1812 **XII** (1st Report), 435); transferred to the Public Record Office from Crown Estate Office in 1960 (NA, MR 1045 and 1047 [LRRO 1/1051 A and B])

32 'Mr Nash was directed, after an interview with the Chancellor … to reconsider the subject, and alter his Design, in the contemplation of fewer Buildings, and a greater extent of open ground … [since the Treasury] cannot approve of appropriating so much [land] to building', *PP* 1812 **XII** (1st Report), 357, 463, 467

33 *Parliamentary Debates* [hereafter *PD*] 1812 **XXIII**, col 72 (7 May): 'the people at large [would have] only one tenth part of the ground on which they were wont to take their recreation.' Building in Hyde Park had been successfully resisted by William Windham, on similar grounds.

34 Glenbervie's diary account of this incident was deleted in Sichel (ed) 1910, 152 (*see note 7*). This section of the diary (vol **X**) has since then been mislaid; the remaining volumes are now in the National Library of Scotland.

35 NA, MPE 902 (6) [LRRO 1/1047 (6)]; *PP* 1812 **XII** (1st Report), 465, 'reduced and drawn from the original by Peter Potter, Kentish Town'; Sichel (ed) 1910, 148, 152 (*see note 7*)

36 *Gentleman's Magazine* **158** (1812) **I**, 34 and **159** (1812) **II**, 370; *PD* 1812 **XXIII**, col 879 (2 July); for details of both barracks, *PP* 1812 **IX** (April), 103–5. The Duke of Portland, owner of the nearby Barrow Hill estate, also used his influence in Parliament to secure the relocation of the barracks. The Life Guards ended up in Albany Street and the Artillery in St John's Wood (Anderson 1998, 257–62).

37 *PD* 1812 **XXII**, col 1150–1 (1 May)

38 A related plan, 'taken on the ground' between December 1811 and March 1812, is in BL Maps, Crace Collection **XIV**, no. 30; published 1 April 1812 by I Luffman, 377 Strand.

39 Sold at Christie's, South Kensington, 28 April 2000, lot 245, watermark 1813; referred to as Plan 'No. 4' in *PP* 1812 **XII** (1st Report), Appendix 12, H, 467; engraved by William Faden 4 June 1813. An un-watermarked version survives in the Canadian Centre for Architecture, Montreal (D R 1984, 570), ex Weinreb; similarly, an un-watermarked version of plate 1, prepared by the Regent's Canal Co, combining elements from *PP* 1812 **XII**, 465 and 470.

40 MS note attached to map published 24 May 1813, private collection

41 Thorne 1986 **V**, 573

42 Thorne 1986 **V**, 574

43 Thorne 1986 **V**, 57–8. Downton Hall is only a few miles away from Payne Knight's Downton Castle, Herefordshire.

44 *PP* 1812 **XII** (1st Report), 465: 'Plan of an Estate … called Marybone Park Farm', J Basire, 13 June 1812, Museum of London Collection; 'Plan of the Intended Regent's Park, Marylebone', Edward Mogg, 24 May 1813, pl 3); 'reduced and drawn … by Peter Potter, Kentish Town' (Westminster City Archive T 136, 398, nd)

45 Elmes, J 1827, 11

46 NA, CRES 2/742

47 *PP* 1812 **XII** (1st Report), 435

48 *PP* 1812 **XII** (1st Report), 463

49 *PP* 1812 **XII** (1st Report), 433, Appendix 12G, 113

50 *PP* 1812 **XII** (1st Report), 434

51 *PP* 1812 **XII** (1st Report), 463, Appendix 12I, 116

52 Glenbervie told Col McMahan: 'Mr Nash … has estimated that the value of Marylebone Park will be increased to the amount of at least £15,000 a year if the [new] street shall be made. I believe much more, but as his estimate is to be sworn to he does right to keep within bounds' (Royal Archives, Windsor Castle 19999–20000, 31 August 1812). For a comparison of the relative costs of schemes by Nash and Leverton and Chawner, see BL. Maps, Crace Collection **XII**, no. 18.

53 'For the last five years the great interest which the public Funds have afforded has diverted the capital formerly employed in [building] speculation; [but] as the Funds rise in price the floating capital in the country will flow into other Channels, and should those of building not be dammed up, a part of that capital will most certainly find its way into Mary-le-Bone Park' (*PP* 1816 **XV** (2nd Report, 4 February 1816), 113–4, Appendix 20)

54 *PP* 1823 **XI**, 26, 127, Appendix 24, plan facing page 126 [ie Nash's 4th plan]; engraved by Basire, printed by Hansard 7 March 1823 (4th Report). Richard Horwood's *Plan of London and Westminster* (4th edn 1819: BL Maps, 33 e 24) gives only a speculative indication of Nash's plans.

55 *PP* 1826 **XIV** (5th Report), 11, 137, Appendix 2, 368; James Basire (12 May 1826), as in BL Maps; Crace Collection **XIV**, no. 32; published by E Mogg 1828

56 On either side of the Outer Circle, linked by an underground tunnel; larger buildings were to be placed on the northern side of the road, the land within the perimeter of the park being reserved for 'a highly ornamental Garden, with aviaries, huts, seats, and enclosures' (Zoological Society prospectus, 15 June 1827). Burton's plan (NA, MPE 906); see also Guillery, P 1993 *The Buildings of London Zoo* (London: RCHM).

57 *PP* 1816 **XV** (2nd Report), 17–18, 114; 1819 **XIX** (3rd Report), 10. For Mayor's circus, NA, CRES 2/748 (1812), 2/752 (1812–28), and 2/763 (1818), with plans MPE 1572. The project was rescued in 1819 by John Farquhar, an East India gunpowder contractor.

58 Soane exhibited a design in 1821 for 'a church proposed to be built in the Regent's Park' (RA, 1821, nos. 950, 964, 978).

59 NA, MPE 912 [LRRO. 1/1061]; Summerson 1980, pl 33b; Crook, J Mordaunt 1990 'The architectural image', *in* Thompson, F M L (ed) *The University of London and the World of Learning* (London: Hambledon), 5

60 Burton, D 1840 [report] *Gardeners' Magazine* **16**, 514–16 and BL Maps, 3620 (7): Burton's plan, 1840. For previous schemes, eg by Henry Laxton, R H Essex and Wyatt Papworth, *Civil Engin Architect J* 1837–8 **1**, 359, 559–62; **2** (1840), 173; and **10** (1847), 163

61 Summerson 1980, 125

62 *PP* 1826 **XIV** (5th Report), 137, plan; Summerson 1980, pl 33a

63 Bickley, F (ed) 1928 (*see note 7*) **II**, 199 (16 August 1816). Matters were hardly improved by the fact that Lady Glenbervie was Lady in Waiting to Caroline, Princess of Wales.

64 Farington *Diary* (ed Garlick et al 1978–1984) **XIII**, 4585–6 (18 September 1814)

65 Altick, R 1978 *The Shows of London* (Cambridge, Mass: Belknap Press), 141ff. The Colosseum – demolished in 1875 – was designed by Decimus Burton; its interior panoramas were painted by Thomas Horner and E T Parris. See also *Building News* **XV** (1868), 131–2, 153. The Diorama – which closed in 1848 – was designed by A C Pugin and James Morgan. There was a similar Cosmorama in Regent Street. See also Cook, O 1962 *Movement in Two Dimensions* (London: Hutchinson).

66 Elmes 1827, 23

67 *ibid*

68 NA, CRES 2/767 (1821–3)

69 Summerson 1980, 123

70 NA, CRES 2/781 (1826), and 2/1737 (1824–7), with plans MP1586. *See also* Fig. 9.17.

71 Summerson 1935, 197

72 NA, CRES 2/742 (1832); *PP* 1829 **XIV** (6th Report), 74. *See* Fig. 9.14.

73 Elmes 1827, 11

74 Elmes 1827, 28–9

75 Elmes 1827, 30, 46–7, 50

76 Elmes 1827, 29, 36–7

77 Elmes 1827, 29

78 Elmes 1827, 44

79 Elmes 1827, 88. The connecting tunnel still survives. For Burton's plan of the gardens, *c* 1819 – a geometrical pattern with irregular interstices, Longstaffe-Gowan, T 2001 *The London Town Garden, 1740–1840* (New Haven & London: Yale University Press), pl 239 (Westminster City Archives).

80 [C Ollier] 1823 *Literary Pocket Book* (London: Henry Colburn and Richard Bentley)

81 *The Brownings' Correspondence* **XII**, 317 (11 May 1846), and 323 (12 May 1846) (conflating two accounts of the same incident, written to Robert Browning and Mary Russell Mitford)

82 *PP* 1831 **IV**, 10: Select Committee on Windsor Castle and Buckingham Palace

83 Alexander Baring, *PD* 1829 ns **XXI**, col 1585 (25 May)

84 Sir Joseph Yorke, *PD* 1829 ns **XXI**, cols 1582, 1825, 1826

85 *PP* 1828 **IV** (1828 Report), 386. When it came to royal command, he admitted no choice but 'implicit obedience'; at Buckingham Palace he was 'totally independent of the Office of Works', except for 'measuring, moneying, and making out of the accounts', *PP* 1831 IV, 194, 204: Select Committee on Windsor Castle and Buckingham Palace.

86 John Calcraft, *PD* 1830 ns **XXII**, col 1164 (2 March). In 1829 Nash produced a public statement justifying his actions and explaining the difference between 'an earnest desire to complete the plans in progress … and a grasping desire for unfair emoluments' (Summerson 1991).

87 *Gentleman's Magazine* 1820 **I**, 34. Nash admitted that his Marble Arch was 'a plagiarism of the Arch of Constantine' (Crook and Port 1973, 294 n 7).

88 Crook, J Mordaunt 1972 *The Greek Revival: Neo-Classical Attitudes in British Architecture, 1760–1870* (London: John Murray), 121

89 Disraeli, B 1829 *The Young Duke* (London: Henry Colburn and Richard Bentley), ch ix, 28–9

90 Summerson 1935, 195; Summerson 1980, 124

91 Cockerell Diaries, quoted in Watkin 1974, 68

92 Pinhorn, M (ed) 2000, 8–9

93 NA, MPE. 911 [LRRO 1/1059]

94 NA, CRES 2/778, with plans MR 1905 (1–4); *Survey of London* **XXI** (1949), 653–8, pls 89–99; Tyack, G 1992, 24–5

95 Full plan by Philip Hardwick, 1829 (NA, MPE 907 [LRRO 1/1055])

96 Illustrated in Mansbridge 1991, 256–7

97 *Architect and Building News* 1950 (14 April), 387 –95 (plates and plans)

98 NA, CRES 2/778, MPE 911 and MR 1905/4. See Tyack 1992, 24

99 *Camden History Review* **VII** (1979), 10

100 Colvin 2008, 1054

101 For earlier residential details, Survey of London **XIX** (1938) and **XXI** (1949)

102 Anonymous 1939 *Royal Blue Book Court Guide* (London, Kelly's Directories), 512

103 *Architect and Building News* 1950 (14 April), 387

104 Tyack 1992, 24, pl 11

105 Cockerell Diaries, quoted in Watkin 1974, 68. On the whole, Cockerell disapproved of the picturesque in architecture (*Civil Engin Architect J* 1841 **4**, 121).

6

Reshaping the West End

GEOFFREY TYACK

Metropolitan improvements

John Nash's involvement with the replanning of London stemmed from the need to connect Regent's Park to Westminster and the City: the twin centres of Britain's government and commerce. Without such a link it would be impossible to attract affluent residents to the housing on which the Crown Estate depended in order to realise the improved value of its Marylebone estate. A new street could also ease London's traffic problems and, by removing poor-quality housing from the fringes of the fashionable West End, could promote better sanitation and help control, or at least marginalise, the growing urban underclass: a major preoccupation of improvers everywhere in the 19th century. A project of this magnitude – the building of a major thoroughfare a mile long through a built-up area – was beyond the capabilities of London's fragmented local authorities. Only central Government could raise the necessary funds and organise what was bound to be an exceptionally complex project, more ambitious in its scope than anything built since the Great Fire. Nash's genius was to plan the operation and to carry it through to completion, and for this achievement, Londoners and visitors to the capital still remain in his debt.[1]

By 1815 London was the largest city in Europe, and possibly the world, with a population of over 1.2 million, rising to some 1.6 million by 1830,[2] some of them ostentatiously rich, others industrious and upwardly mobile, many more desperately poor and potentially rebellious. Following the naval victory at Trafalgar, London saw a massive growth of overseas trade, especially with the colonies, evident in the building of vast new docks to the east of the City. There was also a substantial increase of housing, especially on the South Bank following the opening of Waterloo Bridge

in 1817 and Southwark Bridge in 1819. John Gwynn's *London and Westminster Improved* (1766) had already set out a comprehensive blueprint for street improvements in the central areas, including a new thoroughfare leading north-west from Charing Cross to the New (Marylebone) Road, London's first bypass. But it was left to John Fordyce, Surveyor of the Crown's Land Revenues, to revive that project in 1809 as part of his plans to develop the Marylebone estate, beyond the New Road, for housing. 'Distance', he argued, 'is best computed by time; and if the means could be found to lessen the time of going from Marybone [*sic*] to the Houses of Parliament, the value of the ground for building would be thereby proportionately increased'. He therefore proposed 'a great street', 70 feet wide (21.3m), leading from the Park and cutting across the main east-west routes – Oxford Street and Piccadilly – to the bottom of the Haymarket.[3] This was the germ of what was to become Regent Street.

Fordyce died in 1809, and in the following year the Land Revenue Office was merged with that of Woods and Forests, in which Nash had been one of the two Surveyors since 1806. When the 59-year-old Nash supplied his first plans for Regent's Park in 1811 he also prepared a plan for the street, which found favour with the Commissioners of the combined departments and was published in the following year.[4] Then, in 1813, he submitted two more plans, and the one reckoned the more profitable gained immediate approval from Parliament.[5] Compulsory purchases started in 1814, and the street was completed nine years later, in 1823. By then work had already started, under Nash's supervision, on the redevelopment of a block of Crown property next to Haymarket and Pall Mall, and in 1826 a second major phase of works began under a new Act of Parliament, designed to link Regent Street via Pall Mall to

Charing Cross. This project was also master-minded by Nash, and preoccupied him for the rest of his career.

Urban improvement schemes in 17th- and 18th-century Europe were usually the prerogative of absolute monarchs. Regent Street, likewise, has sometimes been seen as an act of monumental self-indulgence by a notoriously extravagant Prince. But, although the Regent gave the project his tacit support, his active involvement was minimal.[6] Under the New Street Act of 1813, responsibility was placed in the hands of Commissioners answerable to the officials in the Office of Woods and Forests and their political masters in the Treasury.[7] Spencer Perceval, Prime Minister from 1809, and Lord Liverpool, who succeeded him after Perceval's assassination in 1812, headed 'liberal Tory' administrations. These attempted, with more success than is often credited, to promote economic growth and to maintain public order at a time of war and social upheaval. It has recently been convincingly argued that they and their colleagues, especially William Huskisson, First Commissioner from 1814, saw the new street as a huge public works scheme, regularly employing 3,000 people over the 10 years of its construction and helping to stimulate the economy by encouraging the building industry and mitigating post-war unemployment.[8] They were certainly prepared to indulge in deficit spending, borrowing £600,000 in the early stages.[9] And, despite the almost inevitable cost overruns, which were equally inevitably seized upon by disaffected politicians and the press, the street brought both short- and long-term benefits: fostering a flourishing service and consumer economy; encouraging the development of London as a tourist and entertainment city; supplying, in due course, a steady source of income to the public purse; and creating or beautifying public spaces – Oxford Circus, Piccadilly Circus, Trafalgar Square, St James's Park – that have become some of the defining features of the capital for residents and visitors alike.

When Nash prepared his first plans he had no direct experience of large-scale urban improvement projects. But he was, both by temperament and by training, well suited to the challenge. He was a risk-taker, resilient, adaptable and financially astute. He had started his professional life as a speculative builder, and he maintained contact with the London building world during his years as a successful country-house architect. Both in his first major building, in Bloomsbury Square, and in his own house in Dover Street, he had glamourised conventional London street architecture with his use of stucco enrichments; echoes of both can be found in his later buildings. His involvement with the Highgate Archway in 1812–13 and with the Regent's Canal, carried out concurrently with the street and park, gave him practical experience of financing large civil-engineering projects. When the new street was nearing completion, Nash became involved in the layout and design of the Regent's Park terraces and the Crown land to the east of the Park: the Park Village and the streets and squares of artisan housing to the south of the Canal basin (*see* chapter 5). And his early exposure to the theory and practice of the picturesque enabled him to turn the problems that inevitably attended the building of a new street through a built-up area into aesthetic opportunities.

Several provincial towns had carried out relatively small-scale improvement schemes during the 18th century,[10] but, when plans for Regent Street and Regent's Park were first sought in October 1810, would-be architects were exhorted to pay special attention to recent developments in Edinburgh and Bath. In Bath, the route from Queen Square to the Circus and Royal Crescent (finished in 1775), with its constantly changing vistas, offered an object lesson in picturesque urbanism. The Pulteney estate, under construction from 1788 to the 1820s, showed how a varied series of palace-like facades could be successfully orchestrated to impressive effect, and Bath Street (1791) gave an indication of how a colonnaded shopping street could be cut through the centre of a crowded city.[11] In Edinburgh, arguably the most spectacular city in the British Isles, the New Town had been laid out on classical lines after 1767, and a further scheme of improvements, including the building of the South Bridge, was launched in 1785–6; large-scale building resumed after 1815, giving tangible expression to the ideal of the Scottish capital as the 'Athens of the North'.[12] In Dublin, the second largest city in the British Isles, the aptly named Wide Streets Commission extended Sackville Street (now O'Connell Street) to the River Liffey, starting in 1785, followed by the construction of new streets through the built-up area south of the river, one of them – D'Olier Street – lined with terraces incorporating shops.[13] And in 1814 and 1815 Nash went to Paris, where presumably he saw the arcaded and shop-lined Rue des Colonnes (begun in 1797), and the Rue de Rivoli (1802),[14] along with monumental projects such as the unfinished church of the Madeleine, closing the formal vista north from the Place de la Concorde; the Arc du Carrousel in front of the Tuileries Palace; and the Arc de Triomphe, also unfinished, at the end of the Champs-Elysée. These showed how architecture could be used both to beautify a modern metropolis and to celebrate national prestige.

By July 1811, when Nash revealed his first plan, it had already been decided to start the new street at Carlton House, the Prince Regent's London residence. From here it would run north-west to Portland Place, London's widest street, developed in 1776–90 on land belonging to the Dukes of Portland. It led to the Park, where nebulous proposals had been aired for a *guinguette* or pavilion for the Prince.[15] A straight line drawn from Carlton House to the southern end of Portland Place would have led through the western fringe of Soho. This was approximately the line adopted in a plan attributed to James Wyatt, which was submitted to the Commissioners at the same time as Nash's and was published by the Duke of Portland's surveyor John White after Wyatt's death in 1813.[16] Nash's route took a more westerly route along the line of Swallow Street, a narrow north-south thoroughfare bordering the fashionable district of Bond Street, Savile Row and Hanover Square. His plan promised to establish a clear 'line of separation', as he called it, between the 'first classes of society' who lived to the west and the 'inferior classes' to the east. '[My] purpose', as he later said, 'was that the new street should cross the Eastern entrance to all the streets occupied by the higher classes, and to leave out to the East all those bad streets, and, as a sailor would express himself, to hug all the avenues that went to good streets'.[17] Nash's route helped establish a system of informal 'zoning' which may or may not have been part of a wider agenda of social control;[18] more immediately, it ensured that the residents of the affluent areas of the West End would not have to enter poorer areas in order to get to the shops, a vital factor in ensuring the street's commercial success.

Nash's first plan was for a straight street double the width of Bond Street, with a slight change of direction north of Piccadilly (Fig 6.1). Like the monumental main thoroughfares of the Roman Imperial cities that it was clearly intended to evoke, it would be lined with colonnades for most of its length. And, as in the cities of the ancient world and of Baroque Europe, there would be impressive public spaces: two Circuses where the street crossed Piccadilly and Oxford Street, and two squares, one in front of Carlton House and the other to the north-west of Piccadilly Circus, enclosing a large but unspecified public building. But the Commissioners balked at the expense, and Nash returned to the drawing board. The first of his two revised schemes (of which no visual record survives) featured 'a square, formed by the North side of Piccadilly on one side and the South side of Jermyn-street on the other, leaving St James church [Piccadilly] on the west side of the square'. In the second, definitive, scheme, approved by the Treasury in March 1813, the square was abandoned, as were most of the colonnades originally envisaged, and the portion to the north of Piccadilly Circus turned into 'a bending street, resembling … the High Street in Oxford' (Fig 6.2) – a city Nash seems to have known well.[19] These changes were dictated by financial considerations. By routing the street through decrepit Crown property to the north and south of Piccadilly – 'old ruinous Houses laid out in narrow streets, the greater part not worth repair',[20] as Nash put it – the potential cost of compulsory purchase was drastically reduced. Further savings came at the northern end, where Nash was forced to change the route he had originally proposed in order to avoid the exorbitant cost of buying properties on the eastern side of Cavendish Square, one of the showpieces of the Portland estate. 'The sinuous path of Regent Street', in the words of one recent writer, 'was not Hogarth's Line of Beauty but the developer's line of maximum profit',[21] and in the building of Regent Street, Nash showed himself to be an exceptionally astute developer. But he turned financial necessity to visual advantage, and the studied informality of alignment gave the street its special character.

Having worked out the line of the street, Nash's tasks were those of any estate developer: purchasing property; estimating compensation for owners and occupiers of premises to be destroyed; organising the construction of the sewers and paving – an essential part of any street improvement scheme; letting the ground to builders; and exercising a general supervision over the choice of elevations and the construction of the buildings. Regent Street was a street of facades, such visual unity as there was coming from the near-uniform height of four

PLAN OF A NEW STREET FROM CHARING CROSS TO PORTLAND PLACE.

PLAN OF A Street Proposed FROM CHARING CROSS TO PORTLAND PLACE DESIGNED BY I. NASH ESQ.

Published With permission of the Commissioners of his Majesty's Woods, Forests & Land Revenue.

By W. Faden, Geographer to his Majesty & to H.R.H. the Prince Regent. CHARING CROSS, MAY 11th 1814.

N.B. The Parts coloured Blue denote the Crown Property.

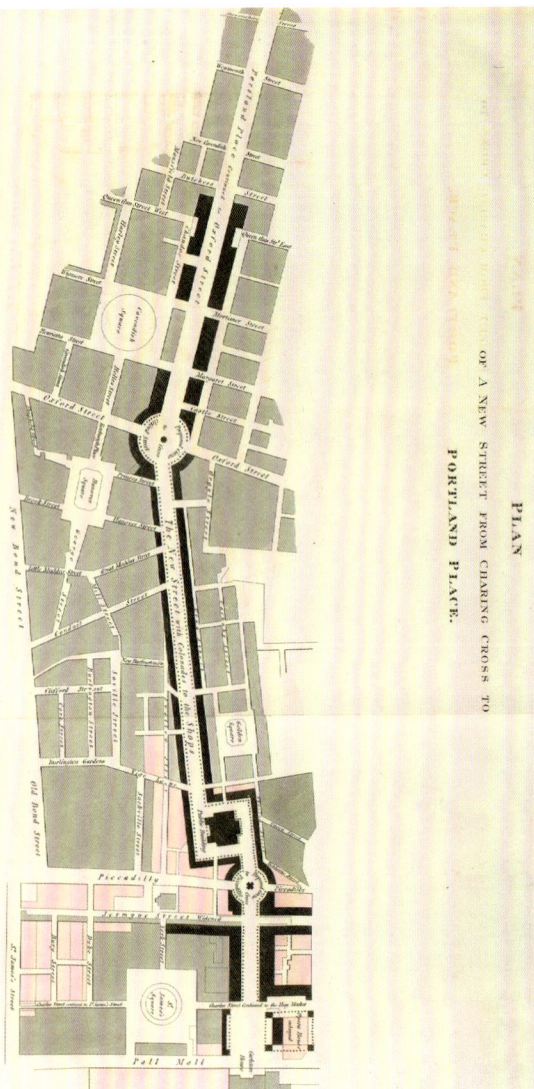

Fig 6.1 (left above)
Nash's first plan for the new street, 1811
(The Bodleian Libraries, University of Oxford, O.Pp.Eng.1812/XII, f. 447).

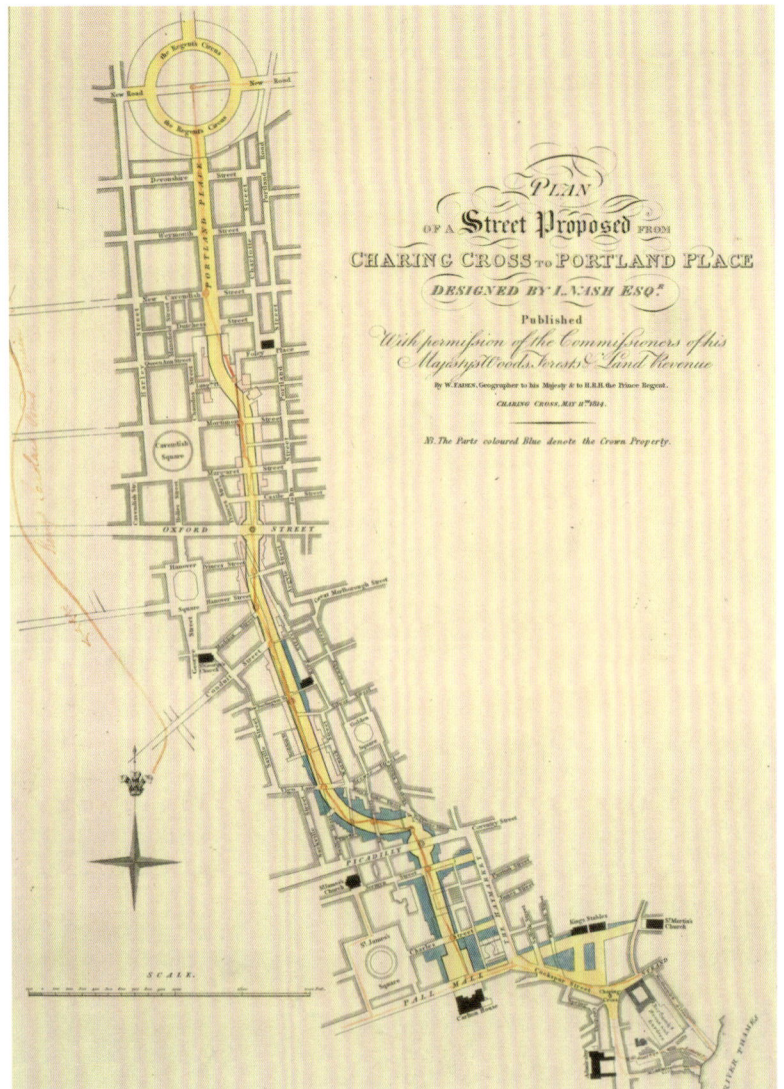

Fig 6.2 (right above)
The second, definitive plan for 'a Street Proposed from Charing Cross to Portland Place, leading to the Crown Estate in Marylebone Park' (Crown property shown in blue), engraved 1813 (© The British Library Board, Crace Collection XII, 16).

storeys, usually with one cornice line above the shop fronts and another below the attic storey, and from the consistent use of stucco (Parker's Roman cement, painted in the colour of Bath stone) to hide the brick construction. Nash had been a devotee of stucco ever since his first building speculation in Bloomsbury Square more than 30 years before; its use was now dictated by a widespread reaction against the alleged dullness of the streets of 18th-century London, and by the high cost of stone. Nash told a Commons Select Committee in 1828 that, with some exceptions,[22] he designed the facades himself. But, he added insouciantly, '[If] a person presents a design for the elevation of a building, and I do not see a material defect, it would be invidious of me to find fault with it; I return it as approved by me.'[23] This inevitably meant that the finer nuances of design were lost

in the eagerness to finish the project quickly so that the shopkeepers could make a profit and the Government reap a return on the ever-increasing costs: something for which Nash was never forgiven by the connoisseurs.

The first part of the project to be constructed was Park Crescent, an elegant semicircle linking Regent's Park to Portland Place; it was begun in 1812, but its builder went bankrupt and it was not completed until 1818–22.[24] Nothing happened in the main part of the street until after the Battle of Waterloo, but then there was a credit-fuelled building boom as the pent-up demand of the war years was finally released, and the street was completed in what seems in retrospect to be a remarkably short time.[25] Much depended on Nash's builders, above all James Burton – one of London's largest building contractors, responsible for the rapidly expanding Bedford and Foundling estates in Bloomsbury[26] – and Samuel Baxter of Carmarthen Street, Tottenham Court Road. Burton took the important site facing Carlton House (Waterloo Place), where work started in 1815, and he went on to build the southern part of Lower Regent Street (Fig 6.3). Baxter meanwhile undertook to build Oxford Circus and the blocks to the north and south. Nash risked both his reputation and his money by taking personal responsibility in 1818 for the Quadrant, the most complex undertaking. He advanced £60,000 – the equivalent perhaps of about £2.5 million today – arranged for the manufacture of the iron columns supporting the Bath stone entablature of the colonnades, and supplied bricks made out of earth from the digging of the Regent's Canal basin.[27] With its construction ensured, Burton could safely contract for the main sites between it and Oxford Circus, finally ensuring the completion of the street as far as Carlton House, albeit at five times Nash's original estimate: chiefly the result of excessive awards by arbitrators and juries for 'goodwill' (loss of business).[28]

The new street became one of the main sights of London as soon as the last coats of stucco were dry. Charles Ollier exclaimed in 1842:

Who that remembers the narrow, dingy thorough-fare called Swallow Street, with its adjacent poverty-stricken alleys, can forbear to rejoice on seeing the wide, noble, and decorated vista of costly shops and other buildings which, in the improvement of London, has risen on the site? … In all London, a finer walk or drive cannot be found than is afforded by Regent Street.[29]

Visitors were primarily attracted by the shops, but there were also some public and semi-public buildings: three churches, one of them (All Souls, Langham Place) designed by Nash himself;[30] a concert hall (the Argyll Rooms),[31] also designed by Nash; hotels and clubhouses; offices, such as the County Fire Office, which terminated the view north from Carlton House;[32] and private houses, of which the most ostentatious was Nash's own at No. 14, part of a larger building, the other half of which (No. 16) was occupied by his cousin and business associate John Edwards.[33] The main shops – milliners, hatters, linen drapers, wine merchants, sellers of prints and musical instruments, etc – were in the central portion between Piccadilly Circus and Oxford Circus, their upstairs floors laid out as 'chambers' or flats, suitable for letting as furnished lodgings; one of the early short-term residents of the Quadrant was the composer Rossini, who lodged there with his wife in 1823–4. The wide pavements meanwhile gave ample space for window-gazers and *flâneurs*, the eye-catching architecture providing an ideal

Fig 6.3
Lower Regent Street under construction, by J C Nattes c 1815
(© City of London, London Metropolitan Archives). The southern part of the street was built over the site of St James's Market, laid out in 1663–6 and relocated in 1817–18 to a new site west of Haymarket.

105

backdrop to the constantly changing street life celebrated by writers and artists from the 1820s onwards.

Regent Street was always intended to be the first part of a route that would terminate at Charing Cross. The second part of the scheme involved widening the eastern end of Pall Mall, removing in the process 'filthy alleys inhabited by abandoned characters',[34] and creating a new open space (Trafalgar Square) on the site of the Royal Mews (stables) at the northern end of Whitehall, with rebuilt barracks to the north to deter or quell potential unrest (Fig 6.4).[35] Work began in 1816 on long-matured plans for redeveloping a block of Crown property to the east of Lower Regent Street, including the Royal Opera House, one of the main centres of London's musical and social life.[36] Nash went on to rebuild the Haymarket Theatre and, following the termination of leases in 1820, to redevelop a run-down pocket of Crown land on land originally taken by John Edwards in and around

Suffolk Street, behind the theatre.[37] Then, in 1822, the King, as he had now become, decided to abandon Carlton House – recently extended and beautified by Nash – in favour of what was to become Buckingham Palace. After the demolition of Carlton House in 1825 Nash extended Waterloo Place southwards over the site, with new clubhouses on either side, one of which (the United Service Club) he designed himself,[38] and two giant blocks of housing (Carlton House Terrace) at the southern end, begun in 1827.[39] From here there were views over St James's Park, which Nash went on to transform in the picturesque, Reptonian manner he had employed to such good effect in Regent's Park (Fig 6.5).[40]

Under plans formed in 1819, followed by legislation in 1826, Nash now turned to the creation of Pall Mall East and Trafalgar Square: a project that was achieved within his original estimate of just over £1m.[41] In 1824, the royal stables were moved to their present premises –

Fig 6.4
Plan showing the second stage of Nash's improvements, from Lower Regent Street to the Strand (redrawn by EH from OS 8in to the mile 1986, with amendments from earlier OS editions; © Crown Copyright and database right 2012. All rights reserved. Ordnance Survey Licence number 100024900).

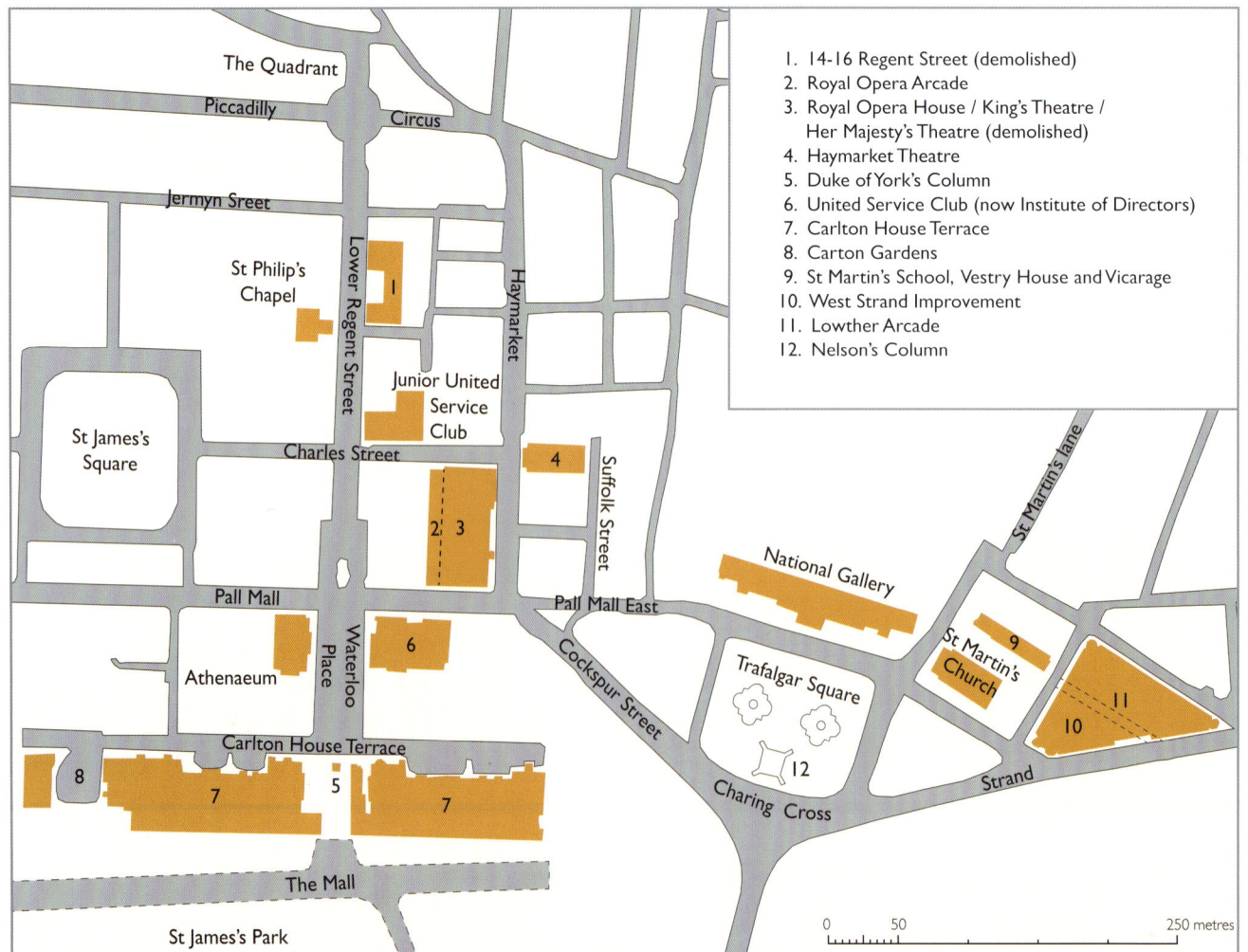

1. 14-16 Regent Street (demolished)
2. Royal Opera Arcade
3. Royal Opera House / King's Theatre / Her Majesty's Theatre (demolished)
4. Haymarket Theatre
5. Duke of York's Column
6. United Service Club (now Institute of Directors)
7. Carlton House Terrace
8. Carton Gardens
9. St Martin's School, Vestry House and Vicarage
10. West Strand Improvement
11. Lowther Arcade
12. Nelson's Column

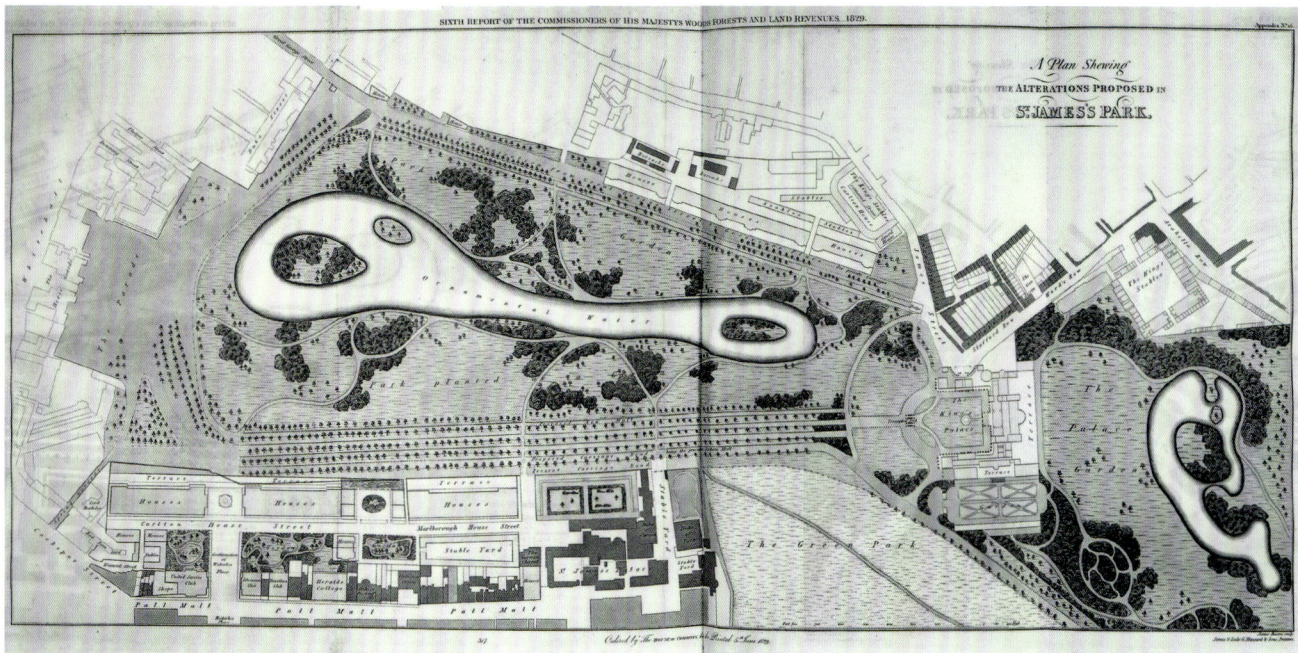

SIXTH REPORT OF THE COMMISSIONERS OF HIS MAJESTYS WOODS FORESTS AND LAND REVENUES. 1829.

A Plan Shewing
THE ALTERATIONS PROPOSED IN
ST JAMES'S PARK.

designed by Nash – next to Buckingham Palace (*see* Fig S.3),[42] making it possible to open a route from Regent Street to the Strand, with traffic for Whitehall and Westminster disgorging from a widened Cockspur Street into the southern end of the new square. Nash thought that this was 'the finest site in London for a public building',[43] and he prepared designs both for a Royal Academy in the middle of the open space, where Nelson's Column now stands, and for a new National Gallery on the north side, neither of which were executed.[44] His plans for the layout of the square were not implemented either, and a proposed street leading north to the British Museum was also shelved, later falling victim to a new spirit of public parsimony when the Whigs came to power after the King's death in 1830.[45] Yet by creating the square, presided over by James Gibbs's church of St Martin-in-the-Fields, he helped to redefine the visual character of what is seen by many people as the centre of the metropolis.

Nash's plan for the 'Proposed Improvements at Charing Cross, St Martin's Lane, and the Entrance to the Strand' (1826) showed a new arrangement of streets to the north and east of St Martin's church. To the north, he designed a new vicarage, Vestry Hall and *palazzo*-fronted Parish School in 1827–30, on land conveyed to the church authorities by Commissioners of Woods and Forests. And in 1830–2 he carried out the 'West Strand Improvement' as a joint venture with the builder William Herbert of

Farm Street, Mayfair: a new layout of the streets replacing an area of 'wretched courts and alleys, dens of infamy and haunts of thieves' to the east of the church.[46] Here Nash designed a triangular block of shops and chambers bisected by the Lowther Arcade, famous for its toyshops.[47] The arcade, alas, has gone, but Nash's stuccoed facades and 'pepperpot' towers at the corners survive, cheering commuters as they emerge from Charing Cross station. They represent Nash's swansong as an urban designer.

An architectural promenade

Although more of Nash's London survives than is generally realised, his improvements can nowadays be fully appreciated only through pictures.[48] Here, the historian is fortunate, because few streets in any city have been more thoroughly recorded than Regent Street, first by topographical artists and later by photographers, some of whom had their premises there.[49] Nash's approach to architecture was fundamentally pictorial, and his route was designed to be experienced episodically, as a series of constantly changing spectacles enhanced by carefully placed visual incidents, as in a landscape garden or along the Grand Canal in Venice. The illustrations that take up most of the remaining space of this chapter have been chosen to recapture that effect. The route taken is from north to south, starting at Park Crescent and terminating in the Strand.

Fig 6.5
St James's Park,
Buckingham Palace and
surroundings as landscaped
by Nash; north is at
the bottom
(The Bodleian Libraries,
University of Oxford, O.Pp.
Eng.1829/XIV, btw 162–3).

Fig 6.7 (above)
Houses on the west side of Park Square (1823–4),
looking south to Park Crescent. Park Square and Park
Crescent mark the transition between Regent's Park
and the new street. Beyond Park Crescent is Portland Place,
the residential thoroughfare developed by the Adam
brothers in 1776–90
(DP104286).

Fig 6.6 (above)
Park Crescent and the New Road with the new
Marylebone parish church in the distance: aquatint by
an unknown artist published by Rudolph Ackermann
1822 (© Trustees of the British Museum, Crace
Collection **XXX**, 136). Nash originally conceived the
Crescent as half of a giant Circus bisected by the New
Road (Marylebone Road), with a church, replacing the
old parish church of St Marylebone, in the middle.
But the northern half was never built, and the church
(by Thomas Hardwick, 1813–17), was placed farther
to the west.

Fig 6.8 (below)
Langham House from the south, watercolour by
Thomas Shepherd (© Trustees of the British Museum,
Crace Collection **XXIX**, 51). The house, at the southern
end of Portland Place, was built to Nash's designs in
1813–15 on property he had astutely purchased from
one of his creditors, Lord Foley – his client at Witley
Court (Worcestershire) – in order to secure the line of
the new street. It was replaced by the Langham Hotel
in 1863.

Fig 6.9 (above)
Langham Place looking south, lithograph by William Stirling
c 1830 (© Trustees of the British Museum,
Crace Collection **XXIX**, 48). The house on the left stood on the
site of the BBC's Broadcasting House. Next to it is All Souls
Church (1822–4), the only Nash building to have
survived the comprehensive rebuilding of the main part
of Regent Street in the 20th century. It is entered through an
Ionic rotunda surmounted by candle-snuffer spire, which
terminates the vista north from Oxford Circus; C R Cockerell
thought the exterior 'too homely … reminding one of a village
church & not such as fits a metropolis' (Watkin 1974, 68).
Beyond the church in Fig 6.9 is the London Carriage Repository
and on the extreme right the grounds of Langham House.

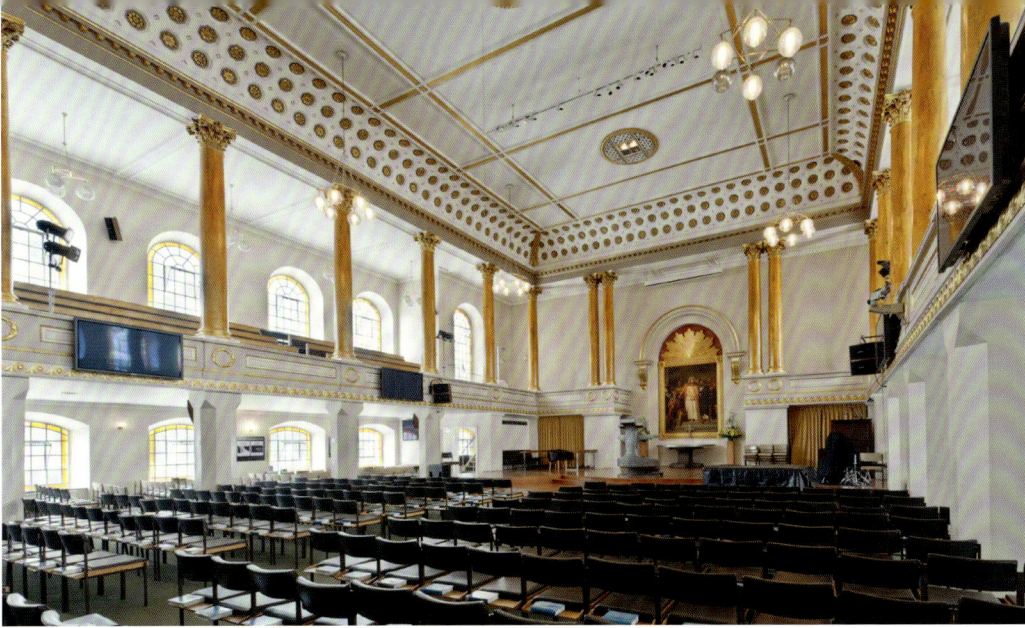

Fig 6.10 (above)
The interior of All Souls Church: a spacious, galleried preaching-box with Corinthian columns supporting the coved ceiling. The altarpiece ('Ecce Homo') was painted by Richard Westall and presented by the King in 1823 (DP104367).

Fig 6.11 (right)
The north-eastern segment of Oxford Circus, photograph by Bedford Lemere c 1910 (B l20981_022). Elmes (Metropolitan Improvements, 98) drew attention to the 'broad showy shop-windows … wherein goods and manufactured articles of the most splendid description … may be displayed to the greatest advantage'. They were made possible by recent advances in iron construction.

Fig 6.12 (left)
*The northern part of Regent Street, drawing by William Westall, brother of Richard Westall, 1825 (© Trustees of the British Museum, Crace Collection **XXIX**, 35). The domed structure on the right is the entrance to the Argyll Rooms, home of the Harmonic Institution (ancestor of the Royal Philharmonic Society). They were rebuilt by Nash after the existing building had collapsed in 1819; in the concert hall upstairs, reached by a top-lit staircase, Carl Maria von Weber and the young Felix Mendelssohn conducted concerts, and Beethoven's ninth symphony received its first British performance. Next to it is the Society's music shop, entered through a colonnade of 'terms' (posts surmounted by heads), sculpted in artificial stone by James Bubb, one of Nash's regular collaborators. The Rooms – two first-floor concert rooms, an assembly room and an ante-room, reached by a curved top-lit staircase – fell victim to fire in 1830 and were replaced by a more conventional block of shops and chambers. All Souls Church can be seen in the distance.*

Fig 6.13 (left)
The view south from Oxford Circus, with the Argyll Rooms in the left foreground and the portico of the Hanover Chapel on the extreme right, from Sheppard and Elmes, Metropolitan Improvements, 1827 (© Trustees of the British Museum, Crace Collection *XXIX*, 37). Here the street veered south-east towards the Quadrant and Piccadilly Circus.

Fig 6.14 (above)
The central section of Regent Street looking south, with the Hanover Chapel (1823–5) – C R Cockerell's first major building – on the right and the Quadrant in the distance, from T Shotter Boys, Original Views of London, 1842 (© Trustees of the British Museum, Crace Collection *XXIX*, 38).

Fig 6.15 (above)
The central section of the street was dominated by a sequence of large and stylistically varied palace-like façades. The eclectic façade of Nos 224–240 on the east side, shown here in a photograph by Bedford Lemere c 1910 (B l20981_048), is a cross between the idiosyncratic architecture of Sir John Soane – who designed Nos 156–70, a little to the south, himself – and the later experiments of 'Greek' Thompson in Glasgow.

Fig 6.16 (left)
The long frontage of Nos 171–195, on the west side of the street, was articulated by giant Corinthian pilasters, with the shop-fronts squeezed in between. It is shown here in a drawing of 1829 by George Scharf. The Hanover Chapel can be seen in the distance. (© The British Library Board, Add.36489A, f 79).

Fig 6.18 (above)
Nos 132–154, on the eastern side of the street, was a carefully detailed neo-Palladian composition with a Corinthian temple-front in the centre and projecting end pavilions. The tall building to the right is a later intrusion in this photograph of c 1900 (BB 71_04053).

Fig 6.17 (above)
The upper floors of Nos 153–165, also on the western side of the street had paired pilasters enclosing round-headed windows with scallop-shell decoration in the tympana – a favourite Nash motif (B l20981_015). By the time Bedford Lemere took this photograph the original shop-fronts had been replaced by larger ones with plate-glass windows.

Fig 6.19 (left)
A view of the central section of the street, looking north from the Quadrant c 1870 (BB 83_01009a). The rotunda in the left foreground echoes that of the Argyll Rooms farther north.

111

Fig 6.20 (right)
The Quadrant looking north, etching by G H Jones c 1830 (© Trustees of the British Museum, Crace Collection X, 149). In the foreground is the County Fire Office, an accomplished Renaissance palazzo designed by Robert Abraham, with modifications imposed by Nash; it was based on the Queen's Gallery at Somerset House (1662–3: demolished 1776), once thought to be by Inigo Jones, but now generally attributed to John Webb.

Fig 6.21 (left)
The Doric columns of the Quadrant were of iron coated in stucco, and supported a terrace from which visitors, and the residents of the upper floors, could look down on the street below, as shown in this watercolour of 1825 by George Scharf (© Trustees of the British Museum, Scharf, Book 4).

Fig 6.22 (above)
The County Fire Office and the Quadrant after the removal of the colonnades, photograph by Bedford Lemere c 1910 (B l20981_037). The colonnades were removed in 1848 following complaints by the tenants of the shops that they darkened their windows and encouraged loitering prostitutes and social deviants.

Fig 6.23 (above)
The north-west segment of Piccadilly Circus c 1900 (BB 65_03118). The architecture is plainer
than that of Oxford Circus, with pilaster-strips to the upper floors.

Fig 6.24 (above)
Lower Regent Street looking south from Piccadilly Circus to
Carlton House, engraving by William Westall c 1820–5
(© Trustees of the British Museum, Adams (London) 147.38).
The portico and Grecian rotunda halfway down on the right
belong to St Philip's chapel, designed in 1819–20 by George
Repton, whose brother was the first incumbent.

Fig 6.25 (above)
The east side of Lower Regent Street, looking south to Waterloo
Place and the Duke of York's Column; late 19th-century
photograph (CC 97_01525). In the left foreground are Nos 14–16,
built by Nash in 1819–22 at a cost of £30,000. Closer in character
to a Parisian hôtel particulier than a London town house, the
central block was set back from the street, with wings projecting
forward. Beyond is Decimus Burton's Club Chambers.

Fig 6.26 (above)
The Gallery at No. 14 Regent Street, from Britten and
Pugin, Public Buildings of London. Nash sent Richard
Evans, one of Sir Thomas Lawrence's assistants, to Rome
in 1821 to copy Raphael's paintings in the Vatican loggia.
There were also casts after the antique and a set of
specially commissioned architectural models by the
Parisian model-maker Jean-Pierre Fouquet. The room
was taken down and re-erected at East Cowes Castle in
1834, but was demolished along with the rest of the castle
in 1960.

Fig 6.27
Nos 17–25, on the western
side of Lower Regent Street,
photograph by Bedford
Lemere c 1910
(B l20981_004).
The pilasters are of the
'Ammonite' order, first used
by George Dance at the
Shakespeare Gallery
around the corner in Pall
Mall (1782).

Fig 6.28
Lower Regent Street looking
north from Charles Street,
Piccadilly Circus,
photograph by W H Fox
Talbot c 1845 (BB
67_08242). Robert Smirke's
Junior United Service Club
(1817–19: remodelled by
Burton in 1830) is on the
right and the County Fire
Office in the distance.
The club, intended for
officers discharged from the
armed forces, was the first
of a new generation of
gentlemen's clubs that gave
a distinctive character to the
southern end of Regent
Street and Pall Mall.

Fig 6.29 (above)

The eastern part of (above) Charles Street as seen from Lower Regent Street, watercolour by an unknown artist 1822 (© Trustees of the British Museum, Crace Collection **XI**, 103). By extending the street to the Haymarket Nash managed to contrive a cross-vista to the portico of the new Haymarket Theatre, which he also designed. To its right is the northern flank of the Royal Opera House, and the (Junior) United Service Club is on the left.

Fig 6.30 (below)

Waterloo Place looking north, engraving by A C Pugin 1817 (© Trustees of the British Museum, Crace Collection **XI**, 79). A French-inspired Grande Place, Waterloo Place was compared by Elmes (Metropolitan Improvements, 121) to 'a fine estuary opening from the sea, and forming the mouth of a great river'. Its receding planes framed the entrance to Lower Regent Street, with the County Fire Office in the distance.

Fig 6.31 (above)

When Carlton House was demolished Waterloo Place was extended south, flanked by two club-houses: Decimus Burton's Athenaeum, and Nash's United Service Club (1826–8, now the Institute of Directors), shown here (DP104307). Nash's Renaissance-inspired clubhouse was built after Smirke's original club in Lower Regent Street had become too small for its membership; the exterior was altered and the frieze added by Burton in 1858–9. To the right is the Duke of York's Column, built in 1831–4 to the designs of Benjamin Dean Wyatt: in many ways a more satisfactory termination to the street than Carlton House had ever been. Nash first proposed a domed rotunda on the site, supported by Corinthian columns from the portico of Carlton House, but was overruled by the Commissioners of Woods and Forests; the columns went instead to the National Gallery.

Fig 6.32 (below)

The staircase of the United Service Club, photograph by Bedford Lemere 1913 (B l22354). Nash may have originally intended to re-use Henry Holland's oval-shaped staircase from Carlton House, but this plan was abandoned and the staircase now consists of a single flight leading to two arms, which ascend to the gallery, giving access to the library overlooking the garden. George IV's younger brother, Frederick, the 'grand old Duke of York', occupies the niche at the top of the first flight.

Fig 6.33 (below)
The eastern block of Carlton House Terrace, late 19th-century photograph (DD 97_00204).
The Terrace (1827–33) is the grandest of all Nash's residential developments, and soon
attracted wealthy residents, some of whom, like the Earl of Caledon (at No. 5) had employed
Nash elsewhere. The two blocks of 'Dwelling-houses of the First Class' are separated by steps
leading from Waterloo Place to the Mall, still unencumbered by traffic when this view was taken.
The houses are entered from the north, but the Parisian-inspired main façades were designed to
look south over St James's Park; the capitals of the Corinthian columns (which have iron cores)
were copied from those inside the Pantheon in Rome, drawn by the young James Pennethorne on
his extended study-tour to Italy. The main rooms look out onto a terrace, beneath which are
vaults with squat Greek Doric half-columns (also of iron) fronting the Mall.

Fig 6.34 (above)
The fireplace of one of the upstairs rooms in No. 13 Carlton
House Terrace, photographed in 1971 (BB 71_06490).
The internal design of the houses in Carlton House Terrace
was left to their lessees and their architects, who included
Nash himself; his surviving interiors contain heavy
neoclassical chimneypieces and richly plastered ceilings,
characteristic of his late domestic work, and, in some cases,
staircases and corridors with glazed domes on pendentives:
a motif he had employed in his first town houses in
Bloomsbury Square 50 years before.

Fig 6.35 (below)
The lake in St James's Park looking east to the Horse Guards, with Carlton House Terrace,
Nelson's Column and the spire of St Martin-in-the-Fields to the left, from T Shotter Boys,
Original Views of London, 1842 (© City of London, London Metropolitan Archives).
In Nash's design, which drew on discarded plans by Capability Brown, the formal rectangular
'canal', created in the late 17th century, became a serpentine lake with gently curving banks,
the surrounding 'swampy meadow' giving way to lawns studded with clumps of trees and
shrubs and crossed by meandering paths. Nash also laid out the private garden of Buckingham
Palace in a similar manner.

Fig 6.36 (left)
A late 19th-century view looking east from Waterloo Place along Pall Mall towards the National Gallery (DD 87_00016). On the left of the street, rising above the houses of Waterloo Place, is Her Majesty's Theatre, built in 1891 on the site of Nash and Repton's Royal Opera House; the site is now occupied by New Zealand House. On the right is the entrance to the United Service Club.

Fig 6.37 (left)
The Opera House, Haymarket, from Pall Mall East, late 19th-century photograph (DD 97_00256). The Royal Opera House was founded by Sir John Vanbrugh in 1704–5 and later became one of Europe's main operatic venues. Having been rebuilt in 1782 and again, following a fire, in 1789, it was remodelled externally by Nash and George Repton in 1816–18, with Parisian-inspired colonnaded frontages, lit by gas, to Pall Mall, Haymarket and Charles Street. A terracotta relief, by Bubb, of the Progress of Music 'to its ultimate perfection in the present day' adorned the Haymarket façade.

Fig 6.38 (left)
The interior of the Royal Opera Arcade (DP104294). Nash's arcade, running along the western flank of the Opera House, was London's first covered shopping arcade, lit internally by his favourite expedient of glazed domes over each bay. Inspired by the passages of Paris, the European capital of fashion and consumerism, it has fortunately survived the demolition of the Opera House itself.

Fig 6.40 (right)
The interior of the Haymarket Theatre, by Robert Schnebbelie, 1823 (© City of London, London Metropolitan Archives). The narrow auditorium was described by one contemporary as 'one of the most elegant … in London, but for convenience of seeing and hearing, the worst contrived'. It was reconstructed in 1879–80, and again in 1904–5.

Fig 6.39 (above)
Haymarket looking north, with the Opera House on the extreme left and the portico of the Haymarket Theatre on the right (BB 83/5819). Following the remodelling of the Opera House, Nash persuaded the owner of the Little Theatre in Haymarket to relocate to an adjacent site facing the newly extended Charles Street. Here in 1820–1 he built a new theatre, of which only the Corinthian portico and stuccoed rear elevation to Suffolk Street now survive.

Fig 6.41 (left)
Suffolk Place and Suffolk Street
(DP104384). This modest and little-
frequented backwater still survives intact.
Following the demolition of so much of
Nash's work between the two World
Wars, it is now the best surviving
example of his street architecture.

Fig 6.43 (below)
Pall Mall East looking from the junction with Cockspur Street
towards St Martin-in-the-Fields (1722–6), watercolour by
W H Bartlett c 1830 (© City of London, London Metropolitan
Archives). The royal stables – soon to make way for the
National Gallery – are on the left, and premises newly
designed by Henry Rhodes for Messrs. Hancock & Rixon,
glass manufacturers, to the right.

Fig 6.42 (above)
Suffolk Street in 1827, from Sheppard and Elmes, Metropolitan Improvements (© Trustees of
the British Museum, Crace Collection XI, 123). The street was rebuilt by Nash in 1821–4.
On the east side is his narrow façade to the galleries of the Society of British Artists, founded in
1823, with a Doric portico over an arcade; the galleries themselves (since rebuilt), were
designed by James Elmes above vaults and stables, and extended east to Whitcomb Street.

Fig 6.44 (above)
Nash's first, unexecuted, design for Trafalgar Square,
c 1819–20 (© City of London, London Metropolitan
Archives). The square was laid out on the site of the outer
courtyard or Great Mews in front of the royal stables, designed
by William Kent in 1731–3. Nash proposed to build a Doric
temple-like structure for the Royal Academy in the middle
of the square, flanked on either side by near-identical
neoclassical buildings, only one of which (Robert Smirke's
Royal College of Physicians and Union Club – now Canada
House – of 1824–7, to the left) was built. The Royal Academy
building – the closest Nash ever came to designing a Greek
Revival structure – never got beyond the drawing board,
and in 1840–3 Nelson's Column went up south of the site.
Kent's stables were replaced by William Wilkins's National
Galley in 1833–8.

Fig 6.45 (above)
The southern side of Trafalgar Square, with Hubert Le Sueur's
equestrian statue of Charles I (1629–33) in the foreground
(BB 90_03232). In 1826 Nash was instructed to push the
eastern side of his proposed square farther back, opening up
a view of the portico and spire of St Martin's Church. A hotel
(later replaced by South Africa House) occupied the eastern
side of the square. To the right is the Strand, with one of the
turrets of Nash's West Strand Improvement block just visible
in the distance.

Fig 6.46 (left)
Nash's buildings on the north side of St Martin's churchyard
(DP104300). One of the effects of Nash's improvements was
to isolate St Martin's Church from the buildings that had
formerly surrounded it. His new vicarage, Vestry Hall and
palazzo-fronted Parish School went up in 1827–30 and have
recently been revealed to public view following a welcome
refurbishment of the church and its surroundings.

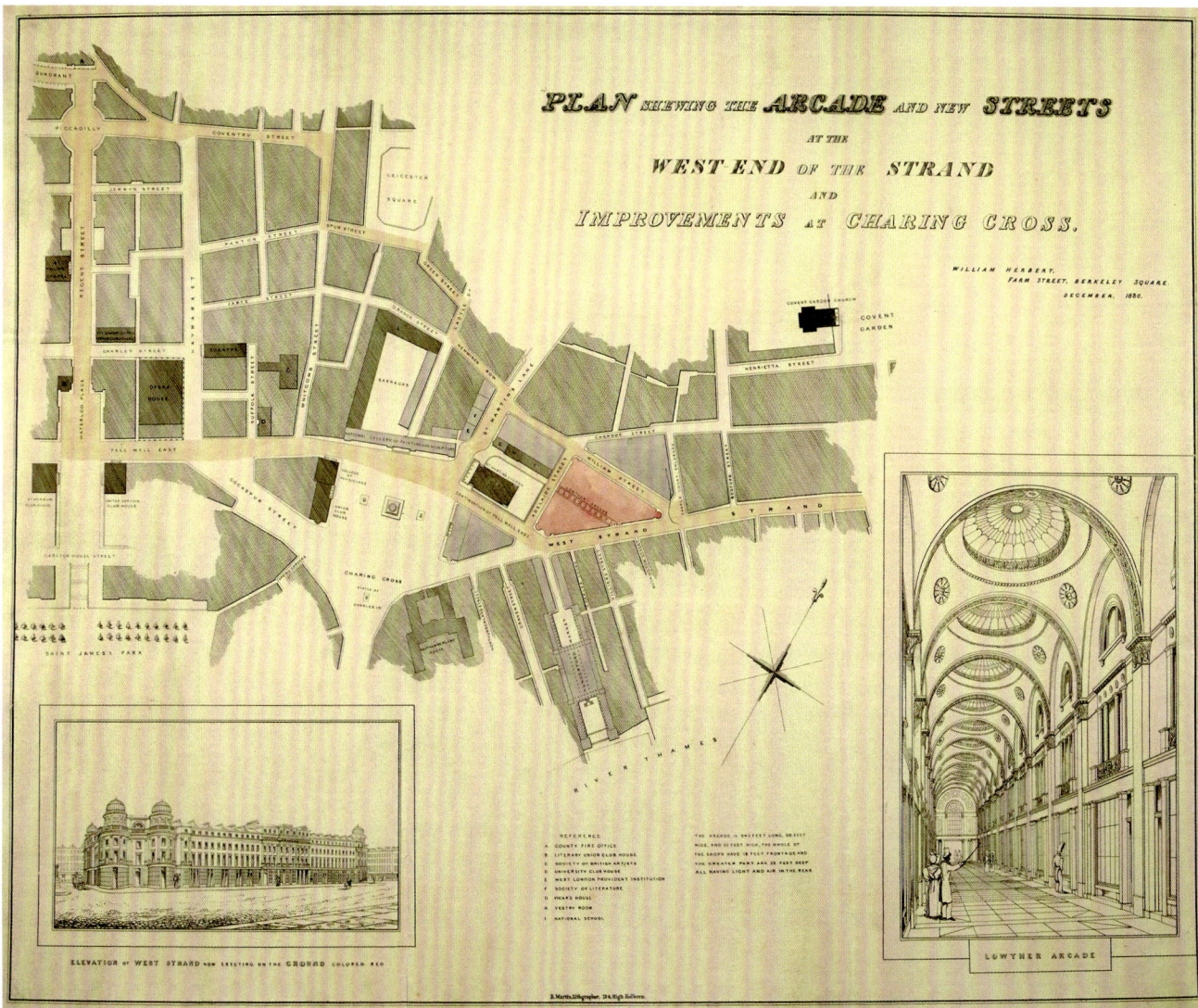

Fig 6.47 (above)
Plan of Trafalgar Square and the West Strand Improvement by William Herbert, 1830 (© City of London, London Metropolitan Archives); Herbert was the builder who carried out the triangular block coloured red on the plan (and illustrated at the bottom left) to Nash's design in 1830–2. The vignette at the bottom right shows the Lowther Arcade – a grander version of Nash's Royal Opera Arcade, which bisected this block. Each bay was roofed by a glazed pendentive dome, more characteristic of Soane than of Nash.

Fig 6.48 (right)
Nash's 'West Strand Improvement' involved the creation of two new streets, named after King William IV and Queen Adelaide, and the building of a new block of shops and chambers in the space bounded by them and the Strand. Most of the detailing is plain to the point of austerity, but visual interest is supplied by the rotundas that mark each corner, each surmounted by a 'pepperpot' turret (DP104388).

After Nash

John Nash made three major contributions to modern urban planning. At Regent's Park, and later at St James's Park, he recreated the urban park as a planned *rus in urbe*. In the Park Village he showed how the middle-class suburb could be laid out on picturesque lines. And in his Metropolitan Improvements he showed how new streets cutting through built-up areas could stimulate a city's economy, enhance its cultural life and beautify its built fabric. As early as 1826 that enthusiastic traveller and gardener Prince Pückler-Muskau could remark that the capital now had 'the air of a seat of Government (Residenz) and not of an innumerable metropolis of "shop-keepers", to use Napoleon's expression.'[50] Yet, for the most part, Nash's architecture proclaimed not the glories of Court or Church, but of a thriving commercial city at the heart of a worldwide Empire. His genius lay in the way in which he worked with the grain of the city, satisfying its utilitarian needs but at the same time creating an uplifting backdrop to the drama of modern urban life. His success owed much to his skill in applying the picturesque devices of surprise and variety within an urban setting. His architecture drew on conventional classical sources, from ancient Rome to modern Paris, but he handled his sources in an eclectic, Baroque manner, delighting in curvaceous surfaces and paying more attention to visual and dramatic effect than to stylistic consistency. The façades along Regent Street, like the Regent's Park terraces, were designed not to be lingered over but to be experienced dynamically. In this respect they conformed to the spirit of an age that, like ours, valued change, mobility and sensation.

Nash was unusual among architects in seeing his vision of a transformed West End of London realised in his own lifetime. His successors were not so fortunate, and the later history of central London is marked by a series of failures to capitalise on his achievement.[51] But his influence can be traced in developments outside the city centre, such as the Grosvenor estate in Belgravia, and also further afield in the stuccoed terraces, contrived vistas and carefully planted open spaces of Brighton and Cheltenham, and in the subtle curves and classical set pieces of Newcastle's Grey Street. And something of his vision can be seen in the Paris of Napoleon III and Haussmann, and in the American 'City Beautiful' movement.[52]

Nash's work in London has generally been admired more by urban planners, and by architects with an interest in urban design,[53] than by the more fastidious architectural critics. One his many 19th-century critics, anticipating the detractors of recent postmodernism, complained that his buildings had 'the appearance of having been erected from hasty unrevised sketches. There is in them a good deal of tawdriness and show, and very little richness'.[54] Nash's use of stucco came in for particular censure, especially when Victorian pundits began to confuse architecture with morals by demanding 'honesty' in construction. His street-scape began to be eroded towards the end of the 19th century as new and taller buildings replaced some of the original blocks. As interest in late Georgian and Regency architecture began to awaken in the inter-war years opinions began to change, and in 1924 A Trystan Edwards could remark that 'Painted stucco is the ideal material for street architecture … One of the most beautiful sights in the world used to be the west side of Piccadilly Circus midday in April after a shower of rain'. But by then the original leases had fallen in and the demolitions had begun, Nash's buildings making way for larger and more lucrative blocks whose overbearing stone facades do little to lift the

Fig 6.49
All Souls, Langham Place, from the south, with Broadcasting House (1931) in the background (DP104369).

spirit.[55] Fortunately, though, Carlton House Terrace was spared, along with All Souls, Langham Place (Fig 6.49) and some of the backwaters around Pall Mall and Trafalgar Square. And Regent Street itself has survived and flourished, as have the parks and urban spaces that Nash created, giving life and vitality to the capital and vindicating his vision, his creative energy and his persistence.

Notes

1 The most reliable published accounts are in Summerson 1980, 75–89, 130–45; Hobhouse 2008; and Crook 1992. The origins and implementation of the project are explored thoroughly in Anderson 1998; see also Summerson 2003, 196–216, and Arnold, D 1995 'Rationality, safety and power: the street planning of later Georgian London', *Georgian Group J* [for 1995], 37–50.
2 The figures are for the area of London County Council as it existed from 1888 to 1965.
3 4th Report on Land Revenues of the Crown, *PP* 1809 **IV**, 28
4 *PP* 1812 **XII**, 71–2
5 BL Maps, Crace Collection **XII**, 17; Summerson 1980, 139. Some minor variations are shown in the MS maps in NA, MR 1/697/1–5
6 Anderson, J 2009 'The Prince Regent's role in the creation and development of Regent Street and Regent's Park'. *Georgian Group J*, **17**, 107–14
7 Anderson 1998, 19–21, 178
8 Anderson 1998, 97
9 *PP* 1816 **XV**, 20; *PP* 1819 **XIV**, 12–13. The loans were repaid in 1824–5.
10 eg Worcester, Taunton, Liverpool, Huddersfield (Girouard, M 1990 *The English Town*. New Haven and London: Yale University Press, 171–80)
11 Girouard 1990 (*see note 10*), 177–9; Ison, W 1948 *The Georgian Buildings of Bath*. London: Faber and Faber, 168–9
12 Little was done before 1806 (Youngson, A 1966 J *The Making of Classical Edinburgh*. Edinburgh: Edinburgh University Press, 133ff)
13 Craig, M (ed) 1980 *Dublin 1660–1860*. Dublin: Allen Figgis, 172–4; Casey, C 2005 *The Buildings of Ireland: Dublin*. New Haven and London: Yale University Press, 44–7, 417–19
14 Sutcliffe, A 1993 *Paris: An Architectural History*. New Haven and London: Yale University Press, 68–73
15 NA, Cres 2/742 (6 February 1832)
16 White 1814; Westminster City Archives, D135(307); Anderson, J 2001 'John White Senior and James Wyatt'. *Architect Hist* **44**, 106–13
17 *PP* 1828 **IV**, 74
18 Arnold 1995 (*see note 1*), 45
19 *PP* 1816 **XV**, 116. Nash prepared an unexecuted design for extending Magdalen College, Oxford in 1801 (*see page* 41) and later carried out minor work at Exeter and Jesus Colleges.

20 *PP* 1816 **XV**, 123. More than half of the houses demolished for the new street (430) belonged to the Crown; another 355 had to be compulsorily purchased (*PP* 1819 **XIV** (474), 12).
21 Crook 1992, 90
22 eg nos. 156–70, by Soane, nos. 176–86, by Robert Abraham, and perhaps others by Decimus Burton
23 *PP* 1828 **IV**, 387. There is an elevation of one block in NA, MPE 1356, but no others appear to survive.
24 Saunders 1981, 81–3. *See also* chapter 5.
25 For the deeds of purchase of individual properties, with names of builders see NA, LR 1/255–265
26 Olsen, D (ed) 1982 *Town Planning in London*. New Haven and London: Yale University Press, 27–96; Arnold 1995(*see note 1*), 29, 84–8
27 Hobhouse 2008, 27, 42
28 *PP* 1819 **XIV**, 16; *PP* 1828 **IV**, 144, 387; Anderson 1998, 207, 218. The final net cost of the street was £1,639,000.
29 Boys, T S 1842 *Original Views of London As It Is, with notices by C Ollier*. London: [publisher unknown], np
30 Port, M H 2006 *Six Hundred New Churches*. Reading: Spire Books, 64–6
31 *Survey of London* **XXXI**, 284–307; NA, Cres 26/108. There are letters from Nash to the critic and impresario William Ayrton, one of the founders of the Institution, in BL, Add MS 52339. I am grateful to Dr Leanne Langley for this reference.
32 NA, Cres 26/134
33 Britton, J and Pugin, A C 1828 *Illustrations of the Public Buildings of London*. London: J Taylor, **II**, 287 (*see* Fig 0.3). The interior of Nash's house is described in Schinkel, K F 1993 (Bindman, D and Riemann, G eds) 1993 *The English Journey*.New Haven and London: Yale University Press, 89–90; *see page* 41.
34 Boys 1842 (*see note 29*)
35 Arnold 1995 (*see note 1*), 47. The barracks were behind the present National Gallery, and there were more barracks to the east of Regent's Park (Douet, J 1998 *British Barracks 1600–1914*. London: English Heritage, 106–9)
36 *PP* 1809 **IV**, 20; *Survey of London* **XX**, 223–50; Nalbach, D 1972 *The King's Theatre, 1704–1867*. London: Society for Theatre Research, 77–9, 92–3
37 *Survey of London* **XX**, 89–100; *PP* 1819 **XIV**, 17; *PP* 1829 **III**, 25–40, 121
38 *Survey of London* **XXIX**, 386–99
39 NA, MPE 891; NA, Cres 2/533; *Survey of London* **XX**, 77–86; Tyack 1992, 14, 20–1. Nash designed the interiors of nos. 2, 5, 8–14, and probably also no. 6 (notes by Sir John Summerson (1966) in the National Monuments Record. Nos. 16–18 were not built until 1862–4, under the supervision of Pennethorne).
40 *PP* 1829 **XIV**, 12–13, 162; NA, WORK 32/75. Nash's proposal to line the southern side of the Park with stuccoed terraces was shelved, and the improvement of the northern approaches to the Palace – including the Constitution Hill Arch and the Ionic screen at Hyde Park Corner – was entrusted to Decimus Burton (Brindle, S 2001 'The Wellington Arch and the western entrance to London'. *Georgian Group J* **11**, 47–92). The Wellington Barracks were built in

1833–4, with elevations by Philip Hardwick, on the southern side of the Park.

41 *PP* 1823 **XI**, 24; *PP* 1826 **XIV**, 12 and Appendix 3; *PP* 1833 **XLIV**, 5. The 'West Strand Improvement' cost another £843,000, according to Wade, J 1837 *The Extraordinary Black Book*. London: Effingham Wilson, 193

42 Crook and Port 1973, 303–6, 351

43 *PP* 1829 **III**, 122

44 For the Royal Academy design *see* Fig 6.45 (LMA, p7506671) and PP 1826 **XIV**, 12 and plan 3; for the National Gallery, Pinhorn (ed) 2000, 127. Neither Nash's 1831 model nor his drawings of his proposed National Gallery appear to survive.

45 It would have followed the line of St Martin's Lane to Seven Dials and Monmouth Street before diverging to the right, with a square, enfolding Nicholas Hawksmoor's St George, Bloomsbury, on the site of the present streets to the south of the Museum (*PP* 1826 **XIV**, plan after page 136).

46 *Gentleman's Magazine* 1835, 438. The new arrangement of streets is shown in *PP* 1826 **XIV**, plan 3. See also a plan engraved by Ingrey and Madeley *c* 1830 (Fig 6.47; LMA, p5424207). Contemporary perspective views are reproduced in Fox, C (ed) 1992 *London – World City 1800–1840*. New Haven and London: Yale University Press, 279.

47 *Gentleman's Magazine* March 1831, 201–7; Stokes, M V 1972 'The Lowther Arcade in the Strand'. *London Topograph Rec* **23**, 119–28. The arcade was demolished in 1902.

48 The best verbal description is in Summerson 1980, 130–45.

49 Webb, D 2001 'The photographic studios of Regent Street'. *London Topograph Rec* **28**, 122

50 Butler, E M (ed) 1957 *A Regency Visitor*. London: Collins, 38

51 eg Tyack 1992, 43–86

52 Napoleon III spent much of his exile in London and, like Nash's political masters, saw the value of public infrastructural works in stimulating the economy and reducing unemployment (Pinkney, D H 1958 *Napoleon III and the Rebuilding of Paris*. Princeton, NJ: Princeton University Press, 31, 37).

53 eg Rasmussen, S E 1937 *London: The Unique City*. Cambridge, Mass: M I T Press; Bacon, E 1967 *Design of Cities*. London: Thames & Hudson; Farrell, Terry, 2007, 'Manifesto for London', *Architectural Review*, issue 1327, esp. 26-7

54 *Civil Engin Architect J* **1** (1838), 219

55 Hobhouse 2008, 113–25

7

John Nash and the Royal Palaces

M H PORT

John Nash's relationship with the Prince Regent might have developed from more than one source. In his Welsh retirement Nash became a close friend of John George Philipps (1761–1816) – MP for Carmarthen 1784–1803 and a zealous supporter of Charles James Fox – a friendship sustained after Nash's return to London.[1] Nash is known to have been in touch with Fox,[2] then closely associated with the Prince of Wales,[3] and this might have led to his exhibiting in the Royal Academy's 1798 exhibition a design of a conservatory for the Prince – or this could have resulted from his then partnership with Humphry Repton. But it was during the short-lived Foxite administration of 1806–7 that he was appointed Surveyor to the Office of Woods and Forests, responsible for Crown lands. Whatever the origins of his connection with the Prince, by 1812 Nash was employed by him as a political agent, and was clearly on personal terms with him.[4]

Royal Lodge, Windsor

The improvement of the royal residence at Windsor Castle having been abandoned after James Wyatt's death in 1813, the Regent needed a convenient residence at Windsor, close to his parents' households in the castle. Most appropriate was the former residence of the Rangers of the Great Park, Cumberland Lodge, but because of the time required to refit it, one of the smaller Great Park lodges – the Lower Lodge – was chosen for a temporary retreat, 'a commission … which well might seem to be of an entirely personal character and to reflect the kind of relationship which clearly subsisted between Prince and architect'.[5] It then transpired that converting Cumberland Lodge would be exceedingly costly, so the estimates at Lower Lodge soared from £2,750 to some £13,000 for permanent occupation.[6]

This work, however, was to be executed officially by Nash as architect to the Office of Woods and Forests. Therefore in 1813–16 he 'fitted up Lower Lodge in a style of splendour, for the occasional residence of the Prince Regent',[7] at a cost, with outbuildings, of some £22,600. He created an overblown version of the *cottage orné*, a genre in which he had displayed versatility (notably at Blaise Hamlet, Bristol, in 1810). The exterior was stuccoed and the roof thatched, a dining room added, with bedrooms above, a gallery, kitchen and offices, accommodation for attendants and visitors (with 29 marble chimney pieces) and a vast cast-iron conservatory about 75ft by 35ft (23m × 11m),[8] a house 'at once royal and rustic; on the outside the simplicity of a cottage, within the rarest union of comfort, elegance and magnificence' (Figs 7.1 and 7.2).[9] But when, in November 1814, he produced a further estimate of nearly £6,000 for cutting down windows, and a variety of ancillary works, management

Fig 7.1
Royal Lodge Windsor, Entrance Front 1813–16; 'called a cottage, because it was thatched, engraving after Delamotte (The Royal Collection © 2011 Her Majesty Queen Elizabeth II).

Fig 7.2
*Royal Lodge Windsor,
Garden Front, with Nash's
conservatory on the left:
engraving after
Delamotte, 1824
(The Royal Collection
© 2011 Her Majesty Queen
Elizabeth II).*

was transferred to the Office of Works, the department responsible for building and maintaining the royal palaces and government offices. Nash's statement accompanying his estimate exposed the chaotic character of the works already done: alterations in the agreed plan, fresh additions, demolition of newly executed work and the materials reused.[10] Then dry rot had to be exterminated. In 1820, now King, and unpopular because of the royal divorce bill, George IV sought seclusion, demanding guard rooms, followed by an entrance lodge, and then extensions priced at £6,800. To pay for Nash's latest improvements, the Great Park timber had to be 'topped and lopped', to a cost of £12,000. Princess Lieven, the Russian ambassadress, found the house still 'very low and damp' in 1823.[11] When, later that year, the King wanted further improvements, he substituted Jeffrey Wyatt for Nash, whose role at Windsor came to an end.

Carlton House

Carlton House in Pall Mall was granted to the Prince of Wales as his residence when he came of age in 1783. It was repaired by Sir William Chambers and substantially reconstructed by Henry Holland in 1784–96. Subsequently, James Wyatt and Thomas Hopper were employed, and a succession of interior decorators kept the interior effervescing under the Prince's keen eye.[12] On Wyatt's sudden death, Nash was promptly put in charge,[13] first completing the internal works already under way. There were rumours that the Prince, now Regent, intended to enlarge the house vastly, and Nash produced designs, both classical and Gothic, for rebuilding (Fig 7.3).[14] Lord Liverpool's government stopped that, so Nash redesigned a range of rooms on the garden front, adding a Gothic dining room (Fig 7.4) to the east, balancing Hopper's Gothic conservatory on the west, an enfilade of 345ft

Fig 7.3 (above)
Nash's proposals for
rebuilding Carlton House,
c 1814: the Classical version,
with portico, dome and
giant order, seen from
Waterloo Place
(The Royal Collection
© 2011 Her Majesty Queen
Elizabeth II).

Fig 7.4 (left)
Carlton House: the Gothic
dining room, engraving
after a painting by Charles
Wild, c 1818. Added by Nash
in 1814, the dining room
was the easternmost room
of the new garden front of
1807–14. The window heads
are turned through 90° to
create the ceiling ornament
(The Royal Collection
© 2011 Her Majesty Queen
Elizabeth II).

(105m). Its Gothic window arches, turned through 90 degrees to decorate the ceiling, and separated by pierced cast-iron brackets, were repeated on the internal side – a clever invention similar (as Summerson points out) to the one he had employed in the hall at Corsham Court in 1797.[15] The estimate for the room was £8,866, including the statuary marble chimney piece designed by James Wyatt and supplied by Richard Westmacott.[16] Adjoining the dining room was the Corinthian, or Golden, Drawing Room (Fig 7.5), lined with fluted, gilded columns, entablature and mirrors, creating a sumptuously rich effect, replicated to infinity. Beyond the Library, at the foot of the Grand Stairs, lay the Anteroom or Lower Vestibule,

Fig 7.5
Carlton House, the
Corinthian Drawing Room,
engraving after a painting
by C Wild. By Nash, c 1813–
14, on the garden front,
immediately west of the
dining room. The opulence
is enhanced to infinity by
huge mirrors
(The Royal Collection
© 2011 Her Majesty Queen
Elizabeth II).

divided by a double screen of *verd-antique* scagliola columns, again with gilded capitals and entablature; ebonised doors with painted panels, and scarlet on walls and furniture, contributed to overwhelm the visitor.[17]

Nash was also employed to execute a range of temporary buildings required by the magnificent public entertainments launched by the Regent in 1813–14 to celebrate the victories of the Allies over Napoleon and the centenary of the Hanoverian Dynasty. Supper rooms were built in the gardens for the reception of the Tsar and the King of Prussia in June 1814, but more spectacular were those added for the fête in honour of the Duke of Wellington on 21 July, dominated by a 'grand circular room'.[18] This oriental-style 24-sided tent of some 120ft diameter (36.5m), 'sd to be larger than … *Ranelagh*',[19] covered in Baber's oilcloth, had a peripheral aisle formed by pairs of reeded iron Doric columns linked by transverse segmental arches.[20]

Despite subsequent heavy expenditure on the permanent buildings, Carlton House failed to satisfy the Regent's mutating tastes: he now wanted 'a general reparation and arrangement of Plan'.[21] But money was tight, the government unhelpful, and only minor repairs were made. The Regent next looked to move to Buckingham House after his mother's death in November 1818, given Nash's report that the ground floor of Carlton House was so weak that it had to be under-propped on reception days.[22]

After the King's accession, Nash told the diarist Joseph Farington that he had taken a dislike to Carlton House.[23] Nash thought in 1822 that even a partial rebuilding would still leave the palace dilapidated and deficient, and the royal attention turned elsewhere. With Buckingham Palace at last under way in 1825, the dismantlement of Carlton House could begin and demolition commence.

The Royal Pavilion, Brighton

The Prince of Wales commissioned a Marine Pavilion at Brighton from Henry Holland in 1787,[24] in the French neoclassical style he then principally affected. When enlargements were planned in 1801, one drawing proposed cloaking the exterior in Chinoiserie.[25] In 1803–6, William Porden built a vast domed riding-house and stables in a 'Hindoo' style.[26] The Prince then invited Humphry Repton to prepare designs in an Indian style for the Pavilion, but they were shelved.[27] When, in 1811, the Prince became Regent, he considered his holiday home inadequate to his dignity and called in James Wyatt, Surveyor General of the King's Works, to enlarge it; but Wyatt was killed in a coach accident in 1813.[28] The capricious Regent had tired of that simplicity which might be 'the charm of the Greek Temples', but which gave the Pavilion a 'mean appearance' not suited to 'the purpose of the building', and awoke to its unfavourable appearance in comparison with Porden's dominating 'Hindoo' stables.[29] 'It was therefore determined by H[is] M[ajesty] that the Pavillion [*sic*] should assume an Eastern character'. Nash not only provided that 'Eastern character' – albeit one more fantastical than Repton had offered – but he also employed imaginative devices and innovative techniques, particularly in the use of cast iron, to raise, as Summerson put it, 'a set of domes of so provocative a shape that they would assert complete dominion and whip the stable into submission' (Fig 7.6).[30]

However, when Nash went to Brighton on 24 January 1815 to meet the Prince,[31] it was apparently with a view to carrying out the enlargement begun by Wyatt. The oriental character seems to have been devised during 1816, using the Regent's copy of Thomas and William Daniell's *Oriental Scenery* (1808) as the source.[32] For the next five years, Nash was engaged in the transformation of the Pavilion into an oriental palace. He offered the Regent

Fig 7.6 (opposite)
The Royal Pavilion Brighton.
Nash's domes (1818–21),
of a provocatively Indian
character, dominate
the scene
(AA 98_04130).

a choice: one design with onion domes over both the central bow saloon and his two new end rooms; the other with a large onion dome over the bow saloon, flanked by two smaller ones over the lesser bows of the drawing rooms either side, and Chinese tent roofs (recalling the Carlton House Waterloo pavilion) over the Banqueting Room and the Music Room.[33] Nash states that the Regent chose the latter (Fig 7.7), but Jackson-Stops thought it more likely that 'the final solution was worked out during the course of the building work'.[34] There is no record of a definite plan; 'changes and additions … were continually made'.[35]

By extending Holland's east or Steyne front – the one most exposed to view – and replacing the angled end rooms of 1802 with much larger banqueting and music rooms, Nash made the Pavilion appear, as Morley points out, much bigger than it really was. He also widened the corridor that lay west of the state apartments to create a spinal gallery (Fig 7.8) 162ft (49m) long – as Summerson points out, a characteristic Nash feature[36] – linking the new rooms and terminated at either end by an imperial staircase of cast iron, the balustrades simulating bamboo

(see Fig 9.4). Cast-iron trusses enabled the construction of large skylights over the gallery, a technique he had employed previously, notably at Attingham, Shropshire. The gallery in turn necessitated a new entrance front. These works of 1815 were accompanied by the reconstruction of a former riding school as a magnificent state-of-the-art kitchen, the great span of its lanterned roof supported by slender cast-iron columns with palm-tree tops (added in 1820). The Banqueting Room and the Music Room followed in 1817–18, and then the great Mughal dome over the circular Saloon. The roofs of all three were daringly innovatory constructions of iron and timber members providing a dome in each room, with an outer skin of sheet iron covered with mastic (see Fig 8.5).[37] The ceilings of the outer, square rooms contrasted interestingly: one with a concave, the other with a convex coving, above squinches in the Banqueting Room (see Fig 9.2), and above a massive octagonal frame in the Music Room (Fig 7.9). These scintillating ceilings match Nash's brilliant designs at Buckingham Palace a few years later. The innovative range of glazed oculi in the saloon dome likewise anticipates the similar

Fig 7.7
The Royal Pavilion, Brighton, the East (Steyne) Front, by Nash, 1818–21. An alternation of domes and tent roofs enriches the skyline, while the diverse elements of the ground floor are tied together by an 'Indian' order of colonnading (AA 98_04127).

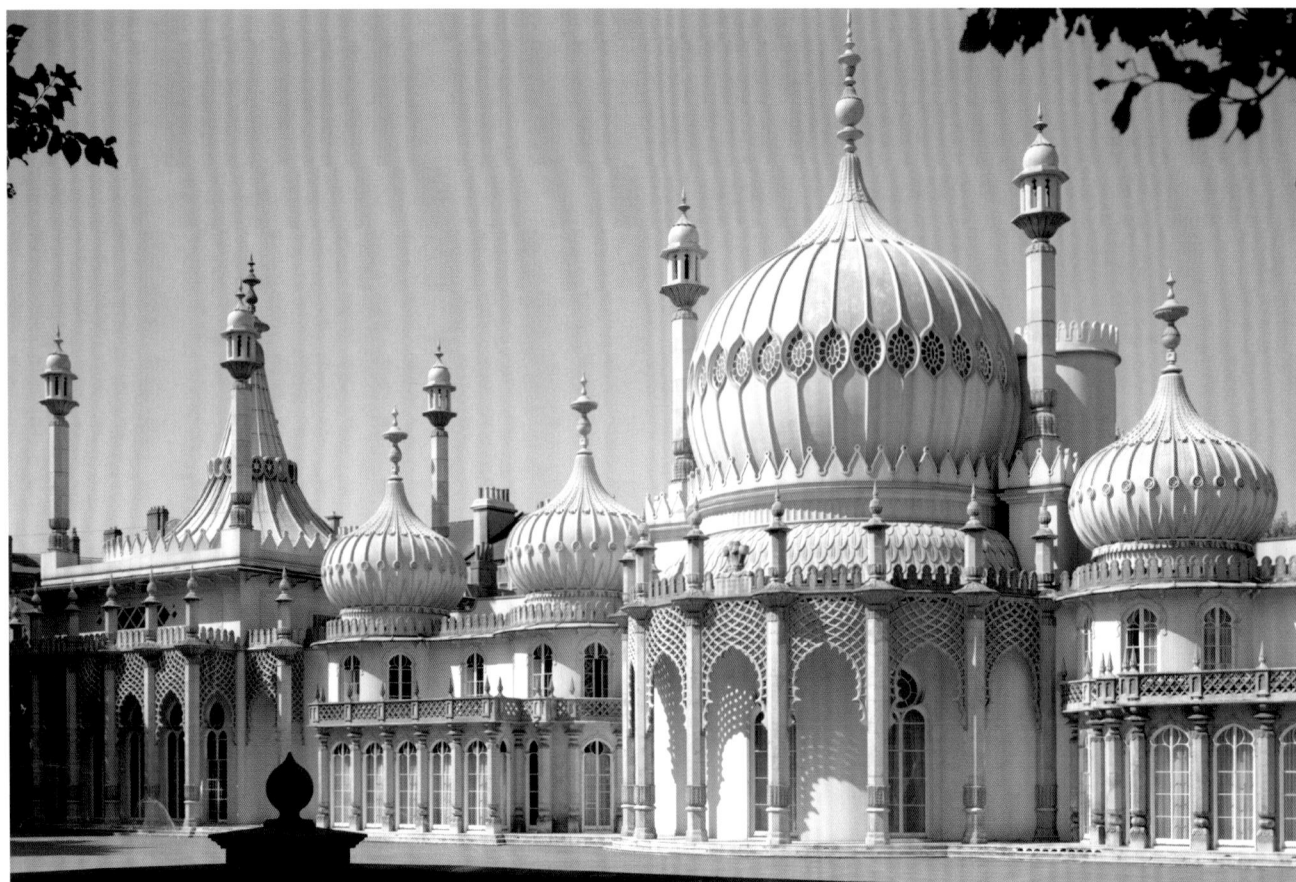

device over the state stair at the palace. Externally, the dome is flanked by iron-cored minarets clad in Bath stone, also used for the Indian-style screen (but of quatrefoil tracery), 'a brilliant invention'[38] that linked the giant Indian columns[39] of the three rooms.

In 1821 Nash used slender iron columns internally to enable him to push out a windowed arcade uniting the twin bows of the two drawing rooms, over which smaller domes were constructed (as noted above) linking up the whole front with an arcade of Indian columns,

Fig 7.8
The Royal Pavilion, Brighton: the Long Gallery or Corridor, by Nash, 1815. Decorated by F Crace, the 162ft Corridor was developed from the old two-storey hall, and was later re-decorated
(Nash, Views of the Royal Pavilion, 1826).

Fig 7.9
The Royal Pavilion, Brighton, section of the Music Room and adjoining rooms, showing the structural elements of the domes
(Nash, Views of the Royal Pavilion, 1826).

similar to, but smaller than, those of the principal rooms. A new North wing for guests (Fig 7.10) bears a general resemblance to the 'Rotas Gur' from the Daniells' *Oriental Scenery*.[40] This linked the East Front with new private apartments on the north-west. Nash also built a new western entrance with a *porte-cochère* similar to the 'Temple on the Ganges' depicted in Forrest's *Picturesque Tour along the Rivers Ganges and Jumna* (1824).[41]

Another innovation was less successful: the use of artificial roofing compositions. Nash was enthusiastic about using compositions for roofing. At Brighton he employed Stanhope's mastic ('powdered chalk, tar and sand, laid on hot and covered with slates') for flat roofs; and Dehl's (supplied by P Hamelin; 'a mixture of litharge, pulverised stone, sand and linseed oil') for the domes.[42] However, in 1822 the Dehl mastic was reported to have 'completely failed', with rain penetrating the Dining Room roof, so Nash incurred royal displeasure.[43] But he had already 'lost the countenance of the King' over exceeding his Pavilion estimates. These were annual assessments of the year's prospective expenditure on the work proposed, and were invariably exceeded to some extent. But unpremeditated works might also be executed, and the various accounts are difficult to reconcile.[44] It appears that from March 1815 to May 1820 Nash's works cost £148,722 16s 9½d: an excess of £11,209 0s 1¼d over his estimates, or a fraction over eight per cent – not a bad result on so complex a building operation.[45]

Nash offered to forgo his commission, but in the end he was allowed the conventional five per cent on some £93,000, a figure for which there is no explanation.[46] In all, expenditure from 1812 to Michaelmas 1821 was about £160,600.[47]

Laodicean Summerson damns Nash's Royal Pavilion as flawed architecture but praises it as an 'unmatched … palace of varieties', and 'a felicitous materialisation of the careless, humorous, audacious genius of its architect'.[48] But it is surely the apotheosis of the picturesque, expressed, amazingly, in the pure geometrical forms and masses of the French Romantic classicists. For Clifford Musgrave, who worked there, 'it equals in evasive loveliness even Shah Jehan's own creations'.[49]

Buckingham Palace

At the Pavilion, Nash worked as the Regent's private architect, paid from the Privy Purse; the building of a new London home for the sovereign had to be on a public footing. After James Wyatt's death, the government had put the Office of the King's Works on a statutory footing, appointing as its head a soldier, Benjamin Stephenson, who had been managing George III's household at Windsor on the queen's behalf. Purely an administrator, he was advised by three 'Attached Architects' – John Nash, John Soane and Robert Smirke – each responsible for a specific group of public buildings, paid a salary of £500pa, and awarded three per cent commission (instead of the usual five) on the cost of

Fig 7.10
Royal Pavilion, Brighton: the North Front, by Nash, 1819, omitting the tented roof and minarets of the Music Room behind, and probably inspired by a Mughal original (Nash, Views of the Royal Pavilion, *1826).*

any new public building on which he was employed. The professional staff of the Office measured new works and dealt with the accounts. Ordinary maintenance of buildings was the responsibility of subordinate architects, who normally employed for each building tradesmen officially appointed by competition. The Attached Architects met quarterly to review the prices paid for such repairs and small works, on the basis of prime costs submitted by the merchants plus fifteen per cent to cover expenses and profit. For major new works, tradesmen of established reputation were invited to compete.[50]

For several years, George IV had been contemplating moving his residence to the Queen's Palace (Buckingham House), which fell in Soane's 'district'. In July 1819, a few months after the queen's death, a Treasury memorandum considered the *modus operandi* on an estimate of £150,000. But the Regent, as he then was, blithely suggested to ministers that they lay before Parliament arrangements for converting the palace for 'the habitation Town Residence and Court of the Sovereign' at a cost of £450,000.[51] Of course, no more was heard of that.

In July 1821, a week before his coronation, the King instructed Stephenson to hand over the palace plans to Nash, to the anger of displaced Soane, with his long-standing ambition to build a royal palace.[52] In October 1821, Nash referred in conversation to the King's wish to move to Buckingham House (as noted above).[53] A few days later, contemplating repairs at Carlton House, Nash warned the surveyor-general that 'whenever authority shall be given to prepare Buckingham House for the King it will take a year at least to prepare it for H[is] M[ajesty's] occupation'.[54] Basic repairs apart, nothing had been done to the palace for some 20 years, and Nash estimated that it now needed £15,000 of maintenance work. The King's intention at that time was to add a few rooms, move the kitchens and raise the ground floor.[55]

In August 1822, a few days after pointing out the inadequacy of any rebuilding of Carlton House, Nash reported to Stephenson that, having 'received the King's instructions and submitted to H[is] M[ajesty] designs for converting Buckingham House into a suitable royal residence', he now transmitted them, with, in obedience to Stephenson's instructions, another set showing the minimum of what was essential for making it habitable for the King.[56] The agricultural distress of 1821–2, however,

imposed strict economy on the government for several years. Then, in 1824, George IV decided to give precedence to improving Windsor Castle; and it was not until 1825 that he revived his London project.

But, as his ideas ripened, the potential work expanded. Nash, alarmed by the scope of rebuilding proposed, tried to persuade the King to build a new palace in a different position. George IV's response was to call his intimate advisor, Sir Charles Long, as witness and declare that he was too old to build a palace, 'but I must have a *pied à terre*' and that was to be at Buckingham House: 'there are early associations that endear me to the spot'.[57]

With a substantial budget surplus expected in 1825, in March of that year Nash resumed tentative designs for the palace.[58] George IV now had three particular improvements in view: a set of State Rooms comparable with those in Carlton House; a set of private apartments on the ground floor; and the removal of the kitchens to the south wing. His penchant for relatively low rooms involved adjusting the height of the floors, so Nash proposed raising the ground floor five feet (1.5m); this allowed him to improve the basement offices – low, damp, and susceptible to occasional flooding from the sewer that ran underneath – raising their floors by half the increased headroom.[59] Other major alterations included building a new west or garden front, so creating space for another of Nash's favoured spinal galleries on both ground and principal floors; a new roof, much of the building being heightened; new wings set further apart; and changes to the entrance front – a Doric arcade with a full-height Corinthian pedimented *porte-cochère* and pavilions – behind an archway and railing.[60] Cladding all this in Bath stone would complete the transformation of the late 17th-century mansion. The design was essentially merely for enlarging the existing structure, at a cost of £200,000, excluding ornamental sculpture, and assuming the reuse of much material from Carlton House. On 25 October 1825, Nash estimated another £30,400, largely for additional works on the south or Pimlico side for the kitchens, and on the north front for the King's apartments. With landscaping, the whole came to £252,690.[61]

What Nash sought was a palace in 'the gusto Greco', with sculpture 'classically treated that is to say as the Antient Artists would have treated them … avoiding the representation of the sentiment by symbols'.[62] What he achieved was

Fig 7.11
Buckingham Palace: the
East Front as first designed
by Nash, 1824–8, with the
garden front dome visible
over the portico, and the
single-storey wings
terminating in two-storey
pavilions, replaced in
1828–9. Engraving by
Wallis from a drawing by
A C Pugin, 1827, for the
Stationers' Almanac, 1828.
(© Trustees of the British
Museum, Crace Collection
XIII, 25).

a unique structure in a picturesque version of French classicism, with an undulating skyline enlivened with statuary (Fig 7.11). The King had always shown strong Francophile leanings, and Nash's trips to Paris in 1814 and 1817–18 gave him direct knowledge of important Parisian buildings, such as Gondoin's École de Chirurgie (1769–75), with its colonnaded forecourt, and Rousseau's Palais de Salm (1783), as well as other late *ancien régime* mansions by Ledoux and Brogniart, adorned with relief panels,[63] and also of the Arc du Carrousel at the Tuileries – indeed, Nash probably cribbed the Marble Arch from Percier and Fontaine's 1806 entrance to the imperial palace, though he told Wellington that it was 'a plagiarism of the Arch of Constantine' at Rome, their common source.[64] The Palais de Salm well may have furnished a prototype: it has a screen to the forecourt, entered through a triumphal arch, the forecourt is colonnaded, and the garden front has relief panels, and statues on the central domed bow.[65] But the garden front of Carlton House also had a central bow: the King had a particular liking for 'a LONG *room*, *with a Bow* IN THE MIDDLE', so that Nash had to repeat it in the private suite on the north front.[66]

Nash's extensive use of sculpture both internally and externally – statues, panels in relief and statuary chimney pieces, employing

the best sculptors and modellers – was an outstanding feature of his designs that had little parallel in contemporary English architecture. Sculptures in the east front pediments were conventional enough; but striking was the array of statues above and reliefs below the pediments and on the turrets, and the Coade stone Virtues around the west front dome – a concept as likely borrowed from Holland's design at Brighton as from the Palais de Salm. The splendid reliefs and ceilings in the State Rooms also struck contemporaries with their novelty.[67] Largely designed by, or derived from, Thomas Stothard, the reliefs, notably nationalistic in character, rank 'among the greatest achievements in the decorative arts of late Georgian England'.[68]

The handsome garden front of the new building (Fig 7.12) was possibly too fragmented for the grandeur of a royal palace; the architect C R Cockerell thought it 'good but [that it had] many defects'. But he joined in the general condemnation of the Mall front: 'total want of order in windows … columns above columns in the Porticoes looking like a scaffolding.'[69] This, the principal approach, appeared as a series of unintegrated items. The purely ornamental dome above the central bow on the garden side protruded above the Mall front's central pediment, looking ridiculous: 'it never occurred

Fig 7.12
Buckingham Palace.
The West Front, by Nash,
1824–31, with dome,
statuary and greenhouses
(that at centre left removed
to Kew that at right
converted to chapel).
Engraving by T Higham,
for the Stationers'
Almanac, *1831*
(© Trustees of the British
Museum, Crace Collection
XIII, 26).

to me that it would be seen from that side', Nash observed.[70] The single-storey, colonnaded wings, with an upper storey in the middle section, and terminating in two-storey pavilions rising above the extruded colonnade to a sculptured attic and pediment – what Summerson calls 'a ludicrous jumble' – were immediately 'deemed to have a bad effect', Nash admitting 'I was disappointed myself in the effect of them'.[71] Christopher Hussey's is a lonely voice in asserting that they were 'singularly felicitous';[72] on the contrary, the contemporary connoisseur Henry Bankes, MP, declared 'every body cried out against the construction of colonnades, or wings, with barn roofs'.[73] In any event, the need for additional bedrooms made rebuilding them essential, although Nash came to the view that 'any wings would take from the dignity of a palace'.[74] However, the heightened wings were a much bolder feature, the terminal pavilions given a giant order resembling the 'ailes Gabriel' at Versailles – an ultimate justification (Fig 7.13).

Nash's problem was that, as at Brighton, he saw himself as the King's personal architect. George IV's greatest pleasure lay in organising and decorating his homes. At Carlton House, '[t]he apartments on all floors were in a constant state of flux'; even chimney pieces were moved about 'with a bewildering frequency'.[75] Altering rooms was his great delight. Walsh Porter

(d 1809), an early aesthetic adviser, who replaced Holland's work there 'in a most expensive & motley taste', declared, 'I have not added or *branched out* into a single thing that was not plan'd by the Prince himself'.[76] All this was done at prodigious expense, but somehow the debts were always settled. Parliament came to the rescue time after time. As King, George cannot have expected that circumstances would change, or that the sovereign would be controlled more strictly than the prince. So, as work progressed, George IV and his advisers, now headed by Sir Charles Long and Lord St Helens, elaborated and varied the designs and arrangements. An early, expensive change was the decision to send the Carlton House properties to Windsor, where Jeffry Wyatt was modernising the castle.[77]

Then, when the new building had been covered in, the King realised Nash's fears that he would make use of it for holding his courts, remarking: 'Nash, the State Rooms you have made me are so handsome'.[78] Nash protested that this was unfair to him as an architect, because the building 'was not arranged in a manner suitable to a State Palace; that no provision was made for the establishment of a Queen, nor for the Office of the Lord Chamberlain or the Lord Steward'. The King, however, advised by the polished septuagenarian courtier Lord St Helens,[79] with Long and his private secretary

Fig 7.13
Buckingham Palace, the
East Front from St James's
Park, as rebuilt by Nash,
1828–9, with the Marble
Arch as state gateway.
This view also reveals the
alterations by Blore in
1832–4: the removal of the
garden front dome; the
construction of an attic
storey decorated with
Westmacott's relief panels
designed for the Arch; and
the addition of Doric screens
at either side to give width to
the wings. Engraving by
T Higham, for the
Stationers' Almanac, 1835.
(© Trustees of the British
Museum, Crace Collection
XII, 27).

Knighton in the background, had already arranged the distribution of apartments, and swept aside Nash's objections.[80]

It is clearly this change in the character of the palace that the Treasury secretary, J C Herries, was referring to in his letter of 22 December 1826 to Sir William Knighton, the King's private secretary:

I have explained the plan fully to Lord Liverpool. He entirely concurs with all of us, who had previously seen it, in admiring the whole of the proposed arrangement; and he is prepared to give the official sanction for carrying all of it into execution, except with regard to that part which embraces the site of St James Palace … He thinks there would be a strong public feeling against the demolition of the State Rooms so recently completed [there] at a considerable expence [*sic*]: and, what is of more importance, he feels that until the King is completely established in His Majesty's new residence, & until His Majesty shall have had some experience of the fitness of the new building for the purposes of State as well as for his domestic comfort, it would be unwise and unbecoming to deprive His Majesty of the only apartments in which he can at present hold his Court in London.[81]

Knighton replied on Christmas Day: 'The King is naturally anxious for the completion of the Palace at Pimlico; and consequently the whole of the arrangements occupy *much* of His Majesty's attention.'[82]

At Buckingham Palace, Nash was breaking the mould set for public building since 1815. As he told the 1828 Parliamentary Select Committee that investigated the Office of Works:

Those designs that I make, are made by the direction of His Majesty, approved by his Majesty, signed by His Majesty, and countersigned by the Minister; … I receive my directions immediately from the king … here I am controlled and interfered with in the details of every part of the building …I pay drawing and other clerks about 1,500*l.* a year, who are principally employed for Buckingham House'[83] … 'every chimney-piece, every detail of moulding, and every ornament about the Palace, is the subject of a distinct drawing, submitted for previous approbation.[84]

Approbation, that is, by the monarch and his friends.

Strictly subordinate to the Treasury under the rules established for the Office of Works in 1814, Stephenson had frequently clashed with members of the royal family, who expected works to be executed as and when they desired. Unsurprisingly, Nash's *ad hoc* methods offended him, and when he saw the first rebuilding accounts, for the third quarter of 1825, he complained to the Treasury that the prices for work were fixed by Nash's agreements with the tradesmen, some written, some merely verbal, all more or less improvidently made. He further complained that Nash had agreed paying 'one quarter under another', in other words with only three months' delay.[85]

Called upon to be more specific, Stephenson responded with a comparison of prices, complained that the public were deprived of the advantages of competition, and also that they were made liable for a penalty if payment were delayed. Moreover, Nash had chosen tradesmen whom the Office would never have invited to compete for major works, 'as from experience it has been found, that it is only amongst Persons, who have a certain command of Capital, that the Public can expect to obtain advantageous Terms, for execution of any extensive Works'.[86] And he further complained that the architect was supplying materials to the tradesmen.

The scene was thus set for the prolonged contest between Stephenson and Nash, which another soldier's ministry was to award to Stephenson. Nash, however, replied to the Treasury at this point, 7 July 1826, with a strong defence of his line of conduct:

> Their Lordships [of the Treasury] are aware of the short time allowed me by The King for executing so vast a Building; it became necessary for me to devise some means for performing the task – I determined therefore to consider the whole not as one but as four distinct buildings and to separate each part by hoarded divisions inaccessible to each other and to employ 4 distinct sets of Tradesmen – so that with respect to the execution it was as if it were only one fourth of the size – a separate Clerk of the Works was appointed to each and His majesty having been graciously pleased to spare me his own Clerk of the Works employed at Brighton, (Mr Nixon) the most efficient Man in that line … I placed him over the whole – and the result of the plan has completely answered my purpose – I am equally satisfied of the economy of the measure … Knowing from the circumstance of so many large buildings carrying on at one and the same time the difficulty which would attend the providing [of] such an immediate quantity of Bath Stone as I shd require and aware of the advantage which would be taken of such a demand as to price[,] the first step I took was to examine privately the state in the market as to the Quantity on hand – and then to see individually every person connected with the Bath quarries and obtain from each of them not only the price; but quantity each individual could supply without letting them know the purpose or the quantity I should require – when I had thus made myself a complete master of the subject I engaged with the most capable and most respectable of them (Mr Freeman) for the whole quantity I should want and at the lowest price then paying (the agreement and the stipulation are in writing).[87]

Nash also arranged for a marble contractor, Joseph Browne, to go to Italy to buy the vast quantities of marble required for 104 columns, the state stairs and floors, an arrangement dogged by misunderstandings, and much investigated by the 1831 select committee of inquiry.[88]

The Chancellor of the Exchequer, the mendacious F J Robinson (later Lord Goderich), had assured the King (30 January 1826) that all was well:

> He has this morning inspected with Mr Nash all the works going on at Buckingham House … all parts of the work appear to be proceeding with the utmost expedition, compatible with so extensive an undertaking. Your Majesty may rely upon Mr Robinson's attention being regularly given to those works, in order that as little delay as possible may occur in providing a town residence suitable to Your Majesty's dignity and comfort.[89]

While some aspects of Nash's contracting were ill-judged, he was not entirely blameworthy, given the innovatory character of several aspects of the palace works. As he noted to the Treasury official, Spearman, 'it is really unfair to expect accurate estimates of such work where there are no precedents of prices nor any thing but my own judgment to guide me'.[90] Apart from the extensive use of iron girders, there was the heating, the use of a new metal, and unprecedented parquet floors.

George Stretton's heating system, chosen by the King, was 'an entire new invention … widely different from any apparatus of its kind ever manufactured'.[91] Stretton, on account of its novelty, refused to give a more precise estimate than £2,000–£3,000. Nash transmitted this to the Chancellor, informing Stretton that a more accurate figure was necessary but that he should be ready to begin work. Stretton understood this as authority to install his apparatus. It is curious that Nash, despite his visits to the palace, was unaware that the apparatus had largely been installed and was functioning during the 1829–30 winter. Presented with Stretton's account, at £3,250, he was so disconcerted that he consulted another heating engineer, John Braithwaite, who put a lower valuation on the work done, as Nash informed the Lord Chamberlain's office, which transmitted the account to the Treasury. There the matter rested until August, when Stephenson successfully urged the Treasury to pay Stretton £500 on account to prevent his being imprisoned for debt.[92]

Not dissimilar was the case of Samuel Parker, who held the patent for a mixture of copper and zinc known as 'mosaic gold'. What he used at the palace, however, was an improvement on that: an invention of his own that he termed 'golden metal'. It was employed for the capitals of the marble columns, the staircase railing (*see* Fig 7.16), the door ornaments, and the frames for the chimney piece glasses, in all about £20,000, largely on verbal contracts with Nash.[93] However, Parker's evidence was less than clear; he claimed to have won the first work – the capitals – by competitive contract at £16 per capital. Subsequent contracts were merely verbal, in gross, for the staircase railing and external gates; but 'a great number of small articles' were executed at 'so much a piece; seven pence a piece was the price of the little fleur de lis.' But confusingly, '[f]or all my work I gave in an estimated expense, not a contract'. The payments he received, however, were 'in the gross on account … put down for the whole'; 'instalments … on a general contract'.[94] He subsequently presented the Lord Chamberlain's office with an estimate for eleven chimney glass frames, to six different 'splendid designs … rather works of art than of manufacture, and which have never been previously executed', for very nearly £7,000.[95]

The matter of the ironwork was different, inasmuch as it was not purely unsatisfactory contracting, though that was one aspect. Nash was among the innovators in the structural use of iron in buildings, from Corsham Court (1797) onwards, declaring, not altogether accurately: 'I have been the principal user, and perhaps I may add, the introducer of cast-iron in the construction of the floors of buildings'. He considered the architect 'the most competent judge of the castings he requires, and their application and strength, and should direct the models by which the castings are made.'[96] So without ado he circularised ironmasters and made his contract with the largest, Crawshay of South Wales. But Crawshay, paying ready money (as Nash could not), sub-contracted for castings with founders both in Staffordshire and in London. London castings, recast in air furnaces, averaged about £3 a ton more expensive than country castings from the blast furnace, though, for large castings at least, there was some uncertainty which were stronger.[97] Unfortunately, in July 1825 the price of iron was at its highest, thereafter falling for the next five years. Crawshay provided £21,000 worth at the

peak price;[98] subsequently a further large contract was made at a somewhat lower price.

Nash's critics laboured to prove that his use of constructional ironwork in the palace was unsafe. The collapse of the iron roof of the Brunswick Theatre in London (1828) seemed to justify their concern.[99] Cockerell had noted the 'striking effects of iron arched Trusses to carry walls' as they went up.[100] Taken over the building by Blore in October 1831, Thomas Rickman commented ambivalently:

> The Ironwork is not accurately described in the Report as there is a great many fastening & Ties which are not described at all yet have considerable influence in the Strength of the whole work[.] Yet there is a recklessness of construction in many parts not required for the execution of the Building as much might have been supported without any difficulty in the lower parts & the bearings are in many instances improperly placed over intervals & openings without regard to adequate support.[101]

The 1831 Select Committee investigating the palace works asked the opinion of the Office of Works' architects, Soane, Smirke (himself an extensive user of iron structurally), and Henry Seward, together with Wyatville from Windsor. But, baffled by 'the extensive and very peculiar use of iron' and the lack of drawings, they in turn sought engineers' advice, turning to the mechanical engineer George Rennie (1791–1866), and the founder engineers John Urpeth Rastrick (1780–1856), who was very experienced in both the manufacture and use of iron castings, and Joseph Bramah junior. Rastrick's lengthy, detailed report was the most critical, but the three differed about the strength of casting necessary to ensure perfect safety in the building. Experiments were made where possible on the beams employed, and none proved defective. The architects, however, apprehensive of the responsibility imposed upon them, recommended other experiments, whereupon Nash proposed filling the State Rooms with soldiers, and made play with the differences of opinion between the engineers:[102]

> I had every casting [of the principal rooms] hammered throughout its surface to prove the soundness by the ring of metal, and Messrs Crawshay the Contractors engaged to prove the whole of the castings before they were delivered at the Building, but for my own satisfaction I proved the girders of the longest bearing; those for the Saloon were proved with 18½ tons, viz. 9¼ tons at 12½ feet from each point of

suspension – and the girders of the Throne Room were proved with 21 tons, viz: 10½ tons at 12 feet from the bearing at each end, the results in both cases were satisfactory to me, for the weights so disposed were equal to a weight infinitely greater, dispersed at as the weight would be, over the whole surface.[103]

Major difficulties in assessing the stability of the palace were the lack of drawings showing the design and the very great difficulty in examining foundations and bearers visually. It is generally agreed that Nash was slapdash in his workings, and the lack of drawings would appear to substantiate that view; his failure to keep office copies was reprehensible. But his request to the King's private secretary, Sir William Knighton, to send him 'the portfolio of the drawings of the Palace, which is in the custody of the page of the King's chamber-door',[104] suggests that, as throughout this history, the King's role was a fundamental difficulty. The evidence of the Select Committee's proceedings suggests that this portfolio was never recovered, though a box of evidently inadequate plans and drawings was submitted to them.[105] Furthermore, Nash complained to the Surveyor-General: 'I was not informed of the intended excavations and cutting of the walls and floors … that I might have had the opportunity of explaining the working drawings by which those cuttings and excavations might probably have been deemed unnecessary'.[106] Nash reported in 1833 that he had delivered to his successor Blore all working drawings relating to the palace.[107]

Having previously carried out the great work of the Regent Street Quadrant as both developer and architect, as also for his own house in Lower Regent Street, and in Suffolk Street, Nash had also at this time taken on the construction of five great houses of Carlton House Terrace East, because the sites had not sold. He sold houses to tradesmen who paid in cement, much of which he used, and some of which he sold on. He also had his own brickfield. Several Buckingham Palace tradesmen took his materials (at unexceptional prices) in order to oblige and in vain hope of advantageous treatment.[108] This gave the opportunity for enemies to accuse Nash 'of gross and direct fraud upon the public', a charge firmly rebutted by ministers: 'if there is one man less likely than another to lend himself to a fraudulent transaction, Mr Nash is the man'.[109] A Commons Select Committee vindicated his conduct.[110]

The 1828 Commons Select Committee's inquiry was into the Office of Public Works and Buildings, and the way it conducted its business; Buckingham Palace was merely one item among many. Their report had criticised Soane's Council Office in Whitehall, concluding that 'the system cannot be good which has produced such a result'.[111] Of the palace, a 'larger and more expensive building', the committee was content to notice the increased costs, met by extra-parliamentary means, and condemn the *modus operandi*: the palace 'is now undergoing very considerable alterations, not originally contemplated, for the purpose of rectifying a defect, which scarcely could have occurred, if a model of the entire edifice had previously been made and duly examined'.[112]

However, the 1831 Select Committee, of a post-Georgian Commons, was specifically charged 'to inquire into Matters connected with WINDSOR CASTLE and BUCKINGHAM PALACE'. This was a punitive committee, determined to bring the deceased King's sins to bear upon his instruments, and determined to smash Nash:

> In the evidence of Mr Nash … various reasons are assigned for the first and second additions to the original Estimate … but no reason has been given … sufficient to account for the great extent of the inaccuracy of the last Estimate, of £496,169. Your Committee are of opinion that Mr Nash … did not use proper caution, either by ascertaining from the different Tradesmen the amount of Balances then due to them, nor the probable amount of what would be so due when the Works by them to be executed should be completed.[113]

Furthermore, they judged that Nash had made improvident contracts, 'and especially with Mr Crawshay for Iron-work'. Although relentless questioning had failed to expose any corrupt dealing by Nash, or loss by the Public, nevertheless, '[y]our Committee hesitate not to express in the strongest terms their marked disapprobation' of the architect's himself 'supplying the Tradesmen with Materials'. So they found Nash guilty of 'inexcusable irregularity and great negligence', but they also condemned the previous (Tory) governments for failing to exercise adequate control.

But despite the Committee's criticisms and regrets that the estimates had not been better controlled and a better site chosen (as Nash himself had wished!), it recommended that the building 'should be finished as a Royal Residence, and ultimately as a Palace for the purposes of State'.[114] The committee had had a report from Edward Blore, celebrated for the reliability of his estimates, 'that the Building possesses great advantages' for the sovereign's residence:

> It would be an act of injustice not to bestow on the principal Apartments all the praise that is due to their number, magnificence and excellent arrangement … the defects appear to me to be trifling; and when remedied, the Palace will, in my opinion, not only become a most excellent residence, but will possess every requisite convenience for Royal occupation, with the power of extending it … for State purposes.[115]

While elements of this 'magnificence', such as the extensive use of scagliola for walls as well as columns, may be ascribed to the King's intimates, Lord Farnborough particularly, and probably Lord St Helens, it was Nash's daring imagination that accomplished the splendid interiors (Fig 7.14), and especially the superb series of ceilings in the State Rooms that puts them on a par with the finest of European palatial interiors.

Nash made great play with lighting differences for daytime effects, provided a magnificent staircase, secured the enfilades so beloved of the *ancien régime*, designed fine parquet floors,[116] appropriate marble chimney pieces, and brilliantly imaginative domed ceilings, sequels to those at Brighton, with unparalleled use of relief panels and statuary. The King's private apartments were on the ground floor, so, to accord with his taste, the Entrance Hall too (Fig 7.15) was relatively low. It was lined with coupled monolithic marble Corinthian columns with gilt bronze capitals, somewhat dim because of the deep portico, and opened to the spinal gallery intended for sculpture. It was brilliantly illuminated by a pool of light from the magnificent domed skylight of the scagliola-lined stairwell at one end. Light shone through the dome's 80 engraved glass panels, a development of the oculi in his Brighton domes. The marble stairs (Fig 7.16) rise between massive gilt bronze balustrades to a landing, from which one flight rises straight ahead to the armoury gallery, while, to the right and left, arms curve round in the manner of the Carlton House stair to return to the doors opening on the east front enfilade through to the throne (Fig 7.17). Throughout the 32ft-high

Fig 7.14
Plan of the principal floor at Buckingham Palace, as completed by Edward Blore in 1838. The chief change in plan from Nash's 1831 arrangement was the rebuilding of room
m *(Nash's Music Room, reconstructed as Blore's State Dining Room) and the corresponding twin rooms,*
o o *(at the north end of the garden front), farther west, out into the garden.*
Key to rooms:
a *Grand Stair;*
b *West Stair;*
c *Gallery;*
d *Armoury/Chapel;*
e *Guard Chamber;*
f *Green Drawing Room;*
g *Throne Room;*
h *Picture Gallery;*
i *Bow Room;*
k *Yellow/White Drawing Room;*
l *Ball Room/Blue Drawing Room;*
m *State Dining Room;*
n *and* **o** *Queen's Private Apartments*
(from Pugin and Britton, Illustrations of the Public Buildings of London ***II*** *(2nd edn), enlarged, by W H Leeds, 1838).*

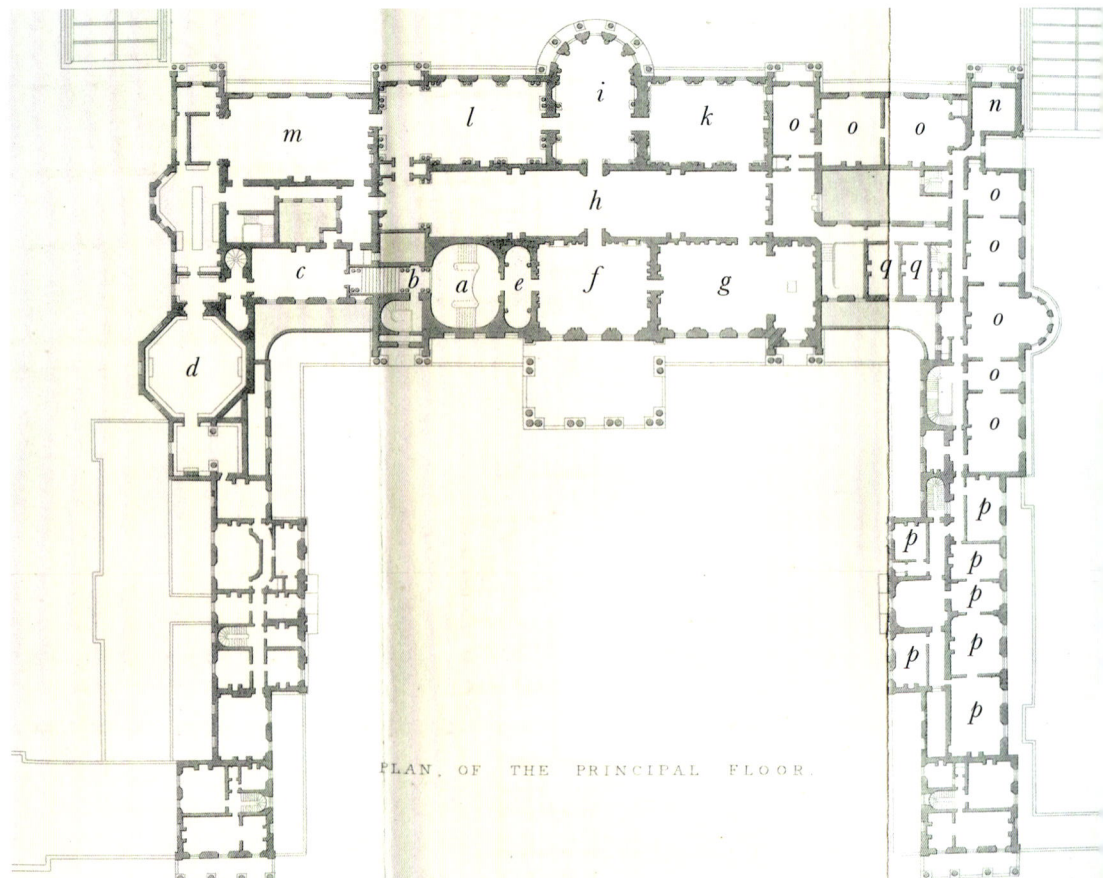

PLAN OF THE PRINCIPAL FLOOR.

(10m) state apartments (in contrast to the low ground-floor rooms) the doors are composed of mirrors framed in Parker's metal and marble work by Joseph Browne.

A tiny, symbolic guard-chamber (Fig 7.18), crowned by another panelled skylight, leads to a central Saloon that opens to the Throne Room, providing a cross-axis view to the Marble Arch and the Mall to the east, and, through the Picture Gallery and west-front Bow Room, to the gardens. Each of these rooms has a magnificent ceiling supported on deep coving above friezes on gilded pilasters ornamented with oak leaves and acorns. In the Throne Room (Fig 7.19) the low-domed ceiling rises from friezes in relief by E H Baily, to designs by Thomas Stothard,

representing crucial scenes from royal dynastic history.[117] The throne itself stands within an alcove formed by piers from which are corbelled out winged genii, modelled by William Pitts and sculpted by Francis Bernasconi, holding gilded garlands from which hangs a medallion with the King's cipher, flanked by pairs of gilded wood trophies from the Throne Room at Carlton House.

On the garden front, scagliola columns or pilasters play an important role. In the Yellow or North (now White) Drawing Room (Fig 7.20), gilded pilasters of yellow scagliola articulate the walls between the four pairs of mirror doors by Samuel Parker; as in the Throne Room, friezes in high relief support the deep coving, but here

Fig 7.15
Buckingham Palace, the Entrance Hall, enriched with monolithic veined marble columns with gilded capitals, looking through to the Marble Gallery, intended for a sculpture gallery. George IV's liking for low rooms governed Nash's ground-floor arrangements (The Royal Collection © 2011 Her Majesty Queen Elizabeth II).

*Fig 7.16 (right)
Buckingham Palace: the
Grand Staircase, rising from
the Entrance Hall, dividing
at the first landing, a central
flight continuing to the
Armoury, and the wings
returning to the balcony
before the Guard Chamber
(CC 97_00775).*

*Fig 7.17 (below)
Buckingham Palace, the
Grand Staircase, looking
north toward the State
Apartments. S Parker's
magnificent balustrade
(1828–30) cost £3,900.
Above Parker's doors
to the Guard Chamber
is T Stothard's frieze of
'Spring' (executed by his
son in 1829)
(The Royal Collection
© 2011 Her Majesty Queen
Elizabeth II).*

it is convex instead of the conventional concave. The adjoining Bow Room (Fig 7.21), in the centre of the front, is dominated by its 18 lapis lazuli scagliola Corinthian columns with gilded bronze capitals, supporting the dome on pendentives, with lozenge-shaped panels displaying the national flowers (Fig 7.22) and a half dome in the bow with its imbricated panels. Dome and semi-dome, set out in plan 'in accordance with geometrical principles', are noted by A E Richardson as innovatory stucco-work.[118] Pitts's reliefs proclaim the Progress of Eloquence. The mirror doors opening to the eastern vista are flanked by marble chimney pieces by Browne. The fine parquet floor by William Croggon is one of the few that survived Blore's economies.

Doubled Corinthian columns in 'bright crimson' scagliola[119] line the Ballroom (now the Blue Drawing Rooom) (Fig 7.23) and articulate it into two compartments with deep coving: the larger of three bays with a low dome to each, the southern bay wider, a protrusion on the garden front. Tympana above the doorways and on the

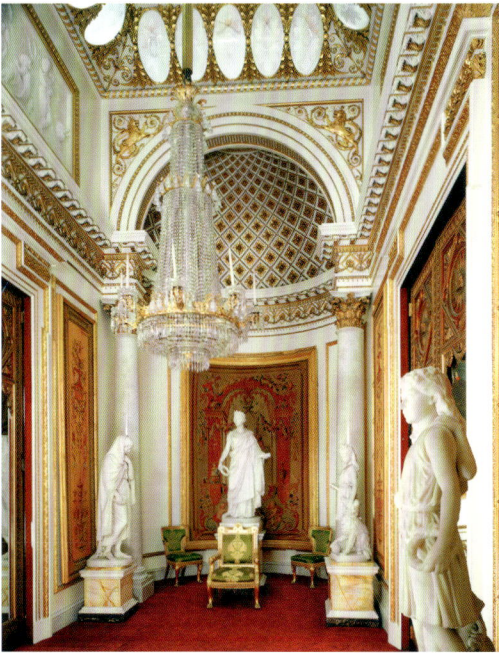

faces of the ceiling-beam marking off the smaller compartment were designed to carry Stothard's designs for reliefs of poets, but William IV rejected them, and those extant were modified and executed by Pitts. The room to the south was designed by Nash as a Music Room, with sculpture enrichments in the ceiling,[120] no doubt indicative of the room's function (like the retained marble chimney pieces, with their instrumentalist caryatides). But it was rebuilt further west, into the garden, by Blore as the State Dining Room (a room Nash had placed immediately below), the design of the ceiling being commonly ascribed to Blore. In general character it follows Nash's pattern of a deep coving, with shallow domes to each bay, as in the Ballroom, but the walls below are unadorned (Fig 7.24).[121]

Nash's spinal gallery on the state floor provided the essential Picture Gallery (Fig 7.25), necessarily lighted from above. Nash contrived

Fig 7.18 (left)
Buckingham Palace: the Guard Chamber. The range of elliptical skylights in engraved glass resembles that in the lantern above the Grand Stair, and follows Nash's innovative skylights in his domes in the Royal Pavilion, Brighton. Domical apses on either side have imbricated ceilings similar to that of the Bow Room (photograph by Derry Moore, The Royal Collection © 2011 Her Majesty Queen Elizabeth II).

Fig 7.19
Buckingham Palace: the Throne Room. Stothard's friezes of scenes of dynastic significance from English history in the manner of the Parthenon frieze embody contemporary antiquarian study of medieval costume. The winged victories supporting the royal cypher in the spandrels of the throne recess were modelled by Pitts and executed by Bernasconi (photograph by Derry Moore, The Royal Collection © 2011 Her Majesty Queen Elizabeth II).

Fig 7.20

Buckingham Palace: White Drawing Room, at north end of the West (Garden) Front. The convex coving echoes that of the music room in the Royal Pavilion, Brighton. Pitts's reliefs represent the Origin and Progress of Pleasure, and were often referred to as 'The Sports of Boys'. The chimneypieces are by R Westmacott (photograph by Derry Moore, The Royal Collection © 2011 Her Majesty Queen Elizabeth II).

an interesting ceiling that has subsequently been much altered. As early as 1800 he had employed cast iron to provide startlingly innovative top-lighting for a picture gallery (then a relatively new type of room) at Corsham Court.[122] In 1807 he had designed something similar for Attingham Park, with coving of a band of oval lights in curved cast-iron framing, gilded. But in building it, continuous glazing on a cast-iron armature was substituted (*see* Fig 8.4).[123] At the Palace, Nash installed a central row of circular lights (closed at the time of his dismissal) flanked along either side by a row of 17 engraved domical lights in the ceiling separated by pendants,[124] a form that

bewildered contemporaries: 'The ceiling … is not only picturesque and splendid, but really curious; possessing all the richness and play of outline of Gothic architecture, produced by a most skilful combination of classic forms'.[125] 'The sub-divisions in the ceiling make the room look narrow, and the drops are not, I think, correct Grecian taste.'[126] 'This imitation of Henry VII's chapel is out of its place here … the light … is false, insufficient, and broken by the architectural decorations.'[127] Soane had employed similar pendants in his picture room at 14 Lincoln's Inn Fields (1823)[128] – but ranged between a central skylight and vertical clerestory windows – and again in his

contemporary Court of Chancery, Westminster. Had Nash been influenced by these examples, nevertheless his glazing of the space defined by the pendants exemplifies the imaginative leaps of which his mind was capable. Blore improved the lighting by opening up the central skylights.[129] The three doorcases (removed in 1914, together with Nash's ceiling) differed from the others in the State Apartments: they were of scagliola with, on either side, large termini with the head of Apollo, figures symbolical of Painting on the pediment,

and medallions of Michelangelo, Raphael and Titian.[130] Nash's five chimney pieces, executed in Italy, each carried a medallion of a famous painter.[131]

The Marble Arch

Nash's design for rebuilding Buckingham House with a much wider forecourt called for some means of closing the court. French patterns suggested a low enclosing wall or railing with a central entrance. It was probably George IV

Fig 7.21
Buckingham Palace: Bow or Music Room, at centre of West Front. Eighteen lapis lazuli scagliola columns are separated by mirrors in frames by Parker. The spandrels contain reliefs by Pitts representing the Progress of Rhetoric. Chimneypieces on either side of the central doorway were executed by Joseph Browne (photograph by Derry Moore, The Royal Collection © 2011 Her Majesty Queen Elizabeth II).

Fig 7.22 (right)
Buckingham Palace:
Detail of Bow Room ceiling,
showing heraldic flowers
of the three kingdoms
(The Royal Collection
© 2011 Her Majesty Queen
Elizabeth II).

Fig 7.23 (below)
Buckingham Palace:
the Blue Drawing Room
served as the Ballroom until
Pennethorne's additions of
1855. The plaster reliefs of
the tympana celebrating
English poets, executed by
W Pitts, were based on
Stothard's designs inspired
by Raphael's 'Parnassus'.
The scagliola columns were
originally strawberry-
coloured
(photograph by Peter Smith,
The Royal Collection
© 2011 Her Majesty Queen
Elizabeth II).

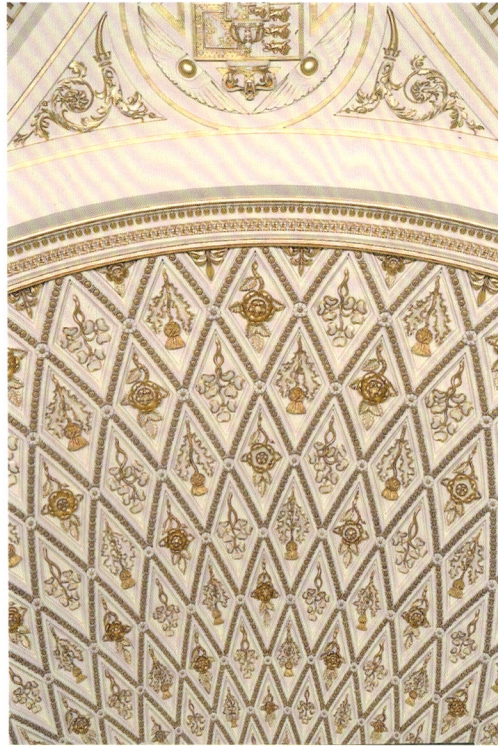

who determined that this entrance should be a triumphal arch,[132] such as Percier and Fontaine had erected for Napoleon at the Tuileries, though Soane, in his design for a royal palace exhibited in 1821, had employed a free-standing triumphal arch surmounted by a quadriga.[133] In the post-Waterloo years, there was much discussion of triumphal arches to celebrate the British victories, with several proposed by Soane.[134] Steven Brindle has discerned the possible influence of a tract by Sir William Hillary, Baronet, suggesting that a military victory monument, in the style of Constantine's arch might 'form the grand approach to the future royal residence'.[135] *The Times* referred on 23 January 1826 to the arch as a celebration of military victory, naming it 'the Waterloo monument'.

Andrew Saint finds the inspiration for copying Percier's Carrousel Arch in Nash's assistant James Pennethorne, who was drawing in Paris in the autumn of 1825, though Nash himself was already familiar with Paris.[136] Nash himself later told Wellington that his arch was

'a plagiarism of the Arch of Constantine',[137] the common source of both arches. Nash had intended to build his arch of Bath stone, concordant with the palace,[138] but it was soon decided to face it with marble, probably a royal decision.[139] Nash was already purchasing marble on an unparalleled scale for the palace interiors, and in an undated letter to his agent, Joseph Browne, sending him drawings of the arch, he stated that that, in consultation with the King and Sir Charles Long, he had determined to have what Browne termed 'ordinary marble'; the capitals were to be carved in Rome, and 12 blocks were to be obtained for figures to surmount the columns and pedestals.[140]

Richard Cockle Lucas (1800–83) made an ivory model from Nash's drawings, but difficulty in arranging his figures drove Nash to seek the assistance of John Flaxman, the pre-eminent sculptor of the day:

[Y]ou will see that I meant Lord Wellington and the group behind him to be insulated figures – and the pedestal on which they stand brought forward instead of receding – but they appeared like actors on a stage and not knowing how to get rid of that impression I made the center to retreat and the gro[up] of Wellington and his aid de camp[s to] be against the circular pedestal of the Tower in alto relievo … I will thank you for your opinion and remarks upon the whole of it.[141]

Fig 7.24
Buckingham Palace: the State Dining Room. Designed by Nash as a music room, as the chimneypiece caryatides indicate, but rebuilt further westward in 1832–4 by Blore, whose ceiling may have been based on a Nash design (photograph by John Freeman, The Royal Collection © 2011 Her Majesty Queen Elizabeth II).

Fig 7.25
Buckingham Palace: the
Picture Gallery. Contemporaries
had difficulty in describing
the style of Nash's system of
overhead lighting, although
he previously employed it
elsewhere, including a simpler
version in the Royal Mews
(1822) and more fully Gothic
in his unexecuted design for
the Waterloo Room at
Windsor Castle, 1824.
The marble doorcases
were by Croggon; the
chimneypieces, each bearing
the bust of a famous painter,
were executed in Italy (The
Royal Collection © 2011 Her
Majesty Queen Elizabeth II).

The ivory model, if completed, has vanished, but a plaster model in the Victoria and Albert Museum shows Nash's ultimate intentions: one front and side were devoted to military (Fig 7.26), the other front and side to naval triumphs. Flaxman died before his designs could be executed, and modifications were made. On the east front, Richard Westmacott was to carve victories in the spandrels of the great arch, and wreaths for the smaller arches; two relief panels above the smaller arches representing the King approving the plan of the Waterloo campaign and rewarding Wellington with the Garter; a long frieze of Wellington's campaigns (with a corresponding marine frieze on the west); and four statues to surmount the giant Corinthian columns that flanked the arches. The short sides were to have one a military, the other a naval bas relief. The naval or west front, entrusted to E H Baily, was to have victories in all six spandrels, two square relief panels, and four statues.[142] The arch was to be crowned with an equestrian statue of King George IV by Francis Chantrey,[143] on an attic pedestal, of which the military side was to bear a relief of Europe on a horse and Asia on a camel supporting a medallion of Wellington by D J Rossi, with a similar allegory of Nelson, flanked by lion, unicorn and Britannia, on the naval front.[144]

The arch was incomplete when Nash was dismissed, and its design was reduced by Blore. Westmacott's friezes were used on the palace itself, the attic reliefs employed on the new National Gallery, and the King's statue erected in Trafalgar Square.[145] When Blore completed his new East Front in 1850, closing the palace courtyard, that made the Arch inconvenient. It was taken down and eventually re-erected at Cumberland Gate, at the north-eastern corner of Hyde Park.[146]

King George IV died on 26 June 1830. Wellington's administration issued a Treasury Minute on 15 October, suspending Nash from his appointments, and on 21 October the Treasury directed the Surveyor-General to stop all works at Buckingham Palace.[147]

John Nash was an architect of genius, but not that type of genius that is 'an infinite capacity for taking pains', such as Soane represented. He scribbled his vision on a scrap of paper for his staff to work up painstakingly, but he did have that vision of what could be contrived in architecture beyond the conventions of his day. It was at once his good fortune to serve a prince who shared his exuberant enjoyment in the capacity of architecture, and at the same time his ill fate to serve a constitutional sovereign, a connoisseur but of inconstant mind.

Fig 7.26
Buckingham Palace: a plaster model of the Marble Arch, as designed by Nash c 1826 as the state gateway to the palace, approach (east) side, celebrating Britain's military glories. Most of Westmacott's frieze of the Battle of Waterloo was eventually placed in the east front of the palace, and Chantrey's crowning equestrian statue of George IV found a pedestal in Trafalgar Square (Courtesy Victoria & Albert Museum, A14-1939).

Notes

1828 Report: *Parliamentary Papers* 1828 (446) IV, 'Report from the Select Committee on the Office of Works'

1831 Report: *Parliamentary Papers* 1831 (329) IV, 'Second Report of the Select Committee on Windsor Castle and Buckingham Palace'

1   Summerson 1980, 14, 25–6, 29; Thorne, R G (ed) 1986 **IV**, 791
2   Summerson, 1980, 57
3   Walpole, Horace (Steuart, A F ed) 1910 *Last Journals*. London: John Lane, The Bodley Hea, **II**, 497
4   Summerson 1980, 90–4
5   Summerson 1980, 94
6   Morshead, O 1965 *George IV and Royal Lodge*. Brighton: Regency Society of Brighton and Hove, 9, 11
7   *Windsor Guide, 1815*. Windsor: C. Knight, 181
8   Morshead 1965 (*see note 6*), 12. Lord Castlereagh defended it in the Commons, remarking that it was 'called a cottage because it was thatched', but was really a substantial house; see Crook and Port 1973, 399, note 5.
9   Morshead 1965 (*see note 6*), 30, quoting Princess Lieven

10   Crook and Port 1973, 399–400 and NA, WORK references there given
11   Quennell, P (ed) 1948 *The Private Letters of Princess Lieven to Prince Metternich, 1820–26*, 276
12   Crook and Port 1973, 307–15
13   NA, LC 1/6, f 340, 29 Dec 1812
14   Illustrated in Mansbridge 1991, 182.
15   Summerson 1980, 97, pl 9
16   NA, LC 1/6, f 346, 18 March1814
17   For Nash's Carlton House interiors, Pyne, W H 1819 *History of the Royal Residences* (3 vols). London: A. Dry, **III**
18   There is a detailed description in *Annual Register* 1814, Chronicle, 63–5, largely reproduced in Crook and Port 1973, 317–8.
19   Farington, *Diary* (ed Garlick *et al* 1978–1984) **XIII**, 4562. (Sir) Thomas Lawrence, who was there, told Farington the diameter was 136ft; Crook and Port 1973, 318 say 116ft.
20   Removed to Woolwich in 1819 for an artillery museum, given brick walls and a leaden roof, this survives today. Nash's instructions for taking it down are in NA, WORK 1/9, 59–61; cf *Apollo* **169**

(May, 2009), 60–1, 'Tent for a prince'; *see this volume, see pages 158–9, 164.*

21 NA, WORK 19/11/5, f 32

22 NA, WORK 1/9, p.309

23 Farington, *Diary* (ed Garlick *et al* 1978–1984) **XVI**, 5741

24 Musgrave, C 1959 *Royal Pavilion*. London: Leonard Hill, 14; Dinkel, J 1983 *The Royal Pavilion Brighton*. London: Philip Wilson and Summerfield Press, 18–24; this book sets out fully the background history, for which see also Roberts, H D 1939 *A History of the Royal Pavilion Brighton*. London: Country Life.

25 Dinkel 1983 (*see note 24*), 25

26 Dinkel 1983 (*see note 24*), 39–41

27 Dinkel 1983 (*see note 24*), 41–4; Musgrave 1959 (*see note 24*), 53–8, pls 15 and 16

28 Musgrave 1959 (*see note 24*), 60

29 RA 34216–19, unpublished preface to John Nash's *Views of the Royal Pavilion Brighton,* quoted in Morley, J 1984 *The Making of the Royal Pavilion Brighton. Design and Drawings*. London: Philip Wilson, 68, which reproduces all the important designs for the interior and exterior of the Royal Pavilion (but see also Dinkel 1983 (*see note 24*) for Nixon's sections). Musgrave 1959 (*see note 24*) quotes 'in full' Nash's MS draft.

30 Summerson 1980, 104

31 Dinkel 1983 (*see note 24*), 52

32 Dinkel 1983 (*see note 24*), 53

33 Both designs are illustrated in Nash, J (Jackson-Stops, G ed) 1991 *Views of the Royal Pavilion*. London: Pavilion Books, 28, and in Musgrave 1959 (*see note 24*), pls 19, 21

34 Nash, J 1991 (*see note 33*), 28

35 Roberts 1939 (*see note 24*), 95

36 Summerson 1980, 162

37 See sectional drawings by William Nixon, the Pavilion clerk of works, reproduced in Dinkel 1983 (*see note 24*), 57–8. Nash's structural innovations at the Pavilion are discussed in more detail; *see pages 158–9, 164 (this volume).*

38 Morley 1984 (*see note 29*), 71

39 These seem 'to be based on Daniell's illustration of a hall at Allahabad' (Summerson 1980, 105)

40 Dinkel 1983 (*see note 24*), 66

41 cf Musgrave 1959 (*see note 24*), pl 25. It is presumed that Nash saw drawings before publication.

42 Summerson 1980, 108. Hamelin's specification is in RA 34068 (5 June 1817)

43 Musgrave 1959 (*see note 24*), 75. The letter (Knighton to Grey, 21 Nov 1822) condemning Nash's experimental roofing is the only one in the Pavilion correspondence bearing the royal sign-manual (Roberts 1939 (*see note 24*), 116)

44 Roberts 1939 (*see note 24*), 112

45 Roberts 1939 (*see note 24*), 113–14. For some items, such as 'Alterations of the 2 Iron staircases', no figure was inserted in the estimates (Morley 1984 (*see note 29*), 76).

46 Roberts 1939 (*see note 24*), 118. For Nash's commission, see also Musgrave 1959 (*see note 24*), 75 (citing RA 33960).

47 Roberts 1939 (*see note 24*), 113–14, based on Windsor, RA 33973–4; Musgrave 1959 (*see note 24*), 160

48 Summerson 1980, 109

49 Musgrave 1959 (*see note 24*), 67

50 Crook and Port 1973, chapter V

51 NA, WORK 19/3/12, 29 July 1819

52 Summerson 1980, 157–60

53 Farington, *Diary* (ed Garlick *et al* 1978–1984) **XVI**, 5740

54 NA, WORK 19/3, f 217, 21 Oct 1821

55 NA, WORK 19/3, f 219, 10 Aug.1822

56 NA, WORK 19/3, ff 219 and 220, 10 Aug and 1 Aug 1822

57 1831 Report, 270–1, Nash to chairman, select committee, 29 July 1831

58 RIBA, MS Nas/1 ('Shide ledger'), 42

59 NA, T.1/3488, f 19080/1830 (estimate of 20 June 1825)

60 The new Mall (east, but without the arch) and garden (west) fronts are shown in engravings (the east after a drawing by Auguste Pugin) reproduced in Crook and Port 1973, pls 6A, 7A.

61 *See note 59.*

62 BL, Add. MS 39781, f 258, Nash to Flaxman, 18 Sept.1826, quoted Crook and Port 1973, 298

63 Kraft, J C and Ransonnette, N 1801, 1812 *Les plus belles maisons et hotels construits à Paris et dans les environs* (2 vol). Paris: [publisher unknown]

64 *Despatches … of the Duke of Wellington* (ns 1867–80), ed. 2nd Duke of Wellington. London: John Murray, **VI** (1878), 3

65 Pevsner regarded the domed bow as 'strikingly unpalatial (Bradley, S and Pevsner, N 2003 *Buildings of England, London 6: Westminster*. New Haven and London: Yale University Press, 637). But a central domed bow is found in several European palaces, eg R de Cotte's Thurn and Taxis palace at Frankfurt on Main, and in grand Parisian houses of the late 18th century. Nash had in 1810 employed the motif at Rockingham (Ireland), which also has a spinal gallery (Mansbridge 1991, 164). For the Palais de Salm, built for a minor German sovereign living in Paris, Kraft and Ransonnette 1801, 1812 (*see note 63*) **I**, pl 74, and Braham, A 1980 *The Architecture of the French Enlightenment*. London: Thames and Hudson, 229–30. It was influenced by Peyre's innovatory project for the Hôtel de Condé (1763) with its triumphal arch in the forecourt screen, as well as by designs of Gondoin and Ledoux.

66 1831 Report, App 12, 284

67 *Fraser's Magazine* May 1830, 385. A full list of the statuary and reliefs is given in Crook and Port 1973, 300–2. Recent precedents can be found in Parisian architecture of the 1770s and 1780s, for example Ledoux, Berlanger, Brongniart (Kraft and Ransonnette 1801 (*see note 63*), eg **I**, pls 5, 6, 29, 40, 74; **II**, pl 1. For Holland's Royal Pavilion Virtues, Kelly, A 1985 'Coade stone in Georgian Architecture'. *Architect Hist* **28**, 71

68 Marsden, J 2001 ' "England's Raphael" and his lost Parnassus'. *Georgian Group J* **XI**, 44

69 Watkin, D 1974, 68 (1 Aug 1826)

70 1828 Report, 60

71 Summerson 1980, 163; 1828 Report, 61. Nash had, at some point, a project of raising an attic crowned by statues over the entire centre building (*Fraser's Mag* May 1830, 384).

72 Hussey, C 1931 'The building of Buckingham Palace', *in* Smith, H Clifford *Buckingham Palace*. London: Country Life, 40

73 *Mirror of Parliament, 1829 session* **III**, 1864

74 1828 Report, 61. There were, of course many French precedents for low wings to an entrance court, notably Victor Louis's Palais Royal constructed for the Prince of Wales' friend 'Philippe Egalité' in 1780, and Gondoin's École de Chirurgerie.

75 [anonymous] 1991 *Carlton House: The Past Glories of George IV's Palace* [exhibition catalogue]. London: Queen's Gallery, 15

76 Farington, *Diary* (ed Garlick *et al* 1978–1984) **VII**, 2745; Aspinall, A 1938 *Correspondence of George, Prince of Wales*. Cambridge: Cambridge University Press, **III**, no. 2078 (quoted in [anonymous] 1991 (*see note 75*)

77 1828 Report, 48

78 1831 report, 271

79 St Helens (1753–1839) had been envoy to Russia in 1783–7, and ambassador in 1801–2 ('parce qu'il connoit le pays, et qu'il est connu et estimé'), G E C [author gives only these initials] (ed G H White) 1949 *The Complete Peerage* **X**. London: St Catherine Press), 314-6, citing Count Woronzow to Lord Grenville, *Hist MSS Comm, Fortescue* **VII**, 5.

80 1831 Report, 271, Nash's evidence

81 Aspinall 1938, no. 1278

82 BL, Herries MSS, 35 (1826–7, Correspondence including York House)

83 Aspinall 1938 (*see note 76*), 47

84 Aspinall 1938 (*see note 76*), 45

85 NA, T.1/3489 pt **II**, SG to Treasury, 24 Dec 1825

86 NA, T.1/3489 pt **II**, SG to Treasury, 26 Jan 1826; Crook and Port 1973, 136–40

87 NA, T.1/3489 pt **II**, no. 13226/26, printed (with typographical differences) in 1831 Report, 200

88 1831 Report, 86–96, 98–110, 290–323

89 Aspinall 1938 (*see note 76*), no. 1227

90 NA, T.1/3488, 19 Aug 1829

91 1831 Report, 170, Stretton to Treasury, 14 May 1830

92 1831 Report, 169, 171

93 This appears to have been another misjudgement by Nash of an innovation: the work had subsequently to be re-gilded.

94 1831 Report, 111–15, 167

95 1831 Report, 168, 17 Apr 1830

96 1831 Report, 274. Nash's use of iron at Buckingham Palace is also discussed in chapter 8.

97 1831 Report, 133, 137, 254

98 1831 Report, 129–32, evidence of Robert Moser, Crawshay's London partner; compare with evidence of other iron masters, J Wyke Fowler and J J Bramah (1831 Report, 135–9). The last claimed that castings made from the second smelting (the air furnace) were much stronger than those from the blast.

99 [anonymous] 1828 *Companion to the Almanac*. London: C Knight, 174

100 Watkin 1974, 68 (1 Aug 1826)

101 BL, Add MS 37800, 25 Oct 1831

102 1831 Report, Appendix, 233–7 (Rennie), 237–58

103 NA, WORK 19/3, ff 114–15. There are drawings of these girders at ff 118–19. Rastrick provides a table of strength of iron beams in the ground floor, with sections, 1831 Report, 255–7

104 Lady Knighton 1838 *Memoirs of Sir William Knighton*. London: Richard Bentley, **II**, 160–2, 6 July 1830

105 NA, WORK 4/30, f 535

106 NA, WORK 19/3, f 123, 19 Apr 1831

107 NA, WORK 19/5, f 943

108 1831 Report, 53, 57–9 (Whitehead); 61–5, 67–8 (Read); 65 (McIntosh); 74–6 (Harrison).

109 Charles Arbuthnot, head of the Office of Woods and Forests, *Mirror of Parliament, 1829 session* **III**, 1861 (25 May). The chancellor of the exchequer, Goulburn, spoke similarly.

110 Summerson 1991, 196–205

111 1828 Report, 7

112 1828 Report, 7–8

113 1831 Report, 3–6

114 1831 Report, 6

115 1831 Report, App 14, 324

116 Several of these fell victim to Blore's economies; that in the Bow Room was executed by George Seddon at a cost of £2,340 (1831 Report, 179)

117 For Stothard's work in the palace, Marsden 2001 (*see note 68*), 29–46

118 Smith 1931 (*see note 72*), 158, note 2

119 Leeds, W H 1838 *Illustrations of the Public Buildings of London … by Pugin and Britton*. London: John Weale, **II**, 302; or, according to Creevey, 'raspberry-coloured' (Maxwell, Sir H (ed) 1904 *The Creevey Papers*. London: John Murray, **II**, 307

120 1831 Report, 183; £649 10s had been paid for these.

121 Included in the list of works ordered by the king, but not begun (1831 Report, 181), is 'Three engraved plate glasses for windows' for the Music Room, which suggests that the circular engraved glass panels in the State Dining Room may have been part of Nash's designs, and taken up by Blore.

122 Ladd, F J 1978, 105–6

123 Ladd, F J 1978, pl 69; Davis 1960, pls 37 and 38. For a history of top-lighting schemes, Compton, M 1991 'The architecture of daylight', *in* Waterfield G (ed) *Palaces of Art*. London: Dulwich Picture Gallery, 37–42. Nash's gallery for Benjamin West, PRA, in 1821, with central top-light screened, and further top-lighting at the sides (Compton 1991, 36, 41), somewhat similar in principal to the palace gallery, was claimed by his sons to be the design of J B Papworth.

124 Described by Nash (1831 Report, 271). William Seguier, Conservator of the King's Pictures, had complained the gallery lighting was inadequate, but could be rectified by centre skylights (1831 Report, 231; *see also* 1831 Report, 175, Paper A, 'Works to be done to complete the Building according to Nash's estimates', which received the sanction of the Treasury: Picture Gallery, '17 ground glass, centre lights, plain'; NA, WORK 3/4, 135, 29 Sept 1832, William Froom, tender for plate glass to Picture Gallery skylights; NA, LRRO 2/1, 182; 1831 Report,

179, Paper C, Works ordered by George IV in addition to estimates sanctioned by the Treasury: '38 engraved glasses for the picture gallery £1080 3s. Credit by instalment £300'. The balance was paid in 1833–4, LRRO 2/2.

125 *Fraser's Magazine* **I**, iv (May, 1830), 385; Nash had designed a similar roof for the Billiard Room at East Cowes Castle.

126 Bamforth, F and the Duke of Wellington (eds) 1950 *Journal of Mrs Arbuthnot 1820–1832*. London: Macmillan, **II**, 343

127 von Raumer, F L G 1836 *England in 1835* (trans S Austin, 3 vols,), quoted *Athenaeum*, 13 Feb 1836

128 Waterfield (ed) 1991 (*see note 122*), 10

129 NA, WORK 19/4, ff 802–4. According to L Kharibian it was Prince Albert who ordered the installation of the central row of skylights, but no reference is given (Kharibian, L 2010 *Passsionate Patrons: Victoria and Albert and the Arts*. London: Royal Collection Publications, 157).

130 1831 Report, 161

131 NA, WORK 19/3, f 346

132 Late in 1816 George as Regent had purchased what Farington refers to as 'a beautiful model upon a small [scale] of Arches in imitation of the celebrated Antique Arches at Rome' (Farington, *Diary* (ed Garlick *et al* 1978–1984) **XIV**, 4921), evidently the marble and bronze models of the Roman Arches of Titus, Septimius Severus and Constantine, now at Windsor Castle, described by H Clifford Smith in *Country Life*, 4 July 1952, 38–9.

133 Bolton, A T (ed) 1924 *The Works of Sir John Soane*. London: Sir John Soane Museum Publications, 123

134 Crook and Port 1973, 294

135 Hillary, Bt, Sir W 1825 *Suggestions for the Improvement and Embellishment of the Metropolis*

(2nd edn), BL, press mark T.1997 (17), cited by Brindle, S 2001 'The Wellington Arch and the western entrance to London'. *Georgian Group J* **XI**, 66–7.

136 Saint, A 1997 'The Marble Arch', *Georgian Group J* **VII**, 77; see also Tyack 1992, 12. It is true that Pennethorne's host, Lafitte, had sculptured panels on the Carrousel Arch.

137 *Wellington New Despatches* **VI** (1877) (*see note 64*), 3–4

138 NA, T.1/3488, f 19080/1830, copy of estimate of 20 June 1825: 'The Entrance archway and circular railing (proposed sculpture of the Archway not included) £8,900' (1828 Report, 15–16)

139 Nash, questioned in 1828, was unable to recall when the change was made (1828 Report, 16). It was not mentioned in an account of the arch given in *The Times*, 23 Jan 1826, but it is referred to in a letter from the marble merchant Joseph Browne to Nash, 22 Feb 1826, printed in 1831 Report, 303: 'I am of opinion that you could not use any better material for the Triumphal Arch than … the ordinary vein or the ordinary marble'.

140 1831 Report, 306–7, letter received in Italy 21 May 1826. The capitals were copied from one inside the Pantheon (1831 Report, 308, Browne to Nash, 23 May 1826).

141 BL, Add MS 39781, ff 254–5, 21 Aug 1826

142 NA, T.1/3488, f 19080/30; T.1/3489, f 1682/29

143 Now in Trafalgar Square

144 On the Victoria and Albert model these attic pedestal reliefs have been transposed.

145 Crook and Port 1973, 295–6, 301, 467

146 Saint 1997 (*see note 135*), 85–91

147 NA, WORK, 4/30, 366–7

8

Pioneering yet peculiar: John Nash's contributions to late Georgian building technology

JONATHAN CLARKE

There is not a single roof in the Pavilion at Brighton which did not from its form require a peculiar construction, differing in all respects from ordinary roofs … (John Nash, 28 July 1831)[1]

[Buckingham Palace] … is a different construction to any building I ever saw of the same nature, it is so strong it must last forever, or go all at once … (George Harrison, builder, 18 March, 1831)[2]

John Summerson was possibly overstating matters in thinking that 'Nash was the last English architect to consider himself not only an architect but an engineer'.[3] Some of Nash's architect contemporaries, such as Edward Holl and Daniel Alexander might be described better as architect-engineers,[4] and a handful of Victorian successors, including Aitchison, I'Anson, Scott, Waterhouse and Norman Shaw, had uncommon appreciation, and understanding, of construction, Shaw even admitting that he was 'intended by nature to be an engineer'.[5] Nash's career began in an era of professional fluidity, when it was possible for men such as Robert Mylne to truly style themselves as 'Architect and Engineer',[6] but it ended at a time when the structural aspects of architecture, and certain building types, were coming increasingly within the purview of civil engineers. He almost certainly always saw himself as first and foremost an architect. To Nash, being a good architect meant being a good constructor, reliant, perhaps, on the services of fellow tradesmen and professionals, but not on their expertise. In 1831, with his own constructional proficiency at Buckingham Palace under scrutiny, he adamantly maintained that '[t]he Architect ought to be the most competent judge of the form of the castings he requires and their application and strength',[7]

also declaring: 'No founder ever furnished me with a design for any casting I ever used.'[8] Although one obituarist (possibly the engineer William Ranger), writing in 1836, was of the opinion that 'Mr Nash seems to have been a better engineer than an architect',[9] Nash would likely not have welcomed the observation,[10] nor the remark that 'Mr Nash's works are not built for posterity (and posterity will, no doubt, thank him for having so much consideration in sparing them the trouble of demolition)'.[11] Nonetheless, the architect, whose only works of real civil engineering (in early 19th-century demarcations) were the Highgate Archway (1812–13) and the Regent's Park Sewer (1813–17),[12] took pride in the fact that he could have, if he had so wished, undertaken more civil engineering projects, recalling 'I had frequent invitations to form piers, docks, and other works, exclusively the province of engineers'.[13] As far as bridges were concerned – still at the beginning of the nineteenth century as much the preserve of architects as engineers – Nash recollected: 'The late Mr Rennie pressed me to give a design for building London Bridge, offering me the use of his survey and section of the river'.[14]

That Nash's engineer contemporaries, including John Rennie, rated his abilities – both in their sole, and their shared, fields of endeavour – testifies to his capability as a designer-constructor, as does his role as expert witness in the inquest into the collapse of the Brunswick Theatre's wrought-iron roof in 1828 (Fig 8.1). Nash, like fellow expert witness Smirke, was described as having 'scientific knowledge and practical skill',[15] yet it seems likely that in Nash's case the latter always surpassed the former. Although Nash was acquainted with the classic

Fig 8.1
Nash and Smirke were
among the experts brought
in to investigate the collapse
on 28 February 1828 of
Thomas Stedman Whitwell's
Brunswick Theatre,
Whitechapel, Nash
concluding 'that the
principle upon which the
roof was constructed was
injudicious, unsafe, and
improper for a theatre'
(London Metropolitan
Archives p7491484;
quotation from Cruikshank,
Robert 1828 'Inquiry into
the fall of the Brunswick
Theatre collapse',
Mechanics' Magazine
9, 201).

works on architecture and carpentry by De L'Orme, Krafft, and Vitruvius, as well as some of Smeaton's Reports, and books by Lacroix on analytic and differential geometry, it is significant that, unlike Smirke's library, his did not embrace works by Tredgold, Barlow or Pasley, or any of the French engineering classics.[16] As James Sutherland concludes, the 'architect who understood his ironwork best was probably Robert Smirke'.[17] But however questionable, in a mathematic or scientific sense, Nash's understanding of structural materials and behavior (betokened, perhaps, by the collapse of the first Teme bridge and the mid-19th-century replacement of much structurally problematic work at Corsham), no other English architect of his era used iron with such ambition, imagination or flair. As Diestelkamp, Dinkel and Summerson have shown, Nash made innovatory, but typically unconventional, use of structural cast iron, and the architectural effects were similarly pioneering, and at times peculiar.[18] Equally, but perhaps less appreciated, he achieved similar levels of innovation in structural timber.[19] The aim here is to draw

together some of the patterns and progressions evident in his known constructive output in iron and timber, focusing largely on the latter because, within Nash historiography, this has received less attention.

Structural iron

Cast-iron beams

Nash declared in 1831 that he was 'the principal user, and perhaps I may add, the introducer of cast iron in the construction of the floors of buildings'.[20] Notwithstanding the pioneering use of cast iron for principal floor beams in the Castle Foregate Flax Mill, Shrewsbury (1796–7), the Salford Twist Mill (1799), and the Meadow Lane Mill, Leeds (1802),[21] it seems almost certain that John Nash was the first architect to employ cast-iron beams and joists covertly within the fabric of polite British architecture. Certainly he was ahead of Smirke in this respect.[22] He probably did this as much for reasons of stiffness – creating floors that did not sag or bounce[23] – as for non-combustibility. He also had a lively interest in extending the structural uses of a metal with which he had some early association: his family originally came from Broseley in Shropshire, and he might conceivably have experienced, at first hand, casting technique at the foundries of Coalbrookdale and Bersham.[24] Corsham Court, Wiltshire, seems to have been the earliest recorded recipient for cast-iron beams; here, as part of his transformations and additions to the Elizabethan house from 1797 to 1802, Nash specified the use of 'girders in all floors of the north front except the ground floor'.[25] He employed them also at Luscombe, Devon (1799–1804), 'to support the weight of the upper brickwork';[26] at Aqualate Hall, Forton, Staffordshire (1806–9), as part of a 'fireproof' floor structure; and at Barnsley Park, Gloucestershire (1806–c 1810), to span over the library.[27] Doubtless he used them also in many of his other lesser documented, or investigated, town- and country-house commissions, as well as large

Metropolitan Improvement works, including the United Service Club (1826–8).[28] Available evidence suggests that Nash almost always employed hog-backed solid inverted T-sections, similar to those pioneered by George Lee at Salford or Charles Bage at Leeds.[29] He did this, it seems, not because it was more geometrically rational (prefiguring, in some senses, Hodgkinson's 'ideal' asymmetrical I-section of 1831, albeit based on less precise rationale), but because the enlarged lower flange gave a greater bearing surface, and a shelf for joists. Evidently he was unconvinced by Tredgold's equal-flanged I-section of the early 1820s, a form based on the erroneous assumption of equal strength of cast iron in tension and compression. The beams that Nash designed for Buckingham Palace, dated 1 July 1825, were primarily inverted T-beams spanning from 16ft to 38ft (5m to 12m), although he did employ I-sections within the Saloon, spanning 38ft (12m) between bearings (Fig 8.2). Unlike those utilised by Smirke in the British Museum, designed by J U Raistick, the

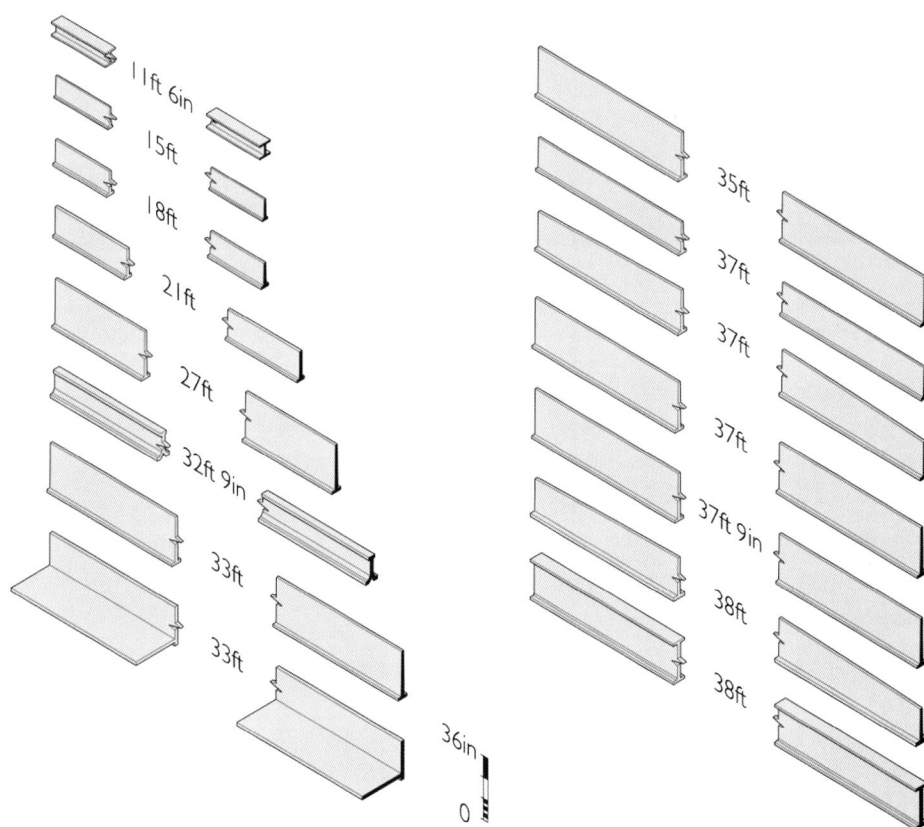

Buckingham House (Palace)
Cast-iron beams, 1825

Dimensions refer to the span. Overall length would be 18-24in longer

Fig 8.2
Nash employed a great variety of beam profiles at Buckingham Palace, including I, Y, L and inverted T forms in lengths up to 38ft (drawing by Andy Donald).

flanges of Nash's beams did not enlarge at the ends – a feature that was criticised during the enquiry because it rendered them less laterally secure, and offered an insufficient width of bearing.[30] For Buckingham Palace, Nash also designed huge L-section beams spanning 33ft (10m) between brickwork, and, more significantly and more efficiently in terms of geometry, inverted Y-shaped girders to carry the Portico of the East Front (Fig 8.2). This form, and the inverted-V shape, later became known as 'skewback' girders, and were specifically cast for employment with jack-arched floors, as they provided the requisite angled abutment to resist the outward thrust of the arches. That the ironwork, contracted from Crawshay's Cyfarthfa ironworks, Merthyr Tydfil, was supplied in 1826 makes Nash a good candidate as the originator of this popular form, used for example by Charles Parker at Hoare's Bank, No. 37 Fleet Street (1829–30), and by Jesse Hartley throughout Albert Dock Warehouses, Liverpool (1843–6).

Modular design

The collapse of Nash's first iron bridge, 'a most light and elegant thing …'[31] spanning 98ft (30m) over the Teme at Stanford (1795),[32] seems to have occasioned a more cautious approach to long-span construction in cast iron, but with the benefit of introducing an element of modularity within his structural vocabulary. Its replacement, built in 1797 and surviving until 1905, 'was really a unique contrivance with cast iron arch ribs and road plates, but with hollow brick cylinders through the spandrels'.[33] It was loosely based on a patent he took out in February that year (no. 2165, 1797) for iron bridges, made up of hollow-box cast- or plate-iron voussoirs, bolted together side-by-side and that could be filled with ballast, with hollow iron sections in the spandrels.[34] By emulating a stone-arch bridge, with bolted iron boxes forming the whole width and span of the arch, the patented design timorously avoided the tensile deficiencies of cast iron. Summerson remarked that '[s]uch a bridge could scarcely fail to stand up if properly carried out with adequate abutment'.[35] Despite some ornamental iron bridges,[36] the replacement Teme bridge was Nash's last major excursion into bridge-building, and he did not take out any further patents. Yet, as Diestelkamp points out, the idea resurfaced at Brighton. The minarets flanking the central dome were formed from hollow cast-iron cores

clad in rings of coursed Bath stone.[37] Standing 34ft (10.4m) high, these cores were formed from two sections, the upper, tapering section bolted onto a lower, 2ft 6in (0.8m) diameter cylindrical one, which was in turn bolted onto a grillage of cast-iron trusses that spanned the cast-iron columns embedded in the saloon's brick walls (see Fig 7.7).[38]

Coved clerestoreys

One of the most inventive and influential uses Nash made of cast iron was for overhead coved window framing, enabling, for the first time, pictures to be hung on all four walls of picture galleries. The music room cum picture gallery at Corsham Court (1797–1802) was probably the earliest top-lit example in this country, with cast-iron coving supporting a large oblong ceiling and oval lights on all sides. Nash proposed a similar design for the picture gallery at Attingham Park, Shropshire, with continuous oval glazing, but instead evolved a more refined technique of cast-iron arched ribs supporting horizontal glazing bars of the same material (Fig 8.3). Eschewing the side windows used in Palladian galleries, and therefore providing additional wall space, and a more diffuse lighting effect, these archetypes foreshadowed later picture galleries, including that at Nash's own house in Regent Street (1819–22), as well as those in Buckingham Palace (1825–30; see Fig 7.25),[39] and those of the Victorian era also.[40] As with the second Teme bridge, the castings for Attingham and Corsham were supplied from Coalbrookdale, to which Nash paid several visits.[41]

Framed transfer structures

Nash's most ambitious, and innovative use of structural cast iron was the creation of skeletal frameworks that floated smaller floors over larger ones, or carried new spaces over existing ones. Again, Corsham Court seems to have been prototypical of subsequent developments. Although based on written estimates and accounts, rather than drawings or fabric (Nash's work being largely removed and replaced in 1846), the octagonal saloon at the centre of Nash's Gothic Tudor elevation was seemingly wholly reliant on cast iron (see Fig 4.1). Measuring 40ft (12m) in diameter, and 24ft (7.3m) in ceiling height, the saloon carried two narrower floors of bedroom accommodation

Fig 8.3
The Picture Gallery at Attingham Park, Shropshire (1806–9) (National Trust, NTPL_497096; © National Trust Images/ Andreas von Einsiedel).

Fig 8.4 (right)
The birdcage-like cast-iron skeleton framing the central portion of the east front of the Royal Pavilion, Brighton (1817–18)
(Brighton Royal Pavilion and Museums dmas_ rg000301_d02.tif).

Fig 8.5 (below)
Within the Onion Dome, Brighton Pavilion, showing the cast-iron skeleton, timber secondary framing and brick skin
(DP 132101v2).

above (styled on Henry VII's Chapel at Westminster Abbey) by means of, in Nash's words, 'iron frames' and hefty 'perforated flying Gothic brackets of cast iron'.[42] Whether the brackets were affixed to iron stanchions concealed within the corner turrets is unclear,[43] but it seems entirely plausible, given the loads and stresses involved, and that techniques of jointing were fast evolving in bridges, aqueducts and contemporary iron-framed mills. The flying buttresses on the exterior were largely decorative, and of Bath stone, not iron.

Nash employed single and clustered columns with large perforated bracket capitals spanning three ways to frame his Gothic dining room at Carlton House (1813–14), but his *tour-de-force* of cast-iron construction is that which frames the central portion of the east front of the Royal Pavilion, Brighton (Fig 8.4). Nash needed to add a first-floor billiard room with domical roof on top of Henry Holland's pre-existing circular saloon, without loading the external walls or interfering with the interior space. Structural cast iron was daringly used to frame this upper floor and dome (Fig 8.5) and transfer its entire weight – 'computed to weigh upwards of sixty tons'[44] around the walls to the ground by means

of encircling array of stanchions, a very early instance of multi-storey skeleton framing.[45] The erection of this birdcage-like assemblage of T-section ribs and stanchions, ring beams and ogee arch trusses must have been quite a spectacle, and one not missed by the Prince Regent, Nash and 'several eminent architects'.[46]

Buckingham Palace seems to have provided the opportunity for Nash's final essay in framed iron construction, albeit in a far more disjointed and incomplete manner than at Brighton. So 'extensive and peculiar' was the architect's 'use of Iron' that one of the builders involved declared to the Commons' Select Committee that 'the Palace itself is a different construction to any building I ever saw of the same nature; it is so strong that it must last forever, or go all at once ...'.[47] This was particularly true of the central portion of the west, or garden front, comprising the ground-floor bow room and its flanking state rooms, and above that, on the first floor, the great domed 'Music Room' (see Fig 7.21), between the 'White' and 'Blue' drawing rooms. Framed by 18 cast-iron ribs, with timber trussing between, the weight of the 40ft (12m) diameter dome was supported partly by the bow façade (with assistance from concealed iron columns), and partly by cast-iron arched girders resting on cross walls, which themselves were carried on cast-iron bow girders that formed the partitions of the ground floor (Fig 8.6) Nash evidently favoured this 'very complicated system of construction'[48] over simple bearing-wall construction for the variation it afforded in floor areas and openings – but at the cost of indeterminate strength and security. The rest of the west front seems to have been more conventional, with large girders spanning between bearing walls, but the plethora of subsidiary iron beams and armatures, and their questionable structural role and efficacy was a far cry from the elegant simplicity of Brighton.

Miscellaneous iron elements and armatures

Such was Nash's enthusiasm for the structural and fire-resisting possibilities of iron that he employed it in resourceful but often peculiar ways. Cast-iron plates were often employed, used to line chimney throats and hearths, or act as bearers for lintels. Segmental arches made from horizontally aligned plate iron, either wrought (rolled) or cast, and tied with rods or bars, were used to strengthen masonry over wide openings, as at Ravensworth Castle, Co Durham (begun c 1808).[49] By the 1820s, if Buckingham Palace is indicative, this technique may have evolved into a sturdier one of flanged segmental arches of cast iron, termed 'cradles', on which brick arches were turned. Similarly discreet assistance was made of iron for vertical elements also: the interiors of Carlton House Terrace (1827–33) utilise wooden columns with iron cores, a technique in use from the mid-18th century, but one exploited effusively by Nash for the tent room at Carlton House (see below). More visibly, and often showily, Nash used iron castings for window frames (eg Kilwaughter Castle, Co Antrim, 1807); for gallery brackets and balustrades (eg Hereford Gaol, 1792–6); for roof trusses (eg in the Orangeries at Barnsley Park, Gloucestershire, 1806–1810 and at Blaise Castle House, c 1805–6); for staircases (eg Caerhayes Castle, Cornwall, 1808); for ornamental interior columns (Brighton Pavilion being the supreme example of these latter uses); for the shops in Regent Street; and for imposing iron colonnades (eg the Quadrant, Regent Street, North Lodge at Buckingham Palace, and Carlton House Terrace). Prefabricated cast-iron components were of course also used for conservatories (eg the one measuring 120ft (36.5m) at Royal Lodge in Windsor Great Park, 1814)[50] and ornamental bridges (eg those spanning the moat at Helmingham Hall, Suffolk, c 1800–3).

Fig 8.6
Nash employed exceptionally deep cast-iron bow girders, formed from three segments and trussed with wrought-iron rods, to help support the central portion of the west, or garden front of Buckingham Palace (drawing by Andy Donald).

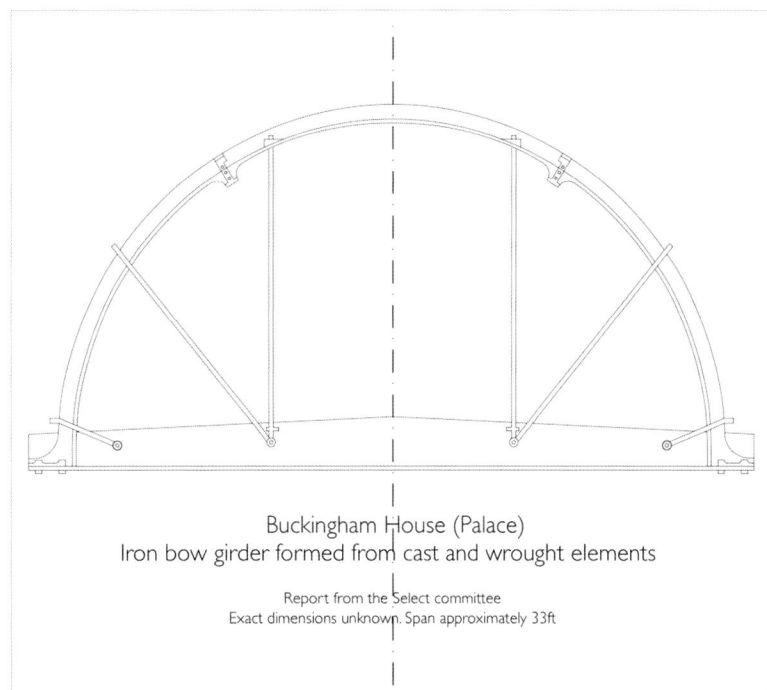

Buckingham House (Palace)
Iron bow girder formed from cast and wrought elements

Report from the Select committee
Exact dimensions unknown. Span approximately 33ft

Structural timber: domes and cones

If Nash was 'quite merciless in his use of cast iron as a general factotum',[51] his use of advanced structural carpentry was more sparing, but equally innovative. For the sake of weight, and economy, Nash almost certainly used timber, rather than iron, to frame the roofs of his town and country houses. Large hipped roofs, with fashionably shallow pitches – such as that set behind the balustrade of the Market House, Chichester (1807–8) – would have demanded techniques beyond ordinary structural carpentry, to prevent movement of timber at the joints, and sagging of the lengthy tie beams or principal rafters under load. Long-span roof trusses were difficult enough; framing domes, hemispherical or otherwise, brought additional problems.[52] As a geometrical form, domes were particularly favoured by Nash, utilised early on, for example, at Casina, Dulwich (1796–7), and at Sundridge Park, Bromley (1796–7). More ambitious examples, as at Rockingham, Co Roscommon (1809–10), where the hemispherical dome spans some 35ft (10.7m) over the drawing room, or those with a quirkier appearance, such as the vast, elongated Tudor domes surmounting the castellated towers of Aqualate Hall, Staffordshire (1806–9) doubtless required yet more creative solutions. Nash was clearly aware of the problems associated with their construction and maintenance. When one of the two domes at Caledon House, Co Tyrone (1808–12), began 'swagging' (slumping), he gave explicit remedial instructions to the owner, demonstrating both his appreciation of timber shrinkage and the value of iron straps:

> … the construction by which the dome is supported is capable of sustaining treble the weight … I am of opinion it will be found that the timbers have shrunk which all timbers will do – & that screwing them up into their place again will bring the whole right again – it is also possible that the carpenter who fixed the framing may have neglected to wedge it up tight or may have omitted the Iron straps …[53]

Nash's most structurally ambitious work in timber, analogous in its innovativeness to his iron-framed east front of the Royal Pavilion, was an enormous conical, rather than domical, structure. His 'Polygon Room', or 'Tent Room', erected in June 1814 in the grounds of Carlton House, was a huge, self-supporting ballroom in the form of a military bell tent, a type introduced in the 1790s and extensively used in Wellington's Peninsular campaigns. In terms of its dimensions, it was one of the largest timber-framed roof structures of the Georgian era, its 116ft (35m) clear span exceeding that of all the wide-span naval slip roofs designed by Robert Seppings in the period 1814–c 1843, and being exceeded by only a small number of roof structures worldwide, notably the gigantic Moscow Riding School, erected in 1790 with a span of 290ft (83m) to designs by Augustin Bétancourt.[54] Following its removal to Woolwich – where it still survives in modified guise (Fig 8.7) – it was described as having 'no equal but the dome of St Paul's Cathedral'.[55] Geometrically, it broke new ground for a framed roof structure, its dramatic catenoidal form derived from the profile of the catenary-curved ribs framing its exterior. Constructionally, it was an early example of the revived use of laminated timber, but, more significantly, it was possibly the first large-scale try-out of a new type of truss configuration, applied, moreover, three-dimensionally. In many ways this peculiar structure, prototypical of the conical roofs at Brighton, characterises Nash's experimentalist approach to architectural construction, and accordingly it is the subject of the remainder of this chapter

The polygonal tent room, Carlton House Gardens (1814)

Hastily designed and erected for the Duke of Wellington's fête on 21 July 1814, celebrating the defeat of Napoleon, the 24-sided Polygon Room, or Tent Room, was the showpiece of the ensemble of interconnecting temporary structures laid out in the gardens to the south of Carlton House. No drawings survive that detail the form or construction of the other temporary buildings, which included refreshment rooms, promenades, giant supper rooms, a botanical arbour, a Chinese pagoda and a Corinthian temple to Wellington, but those of the Polygon Room testify to the skill and ingenuity that went into its design and rapid construction (Fig 8.8). Dated May 1814, the drawings show it must have been erected in 10 weeks or less. Nash was responsible for the overall design, but on structural matters it seems certain that the carpenter William Nixon, his chief clerk of works, aided him considerably.[56] Jeffry Wyatt was most likely the principal carpenter, and both John William Hiort, another Clerk of Works, and

Sir William Congreve, the inventor of the eponymous rocket, may have been involved.

Standing 80ft high (24m) at the apex, and 116ft (35m) across, the Tent Room comprised a sweepingly curved timber-framed roof, sitting astride a double ring of posts and columns (Fig 8.9). Originally covered in painted oilcloth, the roof structure was formed from an array of 24 tapering half-ribs that fan downwards and outwards from the apex. Each half-rib was a trussed assembly of members with curvilinear laminated timber upper and lower chords shaped as catenary curves – the natural curved profile of a hanging chain, or tent roof. They were strapped together at the crown, their bevelled upright members – analogous to king posts – combining to form a cylinder rather like the staves of a barrel. This hollow timber cylinder carried a louvered turret, which helped ventilate the building. The lower ends of the ribs rested on two concentric circular wall plates joined together in the horizontal plane by double-diagonal timber braces. The outer wall plate was carried on and braced to 24 timber posts, which also framed the panel walls. The inner wall plate

was carried on reeded timber columns with cast-iron cores set slightly inside the outer posts. Cast-iron arched braces with open-work spandrels linked these posts circumferentially, and similar but shorter braces spanned between inner and outer posts.

Nash seems to have conceived the roof structure as a three-dimensional divided tie-beam truss, with the central upright timbers of each opposing pair of half ribs forming the giant shared king post, the upper chords acting as the principal rafters, the lower chords as the tie beam. Divided tie-beam trusses were a recent and ingenious arrangement to accommodate raised ceilings, which differed markedly from the usual solution of raising the tie beam above the wall plate. By dividing the tie beam into two lengths and slanting each half upward to the king post, a higher ceiling could be accommodated without the problems associated with the raised tie-beam arrangement, the most acute of which was ensuring sufficiently strong connections to transmit the substantial tensile force between the tie and the principal rafters. As David Yeomans has shown, early 19th-century

Fig 8.7
Interior of the Woolwich Rotunda, formerly the 'Polygon Room', or 'Tent Room', erected in June 1814 in the grounds of Carlton House (BCF 7170; photograph by Derek Kendall 2010 DP 093983).

Fig 8.8
Sectional drawing of the
'Tent Room, Carlton House'
(NA, WORK 43/575),
dated May 1814. Two
accompanying plans
(NA, Work 43/573 and NA,
Work 43/574) are likewise
dated, but unsigned. All
were drawn by Nash and/or
by William Nixon.

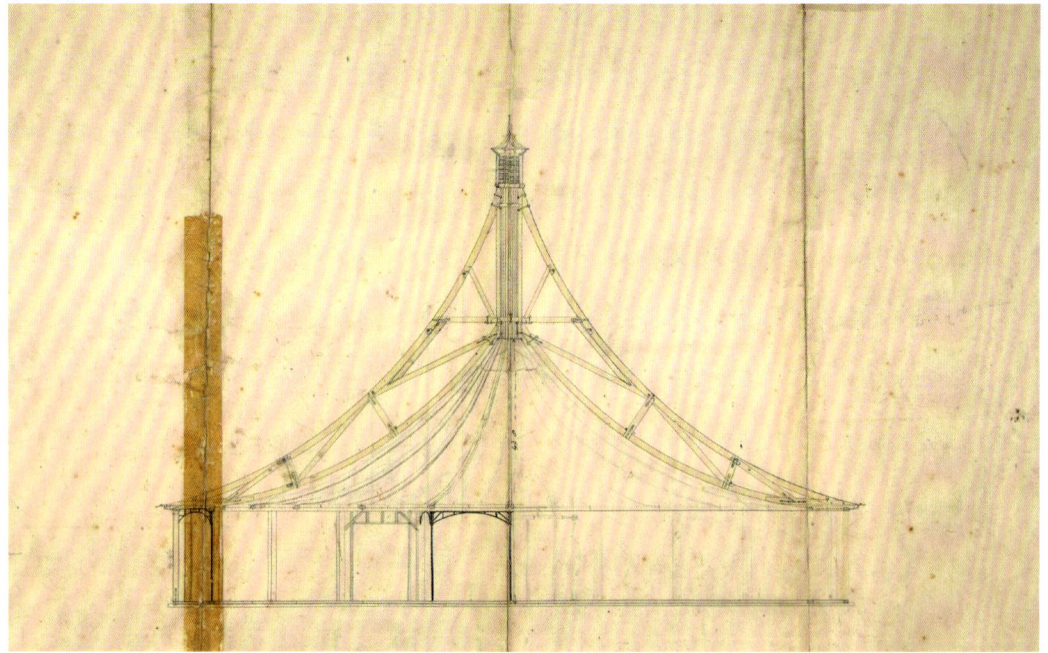

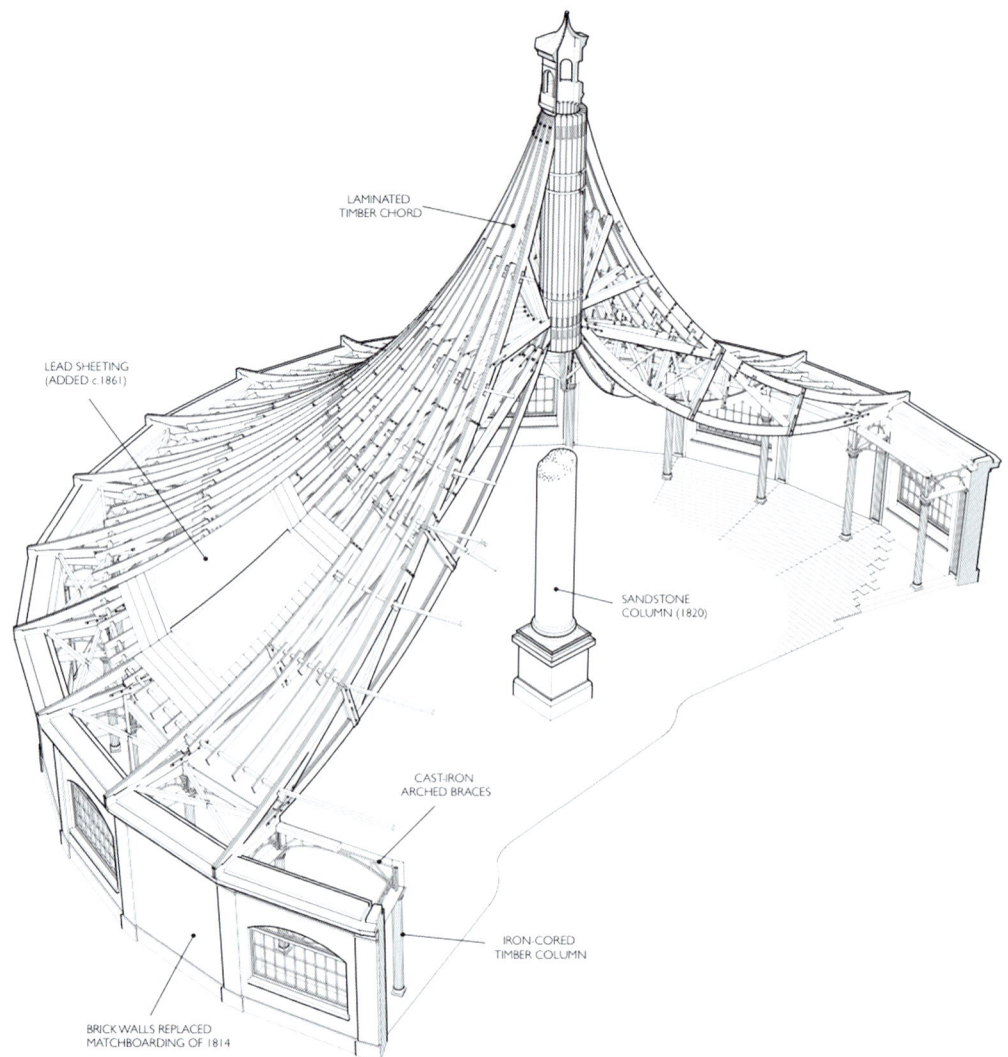

LAMINATED
TIMBER CHORD

LEAD SHEETING
(ADDED c 1861)

SANDSTONE
COLUMN (1820)

CAST-IRON
ARCHED BRACES

IRON-CORED
TIMBER COLUMN

BRICK WALLS REPLACED
MATCHBOARDING OF 1814

Fig 8.9
Perspective views of the
Woolwich Rotunda as it
survives today, showing the
tented form of the roof
structure. Not until c 1861
did weighty lead sheeting
replace the canvas covering
– some 40 years after the
column was introduced
(drawing by Andy Donald).

American carpenters utilised the form, because their churches and meeting houses were timber walled, and hence unable to withstand the outward thrust of low-pitch roofs. The American architect Asher Benjamin, for example, illustrated a divided tie-beam arrangement in the second edition of his *American Builder's Companion*, published in 1811. But there is little reason to suppose Nash was aware of this transatlantic development. However, he, or more likely Nixon, might have drawn on the precedent of a simpler design for a 'circular building' that Peter Nicholson, the prodigious and influential carpenter-mathematician, had published. First illustrated in Nicholson's *Carpenter's and Joiner's Assistant* of 1797, this design simultaneously solved the problems of outward thrust, the intersection of members and the preservation of interior volume and shape (Fig 8.10). Indeed it was possibly because of the latter two circumstances that Nash and Nixon eschewed any possible design based around the more conventional raised tie-beam configuration: to have radially united 12 trusses of raised tie-beam configuration would have been almost impossible, and would not anyway have provided the requisite interior volume or curvilinear geometry. Nicholson's design consisted of a radial array of half trusses, their tie beams connected to the foot of a central, shared king post via a multi-armed iron strap. In this case eight tie beams could be united, but, as he put it, the iron strap could consist of 'as many branches as there are tie beams to be united'. With the strap firmly bolted to the king post, and with the tie beams firmly bolted to the strap, the whole structure would, according to Nicholson, be 'render[ed] … secure and permanent'.[57] It was an adroit divided tie-beam arrangement that, thanks to the iron strap, connected the two halves of each opposing tie as well as the ties to the king post. However, it did not explain how the principals were united around the head of the king post, and it can only be presumed that a similar iron connector was to be employed there also. For stability it also required that the lowest struts were extended below the tie beams to brace against the polygonal walls, circumscribing the open space below the wall plate.

If Nash and Nixon drew on Nicholson's somewhat abstract example, they certainly refined it by contriving their own ingenious technique of binding the whole structure. Bevelling the central upright timbers of the 24

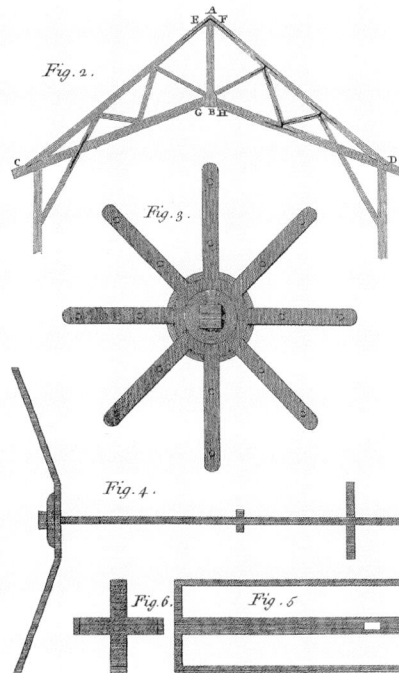

Fig 8.10
Peter Nicholson's design for framing a circular building. As well as being the first recorded example of a divided-tie beam truss, it incorporated an ingenious iron device for uniting the eight tie beams with the king post
(Carpenters & Joiner's Assistant, *1797, pl 77*).

half trusses permitted their radial amalgamation at the crown, an assembly that created a giant, cylindrical king post. Strapped tightly together with wrought-iron hoops and timber wedges, each pair of opposing, curved divided tie-beam trusses was prevented from spreading outwards. To this end, the lower chord or tie beam provided restraint against the outward thrust of the principals, which was quite excessive, given that they curved outwards, rather than being straight or curving inwards. The strength of the joints between the tie beams and the upright timbers forming the cylindrical king post, and the hoops binding these together, was absolutely critical to the success of the structure. Total reliance was placed on the ability of wrought iron to transmit and resist tensile forces at these points. The curved upper and lower chords were laminated, made up from four layers of vertically laminated planks, strapped together so that the inner two 'broke joint' with the outer ones. As well as facilitating the curved profile, lamination conferred great strength. According to Yeomans, Nash may have placed reliance 'on the bending resistance of the laminated ribs to take care of any uncertainties about the behaviour of the structure'.[58] The posts and rafters were also made from laminated timber, although in just three and two thicknesses respectively. An early instance of the revived use of the technique, its use here presaged that at Brighton.

Cones at Brighton

The tented roofs over the music and banqueting rooms at Brighton Pavilion were the direct progeny of the Polygon Room – smaller, but in some ways more refined. Erected c 1818, the two soaring conical timber frameworks span 40ft (12m) between wall plates, each being made up of 20 radial, laminated-timber half-ribs strapped together by their upright inner parts (Fig 8.11). For these lower, flatter ceilings it was possible to tie the lower chords with collars, accomplished by a 20-armed bolted-timber armature that avoided problems of intersection. The feet of the ribs are seated on cast-iron brackets, which project from a timber wall plate that in places is strengthened by iron beams, and which is variously carried on timber squinches, flitched beams and brick walls. This complex 'flying wall plate' construction seems to have been designed to counteract, or safeguard against, the spreading of the timbers. But the most surprising difference between these structures and their prototype is the absence of members connecting the lower and upper chords. Each half-rib has just two posts, with the upper, which is accessible to view, being of doubled form, as in the rotunda, with timber bridging pieces between (Fig 8.12). This paucity of web members is possible because the laminated upper and lower chords were considerably stronger, made up for the most part of five thicknesses of closely fitting planks. Only in the higher part of the upper chords did they reduce in thickness to three planks. Consequently, the laminated chords are better equipped to resist bending, with less need of support along their length. Unlike in the Tent Room, the planks were cut to the required curve, and, it is worth noting, the overall quality of carpentry is greatly superior.

Perhaps Nash placed greater reliance on the inherent strength of laminated timber chords, rather than trussing, because he had seen William Porden's remarkable Brighton stable block. Erected in 1803–8, this dome, of 80ft (24.4m) diameter, was framed using 24 vertically laminated timber ribs, each measuring just 12 inches by 9 inches (305mm × 229mm) at the bottom, diminishing to just 9 inches square at the top. Porden, a pupil of James Wyatt and a friend of Nash, had based his design on the celebrated dome of the Halle au Blé (Corn Market), in Paris. That structure, erected in 1782–3 by master cabinetmaker A J Roubo to designs by J G Legrand and J Molinos, was itself the first major exemplar of the technique in over two centuries, reviving and improving methods pioneered by Philibert de L'Orme. The acclaimed French dome even inspired Thomas Jefferson to give his home, Monticello, a laminated timber dome in c 1800, thereby introducing the technique to America. Nash himself never got to see the Halle au Blé during his first recorded visit to Paris in 1814, as it had already burned down. He did, however, see and admire its replacement – a virtual facsimile in cast iron – and it is tempting to think that this might have inspired the elaborate iron structure framing the Pavilion's centrepiece: the great dome over the Saloon. Curiously, the drawings for this, like so many of the others held at Brighton, are not signed by Nash, but carry the words 'Drawn by William Nixon, 1827' in the corner. Whether this was the hand of Nixon, in his final months, or else his son, Nixon junior, is unclear, but either way it perhaps affirms the crucial role of his trusted clerk-of-works in the Pavilion's structural design.

The Woolwich Rotunda, and tented progeny

Although designed for the spectacular fête at Carlton House in the summer of 1814, such was the Prince Regent's delight with the Polygon Room and the three adjoining apartments that they saw further use beyond 1815, when most of the temporary buildings were dismantled. Moreover, the Tent Room, unlike the adjoining buildings, was destined for a permanent

Fig 8.11
Section through the Banqueting Room roof, Brighton Pavilion, drawn by William Nixon, 1827 (Brighton Royal Pavilion and Museums dmas_ rg000306_d01.tif).

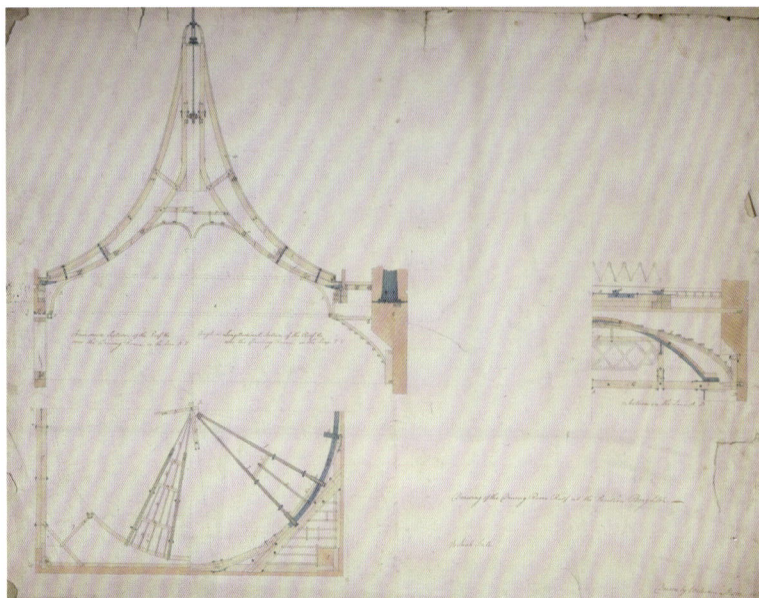

existence thanks to Sir William Congreve, who secured its transfer to Woolwich in late 1818 to serve as a permanent museum for the Royal Artillery, housing the spoils of war. Nash, working at Brighton, had seemingly hoped it might be reused as a church,[59] but he cannot have been too disappointed, considering the building 'applicable to many purposes … indeed I think it would be a useful building in any of the dockyards and other government establishments'.[60] He advised on the dismantling of the structure, making Nixon available on site so that the carpenter could 'explain the construction of the building and advise on the taking of it down'. However, he was adamant that '[Nixon] cannot stay longer than Monday or Tuesday as the works at Brighton are extremely urgent and so difficult of execution that I cannot trust him a moment to be away'.[61] In 1819–20 it was reconstructed in the Repository Grounds, where it survives as the most prominent surviving element of a 19th-century military-training landscape and pleasure ground. Despite the introduction of a brick outer wall, additional roof timbers, a central column and other modifications from the later 19th century, Nash and Nixon's bold, peculiar structure mostly survives.

Besides Brighton, Nash and Nixon's innovative tent room may have produced further offspring, such as the Tent Room of Hertford Villa (later St Dunstan's), in Regent's Park (1827) (Fig 8.13). Designed by the young Decimus Burton, a protégé of Nash, this free-standing convex enclosure was used by Lord Hertford, 'the Caliph of Regent's Park', to stage 'his extravagant and costly entertainments on a scale that only crowned heads could afford'.[62] Unfortunately, Burton's surviving drawings do not show the structure, but it probably relied on divided tie-beam trusses, if not laminated timber. Certainly his Colosseum in Regent's Park (1823–7) used vertically laminated timber for the ribs framing the 132ft-diameter (40m) dome,[63] and it is tempting to think that the young Burton might have drawn on the cones and domes at Woolwich and Brighton, if not under instruction from Nash or Nixon. Other structures comparable to the cones at Woolwich and Brighton were doubtless either built or conceived in this period,[64] but thereafter Victorian sobriety most likely saw the demise of the quirky, concave-curving tented roof, and with it a particular strand of timber engineering.

Fig 8.12
Upward view toward the apex of the laminated-timber roof over the 'Music Room' at Brighton Pavilion (photograph by Derek Kendall 2004, FR10935).

Conclusion

Not long after Nash's death, with his reputation as an architect still at a low ebb, one commentator conceded that the architect's works exhibited 'bold invention and ingenious design'.[65] In some senses this isolated, passing comment is quite remarkable, given the 'dense blanket of indifference [that] obscured Nash's memory'[66] for decades after his death. While directed at the stylistic and planning content of his rich catalogue of designs and schemes, it might equally have applied to their constructive component also – a less visible thread that, in many senses, continued more seamlessly into the Victorian era. The use of structural iron in building construction expanded in the mid-19th century out of all proportion to its earlier decades: methods of construction that were extraordinary in the 1800s had become quite ordinary by the 1850s. This was most palpable in the use of cast-iron beams; with widening availability and appreciation of their merits, they became part of normal working practice, finding routine employment in the architecture of commerce, institutions and leisure. Until proven otherwise, Nash deserves credit for first transposing cast-iron beams from their industrial-vernacular origins to the realm of polite architecture, at Corsham Court in the late 1790s. And his consistent use of iron beams conceivably influenced his contemporaries, such as Smirke, who sustained the

Fig 8.13
The south front of
St Dunstan's, Regent's Park.
Decimus Burton's
self-supporting
quadrilateral Tent Room
(1827), which probably
borrowed carpentry
techniques pioneered at
Carlton House gardens,
marked the end of the line of
Regency tented structures
(Wallace Collection;
The Architectural
Association
728.84.035(42.1)
BUR Ref-Lo).

gradual process of change through their own adaptive applications.

Nash's more ambitious uses of structural iron, in linked assemblages of beams, columns, ribs and arches, were similarly anticipatory of mid-19th-century developments, where such elements were increasingly used to frame lower floors, galleried atria, and domes in commercial and public buildings. Brighton and Buckingham Palace may, by the architect's own admission, have demanded peculiar construction, but they embodied techniques that became both refined and routine in the Victorian era. Similarly, Nash's use of cast iron to frame the 120ft-long (36.5m) conservatory attached to the Royal Lodge in Windsor Great Park, and to form coved clerestoreys, saw continuity in the conservatories, glasshouses and picture galleries of the later 19th century, many of which used cast iron long after the introduction of wrought iron. Ironically, perhaps, Nash's most innovatory structure, the Carlton House tent room, was also the shortest lived. Like the long-span shipbuilding roofs introduced by Seppings, this was a radically new structural form, similarly introduced for quite extraordinary circumstances. While it enjoyed a short spell of life in the second and possibly third decades of the 19th century, unlike the shipbuilding roofs, which remained functionally important and were re-engineered in cast and wrought iron, it failed to cross over into the Victorian era. Perhaps partly because of this, and the more

concealed and understudied nature of his structural carpentry, Nash the constructor has been linked with iron by 20th-century historians to the virtual exclusion of timber. Not so to some Victorians, who thought that his occupation up to, and including the Brighton Pavilion, was as a carpenter![67]

Notes

1   Report from the Select Committee on the Office of Works and Public Buildings, PP 1831 **IV**, 286
2   PP 1831 **IV**, 77
3   John Summerson, in Mansbridge 1991, 15
4   Edward Holl (d 1834), the Navy Board's Surveyor, was arguably the most committed, and innovative Georgian architect working with iron. Holl was directly responsible for at least fourteen dockyard buildings with significant quantities of structural iron between 1812 and his death in 1824, including four large multi-storey iron-framed warehouses, and, in conjunction with Rennie, the celebrated Smithery building at Woolwich dockyard (1814–16) with a complete cast-iron frame of columns, arched girders and cast- and wrought-iron roof trusses. Daniel Asher Alexander (1768–1846) made innovative use of iron for the Tobacco Warehouse at the London Docks (1811–14), and also designed docks, lighthouses and bridges.
5   Saint, A 1976 Richard Norman Shaw. New Haven and London: Yale University Press, 114
6   The inaugural volume of the Transactions of the Institution of Civil Engineers in 1836 noted that 'Robert Mylne may be looked on as the last practitioner of note, who combined in a considerable

degree the avocations of the engineer and the architect. The professions have since become almost entirely disjoined …' *Trans ICE* **1**, x.

7   *PP* 1831 **IV**, 57

8   *PP* 1831 **IV**, 274

9   R[anger], W A 1836, 29. William Ranger (1800–63), a civil engineer best known for his system of precast concrete units, probably knew the architect well and was likely the author of this memoir. He was the son of a William Ranger, a builder and surveyor of Brighton – active at the time of Nash's Pavilion (1815–22). Ranger's agent on the concrete wharf walls at Chatham and Woolwich in the 1830s was Charles Nixon (1814–73), whose father, William Nixon, was Nash's carpenter and Clerk of Works at Carlton House, Brighton and Buckingham palace (Chrimes, M 2002 'Ranger, William (1800–1863)', *in* Skempton, A W (ed) *A Biographical Dictionary of Civil Engineers in Great Britain and Ireland, 1*. London: Thomas Telford for Institution of Civil Engineers, 543).

10 For example, Nash was critical of the engineers' evidence during the select committee inquiry into Buckingham Palace, stating that 'not a single experiment' justified their concerns over the soundness of the iron construction. His dislike, or non-understanding, of scientific rationalism, is evident in his statement that 'It is impossible that Engineers can have been acquainted with the construction of the Bow [Drawing Room], or they would not have attempted to make any calculations of the weights these Columns have to carry; to do so it *utterly impossible*' (*PP* 1831 **IV**, 276).

11 R[anger], W A 1836, 26

12 An essential part of the New Street (Regent Street) project, entailing the reconstruction and re-alignment of much of London's longest sewer, the King's Scholars Pond Sewer (formed in 1724), was considered by Telford to be 'upon the whole very substantially constructed' (Summerson 1949, 128, 134 (quotation); White, J 1814, 55–76, 111; London Metropolitan Archives 1817. Regent's Park Tunnel Sewer WCS/PR/48–51; Report from the Select Committee on the Office of Works and Public Buildings, *PP* 1828 **IV**, 103, 105–8). The engineer for the Regent's Canal was James Morgan.

13 R[anger], W A 1836, 28

14 *PP* 1831 **IV**, 286

15 Anonymous 1829 *A Picturesque Guide to the Regent's Park with Accurate Descriptions of the Colosseum, the Diorama, and the Zoological Gardens*. London: for John Limbird, 203

16 Catalogue 1835; copy in Sir John Soane's Museum

17 Sutherland, R J M 1990 'The age of cast iron, 1780–1850: who sized the beams?, *in* Thorne R (ed), *The Iron Revolution*. London: RIBA exhibition catalogue, 30

18 Diestelkamp, E 1988 'Building technology and architecture 1790–1830', *in* White R and Lightburn, C (eds) *Late Georgian Classicism*. London: Georgian Group, 73–91; Diestelkamp, E 1990 'Architects and the use of iron', *in* Thorne 1990 (*see note 16*), 15–23; Dinkel, J 1983 *The Royal Pavilion Brighton*. London: Philip Wilson; Summerson, J 1945 'Records of an

19 Clarke 2005–6, 43–63

20 *PP* 1831 **IV**, 274

21 Skempton A W and Johnson, H R 1962 'The first iron frames'., *Architect Rev* **March**, 175–86; Fitzgerald, R S 1988 'The development of the cast-iron frame in textile mills to 1850' *Indust Archaeol Rev* **X**, 127–45; Addis, B 2007 *Building: 3000 Years of Design Engineering and Construction*. London: Phaidon Press, 285–7

22 The earliest documented use of cast-iron beams by Smirke seems to be 1810, when he 'used built-in cast-iron bearers at Cirencester Park which were over 30ft in length' (Crook and Port 1973, 416 citing *RIBA J* 1867, 207; and Papworth, Wyatt (ed) 1852–92 'Iron', *in Dictionary of Architecture*. London: T Richards for the Architectural Publication Society, [unpaginated].

23 Sutherland 1990, 1–3

24 Summerson 1949, 44; *see page 2 and note 41*

25 Ladd 1978, 103, note 73, quoting document 6011 (undated), page 17

26 Nash's specification. Two long-span iron beams were employed, one in the middle section, the other over the arch of the porte-cochere. All other beams were timber. I am grateful to Geoffrey Tyack for his cross-sectional sketch of Luscombe, based on working drawings in Hoare's Bank, Fleet Street, London.

27 Bodleian Library, Oxford, MS DD Wykeham Musgrave c.53 (3 July 1807); Geoffrey Tyack, pers comm

28 'In the United Service Club are two rooms of 150 feet by 50, the floors of which are constructed of cast-iron girders' (Anonymous 1828 'United Service Club-House'. *The Mirror of Literature, Amusement, and Instruction* **12**, 210)

29 There is some disagreement as to whether plain inverted 'T' section beams were first used in the Salford Twist Mill; Fitzgerald 1988 (*see note 20*), 128–9.

30 *PP* 1831 **IV**, 245

31 Summerson 1980, 18, quoting Sherwood, H 1910 (Darton, F J Harvey ed) *The Life and Times of Mrs Sherwood (1775–1851)*. London: Wells Gardner, Darton and Co, 171

32 Built for Sir Edward Winnington of Stanford Court, Worcestershire, it spanned 98ft between stone abutments and seemingly relied upon four extremely shallow segmental-arch ribs, each only about foot deep. Unusually for the time, it was not cast at Coalbrookdale; for an illustration, and a graphic contemporary report of its collapse, Ruddock T 1979 *Arch Bridges and Their Builders*. Cambridge: Cambridge University Press, 140–1; Raistrick, A 1989 *Dynasty of Iron Founders: the Darbys and Coalbrookdale* (rev 2nd ed). York: Sessions Book Trust, in association with Ironbridge Gorge Museum Trust, 204); and chapter 2 of Raistrick.

33 Chrimes 2002 (*see note 9*), 474

34 'Construction of plate iron bridges', Patent No. 2165 (1797); published, for example, in *The Monthly Magazine* **3** (March 1797), 221

35 Summerson 1949, 54

36 For example, Nash's two cast-iron flattened-arch bridges of *c* 1800–3 across the moat at Helmingham

Hall, Suffolk, which replaced brick predecessors (Mansbridge 1991, 93–4)

37   Diestelkamp 1988 (see note 18), 88–9

38   Although Diestelkamp states that the cores were formed from three sections, and were fixed onto 'plate iron hollow box girders', according to the notes and annotated sketches of the late Alan Allnutt, MICE, of the Sussex Industrial Archaeology Society, they are formed from just two and are supported on a grillage of parallel open-web cast-iron girders connected top and bottom by intermittent bridging members or ties. I am grateful to Malcolm Tucker for sharing both this material and his thoughts on the matter, including his observation that the intersecting semicircle design of the girder webs was 'attractive but wholly unscientific' (Malcolm Tucker, pers comm).

39   Designed by Nash, but completed by Edward Blore, this employed a series of glazed domes at the ceiling's margins, carried on pendentives decorated with hanging pendants. The whole ensemble, recalling a hammerbeam roof, is depicted in Morison, Douglas 1843 The Picture Gallery at Buckingham Palace (1843), reproduced in Robinson, J M 2000 Buckingham Palace: The Official Illustrated History. London: Royal Collection, 56.

40   Diestelkamp 1988 (see note 18), 77–8; Ladd 1978, 105–6

41   Raistrick 1989 (see note 32), 207

42   Quoted in Ladd 1978 (document 6011, 17, undated), 103

43   Document 6011 (see previous note), the largest estimate at Corsham, makes no mention of this (Ladd 1978, 95, note 51). Some pages of the document, however, have been lost.

44   The New Monthly Magazine 10 (1 October 1818), 275

45   see pages 128–32; for a detailed description of the structure, Diestelkamp 1988 (see note 18), 86–9

46   Summerson 1980, 105, citing Bishop, J G 1875 The Brighton Pavilion and its Royal Associations. Brighton: Fleet and Bishop, 66–8

47   PP 1831 IV, 77. 'Many columns of cast iron, 18 feet in height, and of five tons' weight each, are already raised, and from the quantity of Iron used, and the substantial manner in which the floors and walls are constructed, we may infer, that stability, and security against fire, are provided for by the architect' (['J.B.'] 1827 review of Anonymous 1827 'Original picture of London'. Gentleman's Magazine 97, 54; see pages 138–9.

48   PP 1831 IV, 234

49   RIBA, SB 54/5/1; SB 5/1/14; see pages 49–50

50   Diestelkamp 1988 (see note 17), 77

51   Summerson 1945, 235

52   Yeomans, D T 1992 The Trussed Roof: Its History and Development. Aldershot: Scolar Press, 125–7, 148–56

53   Autographed letter from Nash to the Earl of Caledon, Co Tyrone, dated 25 November 1815 http://manuscripts.co.uk/stock/20442.HTM

54   Yeomans, D T 1997 The Development of Timber as a Structural Material. Studies in the History of Civil Engineering VIII. Aldershot: Ashgate, xxvii; and Addis 2007 (see note 21), 310–11

55   Hunt, T F 1830 Exemplars of Tudor Architecture, Adapted to Modern Habitations. London: Longman,

      Rees, Orme, Brown, and Green, 97

56   Clarke 2005–6, 56–7

57   Nicholson, P 1797 The Carpenter and Joiner's Assistant. London: Printed for I and J Taylor, 66

58   Yeomans, D T 2005–6 'The behaviour of the structure'. Construction Hist 21, 67. Because of this, and of other aspects of the structural design, including uncertainty as regards the transmission of tensile forces among the members, Yeomans suggests 'One must assume design by analogy rather than any kind of formal analysis'.

59   NA, WORK 19/11/5, f 39

60   NA, WORK 1/9, 61; WORK 19/11/5, f 38

61   NA, WORK 19/11/5, f 41

62   Mallett, D 1979 The Greatest Collector: Lord Hertford and the Founding of the Wallace Collection. London: Macmillan, 25

63   Externally, the dome measured 132ft in diameter; its greatest internal diameter was 126ft. Its construction was described thus: 'At sixty feet above the footings spring the principal ribs of the dome. They are 48 in number, and are formed with six thicknesses of inch-and-a-half plank; at bottom, fourteen inches deep. At top, there are only four thicknesses, all securely bolted and spiked together, and the heading joints everywhere alternately. They are let into cast-iron shoes at bottom, secured to a strong plate, which in the manner of a hoop, binds the whole together. There are eleven tiers of intermediate hoops, or enterties [sic]; and the whole of this framing is filled in with strong diagonal bracing. The ribs abut at top against a strong circular curb; and a perfect equilibrium has been maintained throughout' (Anonymous 1829, 25 [see note 15]).

64   The tented roof of a design for a new Chinese-Indian style façade to Thomas Sandby's (1721–98) Forest Lodge (formerly Holly Grove), Windsor Great Park, might, if executed, have been another descendent of the Carlton House 'Tent Room'. Although attributed variously to Joseph [sic] Nash (Mansbridge 1991, 309) and Humphry Repton, c 1797 (Roberts, Jane 1997 Royal Landscape. New Haven and London: Yale University Press, 300–1), the drawing entitled 'Design for Mrs Jennings, Windsor Park', and illustrated by Mansbridge, might plausibly be by John Nash. That a drawing of 'Miss Jennings' villa in Windsor Park' was included in the sale of Nash's books, prints and drawings lends support to this attribution, as does his documented involvement with Royal Lodge in the Great Park.

65   The Architectural Magazine 4 (March 1837), 151

66   Summerson 1980, 190

67   For example, 'In early life he was a carpenter, and being employed at the Pavilion, Brighton, he attracted the favourable notice of the Prince of Wales' (Gaspey, W 1851 Tallis's Illustrated London. London and New York: J Tallis and Co, 151); 'He was originally a carpenter employed at the Brighton Pavilion, where he attracted the favourable notice of the Prince of Wales, who gave him the appointment of architect to the Board of Works' (Wheatley, H B 1870 Round about Piccadilly and Pall Mall. London: Smith, Elder and Co, 176)

9

Nash in context: links with Schinkel, Percier and Fontaine, Soane and Cockerell

DAVID WATKIN

If we have a sneaking feeling that Nash is a superficial, slapdash, and make-believe architect, it might help us to make up our minds about his achievement if we consider the reaction to him of three distinguished architects, all of whom knew him, though all are today regarded as greater than him: Sir John Soane (1753–1837); Charles Robert Cockerell (1788–1863); and the great German architect, Karl Friedrich Schinkel (1781–1841). Soane was Nash's contemporary; Cockerell and Schinkel 30 years his junior. In addition, we also have Schinkel's opinions of both Nash and Soane, as well as the reaction of all of them to Charles Percier (1764–1838) and Pierre-François-Léonard Fontaine (1762–1853), Napoleon's chosen architects. The careers of Soane, Schinkel and Cockerell, were influenced in various ways by Napoleon, while Schinkel and Nash were the architects of two leaders in opposition to him in the Napoleonic Wars, respectively King Friedrich Wilhelm III of Prussia, and George IV as Regent and King.

Schinkel

From 1815, Schinkel transformed Berlin into a cultural capital for Friedrich Wilhelm III, with superb neoclassical public and private buildings such as the Schauspielhaus and Altes Museum, in a way that would have filled Nash and Soane with envy. In 1826, as an agent of the King and the Prussian government, Schinkel toured France, England, and Scotland, studying the recent display of antique sculpture in the Louvre and the British Museum as models for the arrangement of the Altes Museum in Berlin. He was also required to provide information on the latest English developments in industrial design and the manufacture of goods, and was even expected to purchase furnishings for the palaces that he was designing for two of the King's sons, Prince Karl and Prince August.

Investigating the display of sculpture in England, Schinkel found much to admire in Nash's house and gallery in Lower Regent Street (*see* Fig 6.26), but little in Soane's house and museum in Lincoln's Inn Fields. Describing the latter, he began by claiming – wrongly, having been in London for only about a fortnight – that 'Like all private houses in London this house is small.' He went on to note that:

> it contains a great number of casts, fragments of antique statues and buildings, vases, sarcophagi, little panels and bronzes … in the smallest of spaces lit from above and the side, often only 3 ft wide. Mediaeval, antique and modern works are intermingled at every level: in courtyards resembling cemeteries, and in chapel-like rooms, in catacombs and drawing rooms, ornamented in Herculanean and Gothic styles. Everywhere little deceptions.[1]

Soane's house did not greatly appeal to Schinkel's mind, but he and Soane were wholly serious in outlook, and wholly professional, unlike Nash, who could be very casual. For example, Joseph Scoles (1798–1863), the executant architect at Gloucester Terrace (now Gloucester Gate), Regent's Park, had shown 'his independence by varying the proportion of Nash's details (and especially of the cornice)', but all Nash said when he passed it was that 'the parts looked larger than he expected'.[2] Soane and Schinkel devoted their entire lives absolutely and entirely to the cause of architecture and to the idealist 18th-century belief in the ennobling cultural role of high-quality architecture. They lived and died in what was wholly (for Schinkel) or effectively (for Soane) a school of architecture, designed by themselves: the Bauakademie in Berlin, and the Soane Museum in London.

Visiting Nash's house, Schinkel observed, 'He lives like a prince', probably not a term of praise from this workaholic architect, but he did greatly praise Nash's use of new artificial materials, noting on the staircase the 'walls covered in beautiful imitation green porphyry … [with] excellent imitation wood in the doors.' In the Gallery he admired 'Raphael's Loggie pilasters and pediment finely painted,[3] faithful purple background of the side niches, where casts have been mounted of the best statues and busts of antiquity … Plaster architectural models on the tables, lighting by means of openings in the ceiling and small lamps at the side' (Fig 9.1).[4]

Schinkel records that, with Edward Solly, whose picture collection had been acquired for the Altes Museum in 1821, he 'went to Regent's Park … in glorious weather to see the new building there. Immense plan, all private houses built in palace-like terraces, which have a view of the whole park with beautiful hills behind. There are artificial lakes and ponds in the park. Marylebone Church is not without effect.'[5] It was on the Corinthian portico of St Marylebone New Church – built in 1813–17 from designs by Thomas Hardwick – that Nash chose to align the two facing ranges of York Terrace to form a theatrically grand entrance to the park at York Gate in 1822 (see Fig 5.9).

Schinkel also admired and sketched Nash's Military Museum at Woolwich, an elegant and innovative rotunda in the form of a dodecagon with a diameter of 116 feet, covering 10,600 square feet.[6] Its conical tent-like roof was supported on a timber frame designed on a prefabricated principle (see Figs 8.7 and 8.9). It had begun life as a ballroom in the gardens of Carlton House, designed by Nash for the Prince Regent as part of the celebrations to mark the Peace of Paris in 1814. It was moved to Woolwich in 1820, but it is unclear from Schinkel's diary whether he was aware of either its architect or its history.

On separate occasions in the summer of 1826 both Schinkel and Cockerell witnessed progress on the transformation of Buckingham House into Buckingham Palace, begun by Nash in the previous year, when he was 73. Cockerell's reaction will be considered later, but Schinkel simply recorded in his diary: 'looked at the new palace by Nash, very ordinary architecture, the plans may not be seen, nor the building site, the King has expressly forbidden it.'[7] Between the two projecting wings that Nash added on the entrance front, he built a free-standing triumphal arch (see Fig 7.13).[8] This was evidently inspired by the Arc du Carrousel, which Percier and Fontaine had built in 1806–8 as the entrance to the Tuileries Palace, Napoleon's residence in Paris.

Perhaps surprisingly, Schinkel found much to admire in the Brighton Pavilion, amazingly transformed by Nash in 1815–22 from the chaste neoclassical villa built for the King as Prince of Wales by Henry Holland in the 1780s. The Lord Steward of George IV's Household, the Marquess of Conyngham, turned down the request from the Prussian Ambassador to allow Schinkel to visit the Royal Pavilion, but he was persuaded to write again. As a result, so Schinkel rather smugly recorded, 'apparently when the King heard it was me he then gave his permission.'[9]

Soon becoming bored with Henry Holland's Pavilion, the Prince commissioned Humphry Repton to rebuild it in a Moorish style in 1805. As presented in his Red Book with his usual flaps, Repton's Pavilion much influenced that built by Nash, whose earlier professional partnership with Repton had a profound effect on his understanding of the picturesque. Schinkel began his diary entry for 10 June 1826 by exclaiming of the Pavilion: 'The interior of the building is magnificent'. And in the longest description of any single building in his diary, it is fascinating that he should begin with the kitchen:

> First the kitchen, all the apparatus for cooking with steam, very fine; table with an iron plate into which the steam can be fed, on which everything can be kept warm. Iron pots, into which the steam is fed inside double walls, with stopcocks to siphon off the condensed water … The kitchen is held up by 4 [iron] palm trees. Sheet-metal dome.[10]

Fig 9.1
Nash's Gallery, at No. 14 Regent St, sketch by Karl Friedrich Schinkel (1826) (D Bindman, Schinkel Journey, pl 66).

Fig 9.2
The Banqueting Room at the Royal Pavilion, Brighton (Nash, Views of the Royal Pavilion, 1826).

He went on to describe the two amazing interiors built in 1817, 40ft (12.2m) square and 20ft (6.1m) feet high: the Music Room and the Banqueting Room (Fig 9.2), representing the Prince's principal interests, music and eating. As at Nash's London house, Schinkel was fascinated by simulated materials, so he wrote of the Pavilion: 'State Banqueting Room. Wall-covering of shimmering silver material (painted).'[11] He made drawings of the complicated iron construction that made such an interior possible. In the Banqueting Room and Music Room, concealed segmental arches of brick clad in iron carry the thrust of the conical superstructure, above which is a tall laminated timber framework from which the dome is suspended, standing on a ring of cast iron.

The poetry of rooms such as the Saloon was made possible by revolutionary constructional techniques in which a superimposed cast-iron armature supports the central dome, which is actually over the dome of Henry Holland's saloon of 1786 (*see* Fig 8.5). The oriental profile of Nash's dome is formed of sheet iron covered with Hamlin's mastic. Less successful was his covering of the roofs with patent mastic of two kinds: one made of pulverised stone, sand and linseed, another of powered chalk, tar and sand applied hot; but they failed, and the domes leaked.

There are two principal reasons for Schinkel's admiration for Brighton Pavilion, neither related to its exotic style: one is Nash's novel use of cast-iron construction, the other his skill in transforming an existing building with all the skill of a conjuror. Iron-frame structures were developed in Britain to deal with fire problems in the new cotton mills in the 1790s. Schinkel admired Stanley Mill of 1812 on his visit to Stroud (Fig 9.3), while at Brighton Pavilion he saw, for the first time, iron staircases used in a private residence, noting '[t]he banisters are of cast iron, in a delicate imitation of bamboo tracery'[12] (Fig 9.4). Nash made extensive use of cast iron at Buckingham Palace, and there are Greek Doric cast-iron columns at his monumental Carlton House Terrace of 1827, which show his interest in new technology. At the

it to Berlin for the first time in the staircases of these palaces, which were inspired by his study of Brighton Pavilion and English mills. At Prince Karl's palace in the Wilhelmsplatz (1827–8),[13] the cast-iron structural elements of the staircase included slender columns of the exceptional height of some of Nash's at Brighton Pavilion. These columns recur in the much more ambitious iron staircase on the imperial plan, filling a vast hall in the Baroque mansion in the Wilhelmstrasse whose interiors Schinkel completely remodelled in 1830–4 for Prince Albrecht (Fig 9.5).[14]

Schinkel was justly proud of his skill in remodelling earlier buildings, publishing before-and-after engravings of the old-fashioned manor house with high mansard roof built for himself by the architect Johann Gottfried Büring in 1756–8, which Schinkel transformed for the Crown Prince as Schloss Charlottenhof, Potsdam (1826–33) (Fig 9.6).[15] In 1832–5 he built Schloss Babelsberg, near Potsdam (Fig 9.7), for the King of Prussia's second son, Prince Wilhelm, first German Emperor from 1871–88.[16] With its

same time, the Terrace overlooks St James's Park, which he replanned in the Reptonian manner as the picturesque rural park we know today.

Back in Berlin, Schinkel pursued his role as architectural conjuror to the Prussian royal family, following Nash's example by brilliantly transforming existing buildings, including two palaces for the King's sons. Anxious to make use of cast iron, he found an opportunity to introduce

irregular plan pivoting on an octagonal vaulted dining room, Schloss Babelsberg is close to Nash's house plans, notably that of his own house, East Cowes Castle, Isle of Wight (1798– c 1820) (see chapter 3). In the selection of both the site and the style of Schloss Babelsberg, key roles were played by two figures who both made their own designs for it: Prince Friedrich's anglophile wife, Princess Augusta, and his older brother, Crown Prince Friedrich Wilhelm, King of Prussia from 1840–61, an amateur architect who had been taught by Schinkel.

Princess Augusta, who had supposedly sketched Gothic castles as a child at Weimar in the company of Goethe, proposed as a source for Babelsberg plates in English pattern books, notably by Lugar and Papworth.[17] Lugar seems

Fig 9.5 (left)
Schinkel, Prince Albrecht Palace, Berlin, staircase (Sievers, Bauten für den Prinzen, 152, pl 119).

Fig 9.6 (left)
Schinkel, Schloss Charlottenhof (Geoffrey Tyack).

Fig 9.7 (below)
Schinkel, Schloss Babelsberg, engraving (Schinkel, Sammlung architektonischer Entwürfe, 1838).

Fig 9.8
Schinkel, sketch of Windsor Castle, sketch (Bindman, Schinkel Journey, pl 99).

to have been an early associate of Nash, in whose castellated Gothic style he built several country houses, while Schinkel's Schloss Babelsberg, also close to Nash, was the most English building of his career.[18] Indeed, it may be specifically dependent on '[a] design to exemplify irregularity in Castle Gothic' by Nash's former partner, Repton.[19] It probably also owes something to Windsor Castle, which Wyatville had been remodelling in castellated Gothic from 1824. Schinkel saw Windsor on two occasions in 1826, making a sketch of Wyatville's East front (Fig 9.8) and noting in his diary that the castle 'made again an impressive sight in the distance.'[20]

Queen Victoria and Prince Albert stayed at Schloss Babelsberg in August 1858, following the marriage of their daughter Victoria, the Princess Royal, to Prinz Friedrich, who became Emperor Friedrich III in 1888, but died from cancer of the larynx in the same year. Queen Victoria loved Schloss Babelsberg, of which she commissioned watercolours and recorded that 'everything there is very small, a Gothic *bijou*, full of furniture, and flowers (creepers), which they

arrange very prettily round screens [known as *Zimmerlaube*, ie room arbours], and lamps, and pictures. There are many irregular turrets and towers and steps.'[21] The extensive, wooded, land-scaped park in the English style at Babelsberg was begun in 1833 from designs by the court landscape architect, the anglophile Peter Joseph Lenné. A remarkable Reptonian link is that Humphry's eldest son, John Adey Repton, who had been in Nash's office from 1796–1800, came to Prussia in 1822 to give advice to Lenné.[22]

Percier and Fontaine

Schinkel saw much of Percier and Fontaine from his first meeting with them on 30 April 1826, the first day of his stay in Paris, recording that on the next day, he '[w]ent through the whole of the Louvre' with them.[23] Meeting the two architects again at a lecture on Vitruvius by Quatremère de Quincy at the Institut de France, he found that 'Percier was very friendly' and thanked him and Fontaine for sending him 'the sketch of the rooms displaying sculpture in the Louvre.'[24] He would have seen their Arc du Carrousel (Fig 9.9), standing between the Louvre and the Tuileries palaces, and also seems to have visited in the Marais 'the workshop of the skilled bronze founder, Crozatier.'[25] It was the sculptor and bronze-caster, Charles Crozatier (1795–1855), who had provided the quadriga on the Arc du Carrousel which replaced the horses of St Mark after they had been returned to Venice in 1815.

Nash would have seen the Arc du Carrousel on his visit to Paris in 1814 while his protégé, James Pennethorne, a cousin of his second wife and his future chief assistant, had undertaken a six-month course in draughtsmanship, at Nash's expense, with Louis Lafitte, designer of the sculptural panels on the Arc du Carrousel.[26] Pennethorne doubtless transmitted details of this monument to Nash, who also acquired Lafitte's book, *Description de l'Arc de Triomphe*

Fig 9.9
The Tuileries with Arc du Carrousel in the foreground (Garnot, Tuileries, pl 105).

Fig 9.10
'John Bull & the arch-itect wot builds the arches, &c', caricature by William Heath, 1829.

de l'Etoile (1818), of which Soane owned as many as three copies. The Arc du Carrousel and Nash's arch, known as the Marble Arch, were almost the same size, the latter slightly larger, and both were closely modelled on the Arches of Septimius and of Constantine in Rome.

With his keen interest in the work of Percier and Fontaine, Nash bought their principal publications, including their *Cérémonies et Fêtes pour le couronnement de Napoléon et Joséphine* (1807), a book which Soane also owned.[27] Nash also owned books on Versailles, in which context it is interesting that his flanking wings on the entrance front at Buckingham Palace were clearly modelled on those designed for Louis XV in 1772 by Ange-Jacques Gabriel for the entrance front of Versailles to replace the 17th-century Aile Nord and Aile Sud. These long pavilions by Nash and Gabriel terminate in tall, three-bay façades with a first floor featuring four free-standing Corinthian columns below a pediment. In fact, Gabriel's Aile Sud was built for Louis XVIII (1814–24) by Charles Percier and Alexandre Dufour, shortly before the similar range at Buckingham Palace.

Buckingham Palace was incomplete when George IV died in 1830, and there had been growing outrage at the cost, which had risen to well over half a million pounds. An 1829 caricature of 'John Bull and the architect wot [sic] builds the arches', shows Nash as an illiterate artisan with a mason's apron and a prominent trowel (Fig 9.10). He is being quizzed by John Bull, who complains: 'here's a bill for building the wings, here's another for pulling them down, and a third for building them up again. But the bill is more than double the estimate.' Nash replies in cockney: 'Oh Yers, that was always wrong, but we never minds no estimates'. Accused of negligence, Nash was hauled before a hostile Select Committee of the House of Commons in 1828, dismissed from the Board of Works, and not given the long-expected baronetcy. It is inconceivable to imagine such a narrative in the career of Soane, Cockerell or Schinkel, all known for their professionalism and probity.

Soane

Soane was so hostile to Nash for a range of reasons, principally jealousy, that he did not include a single one of his works in the many hundreds of illustrations of modern buildings in London that he had his pupils make to show at his lectures as Professor of Architecture at the Royal Academy. However, he had illustrations made of Covent Garden Opera House by Smirke to accompany his attack on the building in language so strong that he was forced to cease lecturing for a considerable time. Soane did not mention Nash's name once in the lectures, though from his private notes we know that he condemned Payne Knight's Downton Castle, Herefordshire (1772–8), which so much influenced Nash. Soane was disturbed by the lack of unity caused by the contrast between its castellated Gothic exteriors and its neoclassical interiors.

The only reference in his notes to a London work by Nash was a comparison between Napoleon's striking contributions to Paris, such as the Rue de Rivoli by Percier and Fontaine, which he greatly admired, and Regent Street, which he condemned. Indeed, the only comment he could bring himself to make on it was, 'the least said the better.'[28] Part of his hostility was, of course, rooted in an understandable envy of Nash, because the commission for Buckingham Palace should rightly have gone to him, as the building was in his charge in his capacity as one of the three attached architects to the Board of Works.

Soane had anticipated the rivalry with Paris and Napoleon expressed by Nash's Marble

Arch at Buckingham Palace. For example, in his eleventh lecture at the Royal Academy, first delivered in March 1815, he declared:

> the palaces of the Louvre, the Tuileries, and Versailles … present an assemblage of elegant forms and an appearance of princely magnificence such as cannot fail of making a strong impression on the minds of foreigners. If those truly royal residences are contrasted with St James's Palace, and Buckingham Place, what a falling off is apparent.[29]

An even more significant forerunner of Nash was Soane's proposed palace for George IV of 1821, approached through no fewer than three triumphal arches, including a centrally placed free-standing one (Fig 9.11). He falsely claimed in a manuscript note that such an arch had never been used 'for the entrance to a Royal Palace',[30] though he must have seen Percier and Fontaine's Arc du Carrousel on his visits to Paris in 1814 and 1819, and chose to include it in a remarkable illustration made in 1820 for his Royal Academy lectures.[31]

If Nash was inspired by Percier and Fontaine as well as by Soane in creating his own version of the Arc du Carrousel, Nash's Picture Gallery at Buckingham Palace (see Fig 7.25) had unusual side lighting from small domes in pendant arches or canopies recalling those by Soane in his now demolished Court of Chancery (Fig 9.12) in the Law Courts (1822–5) and Picture Room (1824) in his house in Lincoln's Inn Fields. Nash's Picture Gallery has since been remodelled, but something of the dramatic effect of its top-lit side compartments can be appreciated in his Royal Opera Arcade of 1821 (see Fig 6.38).

Cockerell

C R Cockerell began as a pupil in 1809 in Smirke's office, working on his Covent Garden Opera House. This put him off the Greek Revival, just as it had Soane. Farington recorded that, while staying with Nash at East Cowes Castle in 1821, 'Mr. Nash spoke highly of Cockerell, Junr.', and 'thought this young artist was very greatly superior in professional ability to another who is high in public opinion and practise.'[32] Perhaps this unnamed architect was Robert Smirke. After dining with Nash in 1822, when Cockerell was a young man of 34, and Nash 70, Cockerell gave a charming vignette portrait in his diary, 'Mr. Nash always same, amusing, naïve, but making the same quotations, telling the same stories.'[33]

*Fig 9.11 (below)
Soane, design for royal palace, 1821
(Clifford Smith,
Buckingham Palace,
page 38, fig 26).*

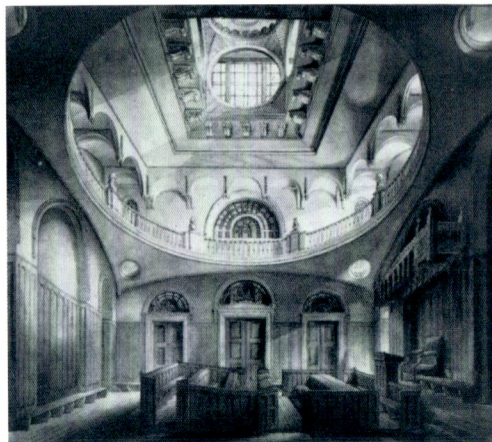

*Fig 9.12 (right)
Soane, Court of
Chancery (Gandy)
(Stroud, Soane, 1961,
page 207).*

Four years later, in August 1826, Nash took Cockerell to see the rising Buckingham Palace, but he shared Schinkel's low opinion, noting 'west [garden] front good but many defects. total want of order in the windows of East front. col[umn]s above col[umn]s: bad in the Porticoes looking like a scaffolding.' He complained of 'cast iron doric col[umn]s where stone is to be had.'[34] Nash's All Souls Church, Langham Place (1822–4), also failed to please Cockerell, who found that 'the spire had an inapposite association, reminding one of a village church & not such as fits a metropolis. for this purpose it is too homely.'[35] He added that he 'had heard the arch[itectur]e praised, think it very good for those who know nothing about it [architecture]', but this does not do justice to Nash's skilful placing of the church to conceal the awkward angle where his Regent Street met the already existing Portland Place by the Adam brothers to the north west. Like a temple in a landscaped park, the church acts as an oiled cogwheel to turn us gently round the corner. However, Cockerell's condemnation is echoed in 'Nashional Taste', a caricature of Nash published in April 1824 after a parliamentary debate in which the church was criticised.[36] He is shown sitting on the top of the spire, painfully impaled by it (Fig 9.13).

Of Regent Street, Cockerell observed in 1821 that: 'it is evident that all has been done hastily – hastily thought, hastily executed, Nothing more necessary than a leisurely habit. Festina lente [is required], working at the same time with diligence. nothing profound can otherwise be attained. all must be flimsy & deficient in principle.'[37] He attempted to improve Regent Street in the design of his own Hanover Chapel (see Fig. 6.14), built in 1823–5 on the west side of the street just below Oxford Circus. It was the most distinguished building in the whole street, and his drawings for it shows the care with which he related its Greek Ionic portico and twin towers to the line of Nash's new fashionable street.[38] The day before the foundation stone was laid, he went to an exhibition that included Claude's seaport paintings, notably 'The Embarkation of St Ursula', which he thought must have been the inspiration for his façade. Such an approach to design was, of course, extremely close to the pictorial approach of Nash. Cockerell recognised this when he said that the Regent's Park terraces:

> … may be compared to the Poetry of an improvisatore – one is surprised & even captivated at first sight with the profusion of splendid images, the variety of the scenery & the readiness of the fiction. But if as many were versed in the Grecian rules of this science as there are versed in those of Homer & Virgil this trumpery would be less popular.[39]

Nash's Cumberland Terrace (Fig 9.14) is both a fiction and splendid: a row of houses not a palace, its pediment is not the end of a roof as it would have been for Soane, Cockerell or Schinkel, and there is nothing behind it, for it is just propped up by an iron rod. Cockerell said of the terraces that there was 'something mortifying & humiliating in seeing the profusion of ornam[en]t & badness of the arch[itectur]e'.[40] This seems unduly harsh, while Cockerell did not do justice to the fact that behind the great terraces on the east side were three market squares for hay (Cumberland Market, 1819), for vegetables (Clarence Market, 1824) and for meat (York Market, 1812–23); although, when executed as Munster Square, the last was wholly residential. There were arrangements for the transport of produce by canal, and even a large commercial icehouse under the western side of Cumberland Market, holding 1,500 tons of ice brought by ship from Norway.[41] These open markets were surrounded by modest houses

Fig 9.13
Nash impaled on the spire of All Souls, Langham Place, caricature by George Cruikshank, 1824.

Fig 9.14
Cumberland Terrace,
Regent's Park
(Shepherd & Elmes,
Metropolitan
Improvements, 1827).

(Fig 9.15), which were all sadly destroyed in 1951 following bomb damage when the canal that served them was filled in.

Possibly the first garden city, Regent's Park could have been inspired by the Ideal Town of Chaux by the leading French neoclassical architect, Claude-Nicolas Ledoux, who published it in 1804 in a great book of which both Nash and Soane had copies,[42] the latter studying it carefully. Following Ledoux, Nash's garden city had houses of different classes from the rich down to the poor, as well as a public house for the working classes and barracks on the east side. However, the setting of the grand terraces was threatened in 1945 by a nightmare proposal for over 25 towering slab blocks, each 110 feet high, arranged in a grim and inhuman geometrical grid. Designed by Mr C Bainbridge, St Pancras Borough Surveyor and Engineer, this Stalinist project was welcomed as 'a good new plan' by Sir John Summerson, who complained that Nash had designed 'for a very thin social stratum.'[43]

If Cockerell was critical of the clumsy detail of Nash's Regent's Park terraces, he reacted sensitively to his Blaise Hamlet (1810–11) (Fig 9.16), explaining that:

> Nash has always original ideas. he recommended to Mr. Harford to build his alms Houses in a picturesque manner & in a retired spot & not in a row .... he built therefore irregular cottages with all those little penthouses for beehives, ovens &c & irregularities which he found in peasant's cottages & they are so beautiful that it is a sight visited from Clifton & I have always called it Sweet.[44]

Having created at Blaise Hamlet what we might call the first 'beauty spot', Nash later brought its narrative principles to London at Park Village East (1824–34) (see Fig 5.16) and Park Village West (1832–8) next to Regent's Park.[45] As no developers were initially interested, Nash took up the leases himself and built what he called 'copies of Blaise Hamlet.'

What Cockerell perceptively identified as at the heart of Nash's achievement is what we might call 'architecture as if'. For example, Nash designed the new Regent Street as if it had grown over time, for he explained that his model

Fig 9.15 (left)
Munster Square in the 1930s
(B 9101).

Fig 9.16 (below)
A 19th-century photograph
of Blaise Hamlet
(BB 83_02061).

Fig 9.17
Chester Terrace,
Regent's Park
(Shepherd & Elmes,
Metropolitan
Improvements, *1827).*

was the High at Oxford which, incidentally, Turner painted at about this moment in 1809. Nash closed the north side of his Piccadilly Circus with a close copy of a building then attributed to Inigo Jones, the Queen's Gallery at Old Somerset House, whose demolition was regretted when it was replaced in the 1770s by Sir William Chambers' Somerset House (*see* Fig 6.20). Nash's building was only a fire insurance office, but its royal style was suitable, for it faced the Prince Regent as he drove north from Carlton House to Regent's Park. Yet this sort of fictive architecture was combined with modern technology, so that the 154 columns of the adjacent Quadrant were of cast iron.

A recent parallel to the kind of narrative, pictorial and associational architecture represented by the echo of the Somerset House Gallery of 1662 is Quinlan Terry's Richmond Riverside, with specific references to earlier buildings by Palladio and William Chambers, both relevant to this riverside site. It has become so popular with residents and visitors that it appears on the town guide as one part of historic Richmond, so tourists come to see it as well as Nash's echoes of peasant cottages at Blaise.

Nash took Cockerell's opinions and talents seriously so that when, as we have seen, he sent James Pennethorne, to study for two years in France and Italy at his own expense from 1824

to 1826, he arranged for the young man to call on Cockerell for his advice before setting out. Pennethorne recorded his gratitude in 1857, recalling that it was on the recommendation of Cockerell 'that he had studied the works of the modern rather than the ancient architects of Italy.'[46] The occasion was a meeting to award the Gold Medal of Sir William Chambers to Pennethorne. Cockerell, who was also present, observed that, 'With all his defects, Nash was a courageous little man, and it was a matter of regret that no proper biography of him had appeared.'[47] This praise, though doubtless sincere, was expressed in a rather patronising way, while Cockerell's surprise that no biography of Nash had been written is astonishing in view of the fact that Wren was at that time the only English architect of whom a biography had been written.[48]

Despite Cockerell's criticism of the Regent's Park terraces in 1821, 30 years later he rather sensibly chose to move to 13 Chester Terrace (Fig 9.17), where he died in 1863. Nash had boasted of Chester Terrace (1824–5), which was the longest of all at almost 1,000 feet, that it was 'nearly as long as the Tuileries.'[49] This palace was, as we have noted, the chosen residence of Napoleon, whose taste George IV rightly admired, even though he was his arch enemy.

Notes

1   Schinkel, Karl Friedrich (Bindman, David and
    Riemann, Gottfried eds; Walls, F Gayna transl) 1993
    *'The English Journey': Journal of a Visit to France and
    Britain in 1826*. New Haven and London: Yale
    University Press, 114

2   *ODNB* **XLIX**, 315

3   Nash commissioned these copies of Raphael's
    celebrated grotesques in the Vatican from Richard
    Evans (1784–1871), portrait painter and copyist,
    who was painting them for him in Rome in
    November 1821 (Farington *Diary* (ed Garlick *et al*
    1978–1984) **XVI**, 5745 (November 1821).

4   Schinkel 1993 (*see note 1*), 89–91

5   Schinkel 1993 (*see note 1*), 116

6   Crook and Port 1973, 317–18; Mansbridge 1991,
    198–9. *See pages 160–3, 164–5*.

7   Schinkel 1993 (*see note 1*), 91

8   Popularly known from the start as 'The Marble Arch',
    it was removed in 1851 to what is now a traffic island
    at the end of Park Lane (Saint, A 2007 'The Marble
    Arch'. *Georgian Group J* **7**, 75–93).

9   Schinkel 1993 (*see note 1*), 104

10 Schinkel 1993 (*see note 1*), 108

11 *ibid*

12 *ibid*

13 Sievers, Johannes 1942 *Bauten für den Prinzen Karl
    von Preussen*. Berlin: Deutscher Kunstverlag, 174–
    244 and pls 178–82

14 Sievers, Johannes 1954 *Bauten für die Prinzen
    August, Friedrich und Albrecht von Preussen: ein
    Beitrag zur Geschichte der Wilhelmstrasse in Berlin*.
    Berlin: Deutscher Kunstverlag, 154–8 and pls 119–
    23; Schinkel's columnar entrance screen (143 and
    pl 111) at this palace was probably inspired by that
    by Henry Holland at Carlton House.

15 Schinkel, Karl Friedrich 1819–40 *Sammlung
    architektonischer Entwürfe*. Berlin: Ernst und Kom

16 Sievers, Johannes 1955 *Die Arbeiten von K F Schinkel
    für Prinz Wilhelm, späteren König von Preussen*.
    Berlin: Deutscher Kunstverlag, 156–206; after
    Schinkel's death, Schloss Babelsberg was completed
    and extended in 1844–9 in a somewhat heavier
    manner by Ludwig Persius and Heinrich Strack
    (Sievers 1955, 207–18).

17 Lugar, Robert 1805 (reprinted 1815 and 1823)
    *Architectural Sketches for Cottages, Rural Dwellings,
    and Villas*. London: J Taylor; Papworth, John
    Buonarotti 1832 *Rural Residences* (2nd edn).
    London: R Ackermann

18 Watkin, David and Mellinghoff, Tilman 1987 *German
    Architecture and the Classical Ideal, 1740–1840*.
    London: Thames and Hudson, 108–9

19 Repton, Humphry 1816 *Fragments on the Theory and
    Practice of Landscape Gardening*. London: J Taylor,
    pl facing page 36

20 Schinkel, *'English Journey'* (1993), pl 99 and page 198

21 Anon, *The Empress Frederick: A Memoir* (London,
    1913), 91–2

22 See Gerhard Hinz, *Peter Joseph Lenné: Das
    Gesamtwerk des Gartenarchitekten und Städteplaners*
    (Hildesheim, 1989), and M. Uhlitz, 'Prince Pückler
    and John Adey Repton's visit to Prussia', *Journal of
    Garden History* 9 (4), 1989

23 Schinkel 1993 (*see note 1*), 35

24 Schinkel 1993 (*see note 1*), 43

25 Schinkel 1993 (*see note 1*), 61

26 Tyack 1992, 12

27 *Choix des plus célèbres maisons de plaisance de Rome
    et des environs* (1809–13) and *Palais, maisons et
    autres édifices modernes dessinés à Rome* (1798);
    see Catalogue 1835

28 Soane, John 'Miscellaneous extracts, Crude Hints &c.
    relating to Architecture. J. Soane 1818, Sunday
    October 1821' (Sir John Soane's Museum), cited in
    Watkin, D 1996 *Sir John Soane: Enlightenment
    Thought and the Royal Academy Lectures*. Cambridge:
    Cambridge University Press, 382, note 379

29 Watkin, 1996 *Soane* (*see note 28*), 637

30 Soane, John 1815 'Designs for public improvements
    in London and Westminster'. Unpublished, 3; cited
    by Watkin, D 1999 'Soane: The Royal Academicians
    and the public realm', *in* Richardson, M and Stevens,
    M (eds) *John Soane Architect: Master of Space and
    Light*. London: Royal Academy of Arts, 45

31 Watkin 1996 (*see note 30*), fig 41, showing it with the
    Temple Bar in London and the Porte St Denis in
    Paris, all drawn to the same scale

32 Farington *Diary* (ed Garlick *et al* 1978–1984) **XVI**,
    5745–46

33 Cockerell, C R [diary], cited in Watkin, D 1974, 68

34 *ibid*

35 *ibid*

36 Hobhouse, H 1975 *A History of Regent Street*.
    London: Macdonald and Jane's, pl VIII

37 Cockerell, C R [diary], cited in Watkin, D 1974, 68

38 Cockerell, C R [diary], cited in Watkin, D 1974, pl 29

39 Cockerell, C R [diary], cited in Watkin, D 1974, 69

40 *ibid*

41 Mansbridge 1991, 222

42 Ledoux, Claude–Nicolas 1804 *L'Architecture
    considérée sous le rapport de l'art, des moeurs et de la
    legislation*. Paris: Chez l'Auteur

43 *The Builder* **169** (1945), 332–3

44 Cockerell, C R [diary], cited in Watkin, D 1974, 81

45 Tyack, G 1993 'John Nash and the Park Village'.
    Georgian Group J, 68–74

46 *The Builder* **23** (1857), 288

47 *ibid*

48 Elmes, James 1823 *Memoirs of the Life and Works of
    Sir Christopher Wren*. London: Priestley and Weale

49 John Nash to Alexander Milne, 3 March 1815 (NA,
    Cres 2/1737)

SELECT BIBLIOGRAPHY

For publications on individual buildings, *see also* List of buildings by John Nash (184–92).

Anderson, J 1998 'Marylebone Park and the New Street: a study of the development of Regent's Park and Regent Street, London, in the first quarter of the nineteenth century'. Unpubl PhD thesis, Univ London

Anon 1835 'John Nash' [obituary]. *Gentleman's Magazine* ns **IV**, 437–8

Anon 1836 'John Nash' [obituary]. *Annual Biography and Obituary* **XX**. London, 1836

Anon 1855 and 1856 'Nash and Schinkel: education of architects'. *Builder* **13** (8 Dec), 585 and **14** (16 August), 441–2

Bolton, A T 1927 *The Portrait of John Soane RA*. London: Butler & Tanner

British Parliamentary Papers (PP)

    PP 1812, XII (357), 1st Report of the Commissioners of Woods, Forests, etc

    PP 1816, XV (147), 2nd Rep Commrs of Woods, Forests, etc

    PP 1819, XIV (474), 3rd Rep Commrs of Woods, Forests, etc

    PP 1823, XI (110), 4th Rep Commrs of Woods, Forests, etc

    PP 1826, XIV (368), 5th Rep Commrs of Woods, Forests, etc

    PP 1828, IV (446), Rep of the Select Committee on the Office of Works and Public Buildings

    PP 1829, XIV (317), 6th Rep Commrs of Woods, Forests, etc

    PP 1829, III (343), Report of the Select Committee on Crown Leases

    PP 1831, IV (329) Rep of the Select Committee on … Windsor Castle and Buckingham Palace

Britton, J and Pugin, A C 1825 *Illustrations of the Public Buildings of London* (2 vols). London: J Taylor

Catalogue 1835 *Catalogue of the Valuable Architectural and Miscellaneous Library, Prints and Drawings of the Late John Nash, Esq.* London: R H Evans

Clarke, J 2005–6 'Cones, not domes: John Nash and Regency structural innovation', *Construction Hist* **21**, 43–63

Colvin, H M 2008 *A Biographical Dictionary of British Architects 1600–1840* (4th edn). New Haven and London: Yale University Press

Crook, J M and Port, M H 1973 *The History of the King's Works* **VI**. London: Her Majesty's Stationery Office

Crook, J M 1992 'Metropolitan improvements: John Nash and the picturesque', *in* Fox, C (ed) *London – World City 1800–1840*. New Haven and London: Yale University Press, 77–96

Daniels, S 1999 *Humphry Repton*. New Haven and London: Yale University Press

Davis, T 1960 *The Architecture of John Nash*. London: Studio Books

Davis, T 1966 *John Nash: the Prince Regent's Architect*. London: Country Life

Davis, T 1973 *John Nash: The Prince Regent's Architect* (rev edn). Newton Abbot: David & Charles

Elmes, J 1827 *Metropolitan Improvements: or London in the Nineteenth Century*. London: Jones & Co

Farington, J 1978–1984 *Diary* (16 vols), ed Garlick, K *et al* New Haven and London: Yale University Press

Ferrey, B 1861 (Wainwright, C and Wainwright J, eds 1978) *Recollections of A W N Pugin and His Father Augustus Pugin*. London: The Scholar Press

Gater, G and Hiorns, F 1940 *Survey of London*, XX, *Trafalgar Square and Neighbourhood*. London: Country Life for the London County Council

Gore, A and Carter, G (eds) 2005 *Humphry Repton's Memoirs*. Norwich: Michael Russell

Hobhouse, H 1975 *A History of Regent Street*. London: Macdonald and Jane's

Hobhouse, H 2008 *A History of Regent Street* (rev edn). Chichester: Phillimore & Co

Jones, F 1939 'The hand of Nash in west Wales'. *Trans Carmarthenshire Antiq Soc* **29**, 93–6

Jope, E M 1956 'Lissan Rectory, Kilwaughter Castle and the buildings in the north of Ireland designed by John Nash'. *Ulster J Archaeol* **19**, 121–7

Knight, C (ed) 1856 *The English Cyclopedia: Biography*, **III**. London: Bradbury & Evans, 430–1

Ladd, F J 1978 *Architects at Corsham Court*. Bradford-on-Avon: Moonraker Press

Lever, J (ed) 1973 *Catalogue of the Royal Institute of British Architects Drawings Collection, L–N*. Farnborough: Gregg International

Liscombe, R 1970 'Designs for the church commissioners 1818'. *Archit Hist* **13**, 43–56 and figs 27–32

Lovell, P, and Marcham, W 1938 *Survey of London*, **XIX**, *Old St. Pancras and Kentish Town*. London: London County County Council

Mansbridge, M 1991 *John Nash: A Complete Catalogue*. Oxford: Phaidon

Pinhorn, M (ed) 2000 *The Diaries of John Nash, Architect* (2 vols). Leominster: Pinhorns

Pinhorn, M (ed) 2002 *The Diaries of John Nash, architect* (supplementary vol). Leominster: Pinhorns

R[anger], W A 1836 'Autobiographical passages in the life of Mr Nash'. *Mechanics' Magazine* 24, 26–9

Roberts, J and Godfrey, W 1949 *Survey of London*, XXI, *Tottenham Court Road and Neighbourhood*. London: Batsford for the London County County Council

Saint, A and Guillery, P 2012 *Survey of London, XLVIII, Woolwich*. London: Yale University Press for English Heritage

Saunders, A 1969 *Regents Park*. Newton Abbot: David & Charles

Saunders, A 1981 *Regents Park*, (rev edn). London: Bedford College

Sheppard, F 1963 *Survey of London*, **XXIX–XXX**, *St. James, Westminster, part 2*. London: Athlone Press for the London County Council

Suggett, R 1995 *John Nash, Architect in Wales*. Aberystwyth: Royal Commission on the Ancient and Historic Monuments of Wales

Suggett, R 2009 'The early life of John Nash'. *Trans Hon Soc Cymmrodorion* ns **15**, 59–86

Summerson, J 1935 *John Nash: Architect to King George IV*. London: George Allen & Unwin

Summerson, J 1945 *Georgian London* (rev edn). London: Pleiades Books

Summerson, J 1949 *John Nash: Architect to King George IV* (rev edn). London: George Allen & Unwin

Summerson, J 1980 *The Life and Work of John Nash, Architect*. London: George Allen & Unwin

Summerson, J 1991 'John Nash's "Statement", 1829'. *Archit Hist* **34**, 196–205

Summerson, J 2003 *Georgian London* (rev edn). New Haven and London: Yale University Press

Survey of London, The (available online www.british-history.ac.uk); *see also* Gater and Hiorns 1940, Lovell and Marcham 1938, Roberts and Godfrey 1949, Saint and Guillery 2012 and Sheppard 1963

Temple, N 1979 *John Nash and the Village Picturesque*. Gloucester: Alan Sutton

Temple, N 1985 'John Nash: some minor buildings in Wales'. *Trans Hon Soc Cymmrodorion* [vols are not numbered], 231–54

Temple, N 1987 'Pages from an architect's notebook, Part 1' and 'Pages from an architect's notebook, Part 2'. *Proc Isle of Wight Nat Hist Archaeol Soc* **8**, 82–99 and 81–103

Temple, N 1988 'In search of the Cottage Picturesque'. *Georgian Group J* **[1988]**, 72–80

Temple, N 1993 *George Repton's Pavilion Notebook*. Aldershot: Scholar Press

Thorne, R G 1986 *The House of Commons, 1790–1820* (5 vols). London: Secker & Warburg for the History of Parliament Trust

Tyack, G 1992 *Sir James Pennethorne and the Making of Victorian London* Cambridge: Cambridge University Press

Tyack, G 2004 'Nash, John'. *Oxford Dictionary of National Biography*. Oxford: Oxford University Press

Tyack, G 2005 'Nash the incomparable'. *Country Life* (**23 June**), 112–6

Watkin, D 1974 *The Life and Work of C R Cockerell*. London: Zwemmer

Watkins, C and Cowell, B (eds) 2006 *Letters of Uvedale Price*. Walpole Society **LXVIII**. London: Walpole Society, [whole volume]

White, J 1814 *Some Account of the Proposed Improvements of the Western Parts of London*. London: W & P Reynolds

Whitehead, D 1992 'John Nash and Humphry Repton: an encounter in Herefordshire'. *Trans Woolhope Naturalists' Field Club* **47**, 210–36

LIST OF BUILDINGS BY JOHN NASH

This list includes all authenticated buildings by John Nash, with short bibliographical references. Manuscript and pictorial sources are not included. It should be assumed that a building is extant except where indicated ('dem' = demolished; 'attd' = attributed, 'nd' = not datable). Unexecuted and uncertainly attributed projects are not included.

Frequently repeated sources

Bradley, S and Pevsner, N 2003, *The Buildings of England London 6: Westminster*. New Haven and London: Yale University Press

Brooks, A and Pevsner, N 2007, *The Buildings of England Worcestershire*. New Haven and London: Yale University Press

Brooks, A and Pevsner, N 2012, *The Buildings of England Herefordshire*. New Haven and London: Yale University Press

Cherry, B and Pevsner, N 1983, *The Buildings of England London 2: South*. Harmondsworth: Penguin Books

Cherry, B and Pevsner, N 1991, *The Buildings of England London 3: North West*. London: Penguin Books

Cherry, B and Pevsner, N 1998, *The Buildings of England London 4: North*. London: Penguin Books

Cherry, B and Pevsner, N 1989, *The Buildings of England Devon*. London: Penguin Books

Lloyd, D and Pevsner, N 2006, *The Buildings of England Isle of Wight*. New Haven and London: Yale University Press

Lloyd, T, Orbach, J and Scourfield, R 2004, *The Buildings of Wales Pembrokeshire*. New Haven and London: Yale University Press

Lloyd, T, Orbach, J and Scourfield, R 2006, *The Buildings of Wales Carmarthenshire and Ceredigion*. New Haven and London: Yale University Press

Nairn, I and Pevsner, N 1965, *The Buildings of England Sussex*. Harmondsworth: Penguin Books

Newman, J and Pevsner, N 1972 *The Buildings of England Dorset*. Harmondsworth: Penguin Books

Newman, J 1995 *The Buildings of Wales Glamorgan*. London: Penguin Books

Newman, J 2000 *The Buildings of Wales Gwent/Monmouthshire*. London: Penguin Books

Newman, J and Pevsner, N 2006, *The Buildings of England Shropshire*. New Haven and London: Yale University Press

Pevsner, N 1961, *The Buildings of England Suffolk*. Harmondsworth: Penguin Books

Pevsner, N 1963, *The Buildings of England Herefordshire*. Harmondsworth: Penguin Books

Pevsner, N 1974, *The Buildings of England Staffordshire*. Harmondsworth: Penguin Books

Pevsner, N 1983, *The Buildings of England County Durham* (2nd edn, revised by Elizabeth Williamson). Harmondsworth: Penguin Books

Rowan, A 1979, *The Buildings of Ireland, North-West Ulster*. Harmondsworth : Penguin Books

Verey, D and Brooks, A 1999, *The Buildings of England Gloucestershire I: The Cotswolds*. London: Penguin Books

For other frequently repeated sources, see the Select bibliography

Buildings mentioned in the text

Abergavenny, Monmouthshire, market, 1794–6 (dem): Mansbridge 1991, 49; Suggett 1995, 24–5, 113

Aberystwyth, Ceredigion, bridge (timber), 1793, replaced by stone bridge 1797 (dem): Suggett 1995, 30–2, 112–13

Aberystwyth, Ceredigion, Castle House, built for Uvedale Price, 1791–4 (dem): Suggett 1995, 65–71, 119–21; *also* Webster J R 1995 *Old College Aberystwyth*. Cardiff: University of Wales Press, 1–11; Watkins, Charles, and Cowell, Ben 2012 *Uvedale Price (1747–1829): Decoding the Picturesque*. Woodbridge: The Boydell Press, 91–105

Aqualate Hall, Staffordshire, built for J F Fletcher Boughey 1806–9 (dem, apart from lodges and portion of outbuildings incorporated in present house on site): Pevsner 1974, 133; Mansbridge 1991, 120–1 (with plan); Temple 1993, 56–60;

Atcham, Shropshire, estate cottages built for second Lord Berwick of Attingham (below), and Tern Lodge (attd), *c* 1797–1800: Mansbridge 1991, 74–5, 81; Temple 1979, 112–15, 125–6; *also* Hill, R 1996 *Burlington Mag* 138, 14–15

Attingham, Shropshire, new Picture Gallery, staircase, etc, built for second Lord Berwick, 1806–9: Davis 1960, pls 37–8; Newman and Pevsner 2006, 126–9; *also Country Life* 1954 (21 Oct), 1350–3; Cousens, B 2000 *Attingham Park* (guidebook). London: National Trust Enterprises, plan

Bank Farm, Surrey (*see* Point Pleasant)

Barnsley Park, Gloucestershire, additions, including library and conservatory, built for Sir James Musgrave, 1806–10: Davis 1973, pl 17]; Temple 1993, 88–9; Verey and Brooks 1999, 159, plan; *also Country Life* 1954 (2 and 9 September), 720–3, 806–9

Belmont, Herefordshire, estate cottages built for John Matthews, nd; Mansbridge 1991, 307–8; Temple 1979, 109–12; Temple 1993, 139–43

Blaise Castle, Henbury, Bristol, dairy and conservatory built for J S Harford, *c* 1805–6: Temple 1979, 55–9; Daniels 1999, 230–5; Davis 1960, pl. 118–19, 126; Mansbridge 1991, 64–6

Blaise Hamlet, Henbury, Bristol, layout and cottages built for J S Harford, 1810–11: Mansbridge 1991, 170–2, plan; Temple 1979, 72–103; Temple 1993, 95–107, 112–35 (Fig S.1)

Brighton, Royal Pavilion, remodelled for HRH the Prince Regent, 1815–22: Summerson 1980, 101–9; *also* Dinkel, J 1983 *The Royal Pavilion, Brighton*. London: Philip Wilson; Morley, J 1984 *The Making of the Royal Pavilion, Brighton*. London: Philip Wilson; Musgrave, C 1959 *Royal Pavilion*. London: Leonard Hill; Nash, J 1826 *Views of the Royal Pavilion* (Jackson-Stops, G (ed) 1991). London: Pavilion Books; Roberts, H D 1939 *History of the Royal Pavilion*. London: Country Life; Rutherford, J 2003 *A Prince's Passion*. Brighton: Royal Pavilion, Libraries and Museums

Caerhayes Castle, Cornwall, built for John Trevanion 1808–*c* 1825 : Tyack 2005, 114–17; *also* Neale, P 1818 *Views of Seats* I. London: Sherwood, Neely and Jones; Gilbert, C S 1820 *Historical Survey of Cornwall II*. London: Longman, Hurst, Orre, Rees and Brown, and R Ackermann

Cahir, Co Tipperary, St Paul's C of I Church, 1817–20, and adjoining school (attd): Mansbridge 1991, 216–17; *also* National Inventory of Architectural Heritage, Tipperary South (www.buildingsofireland.ie)

Caledon, Co Tyrone, wings added for first Earl of Caledon, 1808–12: Davis 1973, 52–3 and pls 30–1; Rowan 1979, 161–3; *also Country Life* 1937 (27 Feb, 6 March), 224–9, 250–5

Fig S.1
Dial Cottage, Blaise Hamlet
(AA 98_04337).

Cardigan, Ceredigion, Priory House, built for Elizabeth Johnes, 1788–9 (remodeled; now part of hospital): Lloyd, Orbach and Scourfield 2006, 451; Mansbridge 1991, 66; Suggett 1995, 44–7, 116

Cardigan, gaol, 1791–7 (mostly dem): Mansbridge 1991, 46; Suggett 1995, 27–30, 110–11

Carmarthen, St Peter's church, roof, 1785 (replaced): Suggett 1995, 107

Carmarthen, gaol, 1789–92 (dem): Mansbridge 1991, 40; Suggett 1994, 51–2

Casina, Dulwich, Greater London, built for Richard Shawe, 1796–7 (dem): Davis 1960, pl 57; *also* Bellamy, J 1998–9 'Humphry Repton and "Homes fit for heroes"'. *London Gardener* **4**, 28–32; Worsley, G 1991 *Architectural Drawings of the Regency Period*. London: André Deutsch, 100 and plan

Chichester, Sussex, market, 1807–8 (interior remodelled 1900): Mansbridge 1991, 135 and plan); Nairn, I and Pevsner, N 1965, 179

Childwall Hall, Lancashire, built for Bamber Gascoigne 1806–13 (dem): Mansbridge 1991, 125; *also* Robinson, J M 1991 *Guide to the Country Houses of the North West*. London: Constable, 172; Twycross, E 1847 *Mansions of England and Wales: Lancashire* **III**. London: Ackermann & Co, 22–3

Corsham Court, Wiltshire, additions and alterations for Paul Cobb Methuen, 1797–1802 (mostly removed): Ladd 1978, 75–119; Mansbridge 1991, 76–9 and plan; Summerson 1980, 35–6; *also* Britton, J 1806 *Historical Account of Corsham House*. London: privately published; Harcourt, L 1976 *Corsham Court: A Gothick Dream*. London: Gothick Dream

Cowes, Isle of Wight (*see* East Cowes; West Cowes)

Cronkhill, Shropshire, built for the second Lord Berwick but leased to Francis Walford, *c* 1803–8: Davis 1960, pls 15–17 and plan; Mansbridge 1991, 101–3 and plan; *also* Tyack, G 2004, 'Cronkhill', *Country Life* (19 Feb), 62–7

Dolaucothi, Carmarthenshire, remodelled for John Johnes, 1792–6 (dem): Jones 1939, 93–5; Suggett 1995, 37–42

East Cowes Castle, Isle of Wight, own residence, 1798–1810 (dem), conservatory added *c* 1821–4: Davis 1960, pls 39–42 and plan; Mansbridge 1991, 85–7 and plan; Summerson 1980, 146–50 and plan); *also The Builder* 1 Sept 1950, 270–4; Sherfield, I 1994 *East Cowes Castle: A Pictorial History*. Camberley: Business by Design

East Cowes, St James church, 1831–3 (rebuilt, except for tower): Colvin 2008, 733; Lloyd and Pevsner 2006, 134; Mansbridge 1991, 301

Emyln Cottage (*see* Newcastle Emlyn)

Ffynone, Pembrokeshire, built for John Colby 1792–5: Davis 1960, pls 49–54 and plan; Suggett 1995, 49 and plan, 120–1; Lloyd, Orbach and Scourfield 2004, 313–15; *also* Baker-Jones, D L 1965 'Ffynone, Pembrokeshire', *Trans Hon Soc Cymmrodorion*, 115–36; *Country Life* 1992 (12 Nov), 50–3

Foley House (*see* Haverfordwest)

Garnstone Castle, Herefordshire, built for Samuel Peploe, *c* 1806–10 (dem except for west lodge): Davis 1960, pls 27–8; Mansbridge 1991, 125–6; *also* Neale, J P 1828 *Views of Seats* **IV**. London: Sherwood, Neely and Jones

Glanusk (*see* Llanwysc)

Hafod, Ceredigion, additions, incl library, built for Thomas Johnes 1793–4 (dem): Suggett 1995, 75–80, 121–2; *also* Macve, J 2004 *The Hafod Landscape*. Hafod estate office, Pontrhydygroes: Hafod Trust, with plan; Moore-Colyer, R J 1992 *A Land of Pure Delight*. Llandysul: Gomer

Hamstead, Isle of Wight, own residence, *c* 1806 (dem): Mansbridge 1991, 123 and plan; Pinhorn (ed) 2000 **II**, 137–43; *also* Sherfield, I 1994 *East Cowes Castle: A Pictorial History*. Camberley: Business by Design, 68–70 and plan

Haverfordwest, Pembrokeshire, Foley House, built for Richard Foley *c* 1790: Jones 1939, 96; Mansbridge 1991, 46–7; Suggett 1995, 44 (plan), 46, 117; Lloyd, Orbach and Scourfield 2004, 225

Helmingham Hall, Suffolk, alterations for fourth Earl of Dysart *c* 1800–3: Mansbridge 1991, 92–4; Pevsner 1961, 236–9; *also Country Life* 1956 (9, 16 and 23 August), 282–5, 332–5, 378–81

Hereford, gaol 1792–6 (dem, apart from former governors' house): Mansbridge 1991, 70–1 and plan; Suggett 1995, 27–9, 111 and plan; Whitehead 1992, 211–13; *also* Shoesmith, R and Crosskey, R 1994 'Go to gaol … in Hereford'. *Trans Woolhope Naturalists' Fld Club* **18**, 97–139 and plan

Hereford, lunatic asylum 1793–4 (dem): Suggett 1992, 112; Whitehead 1992, 215

High Legh Hall, Cheshire, alterations and estate buildings built for George Legh, *c* 1798–1818 (dem, except for school, altered): Mansbridge 1991, 82–3; Temple 1979, 115–21, 145–57; Temple 1993, 43–6, 63–5, 108–10

Ingestre Hall, Staffordshire, alterations incl new north front for third Earl Talbot, *c* 1808–13 (rebuilt): Colvin 2008, 735; Mansbridge 1991, 152–3; Pevsner 1974, 154–5

Kentchurch Court, Herefordshire, alterations for Sir John Scudamore 1795–6: Mansbridge 1991, 54–5; Whitehead 1992, 215–16; Brooks and Pevsner 2012, 382–4; *also Country Life* 1966 (15 & 22 Dec), 1632–5, 1688–91

Kew Gardens, Greater London, conservatory from Buckingham Palace re-erected as Aroid House 1836: Mansbridge 1991, 303; Cherry and Pevsner 1983, 509 (Fig S.2)

Fig S.2
The former Aroid House at Kew Gardens, removed from Buckingham Palace in 1835
(CC 97_00409).

Killymoon Castle, Co Tyrone, built for Col William Stewart 1803–9:
Davis 1960, pls 25–6 and plan; Davis 1973, 44–50; Mansbridge
1991, pp. 104–5; Rowan 1979, 334; *also* Northern Ireland
Buildings Database, www.doeni.gov.uk

Kilwaughter Castle, Co Antrim, built for Edward Jones Agnew 1807:
Davis 1960, pl 44 and plan; Jope 1956, 125–7 and plan;
Mansbridge 1991, 138–9 and plan; *also* Northern Ireland
Buildings Database, www.doeni.gov.uk

Knepp Castle, Sussex, built for Sir Walter Burrell 1808 (rebuilt after fire
1904): Davis 1960, pls 72–4 and plan; Mansbridge 1991, 155–7
and plan; Nairn and Pevsner 1965, 254–5; *also* Cartwright, E 1832
Parochial Topography of the Rape of Bramber II, 2. London: J.
Nichols and son, 295–8; *Country Life* 2003 (17 July), 66–71

Lissan Rectory, Co Tyrone, built for the Rev John Staples 1807
(partially dem): Davis 1973, 52; Jope 1956, 122–5 and plan;
Mansbridge 1991, 136–7 and plan; Rowan 1979, 362–3

Llanerchaeron, Ceredigion, built for Maj William Lewis *c* 1794:
Mansbridge 1991, 49–52 and plan; Suggett 1995, 49–58 and plan,
122; Lloyd, Orbach, and Scourfield 2006, 512–15 and plan; *also*
Evans, M Lloyd 1996 *Llanerchaeron*. Talybont: privately published;
Gallagher, J and Garnett, O, 2004 *Llanerchaeron* (guidebook).
London: National Trust Enterprises

Llysnewydd, Carmarthenshire, built for Col William Lewes *c* 1795
(dem): Mansbridge 1991, 123; Suggett 1995, 48–51 and plan,
56, 123

Llanwysc, Llangatwg, Breconshire, built for Admiral Gell *c* 1790:
Suggett 1995, 36, 63, 118

London, All Souls, Langham Place, 1822–4: Mansbridge 1991, 246–7
and plan; Cherry and Pevsner, 1991, 599; *also* Meynell, M 2009,
All Souls Langham Place: An Historical Guide. London: All Souls
PCC; Port, M W 2006 *Six Hundred New Churches*. Reading:
Spire Books, 64–6

London, Argyll Rooms, Regent Street (dem): *Survey of London* XXXI,
284–307

London, Bloomsbury Square, Nos. 16–17, and 66–71 Great Russell
Street, 1777–8: Mansbridge 1991, 35; Summerson 1980, 6–7;
Cherry and Pevsner 1998, 321–2

London, Buckingham Palace, 1825–37 (completed by Edward Blore):
Crook and Port 1973, 263–302 and plan; Mansbridge 1991, 274–6
and plan; Summerson 1980, plan; Bradley and Pevsner 2003,
644–51; *also Country Life* 1993 (5 August), 44–7; Harris, J, de
Bellaigue, G and Millar, O 1968 *Buckingham Palace*. London:
Nelson; Smith, H Clifford 1931 *Buckingham Palace*. London:
Country Life

London, Carlton House, additions built for the Prince Regent 1813–15
(dem): Crook and Port 1973, 307–15; Mansbridge 1991, 181–2
and plan; *Survey of London* XX, 74–5; *also* [no author given] 1991
Carlton House: The Past Glories of the Prince Regent's Palace (exhib
Catalogue). London: Queen's Gallery, plan; Pyne, W H 1819 *Royal
Residences* II. London: A Dry

London, Carlton House, temporary ballroom built for peace celebrations
1814, re-erected as Royal Artillery Museum (the Rotunda) at
Woolwich 1819–20: Clarke 2005–6; Crook and Port 1973, 317–19;
Mansbridge 1991, 198–9 *Survey of London* XLVIII, 353–7; *also*
Clarke, J 2007, 'The Woolwich Rotunda', *Research News* 6:
Swindon, English Heritage, 8–11

London, Carlton House Terrace and Carlton Gardens, 1827–33:
Mansbridge 1991, 296–9; *Survey of London* XX, 77–86 and plans;
Bradley and Pevsner 2003, 439–44

London, Clarence House, built for the Duke of Clarence (later King
William IV), 1825–8 (remodelled 1874–5): Crook and Port 1973,
323–6; Bradley and Pevsner 2003, 601–2; *also* Hussey, C 1949
Clarence House. London: Country Life

London, Cumberland Market, Clarence Gardens, Munster Square, etc,
1812–30 (dem): Mansbridge 1991, 182–3, 222–3, 265; Saunders
1981, 106–9; *Survey of London* XXI, 39, 142–4

London, Dover Street, No. 29, 1797–8, enlarged 1814 (dem):
Mansbridge 1991, 84 and plan; Summerson 1980, 30–2 and plan

London, Great Russell Street (*see* Bloomsbury Square)

London, Haymarket Theatre, 1820–1 (interior rebuilt): Britton, J and
Pugin, A C 1825 I, 262–72; Mansbridge 1991, 230–1 and plan;
Survey of London XX, 95–100; Bradley and Pevsner 2003, 417; *also*
Maude, C 1903 *The Haymarket Theatre*. London: Grant Richards

London, Highgate Archway, 1812–13 (dem): Colvin 2008, 732;
Mansbridge 1991

London, Langham House, built for Sir James Langham 1813–15 (dem):
Mansbridge 1991, 185; Summerson 1980, 83

London, Marble Arch, 1825–6, removed from Buckingham Palace to
Hyde Park 1851: Bradley and Pevsner 2003, 662; *also* Saint, A
1997 'The Marble Arch'. *Georgian Group J* 7, 75–93

London, Pall Mall East (*see* Trafalgar Square)

London, Park Crescent, 1812–22: Mansbridge 1991, 183–4; Saunders
1981, 81–3

London, Park Village East (1824–34) and West (1832–8: completed by
James Pennethorne): Davies 1960, pls 90, 93–7; Mansbridge
1991, 256–62; Cherry and Pevsner 1998, 382–3; *Survey of London*
XXI, 153–8; *also* Tyack, G 1993 'John Nash and the Park Village',
Georgian Group J 3, 68–74

London, Regent Street (with Langham Place, Oxford Circus, Piccadilly
Circus, the Quadrant, Waterloo Place), plans 1811–13, laid out
1815–23 (original buildings dem); individual buildings by Nash
are listed separately: Davies 1960, pls 169–79; Hobhouse 2008;
Mansbridge 1991, 130–4, 204–5; Summerson 1980, 75–89, 130–9

London, Regent Street, Nos. 14–16, built for himself and John Edwards
1819–22 (dem): Britton, J and Pugin, A C 1825 II, 287 and plan;
Mansbridge 1991, 227 and plan; *also* Yorke, J 2001 'Tiny Temples
of Mr Nash'. *Country Life* 2001 (8 February), 66–7

London, Regent's Canal 1812–20 (James Morgan, engineer):
Summerson 1980, 71–3, 117–18; *also* Spencer, H 1961 *London's
Canal*. London: Putnam

London, Regent's Park, plans 1811–13, laid out 1813–16: Saunders
1981; Summerson 1980, 58–74, 114–17; *also* Summerson, J 1977
'The beginnings of Regent's Park'. *Architect Hist* 20, 56–62; Crook,
J M 2001 *London's Arcadia*. London: Sir John Soane's Museum

London, Regent's Park, terraces, 1821–30: Davies 1960, pls 141–67;
Mansbridge 1991, 227–9, 234–40, 242–3, 248–9, 251–5, 263–73,
179–84, 288–9; Saunders 1981; Summerson 1980, 119–26;
Cherry and Pevsner 1991, 618–24; *Survey of London* XIX
(Cumberland Terrace, Chester Terrace, etc); *also Country Life*
1962 (5 July), 20–3 (Sussex Place)

187

Fig S.3
The Royal Mews, Buckingham Palace
(B 118828a).

London, Royal Mews, Buckingham Gate, 1822–5: Crook and Port 1973, 304–7; Mansbridge 1991, 244–5; Bradley and Pevsner 2003, 652–3 (Fig S.3)

London, Royal (King's) Opera House, Haymarket, 1816–18 (with G S Repton) (dem), and Royal Opera Arcade: Britton & Pugin 1825 **I**, 308; Mansbridge 1991, 206–7 and plan; Bradley and Pevsner 2003, 414–15; *Survey of London* **XX**, 98–100; *also* Nalbach, D 1972 *The King's Theatre*. London: Society for Theatre Research

London, St James's Park, laid out 1827–8: Summerson 1980, 166–9; Bradley and Pevsner 2003, 653–4

London, St Martin in the Fields, vicarage, vestry hall and parochial school, 1827–30: Mansbridge 1991, 293–5; Bradley and Pevsner 2003, 325–6

London, Strand, Nos. 430–49 Strand (West Strand Improvement), 1830–2 (with frontages to Adelaide St and William IV St), and Lowther Arcade (dem): Mansbridge 1991, 286–7 and plan, 302–3; Summerson 1980, 143–5; Bradley and Pevsner 2003, 325–6; *also* Stokes, M V 1972 'The Lowther Arcade in the Strand'. *London Topograph Rec* **23**, 119–28

London, Suffolk Place and Suffolk Street, including Gallery for the Society of Artists (with James Elmes), 1821–4: Mansbridge 1991, 232–3 and plan; Summerson 1980, 140–2; Bradley and Pevsner 2003, 432, 434–5; *Survey of London* **XX**, 89–94

London, Trafalgar Square and Pall Mall East, layout begun 1826: Mansbridge 1991, 286–7 and plan; Summerson 1980, 142–3; *Survey of London* **XX**, 15–18

London, United Service Club, Pall Mall, 1826–8: Mansbridge 1991, 244–5 and plan; Bradley and Pevsner 2003, 445–6; *Survey of London* **XXIX**, 386–99; *also Country Life* 1962 (12 April), 832–5

Longner Hall, Shropshire, built for Robert Burton 1805–8: Daniels 1999, 136–9; Davis 1960, pls 85–9; Mansbridge 1991, 106–7; Newman and Pevsner 2006, 342–4; *also* Tyack, G 2004 'Longner Hall'. *Georgian Group J* **14**, 199–213

Lough Cutra Castle, Co Galway, built for Charles Vereker 1811–17: Davis 1960, pls 81–4; Mansbridge 1991, 168–9; *also* Guinness, D and Ryan, W 1971 *Irish Houses and Castles*. London: Thames & Hudson, 177–80 and plan; Rait, R S 1908 *Story of an Irish Property*. Oxford: privately published; National Inventory of Architectural Heritage, Galway, www.buildingsofireland.ie

Luscombe Castle, Devon, built for Charles Hoare 1799–1804: Davis 1960, pls 59–62; Mansbridge 1991, 95–7 and plan; Summerson 1980, 38–40 and plan; Tyack 2005, 112–15; Cherry and Pevsner 1989, 544–5; *also* Hussey, C 1958 *English Country Houses: Late Georgian*. London: Country Life, 55–65

Newcastle Emlyn, Ceredigion, The Cottage, built for Mrs Ann Brigstocke 1792–4 (dem): Suggett 1995, 71–6 and plan, 120

Newport, Isle of Wight, Guildhall 1814–16 (tower added 1887): Mansbridge 1991, 193; Lloyd and Pevsner 2006, 177-

Parnham House, Beaminster, Dorset, additions and alterations for Sir William Oglander 1807–11: Mansbridge 1991, 139–40; Newman and Pevsner 1972, 87–8; *also Country Life* 2005 (1 July), 72–7; Royal Commission on Historic Monuments *West Dorset*, 21–3 and plan

Point Pleasant, Kingston-on-Thames, Greater London, built for Maj-Gen Frederick St John 1796–7 (dem): Daniels 1999, 211–12; Mansbridge 1991, 69 and plan

Ravensworth Castle, Co Durham, built for Sir Thomas Liddell (first Lord Ravensworth) 1808–c 1840 (completed to designs of the Hon. Thomas Liddell; dem): Davis 1960, pls 11–14; Lever (ed) 1973, 106–8; Mansbridge 1991, 142–3; Summerson 1980, 45–7 and plan; Pevsner, 1983, 389–90; *also* Mackenzie, E and Ross, M 1834 *Views of the County Palatine of Durham*. Newcastle: Mackenzie & Dent, **I** 149–53

Rheola, Resolven, Glamorgan, house and cottages built for John Edwards *c* 1812–14: Mansbridge 1991, 186–7; Suggett 1995, 92–9 and plan, 124; Temple 1985, 252–3; Temple 1993, 38–9, 150–5; Newman 1995, 538 (Fig S.4)

Fig S.4
Rheola House from the east
(Geoffrey Tyack).

Rockingham, Co Roscommon, built for Robert King (first Viscount Lorton) 1809–10 (dem): Mansbridge 1991, 164–6 and plan; *also Country Life* 1988 (17 Nov), 116–17; Wheeler, G 2003 'John Nash and the building of Rockingham', *in* Reeves-Smith. T and Oram, R (eds) *Avenues to the Past*. Belfast: Ulster Architectural Heritage Society, 169–90 and plan; MacDonnell, R 2002 *Lost Houses of Ireland*. London: Weidenfeld & Nicolson, 183–90

Royal Lodge, Windsor Great Park, Berkshire, built for the Prince Regent 1813–22 (subsequently rebuilt): Mansbridge 1991, 175–6 and plan; *also* Roberts, J 1997 *Royal Landscape*. New Haven and London: Yale University Press, 311–24; Morshead, O 1965 *George IV and Royal Lodge*. Brighton: Regency Society of Brighton and Hove

St David's Cathedral, Pembrokeshire, chapter house (dem) and repairs, including new west front 1790–3 (replaced post-1862): Mansbridge 1991, 39; Suggett 1995, 22–4, 108–9; *also* Evans, W 1986 'St David's Cathedral: the forgotten centuries', *J Welsh Ecclesiast Hist* **3**, 72–92; Jones, I Wyn 1952 'John Nash at St David's', *Architect Rev* **112**, 263–4; R Suggett, '"Done after the Fantastic Order": John Nash's restoration of St David's Cathedral', *Georgian Group J* **XXI**, 2013, forthcoming

Sandridge Park, Devon, built for Elizabeth Dunning, Lady Ashburton, *c* 1804–7: Davies 1960, pls 78–80 and plan; Mansbridge 1991, 118–19 and plan; Cherry and Pevsner 1989, 719–20; *also* Yallop, R 2009 'An house more worthy of the situation'. *Trans Devon Assoc* **141**, 181–217; *Country Life* 2012 (21 Nov)

Shanbally Castle, Clogheen, Co Tipperary, built for Cornelius O'Callaghan (second Baron and first Vct Lismore) *c* 1810–19 (dem): Davies 1960, pls 18–24; Mansbridge 1991, 218 and plan; *also* MacDonnell, R 2002 *Lost Houses of Ireland*. London: Weidenfeld & Nicolson, 191–6; O'Riordan, E, accessed 2011 'Historical Guide to Clogheen'. www.Galteemore.com

Southborough Place, Surbiton, Greater London, built for Thomas Langley 1808: Davis 1960, pls 3–7 and plan; Mansbridge 1991, 150–1 and plan; Temple 1993, 34–7 and plan

Southgate Grove, Greater London, built for Walker Gray 1797: Davis 1960, pls 29–36 and plan; Mansbridge 1991, 72–3 and plan; Cherry and Pevsner 1998, 462–4 and plan; *also* Eccleston, M 1989 *The Story of Grovelands*. London: privately published; Knight, C 2009, *London's Country Houses*. Chichester: Phillimore & Co, 263–6 (Figs S.5 and S.6)

Stanford-on-Teme, Worcestershire, bridges 1795 and 1797 (dem): Mansbridge 1991, 60–1; Suggett 1995, 33–4, 114

Stoke Edith Park, Herefordshire, parlour 1793–6 (dem) and estate buildings built for Edward Foley: Suggett 1995, 12; Whitehead 1992, 221–7

Fig S.5
A perspective view of Southgate Grove, possibly by Humphry or John Adey Repton c *1796 (AA 48_05225).*

Fig S.6
The Breakfast Room at Southgate Grove
(FF 82_0317).

Sundridge Park, Bromley, Greater London, built for Claude Scott, 1796–7 (Fig. 6): Mansbridge 1991, 84–5 and plan; Cherry and Pevsner 1983, 170–2; *also* Angus, W 1804 *Seats of the Nobility and Gentry*. London: W Angus; Wilson, K *Sundridge Park*. Orpington: privately published; Knight, C 2009, *London's Country Houses*. Chichester: Phillimore & Co, 85–7 (Fig S.7)

Temple Druid, Maenclochog, Pembrokeshire, built for Barrington Price 1791 (largely dem): Jones 1939, 96; Suggett, 53, 118; Lloyd, Orbach and Scourfield 2004, 271

Tenby, Pembrokeshire, Zion House, built for William Routh *c* 1790 (dem): Mansbridge 1991, 43 and plan; Suggett, 43–4 and plan, 118

Warrens, The, Bramshaw, Hampshire, built for George Eyre, 1801–5: Mansbridge 1991, 92–3; *also* Temple, N 1988 'Pages from an architect's notebook', *Proc Hampshire Fld Club* **44**, 95–105

West Cowes, Isle of Wight, St Mary's, west tower 1816: Mansbridge 1991, 99; Lloyd and Pevsner 2006, 120–2 (Fig S.8)

West Cowes, Northwood House, lodges built for George Ward *c* 1805–18: Mansbridge 1991, 99–101; Pinhorn (ed) 2000 **II**, 132–6; Temple 1993, 145–9; Lloyd and Pevsner 2006, 129, 133; *also* Sherfield, I 1994 *East Cowes Castle*. Camberley: Business by Design, 65–8.

West Grinstead Park, Sussex, built for Walter Burrell *c* 1806–8 (dem): Davis 1960, pls 8–10; Mansbridge 1991, 153–5 and plan; Temple 1993, 28–30; Nairn, I and Pevsner, N 1965, 371–2

Whitson Court, Monmouthshire, alterations for William Phillips *c* 1791–5: Mansbridge 1991, 56–7; Suggett 1995, 40–1 and plan, 60–1, 120; Newman 1995, 601

Witley Court, Worcestershire, additions and alterations, incl conservatory, built for the third Lord Foley, *c* 1806 (burned down; ruins survive): Mansbridge 1991, 114–15; Brooks and Pevsner 2007, 325–8 and plan; *also* Harris, J 1971 'C R Cockerell's "Ichnographia Domestica"', *Architect Hist* **14**, 136–7; Pardoe, W 1986 *Witley Court*. [place of publication not given]: Peter Huxtable Designs; White, R 2008 *Witley Court*, London: English Heritage

Woolwich, Greater London, Rotunda (*see* London, Carlton House)

Minor Commissions and other works not mentioned in the text (attributed and unexecuted works are not included)

Ascot, Berkshire, racecourse stand for George IV, 1822 (dem): Colvin 2008, 732; Mansbridge 1991, 240

Bembridge, Isle of Wight, Holy Trinity church, 1827 (rebuilt): Colvin 2008, 732

Betley Court, Staffordshire, internal alterations, 1809–10: Colvin 2008, 735; Mansbridge 1991, 162

Brampton Park, Huntingdonshire (now Cambridgeshire), additions and

Fig S.7 (above top)
Sundridge Park
(RIBA Library Photographs Collection).

Fig S.8 (above)
A drawing by Thomas Pennethorne showing the tower of St Mary, West Cowes, with the Solent in the background, c *1816 (Isle of Wight Record Office).*

alterations, 1806–7 (mostly dem): Colvin 2008, 735; Mansbridge 1991, 126–7; Temple 1993, 70–3

Bristol, Miles & Harford's Bank, Corn Street, *c* 1811 (rebuilt): Colvin 2008, 732

Burley-on-the-Hill, Rutland, home farm, *c* 1795–6: Colvin 2008, 733

Carmarthen, house for himself in Spilman Street, *c* 1790 (dem): Colvin 2008, 733; Picton Monument, 1825–7 (dem): Colvin 2008, 732; Mansbridge 1991, 277; Suggett 1995, 102–4

Chalfont House, Chalfont St. Peter, Buckinghamshire, exterior remodeled, *c* 1800 (rebuilt): Colvin 2008, 734; Mansbridge 1991, 89

Charborough Park, Dorset, alterations, *c* 1810: Colvin 2008, 736; Mansbridge 1991, 163; Newman and Pevsner 1972, 139

Clytha House, Monmouthshire, gateway, 1797: Colvin 2008, 733; Newman 2000, 190; Suggett 1995, 116–17

Cookstown, Co Tyrone, St. Luran's church Derryloran, *c* 1822 (rebuilt, except for tower and spire): Colvin 2008, 732; Mansbridge 1991, 241; Rowan 1979, 215

Goodwood, Sussex, unidentified alterations, nd (pre-1806): Colvin 2008, 734–5

Gracefield Lodge, Co Laois, 1817 (altered): Colvin 2008, 736; Mansbridge 1991, 210–11

Great Barr, Staffordshire, gateway to churchyard, *c* 1801 (dem): Colvin 2008, 734; Mansbridge 1991, 98

Hale Hall, Lancashire, additions and alterations, 1806 (mostly dem): Colvin 2008, 735; Mansbridge 1991, 124

Hampton Court, Greater London, Stud House, alterations 1817–20: Crook and Port 1973, 337–8

Harpton Court, Radnorshire, additions, *c* 1806 (dem): Colvin 2008, 734; Mansbridge 1991, 122

Harrow, Greater London, Flambards House, remodelled 1797–8 (rebuilt): Colvin 2008, 733; Cherry and Pevsner 1991, 269–70; Mansbridge 1991, 63

Hollycombe, Linch, Sussex, *c* 1805 (rebuilt): Colvin 2008, 734; Mansbridge 1991, 116

Hopton Court, Hopton Wafers, Shropshire, alterations, 1811–13: Colvin 2008, 736; Mansbridge 1991, 173; Newman and Pevsner 2006, 309–10

Leamington Spa, Warwickshire, Willes Road Bridge on Newbold Comyn estate (with James Morgan), 1827: Colvin 2008, 737

London, Adult Orphan Asylum, St. Andrew's Place, Regent's Park, 1823–4 (dem): Colvin 2008, 732

Coventry House, Streatham, 1812–14 (dem): Colvin 2008, 736

Newman Street, picture gallery for Benjamin West's sons, 1820–1 (dem): Colvin 2008, 732

No. 14 Grosvenor Square, alterations for Lord Berwick, 1811–13 (dem): Colvin 2008, 736

Opthalmia Hospital, Albany Street, 1818 (dem): Colvin 2008, 732; Mansbridge 1991, 217

St James's Square, garden layout 1817–18, and Ionic pavilion, 1822: Mansbridge 1991, 212; *Survey of London* **XXIX**, 69–70

St Mary's Church, Haggerston, 1826–7 (dem): Mansbridge 1991, 284–5; Port, M W 2006 *Six Hundred New Churches*. Reading: Spire Books, 81

St Mary's Lodge, Greenwich Park 1807–8: Colvin 2008, 731

Meidrim, Carmarthenshire, poor-house, 1791 (dem): Suggett 1995, 109

Merly House, Canford Magna, Dorset, stables, *c* 1805: Colvin 2008, 733; Mansbridge 1991, 113; Newman and Pevsner 1972, 130

Moccas, Herefordshire, lodges, *c* 1805: Mansbridge 1991, 112; Temple 1993, 25–7

Northerwood House, Lyndhurst, Hampshire, additions/alterations, *c* 1810: Colvin 2008, 736; Mansbridge 1991, 163

Nunwell House, Isle of Wight, repairs, 1807: Colvin 2008, 735; Mansbridge 1991, 116–17

Oxford, Exeter College, repairs to Hall (with G S Repton), 1818: Colvin 2008, 732; Mansbridge 1991, 216

Jesus College, alterations to Principal's Lodgings, 1802; alterations to roofs, battlements, etc 1815–18: Colvin 2008, 732; Mansbridge 1991, 119–200

Preshaw House, Hampshire, additions, 1810 (rebuilt): Colvin 2008, 736; Mansbridge 1991, 167

Slane's Castle, Co Antrim, addns, unfinished, *c* 1816: Colvin 2008, 736; Mansbridge 1991, 180–1

Towneley Hall, Lancashire, lodges, 1796 (dem): Colvin 2008, 733

Trecefel, Ceredigion, bridge, 1793 (dem): Colvin, 731; Suggett 1995, 112

West Cowes, Isle of Wight, villa for Sir J Coxe Hippisley, *c* 1825 (rebuilt): Colvin 2008, 736; Mansbridge 1991, 268

West Cowes, Harriet Lodge, for Earl of Belfast 1832 (dem): Pinhorn (ed) 2000, 89

Westover House, Calbourne, Isle of Wight, alterations *c* 1815: Colvin 2008, 736; Lloyd and Pevsner 2006, 103–4; Mansbridge 1991, 190–1

Whippingham, Isle of Wight, St Mildred's church, remodelled 1804–6 (rebuilt), and rectory enlarged *c* 1804 (rebuilt): Colvin 2008, 731; Mansbridge 1991, 110–11, 188; Temple 1993, 68, 81–2

Worcester Park, Greater London, addns, nd (dem): Colvin 2008, 736; Mansbridge 1991, 277

INDEX

Page numbers in **bold** refer to illustrations. Streets and buildings in London are listed individually and not under London. The designation (n) indicates that the reference is in a note.